The Time Of Memory

SUNY Series in Contemporary Continental Philosophy
Dennis J. Schmidt, editor

THE TIME OF MEMORY

———— ❧ ————

CHARLES E. SCOTT

STATE UNIVERSITY OF NEW YORK PRESS

Published by
State University of New York Press, Albany

Printed in the United States of America

For information, address State University of New York Press,
State University Plaza, Albany, N.Y., 12246

Production by Marilyn P. Semerad
Marketing by Anne M. Valentine

Library of Congress Cataloging in Publication Data

Scott, Charles E.
    The time of memory / Charles E. Scott.
        p.   cm. — (SUNY series in contemporary continental
    philosophy)
        Includes bibliographical references and index.
        ISBN 0–7914–4081–8 (hardcover : alk. paper). — ISBN 0–7914–4082–6
    (pbk. : alk. paper)
        1. Memory (Philosophy)   I. Title.   II. Series.
    BD181.7.S36   1999
    128′.3—dc21   98–36638
                                                                          CIP

10 9 8 7 6 5 4 3 2 1

For
Mildred McFall Scott
and
Wilko Buss Schoenbohm

As when water from the sea
Rises,
Becomes a cloud
Driven by north winds and
Falls to rivers
Flowing back to the sea,
So time
Becomes memory
And memory time.

Down the winding cavern we groped our tedious way, till a void boundless as the nether sky appeared beneath us, and we held by the roots of trees and hung over this immensity; but I said: if you please we will commit ourselves to this void, and see whether providence is here also.

—William Blake, *The Marriage of Heaven and Hell*

CONTENTS

PREFACE

Three years ago when I was working on the third chapter of this book, I read its first section, "First Fragmentary Image," to Wilko Schoenbohm. It was twilight in a summer's evening, and we sat on his deck which overlooked a small meadow that fell through a grove of cottonwood trees, down to a stream. Memory and concentration defined serious problems for him as he struggled to remain in touch with the world around him, but his sweetness of spirit came out clearly when he regained from time to time his perceptiveness. When I finished reading he looked out to the tall trees and to a bridge that crossed the stream and, I thought, remembered something that I could not know. The brevity of his memory and the brevity of the moment of which I spoke in the few paragraphs seemed to rise together in a moment of quiet insight. He said, "That is beautiful." I remember that I took his words to refer not so much to what I had read as to the moment in which his memories gave a living intensity to what I read and turned my words into his experience, a brief experience in which I was a participant, but one that his memories and generosity transformed and carried beyond my grasp. And I now remember that bygone event, which is quite beyond my reach, as I commerate him.

Many years earlier, shortly before her death and long after she had lost most of her awareness, my mother's eyes flashed with recognition as her grandchildren walked into her hospital room. Although no longer capable of forming words or syntax, she laughed, reached out to them, and made the same sounds with the same rhythms that had accompanied her words and were tailored to each grandchild when they came to visit her, sounds and rhythms that had welcomed them for many years when she was "herself." She again gave each of them their place of greeting and affirmation in her singular connections with them. Later she hummed along as best she could as we sang familiar songs before she sank back into an oblivion into which none of us could accompany her—only to come back again, now and then, into the light of activated recognition which restored us to her world and which brought with it new greetings and grandmotherly pleasure.

Although this book is about remembering and memory's loss that often happen beyond people's grasp and that are quite nonpersonal, I wish to begin with this dedication to two people who, like so many others, have enjoyed and suffered the time of memory with a stark pronunciation that makes unmistakable its force in our lives. I also wish to remember their undiminished gentleness and kindness in the midst of this force that gives us incomparably rich moments in accompaniment with unspeakable devastation.

The book also figures, usually in undetectable ways, the influence and good offices of many people. Among them are Ashley Pryor, Ashley Green, Michael Jarrett, Virginia Schoenbohm, Toni Mooney, Beth Ondo, Rita Munchinski, John Sallis, John Stuhr, Ben Pryor, Michael Hodges, Idit Dobbs-Weinstein, Dan Conway, Jeff Nealon, Rich Doyle, David Krell, John Lachs, Bob Fancher, Michael Spinkle, Stephen Dedalus Swoyer, David Goicoechea, Dennis Schmidt, and, above all, Susan Schoenbohm.

The acknowledgment:

A shorter version of chapter 2 appeared in *Die Internationale Zeitschrift füer Philosophie* in 1996 under the title of "*Mnemosyne's Loss: Lethe, Gadamer, Heidegger, (and Derrida)*," and a paper that constitutes chapter 3 appeared in *Epoche* in 1966 under the title of "*On Originating and Presenting Another Time*." I wish to thank those journals for permission to publish that material.

CHAPTER ONE

Introduction: Measuring Shadows

Gods of Hellas, gods of Hellas,
Can ye listen in your silence?
Can your mystic voices tell us
Where ye hide? In floating islands,
With a wind that evermore
Keeps you out of sight of shore?

—Elizabeth Barrett Browning, "The Dead Pan"

We know our immediate neighborhood rather intimately. With increasing distance, our knowledge fades, and fades rapidly. Eventually, we reach the dim boundary—the utmost limits of our telescopes. There, we measure shadows, and we search among ghostly errors of measurement for landmarks that are scarcely more substantial.

—Edwin Hubble

The earliest memory I have of an experience of time and space together took the form of a problem. I was nine or ten years old and about to go three blocks from home on an errand to pick up something at a small grocery store—actually at a deteriorating house in which an old man and a young woman had put up a few shelves for cans and boxes of food, a cold box for soda pop, and a refrigerator for milk. I was in a hurry; I wanted to get there before I was there, and I wanted to be back home before I left the store. I wanted to catch up with and overtake some-

1

thing elusive. I experienced the sensation that I could not be at the end of my steps before I took them, and I could not be at the spot I left as I stepped forward. I could not be at the time I had been or, particularly, at the time "ahead" of me. That made things slower than I wanted them to be, and I fantasized that I was Plastic Man and could stretch my body in an instant to wherever I was going. I did not consider a moment's having duration: that was too short to worry about. But I did feel the impact of the longer stretch of time and space in the middle of which I seemed to find myself, and Plastic Man seemed preferable to me to Captain Marvel because Captain Marvel, like Superman, had to fly to wherever he was going and hence faced the same problem in the air that I was facing on the ground. He was considerably faster than I was, but he seemed to be in the middle of space and time in a way that Plastic Man was not. Stretching in an instant seemed faster even than Captain Marvel, and if stretching were an event of time and space, the elements had gotten so refined that I would not need to worry about them. It was like zap and I could be anywhere, any "there."

As I write of this experience, I have a vivid image in my mind. I remember where I was standing: in the summery yard of my home, looking back across the street, across two other yards that were divided by another street, and to the alley down which I would run as a short cut to the store. I remember that I was arrested by the experience, both surprised and captivated by it and surprised and captivated over being surprised and captivated by it—a double moment to which I gave no thought as I went through it, but one that branded itself on whatever in my mind is susceptible to being branded. I remember that the image came back to me occasionally with happy puzzlement. It also came back to me twelve years later when I read Kant's *First Critique* for the first time, when I was reading "The Transcendental Analytic." I could not believe that he thought that space and time were in our minds and not out there in the yards, across the streets, down the alleys, ahead of us and behind us and, I remember thinking, between us and the stars. Or if he *did* believe that, I wondered why anyone bothered to take him seriously. I did not think that time and space had much to do with imagination or "faculties" of "the" reason. I was shocked that my teacher, Harry Prosch, and another teacher, W. B. Mahan, seemed excited by his ideas.

When I had the experience of standing in the yard and looking toward the alley, I felt very distinctly that I had already lost something that I could not gain back and that I could not catch up with something that was in front of me as well as behind me. It was as though what I could not catch up with was behind me like lost time, although it seemed like it was ahead of me, like time-to-come. It seemed like lost time with distance in front of me and behind me. I could not overcome or comprehend it. I felt vague about "it" but I "knew" "it" was there in some sense. What is important to me now is that that is what I felt then and that that feeling is connected with what this book is about.

This scene bubbled up to my consciousness once again while this book was well under way. There are specific things about the event that puzzle me. I might have been wearing a white T-shirt. Maybe I was "bare shirted," that is, without a shirt, a common phrase when I was growing up. I seem to see things in the scene from my position then, standing there, vaguely aware of one shoulder that is peripherally visible as I look across the street. A young tree is to my right, the intersection of East Eighth Street and Brown Avenue is beyond the tree. The two yards, the alley in which Mrs. Patterson grew hollyhocks by her garbage can, and my sense of the stretch of the alley, only a small part of which I can see, stretching long, long up toward Mekusukey Avenue where the store is. (In this remembering I have so many associations with each of these places and parts of these places that I am struggling to stay focused. I am inclined to tell you *and* me stories about each of them.) And I remember vividly the feelings—as though I now experience them—of wanting to stretch over the distances and overcome them. I also now want to stretch—or to be stretched—over the distance to then and find all the details, like a plastic man of time. When the image came to me I first thought that I went to the store to get a loaf of bread—twelve cents a loaf, recently raised from a dime—for Mother, but I am not sure. An old woman—Mrs. Doolan's mother, whom we called "Grandmother Cox"—was bedridden in the house across whose yard I was looking; I had a sense of death when Mother and I visited, and that sense was there then (and is now) as I looked across the yard—it vaguely colored my experience. I suspect that I was barefooted, but that's a guess. I am not entirely sure if an old man and a young woman ran the store. Why do I think so? I do not remember the exact location of the store. The memorial losses are beyond my grasp. But I know of them because of the vividness of a few remembered details and the cartoon quality of the scene that is spare of a living texture.

I believe that my present experience of loss in this memory mimics part of what I experienced then as lost. But if that is right, that *loss* of memory appears to be part of the vividness of my memory, and it carries over with no image at all in my memory of this event. Its inchoate quality seems to compose part of the scenic quality. In the lapse I can recognize several aspects of the experience, but I can only guess that they were connected in the experience that I remember. I do not expect to know for sure whether the connections existed then. I "know" there are losses in the images. I am reasonably clear *that* there is oblivion running through them and *that* I do not explicitly *perceive* the oblivion except by abstraction and supposition; and I assume that abstraction and supposition "have" oblivion as part of their origin. I would say that oblivion lets the remembered, vivid things be vivid and appears as "something" abstract and speculative that gives the gaps, as it were, in which other memories and present happenings provide texture and instance. Oblivion *appears* with a degree of abstractness when I imagine that this now tattered and sketchy scene, in its experiential moment, will die with me, that it has oblivion in its (and my) future. That is why, I suspect, a moment ago I wondered if Grandmother Cox figured inchoately into my experience then. Was I also experiencing tacitly something about death and oblivion as I imagined the stretch of Plastic Man in the context of lost time and unovercomeable distance? I really do not know. But I am sure that's the way it looks to me now.

Perhaps there are ways to speak not only speculatively about loss in memory. Perhaps there are ways to speak performatively and presentatively of such loss, to speak of the occurrence of memory's loss in ways that allow its nonimagistic, nonsubstantive bearing to communicate nonmetaphorically in the midst of images, metaphors, and nouns. Speaking in such a way is like speaking of emptiness that pervades determined experiences and things in the world or of passage of life in the coming of life. I believe that such speaking need not be mysterious or cultic, even if it departs from our usual manners of expression. Memory's loss, like loss of life or incompleteness in the "fullness" of present existence, is quite ordinary in the sense that it accompanies other ordinary occurrences of memory. The issue is one of attention—or mindfulness—before "something" that we are prone to overlook and in that sense to forget, to lose in our dealings with each other and with whatever we confront. Perhaps this overlooking itself manifests an aspect of memory's loss. We shall have to see if that is the case.

Exploration of ways to speak and think perceptively in memory's loss (as well as about it) thus constitutes part of this book's subject, and that requires us to be attentive to its occurrence, to carry out an unusual discipline of attention in order to be aware of a usual aspect of memory.

I quoted Edwin Hubble at the beginning of this introduction because of his clarity about what he and his colleagues do not know, and this is a book that deals in part with what I do not expect to know by means of objectivity. I am not writing about "ghostly errors of measurement," exactly, but the figure of "dim boundaries" does arise frequently, and I suppose that present figurations of past events could compose ghostly errors of measurement. But these "errors" are not ones that I believe will in time be erased by knowledge, and I am looking for manners of expression that give something like a countenance to the erroneousness of the present past. I find myself before "something" that I cannot touch—not quite like the dark matter in the universe that can be seen by telescopes only in its absence, but not completely unlike it either. I hesitate to use the metaphor of *matter* in speaking of past events because they in their past eventfulness do not seem to hold the promise of illumination, much less of touching presence. They "appear" as past and out of sight. Or they appear in remnants of effects and affects and in present expressions and transformations of influence, which I shall call "memories." The dimension of past events includes loss of touch and sight, loss that I shall name "forgetfulness," and it includes a ghostly quality of withdrawn presence. Erroneousness is also in the dimension of past presence insofar as past events are not the present events of their memory. So "erroneousness" might name one measure of past events. However we name them and their dimension, they compose dim boundaries in our knowledge, boundaries that measure loss of experience and occurrence, of sight and touch. They appear in recession before occurrences of their recall and presentation.

In my boyhood experience of my inability to catch up with where I could have been had I started earlier—always earlier and earlier and never catching up—I could never be in the moments that I felt that I had lost. And now I cannot regain the palpability of the events I remember—they are always earlier than I am and other than I am. And yet I feel in touch with them in the vividness of my memory and in the influences that they seem to exercise in my puzzlement and conceptions out of which this book arises. My experience then of a lost future belonging to a lost, past possibility is intensified as I write of those events in what I can now say composes for them a future that both loses them and retains them in a dim and ghostly way.

We may know our immediate neighborhood "rather intimately," as Hubble says, but our knowledge fades in the distance of the past and "fades rapidly," as we reach the "dim boundaries" of presence. The presence of the past events is missing. Or I could say that in the presence of past events *their* happening is missing.

Three of Jacques Derrida's phrases stood out as I thought of this introduction: "and I am paraphrasing here for whomever no longer recognizes me"; "unless it be so that one should no longer recognize me, another way of saying . . . that people finally recognize me"; "forgetting me on the pretext of understanding me."[1] When he wrote those words, Derrida was struggling with Geoffrey Bennington's effort to show a certain, closing systematicity in his thought, and in this struggle he is also mourning the loss of his mother's recognition of him first through dementia and then through death. In this context I note that the one I remember—me, then, as a boy—does not know me or recognize me at all. I suppose that that is characteristic of most memories, excluding those, perhaps, in dreams in which a younger (or older) 'I' or someone else from the past does know me. But even then I am not so sure who is recognized. Dream figures, for example, who are similar to ghosts in some ways, may know and recognize from all kinds of perspectives including that of a persona from the past. But in the above instance, I—the ten-year old—does not know me now at all. I now seem to be doing all the recognizing. Were I to engage in a process of active imagination so that in my vision he turns around from his gaze across the yards and streets to the alley and looks at me and gains voice, addressing me, not from the grave but from the "imagined" yard of East Eighth Street, he would be speaking now, not then. He would now be someone different from then, in quite different circumstances, and however moved or scared I might be before his gaze and in his recognition, I can know that his body and voice and sight are now and not then. That's what makes such events spooky. Something both "real" and "unreal" is happening. Something, along with all of its emotive and psychological power, happens virtually. I do not mean "unreal" when I say "virtual" in this context, but rather, different, not him then. This instance of active imagining does not overcome loss, is not even an instance of Plastic Man reaching back to "then," but, *like* Plastic Man, the subject of the active imagination is subject to imaginary time and space. I then do not recognize me now, and I now do not recognize a palpable him then.

I do not understand him in many important ways. I now identify him (me), but my living event then is quite lost in its remembered moment. I lose him in recognizing him—like a cartoon, I said above. And I now, as I have noted, am utterly lost to him then. That is a lot of loss that figures in the memory. Returning to Derrida's last quoted phrase, I can say that "I then" and "I now" are foreign to each other in the memorial event. In getting what came before there is a loss of recognition: in this memory there is a forgetting. If I believe I now recognize him *then*, I do not understand the memory. And if I believe that "I as a boy" recognizes me now, I now lose touch with myself in that experience. Only by knowing the losses and *in* the losses can I remember with some clarity of understanding.

And yet I believe that I recognize something about myself through this memory, and the losses that I have noted seem to be inherent in the recognition and memory. The combination of memory, recognition, and loss of events composes part of what this book is about.

Nonvoluntary memory, for the most part, is not about truth if by truth we mean accuracy and fact. Nor is the issue one of deceit, lying, or misapprehension. Memory occurs in so many ways other than a process of active, factual recall. We speak of genetic memory, its transmission of a past that reaches far beyond human kind. Racial memory; family memory; womb memory; suppressed and secret memories; lost memories; deep, unconscious cultural memories: the "work" of these kinds of memories has little to do with active recall. When we call up memories by imagining or by associations, when we look for the regions of mind that they seem to inhabit, something quite different from merely looking for mental objects occurs. Our looking already involves memories. We happen as memorial events as we function as agents that look for and find remembered things. Memory appears to be pervasive of the activity of looking for memories, pervasive of perceiving, and in no sense limited to looking for and perceiving objects. Mentation seems to belong to memory and memory to mind. Indeed, *mind* and *memory* might name the same "thing." But whether or not they are identical, they are not separable in our language, and the limits of memories appear evasive, giving one a sense of infinity in their mutable manifestations, their lack of a clearly delineated region or "geography."

Memory's "truth" appears to be its manifestation, not its object or an aspect of its object. Memory seems to occur as the manifestation of things in their significance and meaning—to infuse their meaning and significance—in both their generality and particularity. In terror, for example, memory seems to function in an immediate, "animal" way as an overwhelming reminder of fragility and life-threat and as a nonreflective perception (recognition) of extreme danger and the importance of continuing to live. It is neither right nor wrong. It is sheer perception. Further, a sense of happiness that is associated with the smell of salt in the air is neither right nor wrong, nor is fear of tunnels, love of flying, or attraction to light. But they are all manifest with and in nonvoluntary memory.

I would like to see the extent to which the phenomenological emphasis on appearing and manifestation can help in perceiving and interpreting memory. It is an emphasis that has its own dimension of memory that I will have occasion to consider. It is also an emphasis that will allow me to give disclosure and appearance a privileged place as we consider the truth of memory.

I find an unresolved tension between abstraction and concrete experience as I deal with memory. I can state this issue by saying that memory occurs as feelings, immediate states of mind, lost presence, and determinate senses of life. It happens in the ordinary occurrences of suffering, ecstasy, boredom, recognition of things as some *things*, a sense of identity or lack of it, anxiety, or serenity. Such occurrences do not happen as formulations in their movement and intensity. Abstraction, formulation, and all other kinds of representation have their own memorial dimensions. They too are memorial events. But they are often—I would say usually—different events from those that they address, signify, and understand (or misunderstand). The tension is found in this difference. I wish to underscore, and hence I repeat, that thinking, describing, and formulating are living events, uncircumscribably rich and diverse in their living histories and moments. They too belong to past and future events that they cannot encompass. But most of the time they are not the events that they address—unless thinking discloses with awareness its own memorial dimension and determination as it addresses a given subject matter. One could put emphasis on the limits of thinking, show what it cannot do, establish its finitude. But a further and distinct possibility, a performative one, occurs when thinking gives expression to "what" it cannot intend or "place" appropriately in a formulation. For now I wish to anticipate an effort of attention to what thinking and writing say nonvoluntarily as distinct to what they say representationally—an effort to let them intensify their memorial dimension by cultivation of alertness to thinking's performative, living event, and thereby to sensitize my thinking to unrepresentable memorial events. Perhaps in thinking's nonrepresentational aspect we can encounter occurrences without representation or abstraction.

This effort does not suggest that a thinking event is the same as what is thought about when we address another occurrence, and it does not suggest that if we are alert in the memorial occurrences of thinking we will have immediate access to other memorial occurrences. It does suggest, however, that encounters with what is unrepresentable can occur with alertness and without a dominance of representation or reflection.

Nothing will be captured by the thinking and writing of this book. Rather than a system of memory that can be reproduced, I find memory's escape from systems and formulations: as I describe aspects of memory—especially nonvoluntary memory— the active memorial dimension of the descriptions as well as of what I describe will often elude me, show only a little of their differences as they withdraw from my determinations, and their withdrawal will make ill-advised the idea of their capture by thought or perception (or by words, categories, and systematic laws).

Memory in human life might be likened to a huge sponge in the sea, stretching the extent of the sea, pervaded by the sea, differentiated from the sea, and yet codeterminant with the sea of its "place" and the "water" that it absorbs.[2] But although something like this metaphor, memory is also not at all like this. Lost to its metaphors, lost to its determination, yet disclosive, passing, seemingly everywhere in human life: memory in its loss is the subject of this book.

One kind of movement that occurs in memory is the turning of one thing into another thing, a play of transformation with a carryover, a trace, of what is lost. The word *trace* for this kind of 'carryover' does not do justice to the turning movement that it names. Although one thing's signifying or symbolizing another is an important aspect of memory, I do not have that in mind now. As when love turns into hate, in one of the most astonishing experiences we can have, or equally astonishing, when hate turns to love, an event can turn into its opposite or into something else. There are occasions in which we can show what was the case—show in the probable sense that it is accessible to careful perception and mutual agreement by those who care to look or listen. I do not mean that the aspect of loss in a memorial event exhausts or adequately describes the event. I wish to emphasize, rather, that in memory radical transformations can occur and can be shown to occur, and those transformations are crucial for an understanding of memory. A little boy, for example, can turn in memory into a little girl, or a recorded touch on the cheek can transform in memory to a slap on the mouth. I believe that such transformations are common in dreams and in both voluntary and involuntary remembrance of things past, and often one is not sure when or whether the transformation takes place. It is as though new differentiations were continuously taking place, making transformation available to whatever took place.[3] With these shifts, a specific time can appear to alter in its specificity, bringing with the alteration degrees of disorientation, differences of perspective, a feeling that something unknown is arising out of the bygone event, as though a new future is occuring in the context of a mutated past-present event. One may simply and quietly be aware of being alert and present with the past in a way distinct to his or her awareness before the transformation took place.

The transformation, I shall say, is itself a memorial occurrence for the mind that experiences it. Such transformation shows memory as surely as the presentation of past things does, and it makes questionable any fixed identity that we give to memories as well as to "memory." This transformational fluidity makes questionable my use of the proper noun *memory*— another tension that I struggle with in this book.

This kind of transformation appears also in transferences of meaning from one situation to another. The misidentified 'Giotto' frescoes of Francis of Assisi in the Cathedral of San Francesco, for example, might carry in their attribution to a well-known artist the meanings of deception, regional competitiveness, desire for recognition, and avarice in the presentation of this saint of truth, divestiture of power, and self-sacrifice. Or the etchings of cruel events by Hogarth might carry the meaning of compassion in their commemoration of terrible acts. The therapist becomes the father, the father becomes the mother, the sea becomes the god, and the hero becomes a substitute for my weakness. Memories may also carry and fuse with other different memories and experiences by which memories are borne (and sometimes born) through transformations. And the newly met man might mean to me both father and mother and hero and devil all at once in a flashing complex of memorial associations. Consistency and literal accuracy do not have much value in the transformative dimensions of memories' happenings. Much can be lost in the creative transformations of memories.

Steeped as I am in these thoughts and their experiences of loss and creativity, I feel a sense of sadness and exhilaration at once. So much impermanence, so much dying and fading: the wonder of this man who died, now remembered, his incomparable life, his laughter and pettiness, his presence and density, his struggles and failures and courage, gone as though in a gust of wind, passing and over while I remember him. And yet—listen and look again. She, there, smiling, beckoning, very present with a faint scent of some flower—what was . . . what is that scent? Was it in the field on a spring day?

But there is a severity in these transformations that my nostalgic indulgence does not reach. The severity is found in the coming of memories as well as in their passage. Severity is found in the loss that invests their memorial return, in the loss of presence in the return of what was and now, transformed, is contemporary. It is like the severity of being in an accident, of being confronted by eminent and unavoidable danger, of losing the life of something important, of the futility of wanting "now" to last forever, or the severity of any other passing event. Events take place, make demands, and persist for a while. They are severe in the sense that they are quite singularly as *they* happen to pass, and in their occurrences they seem often to efface other bygone events whose meaning and images they carry. How are we to speak and think of them appropriately before the severity of their coming transformatively to pass? How do we measure the appropriateness of our response? How do events figure a forgetfulness of the other events that they present? How might we recognize and speak of the forgetting that appears to accompany memory? By means of awareness *in* the transformative memorial occurrences? A group of hypotheses of this book constitutes an affirmative answer to this last question.

I do not intend that the word *awareness* suggest a unitary consciousness. Awareness specific to a singular but complex situation is what I have in mind. This intention might not succeed. 'Awareness' might inevitably suggest something too encompassing, something too indebted to transcendental structures, too subjective. My effort will be to show that the "place" of remembrance and awareness is often found in events that are not in subjective actions or states, that memorial awareness is found in arrangements, institutions, rhythms of movement, and lineages of development. By showing that awareness is not necessarily an event that describes individual people, I wish to show that it is characterized by an unencompassable "quality," by difference from an individual's consciousness, and that part of its difference is found *in* events of loss and forgetting. *Indeterminate determination* is one experimental phrase I use in this attempt to describe some occurrences of awareness that accompany nonvoluntary memories. The genealogical projects of Nietzsche, Foucault, and Derrida might help in this descriptive effort. We will see.

Like 'awareness,' 'memory' does not suggest one thing or a unitary phenomenon. It is not a same thing of which there are more or less dominant and subordinate parts—a hypothesis that my language will both suggest and violate on many pages. We cannot say that memory as such "is." So what are the strategies, in the case of memory, to contrast the kind of identity and sameness that the word seems inevitably to suggest?

I am working toward an emphasis on singularity of awarenesses and memories. In addressing remembering and forgetting I will attempt to valorize such occurrences as gatherings and dispersions, differences in gatherings, differences of gatherings, gathering indifferences—differential gatherings—dividing in constituting, and constituting by differentiation. If this strategy succeeds, I will counteract by my language its own direction toward generalization in the descriptive processes. I do not know how else to proceed in order to speak about memory in "its" appearances, "its" multiplicity, "its" difference from an "it" or an "anything." That is part of what I am attempting to do by describing the play of losses in memorial presentations and in my effort to keep memory in mind in our encounters with legacies of mentation and experience. Memories are already "there" when we speak or think, not as an origin, but as inheritances, structures, associations, inevitabilities, possibilities, forms of enactment. Protean, fluid, in constant differential continuities and enablements—we do not seem able to step outside of memories as we speak of them, to bracket them or neutralize them. We seem to be in and through them. They are already "there," in their losses and appearances, stitching us together in a ghostly, changeable fabric of determinations, combinations, and regularities that carry—transfer—memory's nondetermination, a very strange 'already-being-there' that manifests a shadow of 'not there at all' and 'it was otherwise.' Memory I believe pushes us to this kind of language, not because 'it' is an essence, but because 'it' lacks essence in giving determinations. As I address memory's loss, and hence forgetting, I am thus addressing occurrences that are located in situations and that are not fully defined by their situational determinations. But their transcendence of their situations is found in the losses they figure and by a mutability that leaves them without an essence. If one overlooks the situatedness of even our most open events, however, one denies crucial aspects of those events and engenders ideals and language that embody destructively such denial. Even our deepest silences and most radical beginnings bear memories, some of which appear obliquely and faintly and some of which disappear in arousal of other memories. One of my primary contentions is that memory and its loss accompany all events to which we can refer in any way. 'Memory's loss' addresses occurrences of time—happens as timing—and indicates that 'timelessness' is as temporal, as saturated by memory and memory's loss, as is any 'now,' any 'eternity,' any seeming indeterminacy. Loss of memory happens with memory as well as with a dimension of nondetermination; such loss composes a strange occurrence of forgetting and a withdrawal of events in the coming of events. There is no haven of pure loss—that would be death—or pure beginning which in its indeterminacy would be dead too.

This book proceeds in an ambiguous relation to psychology. I have not valorized psychoanalysis or any other therapeutic method of remembering, nor have I paid close attention to neurological accounts of memory. These strategic omissions do not indicate a lack of respect or appreciation. They indicate, rather, a different language and conceptuality from those of these disciplines. I also do not wish to engage in a deconstructive study that shows that these disciplines in fact are permeated by the complex kind of event I am calling "memory's loss." On another occasion efforts to find common ground for translation of the different conceptual grounds could be worthwhile. But not now.

However, I welcome the finitizing and singularizing occurrences that are peculiar to individuals and groups of individuals. I find it apparent that no act of mentation occurs without the direct influence of individual and social "histories." How such influences occur in situations that often have been interpreted in Western traditions as "pure," as free of all singular determinations, constitutes a recurring issue throughout this book. I suspect that the act of bracketing the unique "psychologies" of individuals in association with what they think and how they are able to think (and how they think they think) is an aspect in the production of the idea of transcendental consciousness, a production, I suspect, that carries blindly many inchoate feelings about loss, finitude, uncertainty, instability, and meaninglessness.

Knowledges of both psyche and logos are now in question, and I wish to make a turn toward rethinking such knowledges by considering genealogical thinking, first broadly and then in some of its particularities that are relevant for this study of memory and memory's loss. In this way, I hope to divide the importance of personal and cultural singularities from the dominant value of subjectivity and to allow a singular impact by singularities to engage the ways we understand such generalities as time, memory, and truth. I want to pay attention to ways in which we are ignited in awarenesses, not necessarily into a conflagration of ecstasy or rapture, but into recognitions, evaluations, and insights that are memorial events. It is as though 'we' are like embers, already alight in memories, and thereby subject to burning brighter or to going out. It's a rough image, but perhaps it will lead to something brighter.

I imagine that usually there has been disagreement in Western culture over the question of whether the gods are (or a God is) actually present and if they are, whether they can be understood literally and directly or only indirectly through experiences—like gifts of fiery ecstasy—that cannot be communicated adequately by human speech. People are certainly able to experience passions so intensely that they feel "outside" of themselves, transported to dimensions of "reality" that seem far beyond the limits of ordinary, normal life. In such experiences they might think that they are not the subjects of memorial passions that take them into a reality that is vastly different from any that they otherwise know, that they undergo something that they cannot create or explain. Those kinds of interpretations can lead to all manner of religious or quasi-religious meanings that are attached to the experiences. Some people are overcome by inexplicable desire for another person, so overcome that they have neither justifications nor interpretations, but are drawn and driven by the other as though by a power that they do not own or control. Language becomes simpler then. People do not need the complications or subtle distinctions that theoretical language requires. They can state simply and directly that this is what happened: "I was so overcome by a passion so strong that everything in me was alive, drawn, transformed by this energy. There was only the experience. I was lost to everything else, completely without other thoughts, completely without distraction. I had never before felt so— ALIVE." And that experience can be seen as free of determining memories, as composing something like a thoroughly mysterious participation in a "higher" reality or in another dimension when compared to everyday life. People are transported into ecstasies of love, sight, pure and simple conviction in which something transcendent speaks so unmistakably that normal language appears to be a source of mistake and unworthy of deep trust—as though these "spaces" and "times" were independent of the memories that compose them and make them very much a part of a culture, of an individual's identity, and of one's everyday life.

I could not write as I have in the last paragraph if I were a devotee of such experiences or if I believed that such experiences do not happen. I view them to be as moving and transforming as they can be deceptive and misleading. I think of them as normal under certain circumstances, as reasonably predictable in those circumstances, as utterly human and, in the light of this book's theme, as filled and determined with nonvoluntary memories. Change the memories and the circumstances and possibilities change. Change circumstances and possibilities, and the meaning of the experiences change. But when we deal with nonvoluntary memories we *are* dealing with one of the most elusive, evanescent, and transcending aspects of human life, an aspect that effects and affects bodies, gives power and perception to ideas, and provides senses of reality that can be radically contradictory and hostile to each other. Memories and their syntheses give a sense of illusion in some experiences of reality and a sense of reality under some circumstances of illusion—as when a person in an extremity of fright remembers that he is not about to be abused by a remembered, angry, and powerful individual but is in a therapeutic setting that "holds" the frightful event with him. But we also might not be able to be sure about the edge between "reality" and "illusion" in memories' occurrences. As reality occurs in memorial syntheses, even the idea of empirical occurrences is in question: the "empirical" might well be aborning in the memorial event, and what once seemed so utterly clear now is beginning to appear obscure in a new figuration that provides a different kind of real clarity. Memories' seemingly infinite flexibility (because of their syntheses) gives most (I believe all) experiences to shimmer in nondetermination—in mere capacity for change—as they establish specific and indubitable events. It's not that overwhelming experiences are wrong. It's that they are overwhelming by virtue of very transitory, embodied memories, whether those memories arise out of an individual's past or out of a culture's memorial dimensions. They do not seem to merit the unquestioning certainty or the blind dedication that they can arouse. They can be worshipful if they do not destroy too much or take themselves with metaphysical certainty, but in most cases they become like tyrants or addictions that forget much in their spasms and inspirations of power or pleasure. Memories, on the other hand, with their apperceptive qualities—their alert ways of holding, by mutable syntheses, many things together and providing situations in which recognitions and other perceptions are possible—give experiences of transcendence to states of affairs. They embody processes of transformation and mutation and thereby add a dimension of transformability to any experience or occurrence of awareness. That transformability seems to me to compose, at times, a sense of transcendence and of a dimension radically different from situations in which people find themselves. This is a transcendence of evanescence that allows us to experience the memory-infused instability of any experience, no matter how rapturous or important it may appear. In the work of memories, one need only pause for a while to allow other memories their arrival and displacement of those that had seemed so overwhelming and transfixing—"a while" might be a few hours, a few days, or a few years. We might well call such pausing 'memorial *phronesis*' in which an image of the flow of memories replaces images of "nonmemorial" substance and conditions for experience. Then a practical wisdom concerning memories' occurrences affirms the flow of recognitions and passions and displaces expectations for stasis without memorial synthesis and for a static transcendence of evanescence. This would be a practical wisdom that recognizes in all human events the power of memories and the irretrievable losses they carry, both of which give vital figurations in the depths and heights of awareness, sensuality, and affirmation. In this context, the book addresses apperception *in* memorial events, especially in nonvoluntary memorial events over which usually we exercise no immediate control.

I am writing this part of the book at some distance from city (or town) lights, and the range and brightness of the stars return to my experience with unusual force. I am impressed with the strange process of giving names to stars. They are so distant and other. When I look at them and do not think of their names—either Greek or contemporary names—I am surprised by the intensity of my astonishment in their lack of identity. I do not mean to suggest that my response is either appropriate or inappropriate, and I know that it has a history that goes back as far as I can remember, memory of being held by my mother, for example, wrapped in a blue blanket, in the middle of the night to see a lunar eclipse when I was very young, but also as far back as I can read in literary sources. Memories, both personal and cultural, are already there as I look up at the stars. But "we" know also that some of the lights I see in this clear atmosphere are from sources that have ceased to burn. They "are," "we" know, burned out, not glowing anymore, and the light I see started its traversal of space before *Homo sapiens* were on the earth—possibly before large mammals were on this planet, perhaps even before our solar system took shape. And we give them names such as—MI29476. I can see why, and I can see why our ancestors named them after other figures—such as Orion or Virgo or Draco. As a boy I was always pleased with the names the Big Dipper and the Little Dipper, rather than Big Bear and Little Bear, because the names reminded me of grandmother's house, the well, the bucket, the dippers, and the novelty of no faucets, the happy smell of the dipper and the freshness of the earth-cooled water in summer when it was hot. But here, now, the stars override their names and the associations that come with their names. Their distance in the darkness is so immense, so singular and absolute. And some of "them" shine and are not "there." I suppose I tame them to a degree by thinking that memories are like they are. I'm especially struck by their twinkling, which means intermittence of their light, and by the abstract knowledge, which sometimes seems more concrete than I "know" that it is, that some of "them" are not there anymore, but I still see "their" light. And I know that, while it is not now true but will be true at some distant time, Polaris, the North Star, by which we take our bearings, will not mark the north (although it will still shine for centuries). I also think of memories' bearings and wonder how many still shine in the absence of their origin, burned out signals for knowledge of where we are, markers that will change and mark no longer a stability, light by now dead stars.[4]

Throughout the book I describe and refer to a variety of mythological figures. I find in these figures patterns of memories, experiences, and occurrences that have been exceptionally affective in our lineage. They are also helpful because in them connotations of universality are severely restricted. The mythological figures are diverse and complex in their historical developments and contexts and in their incorporation of events, as well as of many other local and regional figures. The divergence of many elements that define them allows them to figure highly complex and subtle happenings and dimensions of experience and to open up for us many strands of memory and perception in the fabric of our cultural inheritances. Their affectiveness, I repeat, is in their suggestive and disclosive powers, not in universal, narrative forces, and I refer to them heuristically and strategically, not in order to establish something substantive about the world, but rather in order to indicate memorial figurations of culture-forming perceptions and interpretations. In this study I take them as "embodiments" in images and texts—as comprising remembrances of determinate kinds of experiences. These remembrances are carried in part by the dispersed and ununified mythological presentation of the figures. These "presentations" have an illusive and shimmering quality. They are multilayered, frequently composed of opposing elements, held together at times by personae that seem whimsical and daunting in the force of their arbitrariness. Their presentations appear both fragile and compelling, not subject to the clarity of a system, and usually resistant to whatever defines them with objective rigor. Sensitivity to their presentations and their continuation in their complex and divergent identities are germane to the memorial events that are important for this particular writing. They give an opening to several of the questions that arise in this book. To attempt to nail down the origins of the mythological figures or to prove the superiority of one hypothesis over another or to elaborate or contrast the scholarship that makes possible these observations would be inappropriate here, since my intention is to allow these figures in their multiple, often divergent dimensions to help us along our way toward developing language and concepts that expose us to the loss of memory in memorial occurrences and also to expose us to a striking kind of occurrence in which lack of determination in some situations seems also to engender other determinations. As historical, mythological, and familiar in their strangeness, as both not literal and yet disclosive of perceptive, if often inchoate formations, they can indicate experiential directions and dimensions of ways in which things come to appear with us and to appear with more affectiveness at times than characterizes clearer and more manageable concepts. I am looking for a reciprocity among some of these figures and some of the concepts in this study—a region of interplay—that can intensify our alertness to occurrences of memory's loss and to images of 'what' is not an image.

In a word, these figures can enact a combination of contradictory elements—often radically contradictory elements—which occur simultaneously with each other in the figurations and which exclude or resist each other in their differential simultaneity. In such enactments each figure suggests multiple capacities and directions in which opposition, contradiction, or strong divergence takes place. These enactments compose losses by means of differentiations, losses of identity as one aspect composing a figure ceases to be itself and loses its movement and force at the border of its occurrence, loses its effectiveness and reach as one aspect comes to be dominated by another aspect. Apollo's aspect of order and proportion, for example, loses force and fades into the background of the force of his violence and pride as well as before his divination and dream aspects. The "whole" identity of these figures is riven by borders of "internal" differentiation and the losses that occur as one aspect or another exercises its power at the expense of other aspects. These losses are losses in the interstices of differences within the mythological figures, and the losses are embodied in the figures along with the positive power and meaning of these aspects. The figures' mythological enactments thus include considerably more than values and truths. They often include losses of the values and truths that they also enact. They perform losses of their own positive determinations. Mnemosyne, for example, enacts in her figuration, as we shall see, events of presentation and the loss of presentation regarding bygone times. I shall say that the loss of recall is also a kind of memory, one that is to a degree describable, and one that accompanies the divergent elements that determine who these mythological figures are in their connection and differences with other figures.

Although these mythical figures usually do not play parts in contemporary rituals and thus do not compose ritual enactments, they carry in their figurations—in the very complex formations in which they are presented, textualized, and remembered—what we may call "genealogical memories," memories that are embodied *in* the mythological figures. They can show, in addition to their own histories of formation, movements and forms of experience and perception that are deeply a part of our culture. Such mythological enactments can be found in the performances of our cultural activities and awareness. The play of determination and loss of determination, for example, that are found in both Dionysus and Mnemosyne may well carry and show not only something about Western experiences of tragedy and artistic memory but also something about a deep uncertainty in Western culture concerning clarity and oblivion.

The mythical gods were given a more focused and more unified presentation by Homer and Hesiod, who de-emphasized their multifarious, local significances. These limiting presentations in fact increase the genealogical importance of their multifaceted, submitted aspects within their dominant, unifying Olympian identities. Their poetic and political unification as Olympian figures nonetheless retained internal diversity within their personae, bringing to expression a persistent problematic of identity that marks our lineage and one that is germane to this study: Identity is found repeatedly in question by virtue of internal conflicts among incompatible or conflicting forces of memory. The unified figure manifests deep resistance to its own unification. It figures if not a war of differences at least a dynamic struggle of marginalized but nonetheless operative centripetal forces. Those forces are like memories of differences and differentiations in the appearance of established identities. They are affective in their differences from the dominant identity, differences that are "at work" in the constitutive whole. Apollo, for example, is rent by oppositions to the clarity of his shining order, rent by the dark and chaotic aspects of his own figuration and by the juxtaposition in his "identity" of promise and threat. Hermes carried aspects of both deceiver and guide. Mnemosyne carries in her memorial figuration a force of oblivion.

In this approach I thus understand these figures to show more than systems of explanation, classification, and order. They do show varieties of order, but they also show complex interplays of divergent aspects of experience, perception, and presentation. They constitute spacial figurations—regions—of identity and conflict in the forces of which our cultural world is in part manifest. They present aspects of perceptive awareness in our tradition which can be suggestive as we attempt to describe how the world comes to appear as it does. Those figures can suggest to us something about the complex enactments of conflict, question, nonresolution, undecidability, and differentiation in the memorial dimension of our language, thought, and practice, as well as suggest to us something about troubled orders, classifications, virtual presence, and established identities in our lineage. I emphasize their suggestive power. While I presuppose that they show us something about the constitutive elements in our cultural memories, I do not take them to prove anything. They rather show us aspects of our heritage, aspects that are uncovered and expressed more readily in art and story than in conceptual systems that are governed by traditional logics or mathematical formulations. They are closer to works of art than to informational networks. I do not wish to diminish the importance of traditional logic, mathematics, informational systems, or what we traditionally call "systematic philosophy." I wish rather to point out also that the appearing of things happens in a dimension to which we find access in the special language and narration of myth, a dimension that can be, but need not be, experienced religiously and ritually. Mythical figures play an important disclosive part in our lineage, a part characterized by good and ill. They constitute figurative aspects of our historical existence, and they are especially important in their connections to their early, often Titanic lives as instances of ambiguity and conflict in which occur both nonvoluntary memory and loss of memory.

The art of mythological presentation is two-fold in this sense: on the one hand, mythical figures are extremely complex constructions that are like some works of art. They draw from many histories and cultures, and they are given established identity in one culture that is dominant in the "official" figure. Their forms and narratives carry forceful, effective traces of many differential aspects along with their primary meaning. On the other hand, they have, in their complexity, nonvoluntary power in forming peoples' experiences and perception. In addition to their former and now largely dead ritualistic force, their influence is usually in usually unnoticed aspects of language, thought, and practice—in perceptive formations that give contemporary direction, complexity, and prereflective patterns in the appearance of things. In that regard, they compose something like a *techné*, like an art of presentation that is embodied in our culture. Hence their suggestive and disclosive power.

Mythological and nonmythological presentations of nonvoluntary memory interweave throughout this book. One of the reasons for this is found in the emphasis on nonvoluntary and nonsubjective memory that accompanies some of the mythological accounts. Another has to do with their role in shaping our culture's nonvoluntary memories. In our time, a combination of 'nonvoluntary,' 'nonsubjective,' and 'memory' can seem counterintuitive; and subjectivity, when it is interpreted to include conscious and unconscious dimensions, often appears to constitute the only space and mediation of memory. The religious and quasi-theological functions of memory, (in, for example, the cults of Mnemosyne) have faded in our Western experiences of memory, and with *that* fading a strange autonomy that characterizes some kinds of nonvoluntary memories has also faded. As I move among mythological images in connection with remembering and nonmythological language and thought, I retain an emphasis on nonvoluntary and nonsubjective remembering of which some mythical cultures were so aware, while I also give emphasis to nonreligious carriers of memory (such as grammar, money, or disciplined and accepted knowledge) and to nontheological transmissions of memories (such as processes of differentiation, coming to and withdrawing from appearance, and transformations by means of memory's loss in memory's happening). The myths which I address seem to me to embody memorial events of memory's happening, to constitute recall of nonvoluntary aspects of memory, and to re-*member* memory—to reconnect it to its own loss. Loss of memory is a member, as it were, of memory's occurrence. Loss of memory in memory's occurrence carries a weird and remarkable dimension of human experience: our living connection with bygone events also enacts a living disconnection from them. To live in the immediacy of disconnection with connection is not easy. It happens as the immediacy of losses that destabilize our sense of continuity in our experiences of continuity. Nothing appears to bridge the loss or to restore the lost. In many levels of experience we suffer the losses and live in the losses that we suffer. I believe that we humans construct strange and remarkable practices and beliefs in order to effect a transformation of disconnections into connections—we will find such an effort, for example, in the Greek separation of Lethe from Mnemosyne and the transformation of Lethe into a powerful but overcomeable power of forgetful disconnection. By that separation Mnemosyne is allowed an eternal status of pure continuity that transcends death, suffering, and time, and she becomes a goddess who is associated with ascetic, body-denying behaviors as well as with the gift of immortality to accompany divination and infallible insight. She becomes a goddess who bears loss only by being without it. And yet her own figurations, we will find, carry the loss that she is taken to overcome.

From my point of view, to think as I have in the last two paragraphs shows a sharp departure from mythological presentation. While I love mythological presentations, their living power has transformed into language and thought that is not figured by the sensibility that gave rise to the explanations, experiences, and disclosures that animated the gods' presentations. I know of no viable way to love the singularity of myths other than to allow them the distance and difference from us in which they show themselves now in our culture. They carry their own loss as they require our contemporary imaginations for their perception. But the loss that they now figure can find expression in nontheological language. Mythological language holds no exclusive rights to the presentation of what seems mysterious or extraordinary to some ways of seeing things; nor is a mythologically based religious sensibility necessary for a living encounter with dimensions of experience that occur outside the domain of what some might call "reason" or "empirical verifiability." In my opinion, all that I describe and address in this book is ordinary in the sense that it happens in our daily lives without a requirement for extraordinary circumstance or special dispensations of perception. These things that I address require a "special" language only from the perspective of an orientation that is unalert to the range of expression, transmission, and recognition that now constitutes our (nonmythological) culture. Thinking without the gods, without the immediate power of their celebrations and invocations, does not necessarily mean that a person stands outside their lineage. Their lineage is expressed in the losses of their religious power and in their capacity to allow one to recall fallibly and forgetfully a bygone manner of experience and expression—bygone but not comatose in our recognition of it. They are like comets, perhaps, that stir us in our experience of their beauty and mystery regardless of our knowledge that they are composed of ice and herald no message from other worlds. But mythological figures are unlike a comet insofar as these figures compose influences and dimensions of experience that are quite alive in our nonmythological culture.

Another tension in this book operates between a procedure of following the memorial structures and forces in certain texts on the one hand and accounts of awarenesses that are not like texts on the other. In a phrase, not all phenomena are texts. Their differences give rise to engagements and deciphering that are sometimes transformative readings and sometimes descriptions of what occurs that is not written and in that sense is not literal. Not all phenomena are alphabetized. But there is a tension because these different phenomena are related in my accounts of them around issues of memory, and those issues are valorized by signs, meanings, and images, as well as by institutions and organizations, by feelings, inclinations and dispositions, bodily functions, and by intangibles—events we cannot touch or grasp by the senses—and figurations that we "see" by abstractions that lose them. I do not have a meta-term that holds them together other than *memory*, and memorial occurrences, as I have said, refuse the unifying functions that the word gives to them. I do not want to say that memory in "its" hiddenness is a secret and give that word a methodological priority. Memory, as I will show in chapter 7, considerably exceeds a secret because of its manifestness and availability. Nor does the word *mystery* work very well, in this context, given the history of that considerably overworked word. So I live with tensions among very different sites of attention that lack a clear and identifying field that locates them within a measure of stability. With its stops and flows I hope that this book will give an emphasis to the singularity of the events that I approach.

The plasticity of memories, figured by loss, happens in contrast to what we might call "biological" or "genetic memory." The memory of the sea in the salinity of our blood or a primitive one of danger that takes place in the panic of flight or fight or of seasonal "nature" in metabolic changes that accompany changes during a year may well not be as characterized by the re-membering that I have indicated characterizes other kinds of memory.[5] The comparatively static quality and its importance for survival in genetic memory probably constitute their own kind of incomparably important memory, figured, I speculate, among other things by stubbornness, conservatism, and a predisposition to take care of things, maintain things and ourselves, and to take caution regarding highly transitional and dynamic situations. Without this memory, risk might not have meaning. Such memories that constitute genetic and physical structures and processes appear to be static and change, not by internal dynamism but, if at all, by the externally generated mutations of genes. Cellular structures, physical formations, the neurological patterns of sensation, our drives toward social collectivity—our so-called natural bodies—doubtlessly carry kinships with evolutionary formations and circumstances, and many of our deepest feelings and "instincts" are memorial in the sense that they compose a comparatively static witness to a species past that defines our kind on earth. They constitute a memorial grouping that seems to contrast sharply to linguistic and cultural memory. In our lives we forget our bodies' often wild and strange past at our own peril, for that past appears to be lived in our most cultivated, subtle, and self-conscious moments. I feel reasonably sure that we never leave our bodies even in the intensities of our ideals or our visions of God. This book, however, addresses primarily the dynamics of memories that occur in our social and cultural lives, and I will focus on "biological" memory only in one section of the book that addresses some issues in evolutionary theory.

CHAPTER TWO

Mnemosyne's Loss and Stolen Memories

For the longest time conscious thought was considered thought itself.
Only now does the truth dawn on us, that by far the greatest part of our
spirit's activity remains conscious and unfelt.

—Nietzsche, *The Gay Science*

I shall begin this book with a consideration of two mythical figures,
Mnemosyne and Lethe, in a context of events of transmissions and
nonintentional events of memory. Myths seem not only to exceed particular interpretations of them but also to carry with them human questions
and interpretive responses to those questions—such as, where do we come
from? or why does thunder happen? They also present intense qualities
that appear to explain nothing and to present nothing that is intellectually
graspable. I shall say that in their imagery, some myths are able to present
dimensions of occurrences that are not images or objects or subjects. I
believe that they share with language and thought this 'ability' for presentations that do not constitute an intellectual or conceptual occurrence, and
I shall say more about this kind of presentation in the course of this book.
I intend to show that the early myths of Mnemosyne and Lethe, as well as
of Dionysus and Apollo, present what I am writing about nonmythologi-
cally. As I begin, however, I shall situate aspects of Mnemosyne's and
Lethe's archaic myths within a question concerning transmission of meanings, interpretations, and their limits. In attention to these myths, might
we go beyond interpretations to a mindfulness (or perceptiveness) with

noninterpretative and nonimagistic dimensions of appearances? In beginning this way I shall orient the larger discussion by finding in
Mnemosyne's and Lethe's early mythic appearances a presentation of
memory—a memory of memorial figures, we could say—in which
imagery falls away and is lost, while a nonimagistic dimension of the
memorial occurrence remains. This movement into a dimension of presentation that is beyond the disclosive powers of images seems to show a
nonintentional aspect of memory, an aspect that, like the archaic *myth* of
Mnemosyne and Lethe, shows *in* its presentation a loss of memory,
imagery, and meaning. This occurrence of presentation thus seems to
include both memory and memory's loss which constitutes a strange and
paradoxical aspect of memorial events: I shall want to show that memory
of memory's loss composes a dimension of such presentation..

I shall also begin with a tribute to Hans-Georg Gadamer whose
ground-breaking work on interpretation has a considerable if indirect
bearing on this study, especially his concepts of 'transmissions' and 'fusion
of horizons.' My intention is to present a situation of memory—specifically a memory of Gadamer's influence on a direction of thought that gave
rise to this study, but to present the account of that influence in an inter-
pretative situation that is quite different in mood and philosophical context when compared to the context in which he wrote *Truth and Method.*
That part of this chapter will compass a small, self-aware event of horizonal fusion. In this presentative situation, and in the context of
Mnemosyne's and Lethe's complex titanic association, I find an initial
direction of thought that carries me beyond a hermeneutical orientation
and toward a way of thinking that the purpose of this book is to carry out.
The fusion of horizons that I find will direct us away from a central function for the idea of horizon as we consider memory's loss. And in the following chapters, as I concentrate on the lethic dimension of memorial
occurrences, I find both the language of transmission and its metaphors
shifting and transforming—a process that Gadamer's combined thoughts
of transmission and fusion of horizons can lead us to expect, and a process
that allows hermeneutical thought to anticipate its own transformation. It
is also a process in which the figurations of loss gain more complexity and
appear in a different (when compared to Gadamer's hermeneutical
thought) crosshatch of thoughts and descriptions—a process in which figurations of loss come more to the fore as I encounter processes of memory
in events of thought. In this encounter I also meet memorial dimensions
of appearances which figure both a grounding and an ungrounding of

thinking: I meet movements (or *logoi*) of memory that events of thinking appear to embody.

REMEMBERING HANS GEORG GADAMER

In introducing *Heidegger's Ways*, Dennis Schmidt speaks of igniting philosophical imagination, specifically of Heidegger's igniting Gadamer's philosophical imagination with his lectures on Aristotle. I found difficulty moving from that sentence until I followed a flow of images, feelings, and recollections that sprang from reading Dennis Schmidt's phrase. I recalled my first encounter with *Sein und Zeit* in Tübingen in 1957, finding in it something that aroused me in spite of my inexperience as a philosopher, something enlivening and transformative, although I had little enough sense of where or who I was philosophically to know what or who might experience transformation. I believe that a few months later, in the winter of 1958, when I came close to death in a car accident just after reading the section in *Sein und Zeit* on "Sein zum Tode," something about the connection of philosophy and the loss of life—loss of life generally, but also and most particularly my loss of life and the loss of other lives close to me—became indelible in my ability to think.

In the United States at that time and in the impact of Sartre, Kierkegaard, and Camus and with impetus from Bultmann, Binswanger, Löwith, and many others, Heidegger was often read as a transcendental existentialist. That seemed wrong to me. I found more connection between *Sein und Zeit* and *Vom Wesen der Wahrheit* than I did between Heidegger and existential philosophy. But I did not know how to speak carefully, appropriately of the difference except to say that existentialist thought lost the *question* of *quest* of being and that truth as disclosure did not lose it, that *Eigentlichkeit* addressed 'thought' and 'phenomen' in a manner different—definitely different—from a dialectic of *pour soi* and *en soi*, or of transcendental structures of existence or of self-actualization. Heidegger's thought was far more extreme than existentialist thought and far more extreme than the philosophies of Hegel or Husserl as I read them. He had understood something about the extremity of loss in life's coming, something that could not be restored, something in the extremity of loss that gave things to appear as they do and that could not be thought well in the Western experiences of transcendence, existence, or subjectivity.

In this context in the mid 1960s, I encountered Gadamer and *Wahrheit und Methode*. *Wirkungsgeschichte* (effective history), *Überliefer-*

ung (transmission, tradition), and *Horizontverschmelzung* (fusion of horizons) gave a range to *Entbergung* that considerably exceeded what I could say up to that time. Above all, Gadamer's way of linking thought, art, and tradition in a Heideggerian influence pushed my novitiate's thinking far beyond what I had been hearing and reading and thinking. That irritated me. Ignoring Gadamer's own years of effort, I was aggravated that I had been so blind as not to see immediately that only by rethinking the tradition, its enacted remembrances in its performances, approaches, and disciplines, in its perceptive enactments—and rethinking them in a manner that constituted a grave but horizonal and generative process of losses and, for me at the time, painful recognitions—that only by such rethinking could the question of being occur with life and force thought. The body of thought happens in the living tissues that give things to appear as they do in the transmissions of lineages, transmissions that live so closely to us, that are so much of us that they constitute an area of unalert blindness in the clarity of our recognitions. Through Gadamer I found an intimacy of hermeneutics and ontology that was more persuasive than what I found in Hegel, certainly more persuasive than Cassirer or Dilthey or Troeltsch, and one that returned me to the transmissional facticity of tradition as a return of the sources of thought and presentation.

In a phrase, Gadamer ignited my imagination, a gift greater than which no teacher has to give. In speaking of igniting I also speak, of course, of transformation and death, of coming to one's own, of enownment in Albert Hofstadter's word—and of the life of thought. Gadamer introduced me to the *geschichtliche* dimension of Heidegger's thought. His work, shaped in part by my own experiences and emphases, showed me in those years how thought, existence, appearance, and question happen in a radicality of time by which our tradition springs up out of its losses in its transmissions, losses that are extreme enough to allow hermeneutical transformations to appear as though they were conservations. He gave memory of Hermes to live in this American's interpretive work: Hermes the god of boundaries, thieves, deception, and tricksters, the god who is, along with Dionysus, least established, the one most given to humor. Among those who occasion dispersive gatherings, the gift of Hermes usually involves a loss. His border marker—the herm—is the sign of nothing but the marking and its invisible trajectory (or in the language that Derrida uses, the sign of signing). Hermes is the messenger of the gods, the one whose transmissions bear the gap that separates the gods from humans and from each other and in which gappy deception, questions, and illusion can originate and also steal the "reality" that seems to be given. Gadamer allowed me to see, perhaps with more pronouncement than he would have intended, that interpretation is a hermetic engagement, and that allowed me to see what I had not seen before, a smile on the part of the one who introduced the word *hermeneutics*—Aristotle, smiling with Hermes amidst a tradition of destructive forgetfulness in the disappearance of Hermes' smile.

Although I have just played with images in an indulgence allowed by Gadamer's ignition of my imagination as I worked through his writing, I also feel caution around the word *imagination*. I believe that the word has value in its signification of renewed energy, a sense of vividness, and the strange coming of figures that carry with them only the most fragile indication of their origins. In this encounter with Gadamer, I found myself before the figuration of questions that have their vividness in a tradition's insubstantial element of coming to pass. I learned in Gadamer's figurations of tradition and transmission something of Heidegger's meaning for reticence—*Verschweigenheit* and *Verhaltenheit*—as he, Gadamer, wove his thought of tradition's insubstantial element in a most careful, tactful discernment that allowed the tacit dimension of disclosure to become apparent. A determinate indication of *Gelassenheit*, I thought, as I found myself moving with the flow of his words. In a word, Gadamer's work excited in me a sense of both the fragility and the power of a culture's transmissional events. I found through him the thought that "the past" occurs as transmissions. And I found that the concept of imagination is too limited to elaborate adequately transmissional occurrences, which occur in cultural events and not primarily in subjective syntheses.

But I also feel hesitation in using the word *imagination* for the occurrence—or the site of the occurrence—of incitement. I do not wish to ignore the irreplaceable moments in which images abound in a flow of life, a flow that is most easily marked when it is absent in a depression of mental life. Rather, I want to acknowledge from the beginning that both thinking and transmission occur outside the boundaries of images, as well as within their boundaries, that the movements of thought and transmission pass a Hermes-marked border at which one undergoes the loss of images in events of thinking or occurrences of transmission, a border that easily pathologizes the metaphors and images that arise in our philosophical work—shows them both to guide us and to hide from us 'something' that is not imaginable. This pharmacological quality at the border of images can occur in the obliteration of such images as that of word and voice, even the image of image, as well as obliteration of images of *definitive* origin. We are left with an image-evacuating sense—is that a suicidal image?—of thought in the loss not only of important images but of image as such.

There are many possible strategies for carrying out a reticence, a silence, appropriate to the nonimagistic life of thought and transmission, a remarkable possibility for which Heidegger's thought—I must not say "is an image"—I might say, tentatively, "is a living memory." Before turning to his work, I turn to the image of Mnemosyne to find what happens to her image in the process of her enactment, an enactment which is presented in her early mythology as exceeding all possible imagery. In this consideration I hope that we find a way of return to Heidegger and Gadamer, a way on which and not at the end of which we find them, lost, certainly, to their own literal truth, sitting and talking together again. This is my image, after all, so I have them sitting at a table, a way-station, and talking, musing on the ways they have found to thought beyond imagery, drinking wine together and laughing often. I shall offer them small, thin, dark cigars, bring out a bottle of George Dickle bourbon, pour it for Gadamer and let him introduce it to Heidegger. As we muse with them on the way of these passing words, I propose to turn to a goddess of losing and finding in order to find out more about musing and being lost in our memories, dreams, and reflections. In Mnemosyne I find an image that requires not only the loss of her image but also loss of memory if one is to "know" her. She figures an early mythological form of both memory and loss of memory. One aspect of this loss, we shall see, is found in the imagery that presents "her." Further, the elusive element of a myth and a mythological image 'forms' an especially appropriate beginning for this study of memory's loss. We find ourselves before a nonintentional occurrence—memory's loss—in a manner of presentation—myth—that is excessive to intentional consciousness and to personal memories.

MNEMOSYNE AND LETHE

I cannot begin these remarks on Mnemosyne with an invocation in the manner of Hesiod, whose poetic story in his *Theogony* is close to the rituals in which the gods had their lives. I am closer to Byron who began one canto of *Don Juan* with, "Hail Muse, et cetera."[1] And even Hesiod's "solemnity" and "earnestness"[2] are at a distance from these hermeneutical observations. I am, however, affiliated with Hesiod's written account, which is not a recited poem or in the form of an oracle and which is not designed for worshipful performance but for a narrative and genealogical presentation that enacts its difference from both an oral tradition and worship.[3] This is part of the strange situation of memory with which I begin *in* recalling Hesiod: worlds apart from 'what' is presented, but a re-calling nonetheless in which the recalled—Hesiod's genealogical narrative—seems to play a part in my recalling presentation by virtue of its written departure from oral immediacy and religious performance. The archaic myth of Mnemosyne arises in a culture that is quite different from ours (and from Hesiod's) in which our memory happens. And yet we not only engage in something like the kind of occurrence that she and Hesiod's presentation figure as we recall her. We also are in a cultural situation that we may assume has been formed in part by her mythological heritage and imagery. I understand myself to begin, then, in an interplay of dim cultural influences that are carried in the texts themselves, influences *from* that *to* which we return. And our differences in our recall from the culture in which these influences arose are also reflected in Hesiod's difference from the culture he recalled, a culture in which the myths of Mnemosyne and Lethe had their greatest strength.

I also begin with a suspicion that an interpretation based on the structure of signification is insufficient when we think of memory, a suspicion based in part on the Gadamerian observation that what is past returns effectively in something like a fusion at the border of our present and future, a fusion I shall call it, of perceptive return and yet-to-be that gives birth to a horizon, a past present not-yet that might be more radical in the past's return than the unsurmountable slash of signifier/signified. This "fusion" in its allure might give birth—rebirth—to a muse, to an art of speaking and thinking in an enacted memory of archaic Mnemosyne, the flowing source of return. But I am moving too rapidly. For now, let us note that we are attuned to Hesiod's loss of oral presentation and worship—not obliteration but loss nonetheless, a subtle, distinct process of fading figured by his written genealogical narrative, as he gave accounts of the gods and their origins. And since we are dealing with memory let us not count this loss as a deficiency but simply as memory in horizonal articulation, memory of both the goddess Mnemosyne and her loss of divinity through transmissions of her figuration. The future of that loss did not happen so much as a failure but rather as a birth of which this writing—which takes place in the fading of Hesiod's earnestness, solemnity, and closeness to the gods, as well as in the fading of Mnemosyne's immediacy in his writing—is a distant progeny.

Marcel Detienne amplifies the loss of Mnemosyne's immediacy in Hesiod's writing by showing that in the archaic time of Greece she names a power of direct access to "The Beyond."[4] This power is most apparent in poets, bards, and diviners whose knowledge, in Homer's phrase, is "of all things that were, all things to come." 'Mnemosyne' names a power of direct vision, not primarily a recollection of past things according to a temporal perspective. She names a power to "decipher the invisible" and to make temporally real and immediate through stories and song that of which the poet sang or chanted. Or in language different from Detienne's, we can say that Mnemosyne names the self-presentation of invisible things to gifted sight and that her daughters, the Muses, are powers of presentation in time and human life of what comes from outside of time miraculously to awareness. Such presentation is orally memorialized. The singer and poet belong to Mnemosyne's power in both vision and performance. They perform truly the truth they see. Hesiod, on the other hand, is a chronicler, a writer, one who recognizes lineages and deeds and reports them. His vision and presentation are at a distance from the mnemosynic immediacy of the singer and poet, and Mnemosyne occurs more in the recall than in direct perception. Archaic Mnemosyne appears in her loss in Hesiod's classical, written memory of her.

Hesiod gave three invocations to the gods before whom he experienced a degree of awe and wonder. He does seem to undergo or at least to reflect their forces in his writing. I might choose to feel shame before his experience of the nearness of the gods and in that shame find a lineage of lost divine immediacy that also shows itself in his writing at a distance from ritual. But that would be a feeling on my part by which I would project a loss—a tragic loss perhaps—of life-enhancing divinity. I shall forego that option and attend rather to the distance that separates us from both Hesiod and the myths of divinities and attend instead to the life-enhancing aspect of that distance, to the horizonal, resourceful life of the memory that this distance and loss harbor. The memory of Mnemosyne, I shall say, figures a life of thinking and writing in which her mythological life is wildly transformed into a quite different event (a return fitting to a Titan), perhaps no less presentative and originative than her earlier, distant manifestation, but presentative by loss of immediacy rather than by direct perception. In addition to thinking and writing I shall continue to speak of such arts as poetry, music, and dance, but these arts are not *now*, of course, Greek—except in the sense of their occurring in a lineage and having a distant, mutated connection with Greek cultures. For Mnemosyne is not given to simple repetition or exact recall but to a dark transformation indigenous to her mother, earth, Gaea, and given as well to the chaotic lineage of her father, heaven, Uranus, who housed the gods with an infinite distaste for their orders: fecund Uranus, arching over Gaea with spacious noncontent and with discontent for all determinations: Mnemosyne, earthly, heavenly power, giver and taker of forms. Mnemosyne appears to happen originatively in her loss of form, substance, clarity, and identity. Does she ignite her loss? Do we find her in the transformations that we have noted by reference to writing and diminished religious presentation? Do we have access to this strange power in her loss of her archaic image?

The flow of Mnemosyne is affiliated in some aspects of Greek culture with Lethe, the "region" of forgetting and oblivion. In Plato's *Republic*, Lethe functions as an image of forgetfulness, one that Socrates recalls, but in that recall he suggests that it hides itself, that it refuses not only eternal reality but clear imagery and, in its hiding, gives humans to believe that their limited perceptiveness can traverse everything that is, the full range of being. Lethe is imagined as a river, flowing with water that cannot be contained, water that disperses determinations and discriminations and is itself nothing determinable. Drinking its water, souls cease to remember their lineages and lives. They assume a flowing transience, lost to their own stability, lost, strangely, to their own source. This loss is figured by desire: the flow of Lethe is affiliated with a desert without springing life because this water does not nourish or quench. It makes dry, gives no satisfaction, will not become a life-giving source to any organism. Those who drink of Lethe thirst as they consume its water. Lethe, daughter of dissention (Eris), figures something in the direction of chaos by way of continuous evacuation. So far, Lethe appears inimical to life, to give the soul to be "a leaky sieve."[5] The soul in this situation, as Plato writes of it, lives in a futile effort to replenish itself with immediacies that flow away as they come to presence. Its life is like an unremitting effort to be here now, continuously unsatisfied, thirsting for what Lethe gives in withdrawal. In this imagery, Lethe embodies the soul's self-forgetfulness, its withdrawal from itself as it lives out of itself.

Karl Kerényi has a hypothesis that I shall adopt.[6] He says that in its preclassical life, the image of Lethe presented the normal, temporal life of human beings. Lethe is not negative, not something suggesting a need for philosophical or Eleusinian cure. It speaks, rather, of "outflowing." The archaic image of Lethe is that of a spring, and Kerényi suggests that it is "fashioned after the spring of Mnemosyne" that springs forth, originates, and gives something for return as well as for loss. There appears to be an early and inner affiliation of Mnemosyne and Lethe that precedes their separation and externalization.[7] This suggestion is not completely at odds with Heidegger's account of self-disclosing and self-concealing in "Heraclitus' Fragment B 16," as we shall see, and brings Mnemosyne and Lethe together before their religious and philosophical dispersion. But Lethe also remains imagistically apart from Mnemosyne—a spring on the left by the cypress tree, as one figure has it, a spring that is to be avoided by the souls of the dead, whereas Mnemosyne is the spring on the right that provides the water of life, recollection, and balm. Kerényi sees the early Lethe as belonging to the land of Mnemosyne, Mnemosyne who with her daughters is the predominant power that heals the losses figured in Lethe, Lethe who belongs nonetheless to Mnemosyne's eventful region—and puts in question the imagery by which we remember her.

In this account, the *benefit* of Lethe—and hence the dominance of Mnemosyne—is found in the loss of life's disaster. Rather than constituting only disaster and darkness, Lethe also presents their obliteration—something like the withdrawal of the withdrawal of life—and defines an aspect of the muses' power to give Mnemosyne's comfort: "it is only both the elements—giving illumination and letting disappear, Mnemosyne and her counterpole, Lesmosyne—that make up the entire being of the goddess, whose name comes solely from the positive side of her field of power." (*Lesmosyne* is an early name for Lethe.) Mnemosyne in this figuration retains her titanic depths and incorporates darkness in her luminosity in a manner that both defines and makes possible their later separation.

The religious and philosophical transformation of Mnemosyne into a distant counterforce to Lethe is not altogether a surprise insofar as her lethic dimension constitutes a withdrawal of clarity as clarity occurs and makes room for the art of recovery as well as for the disaster of dumbness and oblivion. The taming of titanic Mnemosyne in forgetfulness of her lethic dimension is what her image allows us to expect. Her titanic image, inclusive of Lethe, also allows us to expect that her image is intrinsically forgetful in its power to recall, that "Mnemosyne" also presents nothing that is an image, recalls us to no image at all, no image that is lost to its imagery. From such loss in the midst of determinate images flows incitement to recall, to re-form, to present again. It is not exactly like water in a sieve, but neither is it like ontological perfection. Such loss is resourceful, almost pregnant without prior guarantees, without enduring stability: rather much like art on a horizon that discloses, that is, remembers in its performance, a resourceful loss of happenings as it refigures the happenings of its time.

I am suggesting that forgetting and loss (Lethe)—something like the oblivion of disaster as well as the disaster of oblivion—are inscribed in occurrences of remembering. I understand this to be a hypothetical descriptive claim, incited and itself inscribed in part by the memory of Mnemosyne in our lineage. As I turn to a nonimagistic dimension of Mnemosyne's image and to memory's function in thought, I shall note in a preliminary manner two ways—Heidegger's and Derrida's— to consider such inscription. By this move I understand myself to describe two figures and two approaches that play parts in determining a foreground to our hermeneutical horizon, a foreground that gives us a "before," as when we speak of our being before a hermeneutical horizon. I am also opening consideration of the enactment of Mnemosyne's lineage *with* Lethe in our activity of remembering, and I am suggesting indirectly that not only are aspects of Gadamer's thought significantly remembered and lost in aspects of Heidegger's thought in his later years, but that something of Heidegger's thought is significantly remembered and lost in aspects of Derrida's thought. Although I shall not elaborate these claims, in our context Derrida appears to me to constitute an important development for both hermeneutical and Heideggarian thinking.

HEIDEGGER AND DERRIDA

I make this turn to Heidegger and Derrida in part to emphasize from the beginning of this study that I address memory and memory's loss in the context of nonintentional occurrences that are outside of the jurisdiction of any subject. Memory and forgetting can happen in intentional fields, of subjectivity, of course. But they also happen outside such fields. One advantage of the titanic, mythical Mnemosyne is that the myth presents her outside of the range of human, intentional incorporation and direction. In her, and Lethe too, we encounter destinies in human life that are beyond the control of selves and yet are determinative of human selves. In addition to its nonintentional occurrence I shall also consider memory's loss as characteristic of the ways in which things appear: appearances occur, in their appearing, nonintentionally and nonsubjectively with both memory and memory's loss.

Both Heidegger and Derrida give descriptive accounts of nonintentional occurrences that are directly relevant to this study. One of the difficulties that a person encounters in reading them is formed in part by their language by which they attempt quite intentionally to speak and write of things that are outside of the range of intentions or subjective synthesis and yet which are within the range of . . . and here we find one of the primary issues of this book: words such as *experience, consciousness,* and even *awareness* are saturated with the suggestion of subjectivity and a priori construction. Within which range do nonsubjective, nonintentional occurrences happen?

Up to this pont in this chapter I have put in question uses of *images* and *imagination* when we speak of memory and forgetfulness. I have suggested that Gadamer's combined thoughts of fusion of horizons, interpretation, and transmission, in the context of Mnemosyne's myth, open a direction toward consideration of a dimension of remembering that is obscured by images and that cannot be 'said' by language formed within dominant structures of subjectivity and objectivity. But our options to an orientation formed by a subject-object structure are not clear, and thus nonmythological options for speaking and thinking of memory's loss in a nonintentional context also lack clarity. I turn now, in a preliminary way, to Heidegger and Derrida to begin this exploration of ways of thinking and speaking (and of writing) by which memory's loss can be perceived and interpreted in its nonintentional occurrence in the appearance of things.

Heidegger considers the titanic Mnemosyne in the context of thinking and poetry.[8] He changes the gender for the German word for memory from neuter (*das Gedächtnis*) to feminine (*die Gedächtnis*) to cohere with Mnemosyne's gender in Greek and, I suspect, to accentuate the difference between the contemporary sense of memory from the archaic myth of memory. Myths let things appear, he says—lets them come to shine. They open to occurrences that are otherwise obscure or silent in the absence of words to say them. Myths present to us in "passing light" things that come before us in their own events and that call us to engage perceptively with their events. Archaic myths, in similarity to Parmenides' experience of logos, provide us with something to think and say with alertness, something that has its meaning in its occurrence and its essential importance for human life.[9] Myths and logos in preclassical Greek experience mean the same thing: they name occurrences of presentation that let things appear in their own manifestations. They let things lie before us, draw us into their singularities of appearing, move us to speak and think in their draw and in the passing light that brings them to bear in our lives. For

Heidegger such occurrences can happen like the inspiration of early poets and bards who saw invisible things in their truth, and for him 'in their truth' means in their disclosiveness, in their coming to light from complete obscurity. Poetry and song in that time meant disclosive happenings in which the occurrence of memory "herself" enriched and nourished and made apparent human beings in their own passing light of life. 'Mnemosyne', like 'logos', gives articulation to disclosiveness and self-disclosures in their resonance with the living appearances of humans. Such articulation gives one to "see" with astonishment in the *happening* of things and of human beings. One is drawn by happening as such , by the invisible process of coming to be and passing away, and one finds (remembers), in this draw and astonishment, 'meaning'—a sense of worthwhileness combined with mystery (as far as our usual intelligence is concerned). Myths are thus rich in meaning (*deutungsvoll*), whereas we now after an age enlivened by myths, are poor in meaning (*deutungslos*) and lack "truly" essential meaning for life. 'Meaning' in this context refers to the myths' disclosing and enacting something essential in the living of our lives. In her myth Mnemosyne performs memory of "what" is essential in our being. This myth articulates the occurrence of unhiddenness, Heidegger says, the coming to pass of self-showing, which is the happening of being. Both unhiddenness and appearing come to light before us and with us. The myth thereby brings us to the possibility of thinking and speaking in attunement with the disclosure of what occurs. This also constitutes the possibility for a return to the Muses, Mnemosyne's daughters, and a return of the "musical" to speech and thought: the "musical" which comprises the arts of speaking from and to the invisible occurrence of Mnemosyne's gift of memory of what is essential for our lives. Heidegger speaks of memorial thought, thought within the reach of Mnemosyne, thought that shares with archaic poetry an ability to let the disclosiveness of our lives appear. This is memory of "what" really counts in human events as distinct to recall of past facts and experiences.

The possibility of this kind of thought and the memory of Mnemosyne, however, are at a considerable distance from *our* capacities. They are like something that we can think about abstractly but cannot grasp or hold for reflection. Our lives bear witness, rather, to a withdrawal of Mnemosyne and her Muses even in our recognition of them. We occur like signs of forgetfulness, of lost touch with what is most essential: like signs of meaninglessness and obscurity.

Our lives are in part structured by the loss of myth and the loss of Mnemosyne. Our lives embody a kind of forgetfulness that seems to exclude Mnemosyne's disclosure. But Heidegger, recognizing the importance of Lethe for Mnemosyne, finds in forgetfulness a possible way to the forgotten. If we attend to the forgetfulness embedded in our speech and thought and to the obscurity of Mnemosyne's meaning, we might find a beginning for a Mnemosynic return to the dimension of events that she gives to shine in her myth. In the effort of the return, perhaps the arts of speaking and thinking will begin to develop, arts in which we will undergo the gifts of the Muses who enact their mother's capacity to return humans to alertness in the shining events of whatever is. Perhaps new capacities for thought and speech will be born. How might we think of forgetting as a way of return?

Consider Heidegger's account of forgetting and concealment and the middle voice verb *epilanthanesthai* that he emphasizes in his discussion of Heraclitus' Fragment.[10] The word not only means "to forget." It has also a middle voice sense of "remaining concealed": what remains concealed occurs as—we would say, reflexively occurs as self-concealed. Or we could say that concealing occurs as concealing (itself), as distinct to appearing. Heidegger takes a further step. The dimension of appearing that conceals (itself) and does not appear, the Lethic dimension, *happens* as not appearing. Concealing occurs in appearing and also in excess to appearing. This is close to the observation that what does not and cannot be an image of any kind happens as un-imageable, as with image but at once as other to image. Heidegger says that in forgetting, as "the early Greeks" experienced it, the forgotten—the concealed—*happens* in concealment. We could say that concealing conceals in accompaniment with appearing.

Further, "what takes place in such indifference comes from the *Wesen* [the essence, the coming to pass] of oblivion itself. It is inherent in it to withdraw itself and to founder in the wake of its own concealment."[11] Rather than coming to appear, concealment happens as concealing (something like the occurrence of not only Lethe but also of Hades or, at times, Persephone). It does not *appear* as concealment. Rather it "is" a self-enactment of concealing. It is not subject to appearance, although it occurs with appearance.

In this intransitive middle voice we thus find expression of something other to appearance that "occurs" (i.e., self-conceals) with appearance. From one way of looking at it, we could say that we have a distinction between the self-enactment of appearing and something other to appearing that of itself 'enacts' concealment. Heraclitus finds in the appearing of things something quite other to appearance. Although we could not call this other to appearance "reality" or "being" in postplatonic senses of the words, we could say that Heraclitus finds in appearing/concealing a strangeness of life that considerably exceeds the intelligence of distinctions and 'clear' appearance. We can also say that the middle voice can "say" the *Wesen* of things, the self-enactment of their occurrence. The word *Wesen*, as Heidegger is using it in this context, has a middle-voice sense of self-enactment that is not determined primarily by formation or deformation, by identity or chaos, by being or nonbeing; the sense of the word *Wesen* is determined by the happening of coming-to-appear-withdrawing-from-appearing. Something like self-concealing and forgetting is thus "remembered" in the self-enactment of concealing that accompanies or "belongs to" appearances in language and thought.

Lanthanomai: A middle-voice verb that says, "I am—with respect to something usually concealed—concealed from myself."[12] I occur in self-concealment as I appear with the appearing/concealing occurrence of things. Heidegger is showing by this turn in his discussion that, according to Heraclitus, the one who exists in and with the appearing-concealing of things is not removed from concealment but lives in the occurrence of self-concealment. Concealment and forgetfulness of the appearing of the self accompany the appearing self. As Mnemosyne appears in withdrawal from images in relation to which *"she" is both present and other*, so concealment withdraws from the appearing of whatever is manifest. This memorial withdrawal is like the memory of forgetting. "Forgetting itself slips into a concealing, and indeed in such a way that we ourselves, along with our relation to what is forgotten, fall into concealment. The Greeks, therefore, speaking in the middle voice, intensify it: *epilanthanomai*. Thus they also identify the concealment into which man falls by reference to its relation to what is withdrawn from him by concealment." An individual thinks and speaks in the withdrawal of appearance as well as in the disclosiveness of appearance, and both self-remembrance and self-forgetfulness occur in the withdrawal and disclosiveness of appearance. In this context, to remember is to forget. And, absurdly, to forget is to remember.

How are we to consider this kind of remembering *in* Heidegger's thought? The *again*—the *re* of remember—the *anew* of his mentation takes the form of a search—a listening—for what he cannot actively call to memory by associations among the concepts and images that he knows by textual expertise. He certainly engages in active remembrances. He also uses all of the ordinary philosophical, scholarly, and philological resources that serve his purposes. But they are in the service of a process that lets them fall into question under the impact of something that is both obscure and, in its obscurity, available in its appearing, but it does not fit the rubrics, assumptions, and methods that helped Heidegger along his way. The *re*—the *again*—happens in the obscure appearing of a different thinking and language that speak themselves in the dialogue's middle voice as Heidegger encounters dialogically Heraclitus' fragment. That thinking and speaking—an event within the domain of Mnemosyne's Muses— occur in the listening and mentation that happens *in* Heidegger's engagement as Heraclitus' fragment comes to appear in withdrawal and concealment. In this listening something like an allure or enticement also occurs, like a promise that stands outside one's capacity to say and think, but a promise that can be heard at a distance nonetheless. This situation itself is mnemosynic in its remembering something quite invisible, not subject to its images, and in withdrawal in its appearing.

This struggling language is ragged, unsure, and without authority in comparison to the language and bearing of the archaic Greek poets and bards. We understand them to have had clarity without regard to analyses, arguments, or descriptions.[13] Heidegger's effort is not to return us to archaic Greek practices or to intimate involvement in the myths of that time. "We" are completely outside of that possibility in our culture. But by recalling these myths and the power of the Muses in a distant time, we, in the situation and enactment of recall and in the struggle to encounter the language and meaning of the myths, might eventuate a movement through and beyond the limits of our present intelligence and understanding—beyond the limits of our interpretations—toward alertness in the *happening* of "the" time that our recall traverses. This happening—the appearing of time with the coming and passing that compose it the appearing of time in remembering—*might* give us touch with both concealment and appearance. It *might* provide alertness with 'what' Mnemosyne's myth discloses in images that are without living power for us. It *might* give us touch with both something invisible and forgotten and with the invisible occurrence of withdrawal in time's appearance. Or we might find this language inadequate and inappropriate but still discover ourselves in a loss of memory that accompanies memory within events and trajectories that have neither clear origins nor subjective grounds. We find ourselves in the wake of something outside of our grasp, something that draws us in its withdrawal, something that gives us dissatisfaction with our clarities and assumptions about ourselves and our lives, 'something' that allows us to wish for another language and another beginning for thought.

In this context I would like to consider also one aspect of a short section in *De la Grammatologie* entitled "Le Dehor Et Le Dedans," "The Outside and the Inside."[14] True to Derrida's genealogical intention, this section considers a nonintentional movement that characterizes Saussure's general linguistics, his knowledge of speech and writing, as well as the text of that knowledge. In this account we also encounter an approach and problematic that define the book as a whole. Saussure's knowledge places writing outside of speech—places it as supplementary to speech—by making writing derivative and narrow vis à vis the phonic system of spoken words: writing is a separate system of signs "that exist for the soul purpose of representing" spoken words. As derivative, writing is imperfect and deteriorated speech. So writing is exterior to speech and dependent on it, while speech constitutes a dominant "internal system" of signs. This internal, limited system makes possible, for Saussure, the exteriority of a written system which in turn allows for the emergence of the discipline of linguistics, and *discipline* here suggests systematic and quasi-transcendental purity when compared to the fallen, phonetic and conceptual losses in writing. But writing is like the body that is supposed to be external to spirit: writing, which is supposed to be completely external to speech, has its "place," its meaning—its mark, we might say—inside speech— "an inside relationship," Derrida writes. Writing as Saussure knows it is "imprisoned" outside of spoken language by being housed inside it.

Another way to view this situation of interiority in the phonic system is to say that on Saussure's account the phonic system arises from an immediacy of logos and sound that is not constituted by the signifier/signified division. Conceptuality and sounding are undivided and unbroken in their posited simultaneity, and the phonic system thus constitutes an internal necessity of meaning that is both sounded—voiced—and continuous. Systems of sounds are not derivative vis à vis concepts, but constitute unbroken origination—unspaced and not marginalized, we might say. Silence, margin, or mere differential space without soundability do not mar the logocentric connections of voicing. According to Derrida, however, in Saussure's linguistics writing "usurps" the role, system, and function of the phonic immediacy, "a dangerous promiscuity," he writes, in which the phoné and the graph represent each other and intertwine with each other in the order that Saussure gives them. In Saussure's knowledge of language, the origin of speech and writing become blurred and indeterminate, and "the origin of [Saussure's] speculation becomes a difference." "Writing is the dissimulation of the natural, primary, and immediate presence of sense to the soul within the logos" in this linguistics. A usurpation of logos' presence to speech is taking place in Saussure's knowledge contrary to what he intends to show. The very "tyranny of writing" that Saussure wants to resist takes place by usurpation in the knowledge that he gives of it. Writing, with its broken and supplementary quality, resides in the midst of speech, fragmenting the supposed immediacy and giving a nonvoluntary memory to the lethic dimension of speech's supposed immediate luminosity. The enactment of speaking is at once an enactment of division, separation, and loss of immediacy—Lesmosyne in the midst of remembered presence. The logocentrism of sound is lost at its center.

How does this usurpation, which I shall associate further with Mnemosyne in a moment, happen? On Derrida's account, Saussure signifies phoné and logos not only in distinguishing them, but in ordering them around their difference to writing. Sound cannot happen as silence. Internal necessity requires, in this knowledge, differentiation. Immediacy cannot happen in the connection of significations. Internal to the interiority of the phonetic system is the signification of externality and the signification of internality in a perpetual differentiation. Derivation, which defines externality, occurs within the systematic texture of sounding, and voice-in-immediacy is deferred indefinitely by the knowledge that requires it. Externality conditions internality in the interior of the phonetic system. Differencing appears at the center of this interior identity, a differential space that is not overcome by the meaning and immediacy that Saussure says define it. To the contrary, only by virtue of difference that escapes epistemic identification, only by virtue of difference that traces unpresence in the texture of positive, immediate identity, can the internality occur that gives both definition and identity to Saussure's discipline.

Our emphasis falls on the unintended difference that has originary function according to Derrida's account of Saussure's linguistics. For even as Saussure writes that the origin of the phonetic system of signs is in the natural immediacy of voice and logos, a very different origin is taking place, an origin in differencing that divides and thereby connects writing and speech. In our context we can say that the difference between signifier and signified—the slash of S/s, an image of disjunctive conjunction—provides a de-presencing origin of the presence of speech to writing in Saussure's account of their incommensurability. His knowledge memorializes deferring difference in a formation that intends a denial of such difference in reference to originative speech. Saussure's knowledge remembers—enacts—the différance, the slash of origination as it attempts to establish the absence of difference in the conjunction of sound and logos. It recalls the obliteration of presence as it proposes the unsignified presence of logos. The slash, I believe, enacts itself as this memory. The outside of speech takes place inside it, displacing a rule of logos that would provide unbroken presence before the brokenness of writing: a mnemosynic event, we could say, in this case the unexpected coming of distinctive and brokenness in a text of knowledge that proposes itself without titanic depth and darkness: Mnemosyne's memory enacted in the trace of differencing, a lethic moment at the center of unintended memory in a modern episteme.

In the fusions of knowledge that contribute to our horizon we have a moment of lethic Mnemosyne, the Titan, in a strange event of disciplined memory: withdrawal of logocentric origin occurs in an epistemological founding of logocentric origin, almost like a destiny of memory that takes place in transmission and fusion, beyond intention, certainly other to subjectivity, silent, implacable, inscribed in the language that would deny it. Or we could say that Derrida undergoes Mnemosyne's enactment that is other to his disciplined intelligence as he establishes a knowledge of Saussure in an invisible priority of unestablishable difference: Mnemosyne is inscribed in writing's inscription in speech and in the image—S/s—of unovercomeable difference, an image in which the presence of its meaning is lost.

A NOTATION ON MNEMOSYNIC THINKING

In our horizonal context of transmission and fusion we might speak of the emergence of ways of thinking—do I push us too far by naming it the "birth of a muse?" We can imagine this thinking as Mnemosyne's progeny insofar as it constitutes an art in withdrawal of presence, a comforting art if you see the dominance of presence and a lost touch with Lethe's enactment as carrying with them a body of disasters in Western transmission. I have in mind a mnemonic thinking, one that remembers in its enactment the *lanthanesthai*—the *epilanthanesthai*—of transmission, one in which, we can say with an awkward preliminariness, Mnemosyne remembers herself in withdrawal as things come to appear in thinking. I shall develop that further in chapter 11. Or we could speak of the enactment of *Horizontverschmeltzung* in thought, the thinking of *différance*, or thinking in the withdrawal of being. I speak lightly of these difficult and different things, knowing that fusions, far from being automatic symbioses, happen in a struggle of cultural forces that I would happily, if anxiously, call "titanic." Something like Mnemosyne seems to happen in the differences among hermeneutical thought, deconstruction, and the thought of being's question, as nonresolution and incitement to think again, as gift of images in withdrawal of images, as error in our descriptive and normative clarity, as serene, untroubled absence of fixation—as memory beyond our grasp.

But such thinking, which has ignited a new constellation of images around nonimagistic events, in which musing measures assertions and judgment, and in which reticence, withholding, indirection, and tact figure appearances by withdrawal—this thinking brings a marked artistry of release from overstressed intelligence and volition, from something like panic in aspects of our tradition which has insisted on an endurance inimical to Mnemosyne's field and resourcefulness. Mnemosyne: given to remember what can never be held, holding by releasing the hold, originating in loss of origins.

I return to my image of Gadamer and Heidegger—and now I add Derrida—musing on their way, remembering before a lethic horizon that is filled with passing light, musing if not sculpting or dancing, musing now beyond Hesiod's sobriety—this is my image after all—igniting us to think in Mnemosyne's withdrawal.

If I am right in finding in the fusions of horizons a mnemosynic moment that irritates us as it makes questionable our methodologically based certainties and truths, we arrive at a moment of strange rejuvenation, a fragility that is in its own way a strength. This moment of fusion can give rise to a sense that everything can be lost in a lethic instant, an instant that gives return in loss, not in presence, an instant that returns us by Lethe to Mnemosyne and to the arising—the igniting—of her Muses now in figurations of contemporary thinking, interpreting, and imagining.

STOLEN MEMORIES: AN EXCURSUS
ON MEMORIAL FUSIONS

The memory . . . becomes active without our being aware of it,
calls up earlier states of a similar kind and the causal
interpretations which have grown out of them—*not* their
causality.

—Nietzsche, *Twilight of the Idols*

I will say later in the book more about thought and the loss of memory in memorial enactments. At this point, however, I would like to take advantage of my use of Gadamer's notion of horizonal fusion by concluding this chapter with some observations based primarily on psychotherapeutic events that involve fusions among memories. I take this approach in part because memory is so apparent and plays such an explicit and important part in psychotherapy. But I also want to connect voluntary and involuntary memories in individual experiences, and I find helpful considerations of the function of memories in therapeutic situations in which the issue of accuracy is much less important than the feelings and associations that are carried by the memories. A memory can draw from many sources in its formation and can compose a composite of events and qualities that seem not to have a common origin or even a common occurrence outside the memory that brings them together—a memory can be similar to mythic figures in this characteristic. And a memory can compose at once both voluntary and involuntary strands which can be particularly apparent in therapeutic situations.

The image of loss by theft in this context can be figured mythically more appropriately by Hermes than by Lethe, but I want to elaborate a lethic aspect in memory by means of the image of Hermes the Thief in the context of people's memories in their senses of identity. The lethic fusing of memories and imagined events also makes apparent the limits of imagery and directs our attention to kinds of fusions that seem to be nonintentional and beyond the reach of imagistic presentation. I find here a kind of event for which an image is appropriate (in this case, that of Hermes) that figures its own presentational inadequacy. The figure of Hermes can indicate what I name below "border experiences" in which both imagery and a particular figuration of identity vanish as though a reality were stolen. Hermes in this aspect is neither graspable nor fixable. He is gone as he is noticed, more like a border of transition or a trace of light than a substantial figure. He is like the disappearance of what is stolen and the emptiness left by thievery. 'Stolen' in this context suggests loss (for the victim) and gain (for the thief), origin outside what is properly my own, excess to ownership, not my property, and, from a "normal" social point of view, impropriety. The image of Hermes can thus aid us only if we do not take him literally but find in his image the figuration— and the memory—of thievery and experiences of crossing boundaries in which crossing who one is (and who Hermes is) comes into question as other possibilities arise.

People frequently make the claim that the memories that a person has in psychotherapy are often not literally true. The father might or might not have abused the daughter when she was very young. The young boy might or might not have witnessed the primal scene, as the man reports he did. The man might or might not have stolen the cherries when he was four years old. Or the woman might or might not remember her dream accurately. The important issue, many say, is not whether we remember exactly what happened or undergo a fabrication in a memory of what happened. The important issue is whether the 'memory' carries feelings the therapeutic engagement of which relieves the individual's depression, anxiety, or other distress. The therapeutic consequences of engaging a particular memory rather than the accuracy of the memory draws one's attention.

This position is a difficult one to hold if self-discovery is the therapeutic goal. If I discover myself to have a history of abuse and make my understanding of myself in the impact of that discovery and then later find out incontrovertibly (let us say) that I was not abused as a child, I would be justified in saying that I had reformed my self around false memories and that I had misled myself into feeling that I were someone I am not.[15] In this instance we would say that "accuracy" makes a difference, even though (let us say) my "memories" of abuse were therapeutically effective as I worked through depression. I would like to hold this issue in reserve for now (and return to it later) in order to give attention to the hermetic situation of taking memories that are not our own—I am using the term *stolen memories* to emphasize that memories may come from somewhere other than a literal past—say, from scenes in other memories or from something like imaginative production and figuration—and to emphasize that the processes of vital—*life*-developing—self-formation are not under the jurisdiction of a traditionally moral compunction regarding literal honesty.

In popular imagination and in some fields of psychological knowledge, a person suffering from identity dissociation disorder is unaware as he—let's make the person here male—switches from one persona to another.[16] As the child persona who is petulant, irresponsible, and extremely hostile, "he"—the adult man before us—is not conscious of himself as thirty-five years old, married, and the father of two children. He has tantrums and sees the world as a disturbed four year old. In the persona of a withdrawn and reclusive woman he is not conscious of the child persona, and so on—in this case he has many personae who are unaware of the others. The crossing of one persona to another is without awareness, and the man is dissociative in his identity because he lacks adequate self-consciousness, as we say, and is unable to manage the multiple differences that characterize his life. He crosses many borders, leaving behind one identity or another without awareness in the crossing.

That individual contrasts to another person who is quite aware of his different aspects, who is alert *in* the movements among the voices or the personae to other voices and personae who dwell in him— aware of the child, the mother, the very feminine one, the athlete, the business executive, the one who successfully worked his way through an early trauma, and so on. He is alert in the crossing from the border of one persona to another and has a sense of himself and some degree of self-direction in the passages to different aspects. Although I hesitate to use *integrated* to describe this state of mind, because the word tends to blur the radicality of some of the departures and differences in which he is aware but which are distinct to the individual he finds himself primarily to be, we could nonetheless say that he is in active touch with many of his aspects, he is able to interact and associate with them, and he is alert when one or another of them come into prominence. He is not dissociative in his transitions.

There are many kinds of border experiences. I have just noted the experiences of different personae that an individual finds in his life. There are also experiences of dying in which something living and present becomes something past, of anticipation in which he projects himself as someone definitively different from the way he now is, of the coming of sleep, of various times of ecstasy, of becoming drunk, of living in the arrival of a powerful and new attitude, of significant changes in external circumstances, of being different from one's determinate situation, of animallike "biological" responses—multiple borders that one undergoes in normal living. I am emphasizing that in these lived crossings we experience something lost, such as the priority of this voice or the presence of that perspective, in the coming of something else, and I emphasize that we happen in such loss. The loss is part of the border crossing, a Hermes aspect in the occurrences of our lives.

Memories seem to arise at times with such occurrences of loss. Both the loss and the lost are traced in remainders. They might be traced in feelings that occurred at the time of loss and arise again in other situations or in scents or in words and verbal associations. Feelings, scents, and words often carry as traces much more than we can easily and actively recall.

Other memorial carriers (traces) can be found in attitudes, postures, muscle formations, shifts in body chemistry, the ways a certain kind of person appears (i.e., in structures of recognition), dream scenes, experiences of momentum, situational alertness—that is, situations that trace earlier situations, reflect them, embody them, "mean" them. These memorial happenings are traces of events that are otherwise not at all present, and they can mark multiple transformations in an individual's life.

Memory-in-loss. We have seen that the titanic Mnemosyne and Lethe belong to each other, that memory belongs to a loss of memory and that loss of memory belongs to memory. I have suggested that the figure of Hermes elaborates one dimension of memory's loss, namely that in the loss one can undergo a sense that something is taken away, stolen. In returning now to Hermes I want to suggest that such 'stealing' can be an aspect of memory.

In crossing over to different personae and to quite different regions of experience one leaves something behind. When the radicality of such transition is writ large, as it is in identity dissociation disorders, the traces of the losses are suppressed in the occurrences: one often does not remember or recognize the other persona, the "past," or the transitional happenings. The traces may not appear to be present in the speaking voice, in the dissociative manner of being present and being the "who" that one at the moment is. But in preferable instances, when dissociation does not dominate, one lives in memories of the "others," the "past," and the transitional happening. The traces and the losses that they mark figure in one's present awareness.

Consider this latter way of living. One's awareness is constituted in part by the loss of the traced occurrence. I do not mean that a person is thematically aware of all that has transisted, died to presence, or even of transitional movement. Rather, the person is prethematically available to—hospitable to—the traces and transitions and is available to herself and to the world through them. She is not traumatized when confronted unavoidably with the transitoriness of living, with the quite different, multiple aspects of her "identity," or with the dying that runs through her living. This is like her being open in and to transitional multiplicity, accustomed to living in boundary occurrences, familiar with the fading appearances of traces, accustomed to the happening of unexpected associations, to the shadowy return of what is past (of the dead) and is now traced in her life. She is familiar with Hermes the reiver, the one who steals the present in the coming appearances of all things, the one who gives boundary and origin in taking away what now is, as it were, in her possession, the one who takes away aspects of one's life in personal transformation and transition.

And what happens in this context as memory occurs? I suspect that memory steals in this sense: in addition to presenting traces of bygone events, memories also attach to and draw from other seeming memories and narrations, and this 'attaching' or 'drawing from' is something like stealing. This is distortion so much as taking from other situations, from other traces, from several different "pasts," filling in the gaps, and appearing as remembrances of things as though they had no lost origins, were thoroughly formed and without so much fragmentation. Memories are often presented as though they possessed a plentitude of significance. They seem to forget the fragmentary, lost, utterly incomplete, and often indeterminate appearances of the traces that mark the pastness of what has occurred. Memory can vivify the lost and the dead with presence, with patterns and connections that are taken from elsewhere, seeming to lose the power of death, and figuring by theft from other memories and images coherent, determinate, explanatory formations that help to make sense of who and where we are.[17]

Far from condemning memories for their thievery, I wish to recognize them—remember them—and to be acquainted with this kind of occurrence in remembering. By remembering and recognizing memories in this way I wish to understand selves in their loss and thievery. I believe that in recognizing memory in this aspect I both know something about it and lose something of it—that I know it in its loss—the loss that gives rise to supplements by "stealing" from other memories—as I supplement my own recognitions, for example, with mythical figures in my lineage, and by them add to memories' determinations. I counteract Lethe, for example, by recalling the image of Lethe (thereby making the trace of loss into a determinate figure!). By transforming the losses that mark Mnemosyne's historic images into new, mutated, and supplemented images with new possibilities, I both know her and disclose loss of contact with her. I give this discourse significance and a future in her revised "presence," a presence that arises, as I work on this knowledge of memory, only by the theft of determinations from other memories and by such theft replace her loss with determination and narrational meaning. I have, for example, presented her image in a close association with that of Lethe and by the closeness of this association, which functions in this discussion as a primary narrational thread, I have lost the very oblivion that I want to address. I have also given her figuration a currency that is largely foreign to her inception and mythological development: I have brought her out of her mythological field of meaning and brought her into a distinctly non-mythological discourse. I have also found her disclosive of dimensions of fusions that occur both in cultures and in individual mentation.

There are many assumptions at work in the previous two paragraphs that I cannot properly justify here. I am assuming that the idea that a memory has *a* determinate and unambiguous origin is not adequately defensible—that is, I am assuming that a memory, a trace, occurs in an originary multiplicity of elements—in fluid configurations—and that the idea of a simple, determinate origin for memories is misleading. I am assuming that many—I suspect most—memories occur as living embodiments, practices, words, uses of words, and nonvoluntary images but not primarily as constructions over which an individual has control. I am assuming that we should not use the word *unconscious* systematically because of its paring with *consciousness* in a lineage that divides disastrously mind and body. I am assuming that the best images in the context of a knowledge of memory are those that put themselves in question and jeopardize their use for the purpose of establishing clear, explanatory, and determinate origins. And I am assuming that by this encounter with memory we are encountering traces—indeterminate memories—of simple origins' absence in the determinations of our lives. I have chosen a style of expression that requires continuous indirection in the midst of direct statements, a requirement for recognition of continuous uncertainty and fragility in the midst of declarations and descriptions. That means that theories of transcendental or empirical entities (such as transcendental subjectivity, archetypes, or necessary facts) that provide continuing stability behind and through memories are inappropriate. Such theories seem to add to memories' losses too much theft from other images in our lineage of anxiety over death and fragmentation.

What, then, are we to say about self-discovery? By recognizing memory as intrinsic to our lives, I have suggested the possibility of a knowledge of self that valorizes boundary, mutational events, and both the fragmentation and the reformation that accompany those events. Our ability to recognize multiple things and configurations from the transcendence of a point of view, a dominant complex of images, or a relatively stable identity allows nonetheless for the forces of multiple "voices" and personae that carry their own fluid trajectories and centrifugal movements. A sense of lively identity appears to depend on something like their cooperative interaction, on their disclosures to each other, on hearing, saying, recognizing—something like a defined and open region of communication that has determinate foci and a tolerance for transformation and differentiation. These qualifications—'appears to', 'something like'— carry an intention to maximize fluidity and indeterminateness in the definition of self, to suggest that a self is composed of fragmentary, hermetic, and Lethic aspects that take place in the lives of memories that constitute a self.

Consider again my earlier example of the man who discovers that he in fact was not abused after he developed a knowledge and understanding of himself in the impact of remembering that he was abused. The question revolves around the "facts" that he discovers. The facts appear to stand outside of his memory's occurrence, to provide a stable point of reference for the correction of his "mistake," to allow him the possibility for a self-awareness that is more true to what he experienced than his earlier memory allowed. The facts appear to *be* unremembered, free of theft, unmovable in their determination. This is not a question of how the facts *should* be interpreted or appropriated, but how they as facts are presented and recognized.

I do not want to deny the occurrences of facts. Memory is certainly not everything, although I believe that something like memory qualifies all presentations and recognitions. In the case of our misled man, his memory and recognition of abuse took place not only in a culture in which abuse is valorized, but also one in which what constitutes abuse is considerably broadened in comparison to thirty years ago.[18] But then he discovered that what is defined as abuse did not happen, that there were no events that fit into even the broad definition of abuse. The fact is found in the absence of abuse and in the past occurrences of a nonabusive relation with (let us say) his father. The mistaken memory carried, it seems, another kind of trauma for which the fabricated abuse served as an affective carrier. Was there an abusive dimension to the factually nonabusive relation? Were there traces of abuse in it? Was there an experiential memory of trauma totally separated from his relation to his father, but one that stole the father-son relationship as an affective image of transmission? I believe that one can never know for sure, that memory's loss means uncertainty and indeterminacy *in* the fabric of facts—because facts *mean* something, they occur in complexities of associations and shifting fields of experience that give them remarkable fluidity and a measure of persistent indeterminacy. Facts are never facts with one, unchangeable identity. Whether the man was abused in fact appears undecidable before his memory of experiencing abuse and his experience of release from depression through his confrontation with his memory of abuse, even if one can show convincingly that the father related to the son without doing what the son's memory attributed to him.

Through this horrific experience something else comes to light about the lives of a father and son, something about themselves and their memories. My hope is that they both believe and accept the son's experience of abuse and his release from that experience's hold on his life, that they accept his stolen memory as disclosive of something in his life even in its factual 'error' and likely injustice to his father, that they accept the aspect of indeterminacy not only in memory but also in 'facts,' that they hold open the possibility that the events of a life can be abusive or carry abuse even when they appear otherwise, that there might be something in their relation that made it, in its loving quality, a productive host to the son's memory, that everything remembered—the good and the bad—is both infused with Lethe and Hermes and fused by them. What appears comes shimmering in the losses and thievery that accompany the memory of what occurred and that occur beyond the limits of factuality as people ordinarily think of it. I hope that in a knowledge of memory and thus in freedom from literalization, they would accept the son's successful therapy in the context of loss, error, and stolen memories. Perhaps they can experience such acceptance in a knowledge of memory (a self-understanding) that countenances a theft by which the son is relieved of a measure of suffering by an error.

I turn now to a further consideration of memory with emphasis on its originary and presentative events, particularly Nietzsche's acceptance and mimetic enactment of tragic loss in his study of Greek tragedy.

CHAPTER THREE

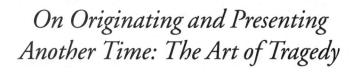

On Originating and Presenting Another Time: The Art of Tragedy

Count no mortal happy till he has passed the final limit of his life.
—Sophocles, *Oedipus the King*

FIRST FRAGMENTARY IMAGE

*I*t seems so long ago since I first saw you. The cottonwoods at the bridge were ashimmer in the summer breeze, making their dark limbs appear stable and alive, stark among the green and silver lights. Or at least the leaves looked like lights. They made me think of Monet and the way he painted lights on canvas. Lights and shadows. One time I touched my nose to one of his paintings, when the guard wasn't looking, to see what the lights looked like up close. They looked like dabs of rough paint.

The cottonwood limbs didn't look like shadows. They looked black and solid. And you were beautiful and unshadowed in the light. I wondered at your long blond hair, at your look of strength, lean as you were, and the light around you seemed to move—to quiver I thought, though probably it was me, my eyes, quivering by the surprise of your presence. But you seemed stable, and everything around you didn't seem stable at all.

I wondered if you would disappear if I touched you with my nose, disappear into something solid but not human, not you. Appear again as something else that I couldn't quite touch.

The water at the bridge was still and green under the trees. The wind was high, and if I had walked onto the bridge and looked down into the quiet water I might have seen the leaves moving in their mirror, moving and not there at all, on the water that was glassy, with reeds coming through its stillness, holding leaves and cottonseeds from the trees, seeming not to move.

A crow called, I remember, during the moment you stood there. The leaves were noisy too, like a rapids. A jet sounded—not quite a roar, but loud enough to give silence between it and the trees. And the crow cawing, sharp, almost in play, below the silence over the trees and above the quiet water.

You listened for a moment, as still as the water by the bridge, almost like a mirror of the things around you. I wanted the wind to move your hair. But it was the silence around you that seemed to move, to shimmer and let you stand.

Then you turned and walked, your light blue dress moving without a sound, over the bridge, leaving a space for a moment that nothing filled and around which the sounds seemed to pause before they rushed in, leaving their own wake, a trace of where they (and you) had been.

I couldn't follow you then. You were gone in the sounds of leaves, a crow and a jet, in the silence of the water. From where I stood I could not see where the bridge joined the bank on the other side. I was surprised that you had been there.

MEMORY-TIME

Memory: presenting another time, the submission of another time to mentation, a submission to now, to the time of remembering.[1] For in remembering, something not now comes now, advening in a different timing and gathering. We might speak of remembering as an advening decision, as a determinant presenting of the remembered in a division from its own happening, as a past event's coming to presence and determination in an occurrence of separation—something like a birth. Is remembering a *production* of separation and suspension? A power to bring forth an encounter of differences that are divided by "now" and "then?" Or is remembering less like producing and more like allowing differentiation to occur? A differentiation from "something" unpresent and hence unoriginal and yet, from something now strangely affective in its re-membered coming? Does remembering include a presentative event of suspending "what" now has to have been and "what" cannot now be as it was? Does remembering thus include the power to begin something that is not except in its coming to be?

Perhaps memory is not so much an occurrence of testimony as it is one of origination. If it were testimony, it would bear witness to something present.[2] It would show us something there, something palpable at least to eidetic sight and perception. By remembering we would find *something* to speak of, to reflect on, to be an object; something to engender methods of recall, exactness, and accuracy; something to itself and yet generous in its power to give rise to knowledge and thought. It would be something decisive in the sense that it would separate us from itself as it made itself available to the testimony of memory. It would set us apart and give us to know our transcendence in our grasp and witness before it.

But the time of remembering is not "then." As remembered, something is presently tensed in its loss. It is *past* presence. It is quite other in its division from now. The remembered was there, but *is* not now.

Or is it? The presently remembered seems to originate in loss of presence and palpability, but in memory something past does seem to be originary. A person remembers something that gave rise to the memory. Whether an experience, a fantasy, or an eidetic, conceptual form, the remembered composes some kind of beginning, an enactment that seems to be tensed by origin as well as loss, a beginning that is presumably indebted in its appearance both to the loss and to what is lost. The remembered *is past*, a strange intensity of not now and most surely now. An intention of time, we might say, not an intention of agency, but an intensity of loss and beginning, an intensity that moves people, affects them, gives them to see things in particular ways. The remembered is not only not now but is at once now and possibily yet to be: a tense-enigma in which we are beyond our intentions as we remember. Remembering hovers in temporal uncertainty, presenting absence of origin and an originary occurrence, positing a loss of the depositer, giving loss to an origination. Remembering seems to compose a place of time.

We have come to the differences that come with timing, the mutual *ecstases* of *being* in presenting uncoming possibilities. In this context I turn to the future of tragedy in Nietzsche's recollection of the sublime in tragic drama, to his recollection of the *ecstasis* of loss in which the time of remembering is tensed to the future by means of the sublimity of lost presence. I want to pay attention to the occurrence, the performance of death and life in the mentation of remembering.

SUBLIME FOREIGNERS

Nietzsche's account of Greek tragedy attempts to describe tragedy without compromising it, while he also exceeds Greek tragedy in remembering it.[3] His account is an incipient genealogy. I mean that Nietzsche gives an account that intends to show the Greek experiences and mythologies that gave rise to tragedy and that turn the suffering of disaster into an affirmation of disastrous life. Greek tragedy, as he finds it, goes beyond the disaster in which it stands. It is an *ek-stasis*, a sublime enactment of Dionysian, festive, musical accomplishment in which an affirmation of disastrous life, rather than nihilistic bitterness, takes place in dramatic movement both in the scene and in the participatory hearing of those present. By this account he shows the loss of Greek tragedy, its coming strangeness in the formation of Western philosophy. He is able to show some of the formative limits in the *life* of Western mentation—limits in the evaluative *power* of Western mentation—in which the unredeemable suffering and disaster of mortal living are either covered over or given transcendental meaning for the sake of affirming something that does not exist in mortal time. In his view Western philosophy is post-tragedy in its replacement of a sense of tragedy with a sense of transcendent, undisastrous life. This sense of undisastrous transcendent life creates values that must deny unredeemable disaster in order to effect untragic affirmations. Thus we have lineages of fiction and deception that are self-identified as lineages of truth. Nietzsche describes our Western sense of life as having a nihilistic consequence in people's denying life's thorough and disastrous mortality in order to affirm it.

Nietzsche's work on tragedy is also proto-genealogical in another of its dimensions. He gives his descriptive account in the awareness that *his* ability to recognize the Greek accomplishment of tragedy is formed by the loss of their experience of tragedy. His disciplined, scholarly memory of Greek tragedy is not the same event that he remembers. It is not a testimony to something present. Although there is a Dionysian aspect in his remembering—he dismembers the Greek experience by his analytical, recollecting gaze, by his hearing of Greek language, and he lets the Greek experience arise again in his German, Western, post-tragedy life of mind—even this aspect is defined by the loss to which he gives attention.

His return to Greek tragedy is tensed by the future reference that he gives the return: he returns in order to turn through the culture of lost tragedy to . . . not to Greek experience but to a sense of life that is differentiated by his memory of Greek tragedy. He turns toward a new beginning, to a different kind of living, to an origin in the ending of Western refusal of tragedy, tragedy which is now lost in its living enactment.

To approach the sublimity of this turning, I recall one of Nietzsche's claims in *The Birth of Tragedy* (a claim that I shall elaborate in the next two chapters). Apollonian and Dionysian forces are forces of nature for the Greeks, he says. Apollo and Dionysus name interdependent, highly differentiated, and unreconcilable powers of dreamlike formation and of energy that moves through the forms, energy that is never sufficiently contained by the forms and that forces the forms beyond themselves in a self-transformative process of transition. In this experience nature and art are joined in a movement of formation and deformation, but in tragedy they are joined in something distinctly human: an experience of intense enjoyment and affirmation that exceeds the totality of the Dionysian-Apollonian combination. This sublimity of excess is, from a genealogical perspective, the focus of Nietzsche's concern. The sublime experience is constituted by disaster, not by a refusing forgetfulness of disaster, but by a turning with it and through it. This turning originates something with the disaster that is more than the disaster: it is an experience of the inestimable value of life, its worth in being, we might say, a standing in and beyond its disaster at once. This is not a sublimity that is occasioned by the presence of *something* to human experience but that is outside of the limits of human experience. It is rather like the 'divinity' of the experience itself; there is an excessiveness among the experiential aspects that, in its excessiveness, is constitutive of the experience. This excessiveness, which occasions the possibility of life affirmation, is like no thing at all; it is rather like death or mere absence. Nietzsche, on his own terms, is to think in a Dionysian manner *with* this re-membered sublime occurrence, and that means that his own thought is to be sublime in the sense that he attends to this excessiveness as the excessiveness is figured by the loss of Greek tragedy and the refiguration of Greek tragedy in his rememberance of it; his thought finds its own moment in an affirmation of tragedy in its loss, which is a loss that composes something like a tragic situation for his own life and culture. By this experience and affirmation, Nietzsche finds that his own patterns of recognition—his conceptual holding patterns—are sublimely transcended in a sense of life that is hostage to no thought or meaning. His way of remembering Greek tragedy composes a dismembering in his own thought, one that initiates a movement to a different way of thinking.

We thus find doubling processes in Nietzsche's scholarly recall of tragedy. On the one hand, Greek tragedy doubles the Greek experience of nature. The disaster of nature takes place as all forms of life are submitted to the fate of degenerative transformation, which in its affective dimension is suffering and in its ontological dimension is dying. Singularity moves toward disintegration as an individual comes into the integration of its own particularity.

This natural course of things is doubled in the artistic creation of tragedy. The art, the *téchne*, that weaves the tragic text is just (*arti*) to nature as it brings forth (*phuein*) the passage of excellent things. It, like nature, produces dreamlike figures that come to pass away in brilliant, shining agony.

In this aspect of art, Apollo's kinship to his twin Artemis is especially apparent. Artemis in her association with the moon and Hecate, and as Artemis Panthenos, in her association with magic, goblins, and the underworld, reflects, as it were, the shimmering, inconstant aspect of the sun god, while he appears in strange conjunction with night as he not only brings dreams to light but also gives rise to figures that shade quickly into nonfiguration. Apollo's *phusis* is mixed with darkness even as he shines. He gives, after all, appearances and not eternal substances.[4]

Art and *phusis* thus conjoin in a jointure of form and force in which things appear as passing away. Such art, according to Nietzsche's account, is true to nature—indeed nature happens in its happening—and when it is embodied in experiences of tragic art, tragedy brings forth that sameness with nature in which humans find themselves, as they lose themselves, in common with everything that is. Such sublimity in this disidentification and dying remembers our human fate and commonality, an experience the strangeness of which is never quite settled or captured by either the Greeks or their successors.

In addition to this doubling of art and nature, we also find Nietzsche's doubling of tragic art in his disciplined remembering of it. He attempts to give contemporary, intelligible form to Greek tragedy, to define it in its lineage of Dionysian festivals and rhythms, to connect it with Greek observations and experiences of natural generation and artistic production. He creates an understanding and interpretation of Greek tragedy. He also intends to produce a body of images that functions in justice to tragedy as he finds it. He finds it to be lost in dominant, Western sensibility (in which he is also participant), to be so counterintuitive that its perceived pessimism seems weak-spirited unless it can be turned into modern optimism. Greek tragedy is both excessive to modern intelligence in its adherence to disaster and sublime in relation to modern spirituality in its vaporous distance, its apparent excellence of accomplishment, and its cultural death. Nietzsche must dismember it to remember it because it is so far removed from vivid and active presence. His primary access to it—even before he can compare it to music—is through the artifacts of manuscripts and printed reproductions. Greek tragedy comes to him in his rememberance of it as a sublime alien.

Nietzsche also wants to initiate an overcoming of the Socratism that motivates his own search for the truth of tragedy, and he wants to give rise to ways of knowing that, far from providing copies of Greek tragedy, are alert to the Dionysian excessiveness of their own particular lifemovements when compared to the patterns of their intelligibility and meaning. He proposes a knowledge of Greek tragedy and its "truth" that is Dionysian in the sense that it is musical and not Socratic, artistic and not primarily theoretical—a knowledge that originates in the sublime loss of Greek tragedy and that moves to the tones, rhythms, and measures of nondiscursive sounds, to the sounds of forces as they break through the forms of theoretical, ideological manipulation and fear of mortality that define our Socratic heritage. Nietzsche attempts in his thinking to double the Dionysian sublimity of affirmation as his thought verges on disastrous deformation and loss of identity. This doubling takes place as he remembers, with all the help of Socratism's disciplines of truth that he can find, Greek tragedy before Socratism.

The imagery of music will go only so far in this project, and we can grant Nietzsche his later confession of the failure of his Dionysian project in *The Birth of Tragedy*. But we should note his doubling of Greek tragedy in his loss of it, his attempt to produce a study that remembers in its performative dimension a dominantly forgotten Dionysian quality that takes place obscurely in the occurrence and life of constructive, artistic, reflective work—that is, in philosophical and philological work—in the Western lineage.

This doubling occurs in the production of appearances and requires a coalescence of art and philosophical reflection. Reflection produces images—appearances—and the process of production is not incidental to either what appears or the manner of experiencing what appears. Whereas for the Greeks the production (the *phusis*) of tragic appearances doubled

natural generation and decay (*phusis* in nature), for Nietzsche the production of the knowledge of Greek experience of tragedy doubled the sublime,
tragic experience of meaningless loss of excellence in character and accomplishment. The loss of Greek tragedy doubles the losses in Greek tragedy;
and Nietzsche's affirmation of the loss and his finding in this affirmation
an opening to a future beyond Socratism—an opening that happens in the
irretrievability of the loss—doubles the tragedy's sublime affirmation of
life in the disaster of its losses (and Socratism, on Nietzsche's terms, is
indeed an embodied disaster of loss, a loss that forecasts Zarathustra's near
fatal nausea before the eternal return of the last man).

You can see that these doubling processes combine alien and familiar
"things." In their texts, the Greeks are far from present. The vivid life of
their language is far removed. We have images and appearances of the
tones and qualities of their lives. But they are foreign to us in our scholarly
familiarity with them— foreign as we come to know them through the
untragic productions of dictionaries, grammars, commentaries, and stably
presented collections that present copies of destroyed manuscripts, copies
that mediate the lost originals to us and that were themselves marked with
letters far after Greek civilization became an inherited dream. The appearances of the Greeks are produced out of indirect encounters, like ancestors
who are remembered in fragments of letters, drawings, memories, and
traits that are embedded in later generations. We draw close to such people
and events in their loss, and we experience their loss as a medium of their
return.

Nietzsche's thoughts of birth in *The Birth of Tragedy* take place in
such loss. The book composes a return to the foreign in which he affirms
its appearing as it is figured by its loss, its dismemberment, if you will.
And this joining of foreign and familiar in his knowledge of them appears
in his thought within the requirements of an image of Dionysus, an
image that Nietzsche loved and one which, like Mnemosyne in this
respect, refuses its own fixated imagery. To be in Dionysus' reign (as I will
show in the next chapter and in chapter 7) is to come to lose him and
one's own identity in the power that the image provides. "He," like Greek
tragedy now, is always alien in his familiarity, and hence he allows
Nietzsche a doubling that finds the truth of Greek tragedy in its tragic
loss, a loss whose coming Nietzsche found himself loving in Greek
tragedy's (and Dionysus') virtuality.

A SECOND FRAGMENT

I felt strange remembering you then, later as I sat beside you. It's as though I heard through you to gone times—no, not times, exactly, but events and moments that were in your presence. Or is it with your presence?

We were together. You there even to touch with my nose as we sat side by side, our arms touching, and listening in the twilight to the sound of a jet as it diminished to vanishing, diminished into a silence the exact moment of which we heard together and upon which we commented. That is indeed a strange moment, hearing the break of sound into silence, marking that loss by comment, together, side by side, in touching presence. In that exact moment, your standing by the bridge under the cottonwoods came back to me in both visual and heard images. There you 'are,' not by my side, but standing in the sounds of the shimmering leaves before you turn and disappear over the bridge away from me, leaving an image and a future that came back to me in the loss of the jet's sound.

MEMORY AND THE FUTURE OF DIONYSIAN THOUGHT
(WITHOUT PROPHECY)

Mind and *memory* have a remarkable history of connection. Consider, for example, that the English word *mind* comes from the Anglo Saxon *gemynd* and is within the kin of the Old High German *minna*. It carries in its lineage the sense of both memory and love (the Middle High German word *minne* means love), as well as the senses of remembrance and consent. In English usage, mind means "thinking," "remembering," or "intending," with occasional overtones of "to admonish or warn:" for example, call to mind, time out of mind, mind me, I have a mind to fish, we are of one mind, my last skiing accident is on my mind, speak your mind, in his terror he was out of his mind. Related words are *amnesia, amnesty* (forgetting or forgiving a past offense), *automation,* and *comment.* The word *mind* also can suggest not only mental disposition or mood or inclination, but also that from which thought originates, or, we might say, a field of consciousness (divine mentation, the American mind, the mind of the South, his turn of mind). Whether such a field is wholly individual or cosmic or regional and historical is not decided in our tradition.[5]

The term *memory* has its derivation from the Latin *memoria,* and its lineage is from the Greek *mermeros* and *merimna. Mermeros* means "care for" and has a sense of being anxious. *Merimna* means "thought" or "solic-itude." The Sanskrit *smarati*, which means "he remembers," is more apparent in the Old French *morain*, I remain, that is, I stay after others have been removed or destroyed, I am left and not included, I endure, I await, I continue to dwell.

Finally, the Old English word *murnan*, which means "sadness" or "anxiety," carries out the meaning of the Latin *mora*, "delay," a meaning evident in *memories, moratory*, and *mourn* as well as in the suggestive power of *remember.* ('I remember her still,' for example, can suggest either happiness or mourning, depending on its context.)

By this excursus I wish to suggest the following: acts of mind have been experienced in our lineage as occurrences of memory; mind and memory both have been connected to experiences of predisposition, antic-ipation, loss, mourning, and anxiety; forgetting as well as nonreflective predisposition and affection are states of mind. Remembering and think-ing have been closely associated in our lineage, and this suggests that in some sense thinking is experienced as also an act of remembering; and thinking, recalling, and caring are also invoked in associations that are involved in our tradition's mentation. I am inclined to believe that a sense of loss, an anxiety in indeterminate opening, and care for things arising out of the likelihood of loss as well as out of the sense of the future's lack of determination all characterized Western experiences of determined mental occurrences, that mentation inevitably, if usually without direct awareness, remembers in its predispositions; and as predisposed, mentation is both determined and indeterminate in its occurrence. This combination of loss, openness to change, mourning and anticipation, determinacy and indeter-minacy in experiences of thought and remembrance suggests the possibil-ity that Nietzsche's attraction to Dionysian imagery and experience is an attraction to a complex situation in Western mentation, that his elevation of art over theory might well constitute an exceptional attunement to our mind's self-enactment, and that the sublime, as I have identified it in the experience of Greek tragedy, describes a perceptive feeling that can arise in the interplay of mental determination, indetermination, loss, and recovery through loss of openness to the future.

In this context, I shall return to Dionysian memory, now with emphasis on vivification and openness to the future. This consideration should so place us that we can directly encounter the future of Nietzsche's Dionysian thought in *The Birth of Tragedy*.

I have emphasized the transformation of a past event in its memory into a present event. Memory figures the loss of the past events's moment and time as memory gives it present appearance. In such presentation a memory is turned by present situations, by predispositions, concerns, and anticipations. Let us now consider another aspect of memory in the form of vivid images. Whereas earlier we considered memory in light of its displacing the life of what has occurred, now we will consider the self-displacement of the agent of memory *in* the occurrence of memory. Even as a certain dismembering of past moments occurs in memory, another kind of dismembering of agency seems also to happen as memory occurs. I address this second kind of dismembering now by means of nonvoluntary, personal memories, which I will also develop further in chapters 6 and 7.

A vivid or vital memory (as I shall call it) comes to individuals in forms such as nonvoluntary images—intense dreams or images of unexpected associations, for example. Vivid memory can also happen as the *emergence* and *force* of meanings, thoughts, and insights that come nonvoluntarily and form recognitions and perspectives or that have the symbolic power of expressing intensely an interplay of signs and meanings. In vivid memories we find figures that speak for themselves, sometimes outside of our control of what they say to us; at other times we find ourselves revived or anxious by the coming of an intense image that we did not anticipate. And I suspect that we are always in the impact of memory-carrying meanings, signs, and symbols that form our minds, that occur outside of our power of direction, and that give us, in part, to think as we do.

Such vivid and nonvoluntary images and formations constitute memories, not memories that we know we have, but ones that arise unconsciously, as we say, or from experiences that appear to be indigenous to our language and culture and hence to our minds.[6] In their vitality they are distinct to other forms of memory, such as storage of information, repetition, holding a group of mental events together, or recalling things that are familiar. In the case of vivid memories, we are approached and addressed by what appears. These kinds of memories displace the continuity of our control and rule over what we call *"our* memories." They indicate a much broader region of remembering than the stretch of our conscious, individual experiences. They seem to indicate something like a gap in our minds between what we might call "our own autonomous memories" and the vital memories that address us.

The experiences of mind that I recalled through the lineages of *mind* and *memory* suggest that much of our experience comes to us in a self-displacing way analogous to the coming of vivid images. Memories, significations—indeed much of the fabric of our experiences—appear to arise from long lineages of complex development. We appear, to a significant extent, to be produced by our lineages—grown by them, we might say, informed and identified in them. I wish to highlight the aspect of self-displacement that occurs in this broad and largely nonvoluntary process of placement. Our minds appear to be constituted by many voices, many different, often countervailing meanings in our language, signs, and institutions. Our minds are multiply predisposed, multiply disposed and impacted by the interplay of forms and forces of differing values, ambiguities of experience, and directions of consciousness. These forces of value and meaning are like vital memories in this sense: they impact us, form us, speak to us, as it were, give us capacities for speech, thought, and community; they are enacted as we act. In that sense, our minds are composed of complex networks of vivid memories that are vital, effective, affective, and often definitive of what appears. As *we* think or remember, as we act with self-conscious intention and interest, our agency is also displaced in our self-direction by these differential, vital forces of mind and memory that are usually outside of our power of either control or recognition; and these gaps of difference in our mental occurrences between self-direction and nonself-direction as well as among the differences of meanings also seem to be mental "states" or, perhaps, nonstates of loss and lapse in mental occurrences. As agents we are displaced in the enactments of our agency, dismembered in the differences of our minds' vital memories.

In this sense we can say that mentation has a Dionysian dimension. In mental formation and enactment there occur—or there are given— multiple gaps of meaning, multiple terminations, multiple deformations. I have highlighted the deformation of agential continuity, and we could consider other mental deformations that occur as values and meanings mutate, transform, lose and gain intensity, carry multiple and incompatible forces, or pass away. The Dionysian festival which celebrates and creates the dissolution of individual identity and a sense of commonality in nonformation among all living things appears now—in *this* memory of the festival—to bring to communal expression a recollection—a re-membering—of the dismemberment that accompanies appearances in their differences and identities. The mood of such festivals was apparently not somber, certainly not burdened with heavy ethical seriousness, in the losses and pains that were suffered. The mourning, if it were there (it was certainly "there" at the "return" of individuality as I will show in the next chapter and in chapter 7), was like a passing cry at the border of lost individuality, a final moan as the transgression into lost singularity happened—a fleeting mood at the border of self and nonself in which people feel that they do not belong solely to themselves, that strangely and, for the religious celebrants mystically, they belong also to the difference of no identity at all.

Sublime is the word we use to translate Nietzsche's *erhabene*. *Sublime* means, innocently enough, "under a lintel." A lintel is something that spans an opening, above, say, a door, carrying the superstructure and holding open the opening. The word also means to come to pass from a solid to a vapor state and back again to solid. The process of vaporization is emphasized when *sublime* is used to name the process of elevation or exaltation. It often is a metaphor for converting something to higher worth or for naming something in its extreme character, such as sublime goodness or even sublime idiocy. In all of its uses it suggests being at an extreme and definitive limit (*limit* derives from the Old French word for limit, *limes*) and being an opening at the extreme limit (*limen* is the Old French for *threshold*). The border experiences about which we have been speaking are, in the Dionysian context, sublime in the sense that they constitute both a termination and an opening, a threshold at the limit of identity and individuality, an opening in which the weight of all that constitutes the past is lifted, if only momentarily, as a threshold of indeterminacy that we associate with futurity, possibility, new life—a threshold that we can say is a remembrance of the future as identity and formation fall away in the caesura of mentation.[7] It is sublime caesura of termination, mourning, anxiety, transgression, opening, and dismemberment, and one that Nietzsche learned to love, it seems, from his way of recalling Greek tragedy, because of what he thought was its intensity and power of rejuvenation. Nothing is in the caesura, and its occurrences seem to give life and appearance another chance.[8]

Nietzsche speaks of the coming of life when he speaks of the birth of tragedy. He does not speak primarily of a classical form or modern form of drama by the word *tragedy*. The word speaks of coming loss, of exhilaration and suffering, of something neither ethical nor opposed to ethics. He speaks also of the life of thought, of the ways in which it comes to loss and might renew itself, of the ways in which it finds its truths with Dionysian limits; he speaks of the limits of conceptual identity, of the restrictions to repetition, of the dangers of fixation, obsession, and truths, and of openings at truths' terminations: he speaks of the ecstasies of mentation and the difficulties of doing them justice in thought. I have been engaged in a reading of Nietzsche, a reading of his reading of Greek tragedy, in which the interruptions and violations inherent to remembering occur as he speaks of them. I have attempted to re-member a dimension of nativity in both tragedy and mentation as I read of a past and unrecoverable artistic birth. I understand this to be an effort toward future thought, toward the coming of thought as an art of recall in the midst of lineages that teach us—and thereby limit us unsublimely—to value identity above all else as we recognize and evaluate things in their strange, memorial dimensions of loss. This is an effort to turn through those teachings that ignore their own lost times to an artistry of thought that finds its vitality through its re-membered losses.

LAST FRAGMENT

You are gone as I sit here at a brown table and write now, amid the talk and clatter of a coffee shop, remembering when I first saw you and when I remembered first seeing you as we listened together to the sound of the jet disappear. You were so present to me both times, once silent and beyond touch and once touching and talking and listening with me. Maybe someone can now doubt that you were there on those occasions. I cannot doubt it. I cannot doubt now your presence then, although many things—thousands of things—have intervened since then in their own occasions. I can recall some of them, image upon image in which you do not appear, and in which you are not present, not to touch, but still in which you give silence and context, like a lost presence.

I miss you now. Your absence hovers among these sounds of the coffee shop. I would like to look up and see you or to hear you say my name. Will you return? Should I hope for that? I could look up, letting go of so many images in a blink, in the shadow of a falling eyelid, and see the man and woman laughing at the table by the window, see them in your absence, feel their laughter in its moment. I would smile then—I know your absence well—and would find something passing beyond these words. In that moment I would know you well, without you, without even your image. You would be more like the wind that gave the cottonwood leaves to shimmer and more like the disappearance of the jet's sound that made your voice so impossibly there, then, when you spoke—you not here now, like an invisible sprite that gives me the two people laughing, gives me to look up and smile and to see beyond them to the people on the street who move in their bright shirts, going to places that I can only imagine.

So many subjunctives and interrogatives—woulds, coulds, shoulds. All without facts in the midst of facts, finding sounds and lives in a disappearance of sounds and lives that gives me to stop writing, to look up and hear again, perhaps to write again with you and without you, perhaps to write of something that you never were and could never be, yet seeing and writing such things because you were.

CHAPTER FOUR

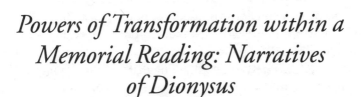

Powers of Transformation within a Memorial Reading: Narratives of Dionysus

You see, what seems to be lacking to me in "*the problematic of narrative*" is the ability to reflect precisely that which makes its very thesis.

—Jacques Derrida

I turn now to memories' losses as they occur performatively in Nietzsche's *The Birth of Tragedy*. In the preceding chapter, I began a consideration of origins and presentations by focusing on loss in memorial transmissions and its valorization in tragic art. I wish now to continue and expand those observations by considering Dionysian memory, Nietzsche's later reading of *The Birth of Tragedy*, and, in the following chapters, Apollo in the context of appearing and thinking: how do Apollo and Dionysus figure the occurrences of appearing and thinking? In what manner does Nietzsche's essay appear as a Dionysian-Apollinian, memorial occurrence? By these considerations I intend to give emphasis to forgetting in the formations of memorial transmissions and to bring thinking into the foreground of our attention.

As I begin to write of the Dionysian aspect of memory and thought, I feel an obligation to Apollo, the bringer of appearances and dreams. His stern requirement of limit, and hence of space, his strange gift of formation, a gift that fades at the margins, gives perspectives in differences and provides no clarity of origin in the shining of the individual thing—his stern requirement of singularity and hence his gift of death: this shining god makes possible the appearance of Dionysus, the most ephemeral of the gods. Dionysus is figured as a mask, as a dream, as a memory, and is no less related to Apollo than Apollo is related to him. But for the moment I shall attempt, thanks to Apollo, to give singularity to Dionysus, the unsingular god, and in the inappropriateness of that attempt I shall, perhaps, give written palpability to Dionysus in his loss of individuation. This attempt provides an entry into Nietzsche's thought on memory and history and into a way of thinking on our part that will attempt to be responsible to Nietzsche's indebtedness to that thinking that he calls "Dionysian." This thinking is close to the event of Lesmosyne that I discussed in chapter 2 and embodies an especially striking enactment of memory's loss in memory's occurrence.

Dionysus, for us who recall him, is an image, an appearance of an aspect (in a pantheon of aspects) of transmission and transformation that occurs in thought and memory. He gives an image to a dimension of preconceptual occurrence in the sense that he is not conceptually constructed in his mythology and allusions. He "naturally" puts in doubt and suspends the civilizing power of careful conceptualization, but in that force he is not an opposite to disciplined thought. Rather, he gives image (with Apollo's irritable but necessary assistance) to a complex dynamic that is not subject to civilization and yet one that inheres in the forces of civilization. If civilization is forgotten (he *is* civilized when he appears as a figure) in Dionysus' enactment, Dionysian force is also often forgotten in the attachments, commitments, and refinements of civilized life. But this double oblivion, I shall say, is conveyed and perpetuated in our social and cultural lives. The transmissions of these kinds of forgetfulness are found in the occurrences of our memories and thoughts, as well as in our other civilized enactments. I wish, in this chapter, to give attention to this "element" of thought and memory—to be responsible to it, I shall say—as I consider Nietzsche's Dionysian work. This is a chapter on and of transmission, forgetfulness, transgression, appearance, and hence of memory and thinking.

DIONYSUS

Dionysus has many shapes. Without *a* nature, "he" is given to transformations.[1] Although I shall use masculine pronouns in reference to him, even his gender—as well as grammatical order in speaking of him—is always in question. His seclusion, disguised as a girl, by Ino in the women's quarters of her palace, where he grew up in hiding from Hera, left him womanlike despite his extraordinary feats as a warrior and commander. He is not exactly phallic or vaginal and leaves unclear whether man and woman are necessary for each other's pleasure or for procreation. Neither 'masculine,' 'feminine,' nor their combination is exactly appropriate for him, since such determination of sexual identity is often absent in Dionysus' life. His tutor was Silenus, half-beast, half-man. He was son of the high god, Zeus, and a mortal divinity, Semele, who herself, as mortal, is also connected to the moon and hence to a kind of inconstant, unself-generated disappearance and resurrection. Like his mother, his life is ambiguous. He was not fully a god in his early life, not even like Jesus—his multicultural progeny—fully god and fully man (according to the Councils of Nicea and Chalcedon). Only later in his life did he become fully god.

He was of many places, of Mount Nysa and Egypt, India, Damascus, Ephesus, Canaan, Samus, Phrygia, Europe, and Olympus. He appears as a kid, a ram, a stag, a lion, a bull, and as mystery. He also appears as dissolute, cruel, generous, fun-loving, snake-headed, horned, panther, savage, joy-bringer, madness-giver. He is friend to Hermes, the god of borders, crossings, and shapeless lights, and of Persephone, Demeter's daughter. Persephone, named by some people as his mother, consort of Hades, goddess at spring's birth, and queen of shapeless dark. He is subject to death and resurrection, to dismemberment and re-membering. He ascended to Zeus' heaven, sat at Zeus' right hand, descended again to earth, resurrected his mother, and gave her ascension to heaven. He gave transition, and he was of transition, being identical with none of his shapes. Always implicated in life *and* death, bestiality *and* humanity, madness *and* sanity, order *and* disorder, and contrary to the grammar, he never provided the continuity suggested by the conjunction *and*. Continuity dissolves in the connections that Dionysus occasions.

Drunkenness was the space of his epiphany, and not only the drunkenness given by wine and beer.[2] He is also associated with the experience of intoxication that accompanies the advent of spring in winter's death. Dionysus was "tree-youth" and connected to the coming of desire, the transposition of latency into lust, and the transposition of quiet darkness into the clarity of passionate movement, growth, and attention. Festival, engorging, opening forth, enlarging, not simply happiness, surely not contentment, but joy, ecstasy, *jouissance*,—swelling, bursting overfullness— are Dionysus' gifts. "Gifted" (*Gift*, German for *poison*), drunken, intoxicated by a chemistry that gave life, strangely, as it took life from the orders that suffered it—Dionysus is found in a catastrophe of hearth and home: the homeland of ordered life lost its ethos in a Dionysian generation of life, a generation that tasted its loss in its coming and that spasmed feverishly in a pleasure more associated with agony than with serenity.

So we associate Dionysus with energetic drunkenness, beyond a civilized "buzz" that makes acquaintances voluble over martinis, other than the depressed stare of a drunk, but an intoxicated release of passion and movement that carries an individual through the boundaries of ordinary life to an unorder of release, rampage, expansion, explosion: Dionysus is not subject to prisons, leg irons, or bondage. He subjects such things to his intoxicated, moonstruck, inflamed, unbounded glory.

Pentheus, King of Thebes, recognized Dionysus as a foreigner to Theben civilization.[3] Pentheus will kill Dionysus, this aphroditic magician who has come to visit his mother's grave, his mother who was killed by Hera, who incited Zeus to use his signature weapon, the lightening bolt, against her because she lay with Zeus, Hera's god-husband. Forget the laughter that Dionysus brings with him, forget his gift of carelessness in spite of life's cares, forget especially his gifts of wine, celebration, and release from worry, anxiety, boredom, and the killing repetitions of everyday life. Pentheus will have Dionysus' uncivilized head for his fraudulent intrusion into tame Thebes. Women warned Pentheus that his civilized piety constituted impiety, that his ethnic knowledge was unwise in its application, that he was ignorant of the blessing that Dionysus brought with his wild, dancing Maenads and the happy ones who hear him. Pentheus, the king, turned a deaf ear to them, refused to follow the blind Tiresias when he was prepared to dance Dionysus' dance, and imprisoned Dionysus, put him under guard in a stable. But not for long. The well-ordered palace was consumed by fire. Semele's tomb quaked and was attended by thunder and lightening. Women ripped live, bawling cattle to pieces with their bare hands and ate the raw flesh. Pentheus himself went insane—and was torn apart by the Maenads, whom he was watching, and who were led by his mother, Agave, who was empowered by Dionysus and was also out of her head. Both she, when she returned to her senses, and his father, Cadmus, were exiled by Dionysus. Nothing happened according to the civilized expectations of Thebes, and Dionysus came vaguely to rule over what, by local standards, were the tragic, hung-over remains of a splendid order.

These remains, however, followed a refusal of Dionysus, not an adherence to him. Thebes is tragic in part thanks to its wisdom, sense of decency, and order, thanks to a civilization that was home to Semele's grave and that knew Dionysus as an alien. I speculate that it was a civilization that expected of itself an unmoonlike stability, that expected of itself no unruly passion in the life of its rules, and that thought it could be human—*we* might even say humane—without bestiality and lust. It, perhaps, was a sober civilization that required an absence of addiction, an environment free of corruption and pollution, one that would eliminate death due to excesses, and one that inchoately thought of grief, mourning, and suffering as isolatable from normal life. So it put Dionysus in a guarded barn and proceeded innocently and secretly to consume its own order in a remarkable, unalert, and utterly mad dionysian revel of cannibalism that at the time appeared to be something quite other to what it was. So innocent was Thebes that Dionysus appeared un-dionysian. They found him fraudulent, a deceptive magician. And in their refusal of him, they failed to recognize what and who they ripped apart. The refusal of Dionysus brought with it its own kind of madness and horror, in this case madness that did not recognize itself.

When people benefit from Dionysus (and we shall see that many of his devotees are not benefitted) they are lighter. They do not necessarily care less in their daily lives, but they care differently when compared to how they care outside of Dionysus' hearing.[4] Consider the kinds of events that Dionysus brings. Many of them are like drunkenness, if they are not literally and totally induced by alcohol, in the sense that an individual is carried outside of his or her boundaries of self-conscious identity by ways and openings that are not ego defined even in their own event. We could use the language of conscience and say that the devotee's superego is neutralized or that one's judgment is impaired. One loses good sense and acts recklessly and without proper constraint. One is close to crazy in his or her moral and rational impairment. Or in the perspective of autonomous individuality, one falls under the control of something outside of one's control, loses control of one's self. Or we might say more hermetically that an individual crosses a border of self-defined identity and enters a different region of only dimly conscious life. In a hermetic perspective we might emphasize the border crossing itself "where" there is an occurrence of differencing that is not under the spell or recognition of any subject, a strange event without categories or kinds of quantities—without calculability or identity, we might say. But pushed to Dionysian language, we would need to speak of blood without pity for the bleeding, of a confusion of living and dying. We might find raucous laughter and shrieking and complex sounds, and certainly we could speak of darkness and light without clear distinction. Our Dionysian language would continuously collapse before bodies in their passionate draw, their savoriness, their rising ugliness and beauty. We would find our bodies in lusting, biting, chewing, swallowing, bleeding, licking, breaking, mingling, wetting, sucking, spasming, churning, expelling, grabbing, wailing, panting, exhausting; in conflicting proximity without love or hatred, in, we might say lightly, reveling without dream and without reality. *Ek-stasis*, we could say, standing out of the holding patterns of ordinary affirmation, love, survival, and behavior.

A lightness, I said, might follow a Dionysian occurrence. It not only filters the hard light of the normal day by a hangover of tiredness, headache, mangled bodies, and shocked conscience. It also can give a loosened sense of ordinary life. Consider, for example, what can happen when an individual is moved most by shock on the day after, the "Oh God, no!" response when one vows never to drink or revel again, when one is frightened and repelled by the fragments of consciousness that remain after the night before, by the guilt of violation and immoderation, by the social and physical dangers that trespassed the boundaries of realism, good sense, and trustworthiness. One then reacts negatively to the revel. One knows the value of serenity, stability, and careful nurturance. One knows that she is fortunate to be alive, that life is a gift not to be squandered, that gratification may come wisely only with discipline and educated intelligence. Dreams are acceptable in their abstraction from waking life, but uncontrolled reveling, like a living nightmare, mocks productivity and the fragility of communal life.

However, when one releases himself to—affirms—the revel, one knows that he is able to kill and be killed, that murder is never so far away, that living is a process that includes killing and being killed, that gratification belongs to life before it belongs to individuality, that blood, bone, and flesh have feel and taste beyond values and words, that foundations rock on a sea without solidity, care, or stasis. One knows of lifedeath together, that to die and kill are not only terror but draws, that terror and living belong together. One might live more lightly with all the good sense that she exercises; her disciplines allow the undisciplined—*know* the undisciplined—in her controls and strategies. That lightness is not like putting Dionysus in a guarded barn. It is like releasing him in the unhold of all that holds her. She knows that she kills as she loves, and she knows that can be a blind part of love's life if modulating care and attention are not given to the Dionysian aspect of living. She knows that life is not a quantity, not a sum total of days and years, that there are worse fates than dying, that life too can be light thanks to its losses.

One also remembers the forgetting that happens in Dionysus' domain. He knows the forgetfulness of care that accompanies caring, that the most important cares are dispensable, that love's labor also can lose love, that release of care can be part of care's life. That is, he knows that forgetting of care in care can be part of one's life, that dismembering belongs to remembering, that deformation accompanies formation, and that much of what is lost is lost forever. He also knows that life's loss can give life's return without obsessive repetition of the same, that broken unities can give rise to other unities to be broken. In his lightness he remembers the loss of memory in the Dionysian event, the death of relationship, the forgetfulness of no identity that identity conceals, the concealment of Dionysus in the good order of the good life. He remembers his forgetting, the other-than-what-he-recalls.

Forgetting. One forgets the whole in the parts; forgets pain, passion, hope; forgets the immediacy of experiences. He forgets the face of the dead beloved, the room where he lived. He forgets himself. He forgets his guilt, deception, his many contrary feelings when he set an image by which to define himself. He forgets his ambiguity when he decided. He forgets as though he eats and dispels what occurs. He forgets in all experiences as he remembers parts and pieces, as he fills in the gaps with narration—and then she forgets that there were gaps (so she writes as though there were no gaps). She is left with images, with reappearances, with fragments, with what is, as it were, stuck in her teeth. He forgets the background as he attends the foreground. He forgets time (and so he keeps a calendar, a clock, a diary, an album; he cultivates memory, creates rituals of repetition and recall, forgetting that they too lose what comes to pass with immediacy, presence). He forgets the boundaries that give him place.

The Dionysian knows such forgetting, affirms it in remembering it (knowing that she will forget it). She forgets as she remembers and remembers as she forgets.

Dionysus is resurrected in such lightness, re-membered in his infusion into the stream of normal life. He rises again as excess in care, constitution, production, and attachment. His epiphany occurs as one remembers that unrecoverable losses occur in the revelry. He is remembered in a letting go that can come with careful association and in separation that can accompany intense joining.

These are strange affirmations in both Thebes and here, now. They have a dimension that is close to Aphrodite who, no matter how penetrated and screwed the night before, awakens to innocent *virginal* likeness, a freshness of life, in full awareness (in her divine case) of what went on in her bed and in and with her body. It can be a renewing aspect, this Dionysian affirmation, a remembering (if one survives) that is not closed in by obsessive protection, repetition, and keeping. It is quite different from a purity that perpetuates itself by holding itself untouched. It can be closer to greeting than to repeating, closer to dis-closing than to closing up, more akin to a flow of tragedies and comedies than to stabilized correctness, more given to its own dangers than to its own rightness, more attuned to its losses of meaning than to its desire for eternal life. And behind it, occasionally, shines a revelry of unhuman, uncivilized consumption, lust, killing, dismembering, and dissolution of life.

DIONYSIAN MEMORY AND THOUGHT

Writing and speaking of Dionysian memory is a strange undertaking, even when, as in this instance, a person wishes to write and speak of a Dionysian dimension in memory and thought and not of remembering the god literally and in the detail of his festivals. *Dionysus* is an aporetic name for "an" unnameable, for "something" of body other to designation and to conscious order, placement, and control. Such writing is further complicated by my intention not to memorialize "life" as a quasi-substance with a nature, even if such a nature were not subject to the movement and categories of reason. I wish to speak of the life of this or that thing, particularly now of the life and movement of remembering. This intention puts me at some odds to claims that Nietzsche makes about nature in *The Birth of Tragedy* and to those claims valorized by his later thought of the will to power. The Dionysian, as we have seen, has to do with blood and flesh and blind desire. And even though it is available through legends, myths, and songs, the availability of the Dionysian arises from quasi-religious practices in which the measure, language, and order of myths, legends, and songs are forgotten in excesses of bodies. This forgetfulness and physicality are borne by the stories and lyrics. I wish, however, to speak of remembering and thinking which are already at a still greater remove from blood and skin than the myths are. We are in the distance of a changed culture, of metaphorical language, of images that do not feel the way bodies feel and that depend in their lives on the civilization that Dionysus disrupts. In the dismembering and re-membering of which I speak and which we enact no individual man or woman tears arms and legs from another, arches their backs, without clear gender, to thrust or embrace a penis, or bear their teeth to bite a bawling cow. We must be satisfied with Dionysus' ghost in this sense, with an appearance that has lost a measure of its bestial and mythological force now when I write of something vaguely like that force in remembering it.

Our Western thought has part of its origins in encounters with transformed remains of Dionysus. He is lost in his wrenching embodiments—another kind of dismembering occurs in our encounter with him. I abstract him in my engagement with the remains of his imagery and festivals. He is already dead as a force that frightened people, sucked them up into a festival of oblivion, and gave them an overwhelming sense of awful divinity that let their intoxication come to expression as a kind of worship, as making sacred the loss of responsible sensibility. We are removed even from his memory in the stories. We encounter the stories with a civilized, scholarly distance that finds its measure in an absence of mythical force. Metaphorically, I can say that Dionysus is three times dismembered and resurrected in my encounter of him, and each resurrection now gives less of the force and life in the experiences that gave him birth. But his loss—his dismemberment—in our encounter of him is not incidental to memory of him. He has his spectral presence in that loss. It—the loss—figures his presence in thoughtful memory; his force in memory is in part a movement of dismemberment that gives rise to remembering him.

In confronting Dionysus, so removed and dismembered in the distance and loss that define our connection with him, we encounter more than a text. The texts that convey his image direct us to a force of disconnection and reconnection, to festivals of physical engagement by means of disengagement from ethea, decency, and social practices. We find our connection with him in reference to such force, not because such force is "universal" or "natural" but because we find it—that is, Dionysus—in occurrences of memory and thought that happen in the lineages of his images and the awareness that his lineages engenders. I suspect that we

find him in such occurrence and thought because images of dismemberment, blood sacrifice, and the excess of forces in social orders have formed
in our cultures and give us an inheritance by which we can perceive, usually inchoately, a nonethical dimension in ethnic life. When compared to a
conception of universal presence or law, Dionysian force is optional in the
weird Dionysian sense that it does not have to be, that it is not governed by
regulated necessity. It is as optional as a forceful but passing image is.
Hence an almost inappropriate (for Dionysian imagery and force) suitabil-
ity of 'Dionysus' as an entry into this study of the disembodying-embody-
ing aspects of remembering and thinking. *Our* confrontation with
Dionysus is thus also an encounter with the coming of his "own" image in
our recollection and thought of him. It is an encounter that I shall intensify by engaging Nietzsche's thought of memory, and one in which we also
engage the force of Dionysus, an encounter that can engender further
thought, memory, and images, that can provide a future for thinking that
originates a re-membering in different thinking and language.

Dionysian images recall more than the spread of beer and wine
throughout the Eastern and Western world. The loss of memory in drunkenness gave way, in some people's early experiences, to memory of dimensions in their lives that were largely forgotten in their day-to-day
civilization. The hallmarks of Dionysian experience, as I have said, are dismemberment, disjoining, separation, falling apart. The cannibalistic rites
and memories that are carried in these stories, rhythms, and songs are
themselves sites of connection with 'something' invisible—something is
celebrated through disconnection, something exceptional is appeased in
blood sacrifice. I believe that we mislead ourselves if we make the change
from blood sacrifice to radical revelry a sign of growing civilization, or if
we give Dionysus the power of an image that explains and presents a power
of nature. Such interpretations are not necessarily false, but they cover too
quickly something in the experiences that is not subject to civilized
progress or explanation, 'something' recalled in disconnection that is lost
to connected states of affairs. More than an unconscious bestiality in
humankind, disconnection from civilization in drunken revelry allows,
under the rule of Dionysus, encounter with a passing of identity and ethics
that appears to constitute human experience and that appears to play a
part in the occurrence of appearance. On Nietzsche's account, such disconnection shows a unifying sameness beyond identity and formation in
the loss of determinant identity. It is sameness without determination—
certainly an aporetic occurrence for civilized eyes that are attuned by net-

works of laws and regulated practices. We could speak in this context of the sameness of loss, indetermination, and (the conjunction *and* remains strange in this thought) death. Sameness and unity happen without anything that is one and the same.

To ritualize the happening of no thing that is repeatable is itself strange. *The Birth of Tragedy* announces Nietzsche's struggle with this conundrum, a puzzle given by Western culture's—and hence Nietzsche's—obsession with nonrepeatability and indetermination, a struggle that is fixed by the occurrence of obsession itself, which repeatedly rehearses that for which no rehearsal is appropriate. This kind of obsession attaches to images of the unattachable and makes the unattachable appear as though it were a repeatable 'it,' an entity that cannot be an entity: a kind of madness for which, according to the myths of Dionysus, he, Dionysus, is responsible—a madness in which the individual cannot see what he, obsessed, is tearing apart and consuming. In this case, something unattachable and uncontainable is consumed by images that hold it in place by meanings and repeatable figurations such as masks. Nietzsche raises this problem in his *On the Advantages and Disadvantages of History for Life* as he shows the kind of retention that kills creative energy, as well as in *The Birth of Tragedy* when he shows that Dionysian energy cannot be kept in the forms that disclose it. Nothing defines Dionysian energy, although Nietzsche later in his life defined it as will to power. Then, on his good days, he laughs.

The Dionysian aspect in remembering and thinking calls our attention here. It allows us to address the losses—the dismemberments—that constitute memory, as well as to address the future aspect of thought and memory in the constructive openings of loss and forgetfulness—I introduce these issues that will recur throughout this book.

AN EXCURSUS ON SANITY AND A SUBLIME ASPECT OF DIONYSIAN OCCURRENCES

Sublime: under the lime. Lime: lintel. A lintel is something that spans an opening, above the opening, carrying the weight of a wall above it, the collapse of which would close the opening. The word *sublime* also has an old and physical verbal meaning of causing of solid state to pass into a vapor state and condense again back into a solid state. Hence it came to mean elevation and exaltation, converting something inferior into something of higher worth. A sublime event gives rise to something of extreme character, such as sublime beauty or sublime goodness. One also could speak ironically of sublime stupidity or evil.

Limes, an Old French word, "a boundary that confines." A *limen* is a threshold. We have in *sublime* the sense of a limited opening by the passing through of which one is transformed in an elevated movement. In the Dionysian context, one enters a higher state by means of a dissolution of ethnic regulation and identity. In the sublime occurrence, something superlative transpires—the blessing of Dionysus, the Maenads said.

In this context of loss of self and sublimity, one can easily speak of self-sacrifice, of sacredness (*sacare*) that is made (*ficare*) to arise through the portal of self-loss. Not a delicate, aesthetic sublimity, of course, that comes from sacrificing worldly attachments and gazing upon otherworldly beauty, or moral sublimity that accompanies a sacrifice of selfishness and desire for the sake of something "higher," or a religious sublimity that characterizes the awe of awareness before God or the Mystery in the soul of an emaciated or drugged or otherwise inspired devotee. Dionysian self-sacrifice names, as we have seen, a sublimity without spiritual loftiness, moral excellence, or obedient responsibility in any usual sense of the terms.[5] It is not the sublimity of goodness or religious accomplishment or apollinian beauty; it is unmarked by stages of spiritual growth and refinement. It is rather more like a rule of losses with nothing determining the loser by either meaning or religious enlightenment. Dionysus ironically is a god of thorough atheism. He does not persist in the sense that he does not provide metaphysical continuity or guarantee of order. He does not give laws. He saves nothing. He determines only in the vague sense that he gives nondetermination. As portal he opens to nothing. In this sense we can speak ironically of self-sacrifice and sublimity: the "self" is lost in Dionysus, and the individual is elevated to nonindividuality in common with all else. That is the sacrifice to mere difference, not to something differentiated by holy otherness.

We may speak now of the sublimity of body without a self-subsistent soul, of the beast without humanity, of killing without conscience, of intoxication in the passage of consciousness, of death without meaning, of life without purpose. But we speak also in this context of resurrection, coming again, re-membering, re-solution, return to determination. Dionysian sublimity dissolves individuals of all kinds into a mere passage of difference and then re-solves them into these differences again—into membered bodies who come again to pass. This is not only or even primarily a sublimity of madness, if by *madness* we mean in modern terms insanity or severe mental sickness. The way in the portal is the way out as reconstitution occurs, and although the festival of intoxication is danger-ous—extremely dangerous—it has in the myth a springlike factor of youthfulness that, at some distance from Senex, issues in blossoming and resurgence. Transgressions and transformations are not separated in this context, and the sublime dimension of Dionysus happens in an unsophis-ticated lapse, something like a spasm of nondetermination, that leaves sev-erance and upsurgence as unclear as Dionysus' gender is.

This doubling factor of nondetermination and determination, ruled by no apparent law (the re-membering process may well not happen), is like madness only in the purview of a one-sided cultural normalcy, a one-sidedness that testifies to its own importance in its perception that its loss is like raging sickness. Dionysus certainly appears to give madness inside the identity of an ethos—he *is* a mad magician in the perception of Pentheus, for example. And his "blessing" is not found in a restoration of the interrupted order. It is found, if it happens, in part in the lightness that I noted, in a re-membering in which Dionysus loses much of his life and memory, in a perceptiveness of normal life without religious meaning. Nondetermination opens to loss of self and rebirth of different life, a rebirth of normal life that is no longer experienced as circumscribed by normalcy. His blessing comes after and through dismemberment and the violent touch of uncivilization and in life that is reconstituted and remem-bered in the spector of "the night before." It is a strange blessing in which the violent loss of "civilization" is transformed into a way of being civilized out of the ashes of Dionysus' upsurgence.

Does that reconstitution provide sanity, sanity that is touched by nonidentity to which it also belongs, by the blindness of a death, experi-ence, a strange power of disempowerment and disappearance, a capacity to dissolve and not to be? Touched by uncivilization, power, lust, inhumane joy in conquest, horror before vacuum, excitement in destructions, con-sumption, abnormality, mere force of passion? I hesitate to name Dionysus' gift a kind of sanity, but I also stop short of the option of giving civilization the final word in naming his gift "madness." He might be sub-lime, beyond both madness and sanity to the extent that he is never blinded by the light of wisdom, charity, piety, or decency. He is, after all, the force of unwisdom in wisdom, the one who hears the uncharity in love, who knows the cruelty of pieties, and whose laughter gives indecent hori-zon to decency. He is the Good's undoing as well as the one to whom order also belongs in unorder. He sublimely opens to the loss of determination, to the nothing-in-particular that every serious soul suffers, hates, and fears and by which in our civilization we also seem to find renewed if different lives. No matter to which gods such good things belong, they belong also to Dionysian indetermination, and his gift comes with the experience of their belonging, too, with him. They are never fully established and stable.

Later in this chapter we will find that in *The Birth of Tragedy* Nietzsche speaks of the sublime only in Apollinian occurrences in which contemplation, serenity, and distance rule in a *techne* or art of appearance. He reserves the word *ecstatic* and not *sublime* for distinctly Dionysian events. But at this point in our discussion of Dionysus, in a context that is not structured by an analysis in *The Birth of Tragedy*, I speak of Dionysian sublimity in a reference to the god's threshold to nonethnic determination, his opening to a dimension of occurrence in which neither identity nor value holds sway—an opening to a "beyond" that grew in Nietzsche's awareness after the publication of his early account of tragedy's birth and one that is as beholden to civilization as civilization is to it.

DIONYSIAN SELF-CRITICISM

I turn now to a strategy for memorial thought, which I will call a "reading," and to carry out this strategy in a reading of Nietzsche's 1886 preface to *The Birth of Tragedy*—a reading by him of his own early work—which he called an "Attempt at a Self-Criticism." His is a Dionysian reading and reconsideration of *The Birth of Tragedy* and one that I shall read in particular responsiveness to its Dionysian aspect.

In the same year of this attempt's publication, *Beyond Good and Evil* appeared with its final section on "my written and painted thoughts." In that section, Nietzsche mourned the loss of energy and immediate life in his thoughts' conception as they found expression in his style and writing. Something uncapturable died, and Nietzsche found his written brilliance dull and depressing in 'the day after' their intoxicating birth. The life of his thinking suffered loss in the life of what remained to be read. His writing was like a process of forgetting the very life that it memorialized in the monument of his script. I believe that something like that experience gave rise to his "self-criticism" as he encountered not only what he said in print in 1872 but also as he encountered it with renewed energy, in another writing now valorized not only by criticism but also by the "health" of renewed laughter—"a dionysian pessimism," he called it—in encountering the remains of his youthful exuberance. In this encounter memory and memory's loss occur in striking ways.

Whereas we might find Socrates' secret irony, Nietzsche says, in his hidden touch of cowardice and falseness in the midst of his apparent courage and truthfulness, we might also find Nietzsche's irony in the limits he undergoes in his engagement with his own writing.[6] His book is at a considerable distance from him as its reader and interpreter, particularly because that book was turned toward music and hence, in this context, toward Dionysus, by "an image-confused, sentimental" young man, who is no longer present, turned in such a way that if the book were to carry out its agenda it needed to have been a masterful work of art. The book's conceptuality placed its thought before something that cannot be stated or read philosophically: music. The book in its philosophical statement requires us to be pessimistic about its own prospects for success. It leads us to expect its failure, its degeneration and decline before what it would say but could never say. *The Birth of Tragedy* suggests the possibility of an artistry of thinking that is excessive to its conceptuality and that finds its inspiration in the inadequacy and collapse of its conceptual relations. It is thus "an impossible book" whose success in interpreting tragedy requires its failure as an interpretive discourse and whose writing, in violating good prose and good thought, succeeds partially in creating a little music of the night that sets at least a tentative if arrogant beat for a Dionysian festival of thought.[7]

Yet, *The Birth of Tragedy* is an exuberant book, a happy, enthusiastic one, at times even a lighthearted one. Nietzsche remembers that it was written in a time of war and personal sickness but that its author was only conditionally concerned with the pressing public and personal events of the time—very concerned and yet unconcerned, he says.[8] The force with which it grapples and before which it fades is not even the civilized forces of war and their consequences. It is the force of music which Nietzsche calls the "unstateable medium of tragedy."

The access to this book that Nietzsche utilizes in reading it is composed of its "questionableness" and its determinate, personal circumstances.[9] The author of *The Birth of Tragedy* had placed a question mark after the phrase, "the alleged 'cheerfulness' of the Greeks and of Greek Arts." In the midst of his own sickness and the instability of a society at war, he was moved by the presumption of largely inaccessible and ancient moods, not in an aesthetic, detached escape from present circumstances, but in their seeming commonality with the ancients, a commonality which he found in questionableness. He reads the book—re-members it—in its questionableness. Even the experience of commonality in questionableness is questionable, questionable most particularly in the context of tragedy and its loss through a lineage in which a nontragic, community-forming cheerfulness emerged in the form of moral and theoretical seriousness: Socratism as the figuration of this commonality. In this lineage Nietzsche finds "an anarchical dissolution of the instincts"—a Dionysian enactment that at once forgets its Dionysian heritage. He finds a dissolution of the body's forces in civilized language, style, and thought, a Dionysian dismemberment of Dionysus in which the strength of pessimism is converted into the optimism and escape from the body's catastrophes, a reversal that protects itself from the perceived sickness of Dionysus by another infection, another "truth."[10] Thebes all over again?

Perhaps we can image the Maenads saying to the 'king' of this reading and writing, "Do not forget the blessings of Dionysus. Remember his awful anarchy, his unmeasured movement, or you too will find a still more terrible curse as you destroy and consume your civilized life in the illusions that belong to cheerful commonality and of civilized behavior." They would be calling us actively to remember what is already figured and hence involuntarily remembered in the formation of our lives.

The questionable life of the book's thought—its involuntary memory of Dionysus—might be read in the questionableness of its own discipline and knowledge, of its disciplinary, scientific character. Nietzsche finds the author of The Birth of Tragedy, youthful, green, arrogant ("defiantly self-reliant"), inexperienced, but also innovative, in touch with a real and original problem that inspired excesses of style and conceptualization in the author-novitiate.[11] The book is a disciplined effort to present scholarly discipline in an encounter with art, an effort that suggests that its success will be found in an artistic presentation of knowledge, theory, and thesis, in an overturning of an espoused theory of tragedy by means of an art, a self-enactment, of remembered loss of tragedy and loss even of its contemporary possibility. That would be an art of the questionable, a Dionysian art in which its discursive presentation holds itself in question thanks to a dismembering of its subject matter that takes place in its memory and thought. It begins in the inadequacy of its knowledge and discipline which is due to the loss of tragedy, a loss that is provisionally discovered by disciplined inquiry. Hence, educated people, in their civilized disciplines, constitute the forgetful body from which The Birth of Tragedy attempts to extricate itself, and this group is the one to which the author belongs as it is dismembered and to which his presentation is significantly indebted.[12] Such a task demands an artist of considerable experience, one who has learned through the Dionysian festivals of thought and memory not to be overcome by the dimension of uncivilized overcoming that pervades disciplined constructions and gives them all to be questionable.[13] It would take a rare artist to convert the Dionysian dimension that is both carried and forgotten in Western culture, to turn that dimension into a presentation that enacts (in a way consonant with Dionysus) alert memory of the culture's active, suppressed Dionysian aspect. The author of *The Birth of Tragedy* was not quite that artist, but in reading the book Nietzsche encounters a force and direction of will that leads one, *almost* lures one beyond the novitiate to the initiated artist. It is a not quite tragic attempt to think in the questionableness—the memory of Dionysus— that moves his preface of 1886.

Did the Greeks, in the midst of their refined culture, practical wisdom, and sublime art undergo a far darker and more painful memory than Apollo's shining destiny could sustain?[14] Did the *rising* of their civilization contain a decline of sensitivity to the pain that gave force to the ascending movement? Perhaps a craving—an obsession—for the unbeauty of life, its barbaric incivility, its evil lack of goodness gave rise to a Greek craving for beauty. Perhaps the flourishing of Greek civilization had its origin—its birth— in suffering the intensity and power of which we can dimly perceive in the vexation of anxious questions about life's meaning. Such questions can be closely related to experiences of a god and a billy goat that are synthesized into one being, a dis-membering–re-membering synthesis, a human-beast that is closely allied with healthful pessimism and a sense of origin in loss.

As Nietzsche raises such questions, hypotheses, and thoughts in his preface-postscript, he not only reapproaches the claims of *The Birth of Tragedy* about Greek life and tragedy. He also reads the book in a much more extensive sense of life than he had in 1872 and in the much clearer connection he sees between morality and intellectual discipline. The emphasis now falls on the losses that characterize the formation of Western morality and intellection, losses that are focused by the fading, that is, relatively quiet dismembering, of tragedy and Dionysus. As Nietzsche questions the significance of morality by reference to life and the significance of the intellectual disciplines by reference to art, he makes both historical and an existential claim.[15] Historically, in our lineage, morality and discipline arose with the kind of energy that marked the rise of Greek civilization, that is, arose in a constructive process that built out of a loss of Dionysian sensibility. This loss is marked by a decline in the very will that drives people toward a culture of powerful presentation, appearances, and orders. The strength of this arising culture, Nietzsche says, is characterized not only by an optimism about reality and life but also by something like a degenerative disease in the energy and orders that emerge.[16] People of normal decency, in their forgetfulness of their own Dionysian aspects, tend subtly and secretly to dismember and consume their own power for rejuvenation and creativity. Their cultural innovations—their moralities and laws—tend to weaken the very power of innovation. *If* such loss were remembered, the questionableness of optimism and a shining culture of moral and intellectual discipline—and the questionableness of 'reality' as it comes to appear in such constructions—would be unavoidable and something very different from Socratism would emerge. But in the absence of such a self-aware memory, a dimension of ordered life is forgotten in the orders, and the Dionysian, dismembering, unmoral, undisciplined, unordered dimension of forgetting and remembering are also lost—consumed—in forgetfulness.

Hence, the marked intensity of the Dionysian aspect in Nietzsche's "attempt." In the self-enactment of questionableness in Nietzsche's thought, a kind of Dionysian dismembering and re-membering occurs in the discipline and artistry of his work. Even the word *attempt* in the context of this preface suggests questionableness and uncertainty as well as, in the German *Versuch*, temptation and lure. The priority of question constitutes a lure to the Dionysian, an unsettling of the certainty that often defines the purposeful energy of our standards and knowledge. It puts in doubt the insistent, authoritative mood of the author of *The Birth of Tragedy* and returns us to the portal before which he—too young for its offered sublimity—wavered in a confusion of quasi-moral, Wagner-inspired enthusiasm. The attempt returns to Dionysus—to conundrums, masks, and unsettlement—in its bemused, subtle analysis by which he takes apart the affections and overwrought conceptual forays of the book. Re-membering Dionysus in the movement of his critique, Nietzsche's language enacts a small Dionysian festival amidst his disciplined thought and artistry. That combination of civilized thought and remembrance of its own uncivilized energy provides entry into a reading that might also enact the "thing" to be thought, a "subject" that undoes, opens, lightens, and rejuvenates the constructive and comprehensive power of the thought that bears it.

I am bringing together the thoughts of self-enactment and art. The art of Nietzsche's preface is found in its self-enactment of the Dionysian through the questionableness that governs his thought. *The* failure of *The Birth of Tragedy* lies in its failure relentlessly to enact the Dionysian in its feelings and concepts. Rather, the young Nietzsche allowed himself to be coopted by "contemporary music"—by Wagner—in a romanticism that was still captive to a Christian, moral vision of life.[17] The young author saw admirably that art gives beauty and value to life—justifies 'life'—through appearances—such as ideas, dreams, beliefs, music, values—that are born to die of their own lively energy.[18] When such art is carried out with full attention to its own unformable upsurge it enacts the Dionysian in the weave of its formation; it knows the Dionysian as it knows things and gives things to appear in a civilized texture. Art is "the truly metaphysical activity" of people in the sense that it presents to significances and meanings in respect to responsibility the absence and loss of significance and meaning that accompanies the creation of civilization. Nietzsche's descriptive claim is that the energy of formations ebbs and flows, like waves of dullness and inspiration. When the formations set themselves in enactments designed to protect themselves from deformation they lose a sense for a dimension of their own energy and violate their own artistry; they force themselves into a vortex of self-repetition that perverts the energy of Dionysus, energy that knows in its liveliness no restrictions and that takes pleasure only in its ebb and flow, its deformations and resurrections.

His further descriptive claim is that Christian faith and morality in our tradition constitute the full power of this perversity. How are we to assess his descriptive claims, his claims that our civilization had its birth in part in Dionysian, physical knowledge of suffering and destruction, that our lineage carries this knowledge largely in its perversions and losses, that Christianity (and in other writings, Judaism) is the major carrier of a fundamental disease in the names of the soul's health, true morality, and salvation? We can say provisionally that the art of Nietzsche's thought must, if it is to be Dionysian, submit such claims to the dismembering ebb and flow of life's upsurge. And he must enact in this thought a continuous caution against the universalization upon which his lineage insists: he must think "in our lineage" with singular energy if, in the context of his thought, he allows the difference Dionysus to appear.

For now, however, he enjoys the ebb of disciplined certainty in *The Birth of Tragedy* and allows his critique to flow into laughter.[19] He also converts the seriousness that he has just excoriated with considerable seriousness on his own part to melt like tender raw flesh in the maul of unbitter laughter. He offers no comfort, invokes "Zarathustra, the dancer; Zarathustra, the light one . . . ," dismembers his own critique in a spasm, and allows Dionysus to appear for a moment in the dissolution—thereby releasing *The Birth of Tragedy* to another reading, another transformation, another thought.[20]

CHAPTER FIVE

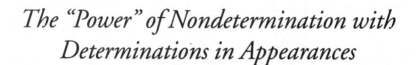

The "Power" of Nondetermination with Determinations in Appearances

I turn to consider more closely Nietzsche's descriptions of Dionysus and Apollo in *The Birth of Tragedy* in a context that modifies considerably those descriptions. My purpose is to expose two aspects of remembering, which for now I am calling the "Dionysian" and "Apollinian," which are writ large in these two figurations. The complex, mythical character of these figures also serves as a continuing reminder of the complexity of memorial events, which I shall develop further in the following chapters. It also composes a reminder of the impact that distance has in memory and of a fleeting, evanescent quality in events of remembering. The figures of Apollo and Dionysus are distant to us both chronologically and in their mythical ways of presentation, and I find their incongruity now in a distinctly nonmythological time and in a distinctly nonmythological discipline to help expose easily overlooked and equally incongruous aspects that happen in the movements—the powers—of remembering. Nietzsche associated Apollo and Dionysus with the inception of tragedy, and he further associated a significant loss of a tragic yet life-affirming sensibility in our lineage with a separation of Apollinian and Dionysian forces. These associations allow me to bring together a certain narrative about these two figures with the narrative of memory that I wish to present.

ENGAGEMENT AND ENCOUNTER

In Nietzsche's short reading of his own book I found an encounter with a Dionysian aspect *in* his memory and thought of this book on Dionysus and tragedy. This encounter enables a renewed reading of the book, a rethinking in an engagement with both a loss of Dionysian sensibility in the book and a resurgence of that sensibility in Nietzsche's way of returning to the loss. As he addresses the book's loss of Dionysian sensibility in *the book's* encounter with the loss of Dionysian sensibility in Western culture, he also enacts the sensibility that the book loses. This enactment takes place in his articulate encounter with the book's distance and pastness and in his rearticulation in a Dionysian manner of the loss of Dionysus. His remembered loss of Dionysus becomes a Dionysian event in which the Dionysian recoils on "itself" in "its" loss. Nietzsche thus finds himself with, outside of, engaged by, and over against the book in an *Auseinandersetzung* (an encounter)—and his thinking arises in the encounter. Reading and thinking in this case occur inseparably. In their enactment something of the Dionysian appears through the loss and remembering—something like Dionysus happens in the performance of the movement of reading and thought. That enactment, I found, passes away, passes "beyond" its civilized formulations in a light and unbitter release of seriousness. This reading-thinking enacts more than an interpretation or a perspective, although interpretation and perspective are involved. It enacts the concrete and strange occurrence of loss (loss of a living, originary event) and the presentation of another event in which the loss and the lost are both evident and transformed. Another appearance happens in which an event that appears in the loss of its life is consumed by its remembrance—and a living event arises in the remembering and thinking.

The divisions and differences among the aspects of the encounter are not overcome in the *Auseinandersetzung*. The difficulties and inadequacies of *The Birth of Tragedy* continue to define the book: it remains in its voice overwrought and overstated, short of its artistic mark, and "impossible." In his own language, Nietzsche does not take pity on it or attempt to "understand" with compassion its struggle to be truly convincing. He offers no generosity toward its weaknesses. But in this unmerciful relentlessness there is also a gathering effect, a *logos* of loss that does not lead to logic or to an overcoming of it but to something like a self-aware carrying of loss in Nietzsche's memory, thought, and language that gives its loss expression and boundary as he brings to bear newer ideas and values. This

Auseinandersetzung is a site in which the loss is determined and remembered as Nietzsche specifies and sets a distance of attention before the distinctive characteristics of his early book. The encounter gives rise to a puzzling continuity, like a marked 'and,' in which the life of the loss through transformation is stretched along in the en-countering. The loss includes his youthful enthusiasm, the truncated Dionysian experience in the book, and the loss of the book's living moment. Now it is more like a memorial that marks something significant but past. There is, in the "Attempt," also an intense process of losing loss as a different writing, moment, and imaginative enactment take place, like an aporetic preservation of loss that dissolves spasmodically through the appearances that hold it.

In this sense Nietzsche's transformation of his book's perspective, experience, and expression includes an overturning of the loss that the transformation also preserves. The encounter is not a debate or an agreement or a systematic presentation. It is more like a performative exchange of voices in a Dionysian chorus in which the voices change rhythms, keys, and modulations but are connected by their responses and initiations; the voices are connected by differentiations that arouse changes among them. A continuity of de-cisions, we could say, that draw out a series of departures, refusals, juxtapositions, passing harmonies, and dissonances: an encounter or *Auseinandersetzung* of voices, as Nietzsche reads, thinks through, and re-members *The Birth of Tragedy*. He does not give birth to another kind of tragedy, but he does carry out a tragic vision that culminates in exuberance and laughter.

The divisiveness in this encounter thus does not lead to a thought of fusion, agreement, or reconciliation or to a feeling of compatibility or an expectation of completion. But it does allow Nietzsche to enjoy a strong, if youthful, opponent and enemy. Or it could draw one to an expectation of continuing life in conflict, a prophetic intelligence that foresees its responsibility in intensifying encounters without regret and with an intention to carry out conflict in a way that arouses energy and enjoyment. That would be an intention to make differences in engagements for the sake of engaging the desires, productivity, and energy to which the encounter gives rise.

In what would friendship and love consist in such a contesting productivity? Nietzsche notably does not find his friends among those who pacify engagements or who affirm the lowest common denominator whereby dissension and initiation quiet and become more harmonious. But the friendship that occurs by means of inciting an opponent is limited in its possibilities. There is also the friendship of the comrade in struggle, the one who returns a love of strength and passion with a similar affirmation, the one who shares the losses. Were Nietzsche's Dionysus to become the only power—the only god—were he totalized, friendship and love would be composed only of the ecstatic experiences of the battlefield, anonymous affections with merely juxtaposed appearing-disappearing bodies in moments of loss and destruction. Affirming the Dionysian dimension goes only so far as to provide affirmation and a sense of sameness in conflict; it provides guiltless enjoyment of those in the conflict; it provides, as Nietzsche says, a yes to life without moral justification and to the unwariness of life in people's desire to *be* as they come to pass. The blessings of Dionysus as Nietzsche experienced them are found in part with those who will not give up because of suffering and final loss of meaning, who love you in your fatal desire to be, those who love you in your losses, and those who do not turn away from you in your destructiveness or in your strength. Your Dionysian friends do not take pity on you in your suffering, although they may stand with you in your pain. They affirm your losses. And they remain, at least for a time, with you as you engage again, if you can, when everything seems to fail and to be consumed in the maul of time.

These are the dangerous friends, in Nietzsche's accounting, whose ways of speaking and thinking remember Dionysus in the midst of harmony and compatibility. They are set apart—*aus einander gesetzt*—by their touch with the Dionysian dimension of families and communities. They are not overcome by the mercy that they practice or by the virtue that they embody. They know something of their own and of your dangerousness and uncivilized madness. One might stop short of consuming you by means of ordered protection and might release you to dangers that could prove fatal, fatal whether in antagonism or in love. One might let you unwisely depart or join. She might incite you to passion that she dangerously shares or cannot share. He might find you beautiful in your tragedy or foolishness. One might refuse to judge you in your indiscretion or might judge you unjustly in an encounter with your good intentions. In his opposition your friend might enrage you to fight or bring you to life in defeat. These are friends who are attuned to the passions of your life and who intensify your life, who give you in passing to feel more alive. Dionysus is not known for nurturance, consideration, or compassion. He prefers terror to simple contemplation and death struggles to justice.

In the midst of refinement and prudence, one feels, on Nietzschean terms, a range of passions that is touched by nothing practical or constructively productive—the madness of love, something that burns below the surface of well-constructed settings for action and foresight, that turns surfaces from familiar repetitions to something inflamed, absorbed by moments of beauty, by an unspeakable intensity that, whether through pain or pleasure, draws us beyond enlightenment to feel alive, to know that we are alive in darklight regardless of the consequences. Our Dionysian friends hear and let us, without piety, hear the consuming blind desire for life that comes with our living. But always there seems to be consumption and lust and blissful refusal of self-knowledge or sustained commitment.

Not only our consuming loves and tragedies can be Dionysian and beautiful. Our virtues also can be so, as they consume us in passions beyond reason, as they drive us to passions of perfection and goodness beyond proper measure. Our religions can lead us to visions of uncivilized splendor (and terror), to outlandish excess. Nietzsche knew that virtue and religion begin to die when humane moderation control them, when they lose kinship with Dionysian laughter and the body's bestiality. They die as they lose touch with their lineages of desire without morality and horror beyond ritual. Virtue and ritual produce few friends of Dionysus. They produce, as Nietzsche sees them, communities of enforced consensus with forceful hierarchies of sober intent and strategies of conservation and survival. Even these communities, however, may in their spasms of excessive conservation, like Agave, remind us, by reversion, of Dionysus as they consume the lives of those they have lived to protect.

Nietzsche's Dionysus is, I believe, without love in our usual Western senses of the word. There is plenty of desire. But Dionysian affirmation does not make a person sacred by the self-sacrifice that it requires; it is not self-sacrificial in the mode of self-giving self-denial. The "sacrificial" dimension happens, rather, as one crosses the border of self-consciousness and social consciousness to desire or urge "for its own sake," a force of life which Nietzsche describes as an immediate desire to be, a desire, in that sense, for "self"-expression. Not self-denial, but expenditure of force. Later I will describe this kind of desire as formed by processes of exclusion, and I will note a significant ambiguity in Nietzsche's concept of 'will to power' around the axes of 'natural' force and a force within a lineage. For now, in the context of Dionysian friendship, I emphasize that Dionysus is for Nietzsche an image of immediate desire that affirms the force of desire and affirms it in that same urge. The nonreflexive occurrence of desire, which I find that I can articulate philosophically only by an abstracting use of reflexive formations, has something to do with immediate (instinctive) urge, however the urge is formed in given circumstances. It suggests a kind of presence that is ecstatic in the multiple senses of being abstracted from pastness—it hardly remembers—from the future—it does not anticipate or project—and it is thoroughly unfocused by daily, present concerns. In the peculiarity of friendship ruled by Dionysus, a friendship with continuous losses in a dimension of immediacy that puts in question the structures of organization, meaning, value and recognition puts in question all considered, reflexive connections of friendship, including those of Nietzsche's own thought about friendship.

In these remarks I do not address the question of what suffices for human life or what constitutes the optimal conditions for humane community. Rather, I am addressing the limited question of the part played by the nonreflective Dionysian energy that occurs, usually inchoately, throughout our peaceful engagements. I am addressing in a limited way the question of dangers to human life when the passions and forces of encounter are forgotten in our ways of establishing supportive communities for human endeavor. It is an issue of remembering the dimension of blind urge and nonidentity in passion and force, and the draw of such force as we engage each other in the orders of our lives. It is, I believe, the issue of remembering the force of Dionysus—letting his order-destroying force appear—in our efforts to stabilize the passage of our lives. This kind of remembering takes place in Nietzsche's "Attempt" as he engages his lost, ordered self in the writing of *The Birth of Tragedy*.

The joining of differences in such encounter also provides a power of disclosure which I noted above as a strange kind of continuity. Dionysian friendship is one aspect of this continuity. Another aspect is found in the way in which exchange or conversation occurs. I have suggested the possibility of an economy of loss and interruption in our manners of speaking and thinking, an economy that occurs as living memory of Dionysus. Part of such an economy is found in the production—the arising or *phusis*—of further (continuing) encounter, a process of giving rise to interest, focus, and passion out of encountered loss. Things appear in this process. They are gathered in the "space" of things passing away. This is an aspect of appearing, I believe, before which our traditional language stumbles and tends toward speech that requires either stable, causal presence by which things continue or a continuity of unlost occurrences. The occurrence of loss and lapse in continuities is hard to think and say in our forgetfulness of Dionysus. We could also speak of a joining in which loss plays a "constitutive" part, a part not consumed by a larger whole or unity, one in which a particular unity belongs as much to its losses as the losses belong to the larger organization. Joining in the encounter—differentiating—carries with it an immediacy of loss that appears to make connections, turning, and addressing possible. It is not as though something past stretches into the present. It is rather more like a stretching out of something past that is broken and remembered in its appearing and that is also re-membered as it is presented in its having passed away.

I am speaking in approximations and comparative metaphors by which I intend to join the issues of continuity and memory. Such speech does not provide an economy of clear connection and an attendant expectation of certainty. It is rather a language that dissolves short of fixation, instantiation, and firm perception. To my philosophical ears its sounds maddening. It sounds vaguely approximate to the appearance of Dionysus in the midst of social orders.

Nietzsche's thought engages Dionysian appearances with approximations that seem to many readers to lack the degree of systematic and analytic discipline necessary for mature philosophical thought. It seems as though he provides a field of experiential richness that requires further conceptualization if its immediacy is to be well thought. Perhaps that is so. But he will not let us forget that highly civilized thought—the kind that promotes its own self-encounter and a systematic account of itself—constitutes an immediate forgetfulness that has its own consuming disasters. There is no elimination of immediacy in energetic events; there are only differently constituted immediacies, and, so the descriptive claim goes, Dionysus occurs in the lineages of those energetic immediacies. So does Agave as she blindly consumes her son in what, at the time, must have appeared to her as an enlightened process of celebration. *The* issue has to do with the life—the immediate occurrences—of manners of engagement that include alertness to the happening of loss in them, and Nietzsche refined this claim in a further Dionysian process in which he conceived of self-overcoming as the rule of movement in our lineage.

I turn now to a complex image of the power of figuration, individuation, and transformation, a kind of power that gives Dionysus to appear and that is able, in its imagery, to figure memory's loss as it gives memories to arise with their specific determinations.

APOLLINIAN FORCE

I began the last chapter with a gesture to Apollo, the one who gives the power to figure the seemingly unfigurable Dionysus, and in this context I will valorize the violence of his figuration: Apollo is a figure who brings determination in the midst of nondetermination and in whose originary violence I find memory of both oblivion and nonorigin. It is no wonder that he is closely associated with Dionysus. The wisdom, foresight, healing, and purification that he brings, the restoration of order through redemptive cleansing, the blessing of catharsis for body and soul—his gifts are proximate to the Dionysian site of extravagance, violation, and destruction. Apollo's gifts can come to the one who has broken laws, who has brought sickness to himself and his community, who has disrupted harmonies in life, who has crossed a border of established patterns and customs or who has been scarred by the ec-stasis of unenlightened revery. But Apollo is not lost to the darkness to which he brings illumination. Much other than light, healing, and order is remembered in his figuration. His mother, Leto, is a divinity of night, and he was born under a panoply of light-quenching water, provided by Poseidon, to protect his birth from the fury of Hera who would have prevented his arrival because of Zeus' infidelity with Leto and fathering of Apollo. In addition to being a healer, Apollo is a bringer of sudden death. As dream giver his element includes darkness. Although he is god of prophecy and the coming of knowledge, the enlightenment that he gives and the contact he provides mortals with radiant Zeus can come in the form of delirium and touch with the mysterious darkness whose interpretation spills forth without grammatical sense or clear meaning (thereby leaving room for self-serving or mad interpretations). While his songs can temper anger and rage, he himself is given to terrible jealousy and terrifying fits of destructive emotion: he is boastful and threatening in his promises; only Zeus could bring a halt to his fight with Heracles and to his murderous intent toward the young Hermes; he killed many Greeks before the Trojan walls because of what he took to be an insult; he flayed Marsyas, the flute player who challenged his musical prowess; and he attempted to rape Daphne. There is little that is clean and clear in this god who hates filth and is noted for his clarity of line and measure.

He was feared by gods and mortals. He was noted for being overbearing and violent, and tyranny is associated with this law giver and founder of new social orders. But much of his violence is found in his history before the full establishment of Zeus' rule on Olympus. His widespread acceptance in many "pre-Olympian" communities, his early Nordic and Asian life, his apparent distance from the Greeks—he supported Troy and was possibly at home among the Hittites—are carried in a figuration that became dominated by his service to Zeus. He is celebrated as protector of herds, patron of young men, deity of warm seasons and spring growth, overseer of the induction of new citizens. But although he is closely associated with social order, his many sexual exploits often have an unrestrained quality. He is found frequently on the boundary of the social order that he also protects. He is not a stranger to the margins where excess begins. There is something odd about this deity in his complex persona of order.[1]

The oddity that I wish to emphasize is found in his gift of structure and clarity. In that gift we find the combinations of order and violence and of determination and indetermination. In this instance we find something like a memory of unorder in the coming of order, something like memory of indetermination in the establishment of the determinate forms. There is something utterly unclear in Apollo's shining clarity, and this unclarity includes memory of the boundaries where sense, significance, and sight fade out, a memory no less radical than Dionysian ecstasy, although its radicality is much less associated with body and is much more serene than that found in the train of Dionysus: a bloodless radicality, we might say, but nonetheless severe and relentless in spite of its association with beautiful form and harmonious social order.

Consider the coming of dreams. In dreamless sleep one seems to undergo something like an oblivion easily associated with a void or mere and undisturbed darkness. But a dream happens. In the midst of no image at all, nothing standing, no movement, there comes an event of images with sound, measure, and, for many ancient Greeks, message. The coming of a dream can be experienced as something coming out of nothing— rather like form coming from a mass of rock minus the hand of the sculptor. The presence of Apollo is felt in the radicality of such interruption by virtue of which the difference between image and no image at all becomes measurable. One is struck by an image, by a form that gives place to an indeterminacy that was no place before the image's arrival. Even if the dream is wild and incoherent, its coming—its happening—gives moment and determination and orders of formations. These passing images provide an order of things.

There is nothing that is sentimental, comfortable, or particularly gentle in such Apollinian events. The strike of light in darkness, like the blow of an arrow, changes things radically. A radical interruption happens, a conversion of uneventful darkness into a site of differences. One might experience relief at the coming of light as when a night guard can see at last what is before him. Or one might experience joy in the sight of a form that answers a search. Or one might be blinded by the light. Whatever the experience, a strange transformation has occurred with Apollo's entry that alters things by way of measure, event, and form. One might well feel tyrannized by the implacability of the enlightening event, by the coming of something previously and utterly absent. Imagine Apollo in Hades' realm of total darkness: light where no light had been, complete change of an element without illumination, the sudden death of what had been. Severe, serene, indomitable giver of determination and thus mortality, Apollo, (not Helios), the coming of light, image, and figuration.

This combination of the coming of light and the coming of form is especially Apollinian. Although one might wish to distinguish and hold apart light's happening and form's happening, the Apollinian figuration is defined by both without separation. The happening of form is enlightening, in-citing we can say awkwardly. Formation gives sight and *site*. It gives appearances to differences by way of identities: it gives differences to appear. And if light and form are combined in this figuration, so are form and darkness by the happening of limit. There is a resistance to Zeus' hegemony in Apollo that I think is inevitable. Zeus tends to unify things under his dominance, to create overarching unification, as though he added unifying totality to the sky's infinite reach. But Apollo, even though he benefits the establishment of social order, citizenships, and colonies beyond the frontiers of a government's jurisdiction, also gives differences by formation and strict limits by individual definition; in this bestowal he carries in his enactment separation that witnesses to absence of definition, identity, and determination. Apollo does not seem to organize or totalize everything so much as he gives things that are never identical to the organizations that arrange them. His gift to universal law, for example, is its individuality, its resistance to its own universal pretensions by virtue of its specificity and individuality. By figuring anything that is (seemingly) absolute, Apollo bestows upon it the gift of both light and darkness in its singularity and limitedness. The terrible gift of Apollo to Zeus, for example, (a gift about which Zeus, I suspect, was never clear) is found in Zeus' mortal limitation as *a figure* of supremacy: Zeus has his domination in his singularity, and his ironic overarching power is in its limitations before everything that it would control. Like all individuals, Zeus finds his power fading exactly at the limits where he exercises it, and that shows an admixture of light and darkness at the boundary of identity: no identity at all where identity fades into undifferentiated difference. Nothing quite fills the gap of differentiation, and darkness "shines" through.

Apollo's gifts of individuation and determination are thus also once gifts of contingency, a fragility that figures obliquely death and absence of determination. And his coming in formations is like a striking event that carries a radicality of creation (in the midst of no determination) and an overflow of arbitrary violence, a quality of strong insistence and dominance in making striking differences. The divine figures had reason to tremble before him: he in a certain sense is the god of their individual figurations and knows their limits and mortality. He rules both individuation and singularity of individual identification.

The coming of an appearance, then, is in tension with the communal stabilities that Apollo also rules. He turns uninhabited places like "what" was to become Delphi or a wilderness into a specific place by settlement, but that process may include the killing of wilderness creatures, such as the dragon, and killing the wilderness itself. Processes of settling a new place, like the coming of appearances, has a striking quality. One can imagine the felling of the first tree ever struck by an axe in an uninhabited place, the conquest of indigenous people in another place, the introduction of human structures into a primeval woods, or the institution of an order where there had been no social, human life. Settlements in their civilization also have their violences, intrusions, and transformations. After they come, nothing is the same. Something else comes to appear.

Apollo is not a comfortable god, not given to nostalgia, paunchy domesticity, or social complacency. Even in his stabilizing functions there are loud echos of instability and unpredictability, of resistance to conformity and obedience in their requirement of order and habituation. One may well expect interruptions of dissension and strangeness in the orders that Apollo gives. As a tree on a plain gives the wind to appear in sound, Apollo's individuation gives unorder, nonlight, and instability to palpability in his founding of ordered particularity. The coming of light may burn what it illuminates, and disharmony is never far away from Apollo's shining orders.

Apollo in his complexity is a god of passing, individuated appearance. In his clarity and light things shimmer not in permanence but in an element closer to dreams than to stable fixations. This is not like Dionysus' world of intoxicated ecstasy, but is a world of particular appearances, of phenomena that bring with them something like a law of light in their shining and fading and extinction. It is a world of figuration that shines with birth and passage for which dreaming is an appropriate metaphor. We can find ourselves arrested by the beauty of things as they come to appear, by their striking presence, by the wonder of their being there, by their rich and seemingly boundless significance, by their singularity and the irreplaceability of their own events. But thanks to Apollo they also shine mortally in their limits and moments and places of appearing. Nietzsche observes that "philosophical men even have a presentiment that the reality [existence] in which we live and have our being is also shining appearance [*Schein*], and that another quite different [existence] lies beneath it."[2] Apollo's shining seems to be pervasive of individuation, which is like artistic figuration—like an art of form in which form, by its artistry, happens in shining complexity and passage. It seems that *what*ever occurs, in its individuation, comes to pass, and that what*ever* occurs has its indeterminate element in its shining, shimmering passage. It also seems that as Apollo's light fades in one figure, his continuing to give figuration kindles other forms in their determinant appearing existence.

Nietzsche's account of Apollo in the first nine sections of *The Birth of Tragedy* emphasizes considerably more than I have the stability that Apollo brings in the process of individuation. Although Apollo brings dreams, Nietzsche observes, he also defines the region of dreaming, a region that can be overstepped and misappropriated if it is taken for nondreaming life. Dreams have their own kind of lives which carries with it—with dream existence—a necessity that it not be another kind. As one experiences dreams, she may also experience joy in their occurrence, in the happening of their lives, even if their content is disturbing or terrible. Nietzsche connects the coming and persistence of things (including dreams) with the possibility of affirming life regardless of its content. The dream's *appearance* is the giver of this possibility. And something in us—"our inner most being"—finds an accord with the appearing of dreams that carries us beyond the travail or happiness of their content.[3] Apollo's gift of shining appearance is associated by the Greeks, Nietzsche says, with "the joyous necessity" of individuated appearance, whether that necessity happens in dreams or, as he will say later in the essay, in tragedy. And joyous necessity is also associated with soothsaying—with telling the truth about life's destiny—and with "the arts generally which make life possible and worth liv-

ing."[4] His thought is that an experience of Apollo in a Greek context puts
one in touch with a "deep consciousness of nature," with a "higher truth"
about life in its shining appearances, and in that touch we may benefit
from Apollo's "fullness of wisdom," "measured restraint," and "freedom
from the wilder emotions" that come with the emerging of things in their
appearances and definitions: "So in the midst of a world of torments the
individual human being sits quietly, supported by and trusting in '*principium individuationis*.' In fact, we might say of Apollo that in him the
unshaken faith in this *principium* and the calm repose of the man wrapped
up in it receive their most sublime expression; and we might call Apollo
himself the glorious divine image of the *principium individuationis*,
through whose gestures and eyes all the joy and wisdom of shining appearance, together with its beauty, speak to us."[5]

Exceptions to this wisdom and calm, for Nietzsche, come from the
Dionysian element in experience and nature. These exceptions are external
to Apollo according to him, whereas I have emphasized that the exceptions
also come from within his figuration. Apollo's direction in Nietzsche's
account includes a separation from sheer energy of life, and thus
Dionysian disfiguration gives rise to sublime ec-stasis as far as the individual is concerned. Dionysus returns us to the nature from which Apollo
separates us and in that return reveals our commonality in an unfigurable
energy of life. Apollo's gift of individuation separates us from nature's
force. I have suggested, on the other hand, that Apollo, in his complexity
of light and darkness, differentiation and differenciation, violence and stabilization, provides a much more complicated figuration and a far more
dangerous and disturbed site than Nietzsche's text indicates. Balm and
healing are mixed with distemper and death in Apollo's realm. The deli-
cacy of Apollo's lines means fading as much as it means illumination.

My departure from Nietzsche's account of Apollo complicates the
idea of sublimity that he develops in *The Birth of Tragedy*. When
Apollinian order, he says, is interrupted by something exceptional to the
order—something foreign to both *the* order and order as such—an individual may suffer terror. In this particular observation Nietzsche has reference to Schopenhauer's description of what happens when the sufficiency
of reason is breached by "the cognitive form of a phenomenon" which
stands outside of reason's ability to grasp and formulate it: something nonrational violates the circumscription of rational power and expectation.
Apollo in this account is identified with rationality and the principle of
sufficient reason, and terror is the overwhelming emotion that an individ-

ual undergoes when *Apollonis rationis* is made contingent in the phenomenal world.

In addition to terror, an individual who is freed from the grip of the order of social individualization and order "as such" may also experience the ecstasy of standing out of the constrictions of order as such and into the flow of sheer life-force. Individualization separates a person from "nature" in its nondetermination, its utter lack of subjectivity, and its deep, earthly fecundity. In the terror of dissociation from identity, from this point of view, one also experiences inexpressible joy in reunion with nature and life power. Nature and human life with it are freed from objectivity and usefulness, from subjugation to purpose and plan, from the stable repetition of patterns and forms, and through the "exception" to reason one crosses a threshold to nonindividualization and undergoes restoration to the inexpressible power that unites everything in nondistinction and formless drive. "How corpse-like and ghostly their so-called 'healthy-mindedness' looks," says an enthusiastic young Nietzsche, "when the glowing life of the Dionysian revelers roars past them."[6]

The intoxication of such ecstasy is transformative, but not, according to *The Birth of Tragedy*, thanks to Apollo. The transformation happens in the violation by excess of Apollo's order. An individual becomes more dreamlike in his departure from ordered figuration, more "natural," more of a force of life in his departure from individuation. "He is no longer an artist, he has become a work of art: in these paroxysms of intoxication the artistic power of all nature reveals itself to the highest gratification of the highest primordial unity."[7]

Although Apollo and Dionysus seem to be at extreme odds, to the point of establishing (!) a dualism, Nietzsche also emphasizes their interplay in their opposition. Together they figure what Nietzsche calls the "artistic energies of nature," "energies in which nature's impulses are satisfied in the most immediate and direct [i.e., nonhuman] way."[8] Dionysus dominates here, however. His "destruction" of the individual "redeems" him "by a mystical feeling of oneness." This redemption overrides Apollo's redemption by means of cleansing and healing an individual. And although Apollo is "the artist in dreams," Dionysian ecstasy turns from dream figurations to something more radical in the deteriorative transformation of the individual in a virtual dream, a dream that happens in an ecstasy of waking life, a virtuality in which individuation and distinctness seem to disappear and the nondeterminant life of nature seems palpable.

The work of the Greek artist as Nietzsche presents him embodies the memory of these two forces of nature—individualization and life force—as the artists gave expression to them both. In Doric architecture, for example, with its ponderous shaft and bold, simple cornice which Apollo ruled, the barbaric Dionysian festivals are held at bay. But in dithyrambic music, Dionysus ruled. And when Apollo and Dionysus achieved a troubled reconciliation at Delphi, each ruling for six months, the cultural basis occurred for their connection in the highest form of Greek art, tragedy. Apollo's art, Nietzsche says, prior to tragedy gave rise to the Olympian figures who adorn the friezes. These figures do not present moral elevation or incarnated spirituality. "We hear nothing here that suggests association, spirituality, or duty. We hear nothing but the account of an exuberant, triumphant life in which all things, whether good or evil, are deified. And so the spectator may stand quite bewildered before this fantastic excess of life. . . . "9 To intensify our encounter with Nietzsche's ideas we might picture to ourselves the severe images of the Doric period, images of powers gathered by figuration and expressing not just abundance but superabundance of life energy. But the expressions are not moved or moving. They are silent and without rhythm. But in the fragmented rhythms of Dionysian music, we hear forms in their violation that stress formations to a breaking point: music which leads people to movements that efface a sense of identity and of particular place and time and that do not yield coherent presentations. In the first instance, excessiveness of life is remembered in severity of form; and in the second, such excess is remembered in dissolution of form. The "dream-birth of the Olympians," on the other hand, with an artistic union of Apollo and Dionysus, provided insulation before the horror and terror of life that were enacted in the excesses of the early, barbaric Dionysian festival and also provided a region for the transference of human misery to gods who were strong enough— well formed enough—to bear it. The Olympians with their terrible disasters and the meaningless suffering to which they gave expression, provided in their stark beauty "a middle world apart" that veiled and transformed, at least to a degree, the agonies of life that gave no basis for hope for the dominance of human value and well being in either nature or the process of human life. And they provided this middle ground by means of beautiful and 'immortal' figurations that expressed the fate of life with transcendent glory. They were the creation of a people who knew that all individuals suffer deterioration and death, that human life is moved by energy that requires indiscriminate destruction, and that affirmation of life can happen, in spite of its fate, in a welling up of exuberant energy in artistic expression.

As we come to terms with Nietzsche's account, we must appreciate the extremity of early Greek perceptions of agony. Neither Apollo nor Dionysus appeared with a blurred vision of suffering's and death's inevitability. Neither forgot the fragmented limits of meaning, and neither was tempted to separate human life into regions of spirit and body that gave to finite individuals significant transcendence beyond suffering and death. Each figured human life through suffering, death, and blind destiny—blind as far as human purpose and interest are concerned. But with Apollo's Olympian accomplishment a will to live with—in spite of—agony gained a remarkable expression. The "higher glory" of the gods gave expression to a will to live in full sight of terrible fate, in full incorporation of such fate for a "wretched ephemeral race, children of chance and misery."[10] Apollo's accomplishment was like "a transfiguring mirror" by which the Greeks justified their living—their energy to live with and in spite of the worst disasters that repeatedly befell them individually and collectively: memory of superabundant life in disaster and of mortifying disaster in life, memory in the formation of glorious gods who saved no one from death and who figured a meaningless desire to endure with the beauty of catastrophe without ultimate meaning.

The *appearing* of Apollo's figuration carried such memory and such intent. The Doric Olympian figures themselves are not dynamic. They are serene in their friezes, cold as their stone element, glistening as light strikes them. But that they are figured, that they have a gathering effect in their unmoving poses, that they come to appear, bear what Apollo can well express: a power of life that drives to well formed expressions, that creates and destroys, that brings disaster with its appearance, that urges more life from the rubble that it throws up in its surge. Nietzsche stresses the remarkable departure in Doric art from barbarian celebrations of savagery in nature and among humans. It is a departure that Apollo's individuation effects and one that creates a power of beauty as the site not only for civilization but also for a resilience that, as we shall see, tragedy brings to an apex of expression.

We find also that Apollinian accomplishment in originating the Olympian gods, an accomplishment that Nietzsche underscores, enacts an *appearance* of gods without the support of a reality or a kind of reality that is fundamentally different from that of appearance. This art, which is paternal to classical Greek culture, figures the appearance of appearing for

its own sake—constitutes a memory of appearing—in a remarkably beautiful expression that fully accepts human suffering without metaphysical
or religious justification. It constitutes a transformation of suffering by
means of art without loss of suffering: an art of mortality in "glorious" figurations, and in this context, an art that transfigures memories of terrible
disasters and continuing fates, an art that re-members sufferings in presentations that "glorify" life by means of beauty. This appearing seems to be a
kind of transformation like transformations that are found in 'nature,' one
that reenacts nature in art. In Apollinian power, the appearing of things is
without grounds. Appearing constitutes its own grounding and shows
nature to be a powerful process of appearing that has the full extent of its
meaning in the appearing events. Apollo shows both art and nature to be
like dreaming: 'things' appear in mortal passage without clarity of origin or
purpose.

The young Nietzsche thus suggested a mimetic connection between
art and nature—art is like nature, expresses it and gives it to appear in
artistic activity. But we can also say, departing from the idea that there is
something called "nature" which presents art and establishes something of
a dualism between art and nature, that Apollo gives nature to occur as
appearance. Just as a dream arises in an element that lacks image, so nature
seems to arise in Apollo's power of figuration and to sink back toward
oblivion in Dionysus' dissolution. We might agree with Nietzsche that for
the Greeks Apollo and Dionysus are powers of nature, but we can also add
that in *their* power nature arises and comes to expression. They turn nature
toward art and make it referable in its figuration. In the young Nietzsche's
interpretation, nature for the Greeks is other to art as a driving force of
growth and destruction, as a meaningless surge of power, and this idea
turns nature into *something*. This turning seems to be an *Apollinian* occurrence (i.e., dreamlike artistry) of which Nietzsche is not quite aware. If he
had appropriated the Apollinian aspect of nature's appearing I doubt that
he would have distinguished Apollo and Dionysus quite so sharply or that
he would have seen nature's force as something so divinely and ecstatically
other—or that he would have moved as he did toward the metaphysical
aspects of will to power. He would have succeeded, I suspect, in thinking
of nature's appearing in a space defined by appearance and found that in
Apollo's wake 'God' happens like nature, that both merely and mar-
velously and disastrously appear without a basis for being something in
itself and sufficient enough to be a Reality. Nature is a figuration, and its
source seems to be in appearing and not in something completely to itself,

with itself behind appearing's occurrence. In a strange turn, Apollo's titanic dimensions give more of what Nietzsche attributes to Dionysus as nature comes to pass in its appearing, thanks more to Apollo's power than to Dionysus.' Apollo gives oblivion, a lethic aspect, to nature in its appeariencial figuration and releases it to the mortal destiny of all appearances. Not a dream, but like one as it arises mortally to quasi-divine status.

Consider this possibility in the following quotation in which I have replaced divine references by the word *nature* and replaced references to the Greeks by Nietzsche's name: "It was in order to live that Nietzsche had to create nature from a most profound need. Perhaps we may picture the process to ourselves somewhat as follows: out of the original natural orders of terror, the Nietzschian experience of primordial joyful nature evolved through the apollinian impulse toward beauty, just as roses burst from thorny bushes. How else could he, so sensitive, so vehement in his desires, so singularly capable of *suffering*, have endured existence, if it had not been revealed to him in his sense of nature, surrounded with a higher glory?"[11] In this interpretation, the impulse that Nietzsche named "art" calls into being a conception and image of nature that are ecstatically Dionysian, a conception and image that "seduced" him to affirm the continuation of life and a conception and image of nature's appearance as a transfiguring mirror of the experiences of human life. In this remarkable artistic work of nature, the forces of nature are found to provide an experiential transcendence (ecstasy) of the meaningless suffering that they also make inevitable; existence itself can become an art, and, in its artistry, it becomes a desire to be for its own sake—existence then is like the figure of nature as the forceful drive of life-seeking-life.[12]

In turning Nietzsche's words this way I have effected a change that is appropriate, I believe, to the Apollinian and Dionysian forces that he describes in the cultural processes out of which tragedy arose. This turning mitigates the likelihood that nature will function either as a self-existent absolute ("the truly existent primal unity"[13]) or as a divine presence for nostalgic explanations of art and beauty that one finds at times in the writings of Schiller, Schelling, and Hölderlin. It allows for an oblivion in the appearance of nature that offsets its function as a replacement for a God— a function that reminds me of the Ass Festival, book 4 of *Thus Spoke Zarathustra*, in which "the higher men," who have not freed themselves from religious and theological passions, conduct a ceremony with a braying replacement for divine presence. When we immerse ourselves in nature's beauty as Apollinian shining, terrible in its appearing power and wonderful in its ability to pass away in each of its determinant manifestations, we remember Apollo's mortal disclosiveness and Dionysus' destruction in the coming to pass of *all* things.[14] We also draw closer to an observation that will inform my discussion of memory in other chapters: memories that appear in "powers" like those of Apollo and Dionysus are said to be without an originary nature, and although 'tragic' does not seem to me to be appropriate as descriptive of all memories, memories do seem to be similar to Greek tragedies in their Apollinian and Dionysian composition.

We see in Apollo's shining an image of things'coming to appear, their *appearing*. Although Kaufmann's translation of *Schein* as "mere appearance" accentuates the difference between appearance and primal reality, a difference that is central for Nietzsche's discussion of Apollo, it does not accentuate adequately the process of the coming to light of things or Apollo's brilliant complexity as the god of individuation. It is true that Nietzsche articulates Apollo's gift of shining in stark contrast to nonvisionary force and in terms of illusion before the reality of primal unity. But he also emphasizes the coming to form—the coming to appear—of dreams, not simply their illusory quality in contrast to waking life but their coming to happen, their illusory coming to light. Nietzsche[15] establishes that Silenus' pessimism—it is better not to be born than to be born, and it is better to die young than to live long—is overturned by Homeric affirmation of life, an affirmation that takes place through artistic presentation. Further, the world of the Olympian gods, "which the Hellenic 'will' made use of as a transfiguring mirror," justifies the lives of human beings. "Existence under the bright sunshine of such gods is regarded as desirable in itself." Two elements dominate this reversal of dark despair, will and light: the Greek will to live and the radiance of art, which gives expression to this will and makes it strong and effective against the force of suffering and death. In the expression of this will through Homeric poetry (which Nietzsche calls the "Apollinian stage" and "naive"), "Homeric man feels himself so completely at one with [existence]!" Titanic violence and monstrous barbarism are overcome by Apollo's gift "through the most forceful and pleasurable illusion," a "consummate immersion in the beauty of *Schein*." We are not dealing here only with figures. We are confronting the transformative power of the shining appearance of art in which people are immersed in the shining—Nietzsche also calls it the "glory"—of life through and in its disasters as presented by way of the Olympian gods. By the shining occurrence, the will to live (which Nietzsche identifies with nature) gains dominance over bitter rejection of life in its sorrows. Transformation, figuration, and transfiguration (of life-will) occur in the medium of Apollo's shining. This is a transfigurative process that Nietzsche presents in terms of mirroring. The Olympian gods are the mirror image of the Greeks by which imagining the Greeks saw themselves with beauty, glory, and life-expressing, disaster-conquering courage. Powerful, beautiful, and naive, Nietzsche says of this art. It is naive by virtue of people's uncritically finding *themselves* in and through the shining of the figurations.

A second aspect in Nietzsche's account is found in his thought of *Wiederschein*, which he describes as the shine of shine—as the re-turn of Apollo's gift, and as Apollo's self-enactment.[16] Naive art expresses the "*Wiederschein*," the re-shining, the shining again, or the re-turn and reflection "of eternal contradiction, the father of things."[17] Apollo expresses, according to Nietzsche, the primal unity by limiting it in processes of artistic individuation. In Raphael's naive art, for example, Apollo's shining is reflected back to itself, a second kind of mirroring in which the transformative work of Apollinian culture is shown to itself in an Apollinian work.[18] Such a return figures Apollo's expression of "primal unity" in individual expression through a person's will, and this figuration of Apollo's work re-ignites Apollo's transformative process, that is, strengthens a person's vitality by the elevated and individualized force of the artistic presentation. Apollo's shining is given expression before itself. The emphasis falls again upon the shining which can transform individual lives. This movement is one in which transformation happens through individuation in images; people are transformed in their energy in the strike of the images, and in such transformation people shine back to the shining in the work of their lives, work that is artistry of will and production in the form of culture. I have complicated and intensified this process by emphasizing that the difference of energy and individuation lies *in* the shining—in the coming to appear—of the individual image or thing, not in an assertion of primal will and departure from its nondifferentiation by means of form.

Where Nietzsche has named the source of Apollo's energy primal *unity*, I have found in Apollo the indication that his engendering work arises out of nondifferentiation with no hint of unity or 'reality' in a primordial energetics. He figures the illumination of coming to pass in illumination, illumination that is oblivious in reference to any *thing* or source or quasi-agency. Apollo memorializes both appearing and Lethic darkness—and even *darkness* says too much—as he gives figuration. This memorialization belongs to shining and gives things to strife and disharmony as well as to order and harmony. In that light, and contrary to what Nietzsche says, Apollo does not redeem human existence vis-à-vis anything. He bestows in the process of coming to light both suffering and a countermanding joy in being. It happens in the oblivion of nondetermination and in the light of singular, related appearances. Apollo, in exacting his measure and his requirement of self-knowledge, exacts struggle with disorder. He also exacts a perpetuation of disorder, whether on Olympus or in Athens or on the frontier, and gives opposing values according to the interests and individualization of different people and situations. The absence of excess that characterizes his aim and the flight of his arrow—the economy and clarity of form that makes the sculpture's great work—is nonetheless, in its severe individuation, excessive to other measures in its vital intensity and force for singularity. He brings to life differences that in their exactness contradict and strike against each other. He gives the destiny of both conflicts and orders in the shining that he enacts, not unlike a major aspect of memories, as we shall see.

I shall return to this destiny in the following consideration of the sublime. For now I note that the clear light of Apollo is intrinsically ambiguous, that it shimmers as it shines, and that his jealousy, rage, cruelty, and inconstancy are not incidental to his measure, exactness, and delimitations. We look in vain to Apollo for confirmation only of simple identity, rarified purity, or a primordial nature. But we can well look to him when we look for a figuration of memoring and memories' losses.

NATURE, ECSTASY, AND THE SUBLIME

Nietzsche remarks in his discussion of naive art that the harmony of existence presented through Apollo is one that is contemplated with longing by modern people.[19] He mentions Schiller, and he could have mentioned many others who found in nature, as Nietzsche himself found in *The Birth of Tragedy*, a primal source for ultimate reference. Behind many of these non-Nietzschean references, I believe, is the Kantian observation that everything ideal and purposeful is based upon the forms of nature that are found in the transcendental categories of the understanding. The form of nature is pure and law-giving if not, taken by itself, fully reflective and self-elucidating. Further, transcendental activity is required to find in nature beauty and purposiveness. Running through these and many other reflections about nature is a common thread of longing for a return to "something" primal, pristine, and, if not differentiated as an individual, nonetheless ultimate, uplifted and uplifting, as well as ontologically revelatory. The return might be in an act of mind or poetic expression, but whatever the means, no matter the terrible conflict or contradictions involved, something in humans that is attuned to The Ultimate Nature is said to happen, and human beings in their travail find themselves connected—unified—in Nature's apotheosis. The dynamics of longing, creating, producing, feeling, or intuiting may return one to a natural movement or energetics or primal source of life, and in such processes, the great thinker or the great poet, the true citizen of the world or the truly religious human is born, radiated by the glory of nature's ultimate reality. Nietzsche, in *The Birth of Tragedy*, had not yet explicitly confronted the spirit of seriousness and the ascetic ideal as definitive of much of modern people's longing. He had not yet appropriated the Dionysian as descriptive of the thought that overturns by the life force within an individual what he identified as the Apollinian. He was, as he said in the "Attempt," overwrought and green, still entranced by a thought of ultimacy that left him prey to ideas of unity and primal nature beyond the oblivion of normal life in its lack of mystery and the promise of apotheosis. Hence, he too looked for entrance into the mysteries of nature by means of sublime and ecstatic experiences. He was bound by a sense of transcendence, its desire for ecstatic disclosure and for redemption through sublime immediacy, bound by a strange forgetfulness of the Lethic by virtue of an inchoate conviction that Dionysus and his destruction of individuation would provide union with nature and, by means of oblivion, would re-member our deepest, most shared commonality.

This paradox of union by means of dismemberment constitutes a strange mixture of elements. On the one hand, it suggests, in seeming contradiction to what I just said, an intense recollection of Lethic oblivion. It means that nothing singular or individuated defines our ultimate commonality, and if he overemphasized Apollo's purity in individuation, he recaptured in Dionysus the titanic aspects that he lost in Apollo. And while one finds in *The Birth of Tragedy*'s account of Dionysus a strong religious aspect, it nonetheless comprises an effort to make a radical turn from determinant theism. On the other hand, the book is saturated by a sense of the presence—even though it is a withdrawing presence—of primal reality, which is present in life as a de-structuring as well as an emerging force, a force figured as Nature, as *common* Nature, return to which constitutes human destiny and the site of people's most significant suffering and affirmation. This conception of Nature, as we have seen, is not yet invested in *The Birth of Tragedy* with the knowledge that it too is like an artistic image in thanks to Apollo, one that provides a sense of the ultimate that is much closer to religious theism than Nietzsche at the time knew. Given Apollo's ambiguity, Nature is an image that in its sense of ultimacy suffers also from Apollo's fate—the passage of appearing and a destiny of fading that accompanies Apollo's light. In *The Birth of Tragedy* Nature and Primal Unity do not mirror themselves in images of individuation that come to pass but rather take their rest in a sense of transcendent necessity that ironically does Kant honor and, as Nietzsche later saw, forgets the Dionysian dimension of its own occurrence. A symptom of this longing for the primal and the forgetfulness that it carries is found in Nietzsche's account of sublime Dionysian experience.

His account of the birth of tragedy requires the opposition of Apollo and Dionysus. Apollinian Doric art, he said, rose up against Dionysian barbarism and Titanic destructiveness, and then found itself in an unresolved, belligerent struggle with the Dionysian. One measure of the naivete of the splendid Doric accomplishment, according to Nietzsche, is found in the absence of Dionysus in the Apollinian affirmation. The movement that Nietzsche wants to chart is toward a union of the Apollinian and Dionysian that will express affirmation in a fully natural movement, a movement that brings together in art what is brought together in nature.

Primitive (i.e., preclassical) Dionysian art is neither pure in form nor serene in mood.[20] It is first and foremost musical and is expressed as lyric and sound. The Dionysian lyric artist "identified himself with the primal unity, its pain and contradiction." It is a repetition (*Wiederholung*) of the world, "a copy of this primal unity as music." This repetition, which is first a subjective mood or sense, quite private and without communication, is presented ("revealed") to the artist in an inchoate Apollinian moment that is similar to a dream image. The combination of an imageless primal unity, pain, and the vague sense of a dream image, Nietzsche says, unites the primal with *Schein*, with appearing, and frees the primal for artistic expression. This combination overcomes the mere subjectivity of painful, private union with the primal by turning that experience of pain and despair into a specific likeness of the primal by means of artistic (musical) expression. In this quasi-Apollinian expression, the artist begins to discover his "identity with the heart of the world," a showing that "in a dream scene . . . embodies the primordial contradiction and primordial pain, together with the primordial pleasure of [Apollo's] shining."[21] Nietzsche thus finds an incipient combination of Apollo and Dionysus in the appearing of musical lyrics, although the combination was not at first thematized or recognized. In the lyric's musical aspect—its mere sounding—there is no image. "The lyric genius is conscious of a world of images and similitudes—growing out of his state of mystical self-abnegation and oneness."[22] Apollinian artists—the plastic artist and the epic poet—live in images, the singularity of the images' definition, and people are given to contemplation of them in the shining reflection of their order and definition. The Dionysian artist, by contrast, instead of maintaining a distance of contemplation in Apollo's shining, is "one and fused" with his figures, which arise from his own private immersion in "the truly existent and eternal self-resting at the very base of things, through whose images the lyric genius sees this very basis." In bringing to light—in the shining—of deeply personal immersion, the lyrical poet exposes something common to us all, something that brings us to the deepest point of individual selfhood where selfhood breaks apart in the primal pain of nonindividuated nature. Here is where shining ceases and the lyricist "celebrates his release" in the shining imagery of the death of shining individuality.

In the work of this imagery, Nietzsche says, one discovers that he is merely an image and artistic projection "for the true author, and that we have our highest dignity in our significance as works of art—for it is only as an *aesthetic phenomenon* that existence and the world are eternally *justified*. . . . Only insofar as the genius in the act of artistic creation coalesces with this primordial artist of the world, does he know anything of the eternal essence of art; for in this state he is, in a marvelous manner, like the weird image of the fairy tale which can turn his eyes at will and behold itself; he is at once subject and object, at once poet, actor, and spectator."

This revelation occurs in a shining movement toward the ending of shining, at the threshold where one finds the "true author" of art: primal nature in its force and indetermination. Art in its occurrence, in other words, is embodied memory of Apollinian and Dionysian forces and, strangely, a memory of its own loss in primal unity.

There is a vestigial connection of Apollo and Dionysus in lyrics and music, Nietzsche says, that is carried out in folk songs in which melody (Dionysian) "scatters image sparks all around" and gives rise to words. The primacy of primordial nature comes to light in the primary force of melody in folk songs. "Melody generates the poem out of itself ever again: that is what the strophic form of the folk song signifies."[23] "Language is strained to its utmost that it may imitate music . . . and the word, the image, the concept here seeks an expression analogous to music and now feels in itself the power of music."[24] This early connection of the two gods in folk songs and the proximity of music to primal unity flowers to full expression in Greek tragedy. Nietzsche's thesis is well known, that Greek tragedy originated in the tragic chorus, that the chorus is a voicing of the Dionysian, and in that voicing it presents to civilized people in a most civilized (Apollinian) manner the tragic dissolution of civilized excellences, a presentation that is at once beautiful and terrible, affirming of life, and without delusion regarding human suffering and loss. In its beautiful affirmation of life, Greek tragedy constitutes a "metaphysical comfort."[25] It also unites us in a common and tragic connection with primordial reality in the lineage of Dionysian "rapture." That rapture is constituted as "annihilation of the ordinary bounds and limits of existence" and give expression to a "chasm of oblivion" that "separates the worlds of everyday reality and of Dionysian reality." But when a person returns from this rapture, Nietzsche says, (contrary to our account of the blessings of Dionysus in the preceding chapter) he or she becomes despondent in the everyday world and "languishes in its non-rapturous and boring, painful mundanity. An ascetic will-negating mood is the fruit of these states."[26] The rapture as well as the horror that Dionysian music reveals gives rise to longing for transcendence of our lives in their separation, absurdity, and death. But tragic art gives a healing affirmation in which the rapture of the Dionysian and the shining of Apollo combine to transform life without denying either the Apollinian or the Dionysian dimension of nature. Nietzsche calls one aspect of this "healing" "the sublime as the artistic taming of the horrible."[27] This healing, in its occurrence through tragedy, constitutes also an embedded memory of the indelibility of loss of life and the suffering that accompanies life. Healing does not restore a sense of ultimate meaning or comfort. It happens in beautiful appearances which are like dreams that do not forget that they happen in an "element" without substance or reality. Healing embodies memory of loss of meaning in the coming of meaning *and* loss of life in life's appearing.

In the previous chapter I gave an account of the sublime by reference to the meaning of the English word and in regard to Dionysian ecstasy. I emphasized the sense of threshold that is found in the sublime occurrence—the sublime as threshold is constituted by a process of disintegration for which dismemberment and oblivion are appropriate metaphors. The German word that Nietzsche uses is *Erhabene*, which places emphasis on elevation and powerful, distant, unreachable presence. Dionysian ecstasy in his account is not itself sublime. Or, to state the point in a different way, in *The Birth of Tragedy* Dionysian contact with nature is not sublime, but it is ecstatic. The sublime dimension of tragedy occurs in "the artistic taming of the horrible" as the Dionysian ecstasy is mirrored to itself in the play's (formulated) scene.[28] The ecstatic dimension of the scene is for Nietzsche a development out of the early, ritualistic, nonimagistic Dionysian experience. The scene brings to brilliant expression the dark loss of individuation and identity in Dionysian ecstasy, an ecstasy that is reenacted by the chorus and by the transposition of individuals into masked characters who are other to the actors' nonstage identities. Unreality and indetermination pass through the tragedy's staging and enactment; and as one joins the drama through imaginative transposition, one sees "oneself transformed before one's own eyes and [begins] to act as if one had actually entered into another body, another character."[29] Dramatic transposition reenacts—performs—the dominant and ecstatic occurrence of loss of individuation. One loses memory of who one "really" is and in this loss of memory finds artistic access to nature before art and other to identification, that is, in this loss one remembers both an indeterminacy that is not subject to direct articulation and one's nature that is revealed in the occurrence of lost identity and in the happening of transposition.

The complicated, contradictory, extremely dynamic composition for Apollo's image, which I described in the previous section, figures his excess to simple identity and makes questionable Nietzsche's description of Apollinian sublimity. Henry David Thoreau has a line in his *Journal* which describes his ascent up a mountain when he "lost [himself] quite in the upper air and clouds, seeming to pass an imaginary line which separates a hill, merely earth heaped up, from a mountain, into a superterranean grandeur and sublimity." Elaborating the imaginary line, Thoreau says, "It can never be familiar; you are lost the moment you set foot there." This aspect of lostness in sublimity points out an important part of Apollo's gift of shining. It does not simply grant the possibility of familiarity in individualized identity, and if we are to attach the name of *sublime* to it we must mean an entrance into a strangeness that is not disconnected from a 'threatening' disclosure of unreality and unform. That is not as distant from Apollo as *The Birth of Tragedy* suggests. The coming of appearance and formation carries with it something to be remembered in thought: something like memory of 'lost-to-form' or 'lost-to-memory,' something that is both Lethic and shining, something that is like a forewarning of complication, deformation, and incompleteness in everything that shines brilliantly in its appearance and palpability.

The issue before us is not whether Nietzsche's interpretation of tragedy's birth is persuasive. I am pointing out, rather, the way in which *indetermination is figured* in his account. A strange phrase—'indetermination is figured'—but one to which we have become accustomed in *The Birth of Tragedy*, and one that will be important in the following discussion. The phrase highlights one of the essay's primary claims, namely, that Greek tragedy has its generation in Apollo's figuration of Dionysian ecstasy. In this sublime figuration Apollo and Dionysus remain locked in struggle, each threatening catastrophic transformation of the other, but they are connected in their resistances by means of an enacted and beautiful affirmation of loss in figuration. In his account an unreal eternity— mere indetermination—is articulated with a strange double emphasis. On the one hand, nature is figured as Dionysian, but as composed by Apollinian, forming power as much as by Dionysian unity without identity. On the other hand, "unreal" eternity is said to be beyond figuration and, as encountered in ecstatic transformations of individuation, to have a trajectory of mere and total oblivion, without brilliance, the possibility of sublimity, or release (redemption). In ecstatic sublimity, in the threshold of "unreal" eternity, time stops, reality lapses, and, Nietzsche's account Nature cannot be formed as "Nature" any more; Dionysus cannot "be" Dionysus, and Apollo vanishes through his appearance. Indetermination is remembered by a figuration whose meaning requires its own meaningless dissolution. It is "fully" remembered in its loss.

Nature has a clearly metaphysical function in Nietzsche's thought at this time to the extent that it provides a reference for continuous presence to human life, no matter how rifted it is by unresolvable oppositions, no matter if its law of appearance lacks unity in its form.[30] But on the other hand, Dionysian ecstasy seems to be a quite nonmetaphysical event in which nothing real or "there" is possible, no presence is spawned and all presence undergoes the catastrophe of oblivion. His thought in conceiving *The Birth of Tragedy* is at least an experiment in the memory of oblivion and loss of figuration in its stark valorization of Dionysian ecstasy. When, in *On the Genealogy of Morals*, Nietzsche allows the Dionysian to mirror itself (to use the language of *The Birth of Tragedy*) in the book's formation of the concept of 'genealogical memory,' and thereby eliminates the possibility of grounding concepts and values, his thought will have achieved the thorough Dionysian quality that *The Birth of Tragedy* lacks because of the way in which nature functions in it. Had Nietzsche conceived of Apollinian power in all its Titanic range he would have had a conception of the force of individuation and appearing that could have eliminated the thought of both primal unity and purity—and with it a much too serene concept of the 'sublime'—a concept that mars the book's attempt at presenting Dionysian thought in its memorialization of irretrievable loss.

CHAPTER SIX

Institutional Songs and Involuntary Memory: Where Do "We" Come From?

> But all of us have, unconsciously, involuntarily in our bodies values, words, formulas, moralities of opposite descent. . . . A diagnosis of the modern soul—where would it begin? By resolute incision into their instinctive contradiction, by the isolation of opposite values.
>
> —Nietzsche, *The Case of Wagner*

*T*here is an important difference between individuals' sacrificing their selves for the sake of something else and their finding emptiness in themselves. In self-sacrifice people give up priority for their own needs, desires, and interests, for the sake of something other than themselves. When they find emptiness in themselves, however—no self at all accompanying their selves—they do not necessarily sacrifice anything. They might rather attend to emptiness and allow by that attentiveness a sense of emptiness to infuse and inform their other experiences, including their self-oriented desires and interests. When that kind of attentiveness happens, their attitudes and feelings and their relations to themselves may well change, but the change happens in association with "nothing" that they find in themselves, and not in association with something outside of themselves in the affirmation of which they sacrifice their own interests and needs. Such sacrificial acts might also happen, but not necessarily because of a sense of emptiness. People might rather experience a dimension that is something like a dispossession that accompanies all that they are and have, a dimension that is not to be grasped or kept, and one that composes a release of determined experiences and things, release in one's involvement with them and care of them. A sense of emptiness can happen like an experience of loss that comes with present, passing events, except this sense of loss is not one of having lost something or given up something. Rather it is like the awareness of being definitely here along with no presence, like being porous in one's singularity, or occurring simultaneously with emptiness and senses of identity and acts of recognition.

Emptiness is a difficult word since it speaks metaphorically of no thing. A report that emptiness "happens" in an individual's life—not the empty feeling of melancholy in an experience of weak (or no) motivation to live, but the emptiness of nothing accompanying other specific experiences—such a report describes what appears to be an extremely private experience and indicates that the individual's life in its event is characterized by radical difference from all of the determinations in his or her life. The issue that I wish to note now is not an epistemological one concerning validation or confirmation. The issue is rather the way in which a person might communicate such a "realization" of emptiness. How can one communicate such a nonobjective and nonsubjective dimension of the particular events that he or she undergoes? Probably only by indirection and in this case indirection that exposes another person to "the" emptiness that one finds. Exposure to no-thing? To indetermination to which one may attend but which does not become an object of attention? To no-thing 'that' 'is' neither active nor passive, neither subject nor object, neither eternal or finite, not a 'this' at all, but happens obliquely like an absence of the signified in a *signifier* or like Lethe that cancels its own image and "communicates" by its passage "beyond" reference and sense? Or like Dionysus who means loss of *all* determination, including his own determination? Or Apollo whose power of determination fades into "darkness" without order or determination, or Mnemosyne who names the coming to presence of "things" in their loss of presence? The difficulty of this aspect is complicated by its imperviousness to the manners of knowing and direct speech by which we usually speak about things, define them, clarify them, and understand them. Although it appears to me that speaking of emptiness should be no more awkward than speaking of bodies, which are also impervious to our direct thought and speech, many people are less accustomed to meeting this kind of difference (from intelligibility) than they are to encountering the resistance of bodies to intelligibility. And we are accustomed to speechless gestures that carry intelligibility, are usually not noticed reflectively, and by which people communicate a good deal of meaning and significance—one's arm moving unconsciously in the air, extending a space of silent communication, expressing any one of hundreds of things that an arm's gesture can "say"—such events are themselves remarkable for the palpability and impalpability that accompany them.

If my observations are accurate, the feelings, issues, and questions that accompany memory's loss (events comprising emptiness as well as determination) are a significant, if seldom noticed, part in our culture's lineage of tacit recognition. And if we are to speak out of these experiences and of them, we face the desirability of speaking and thinking with an indirection that can bring them to the explicit awareness of other people. Direct speech about them can contribute to the processes by which we lose touch with their way of happening and thus mislead us by means of our explicit understanding of them: the greater our abstract clarity regarding them, the more decisive can be our departure and distance from them. In indirect communication, our objectivity and rational good sense can become a conduit to occurrences that do not happen the way objectivity, rationality, and good sense happen, and a conduit that happens as a passing means to occurrences that often are not recognized in our ordinary and well-functioning sensibility.[1]

I would like to show in this and the following chapters how some kinds of thinking can be comprised of an indirect communication in which "something" like Lethic "space" that is unfixed, devoid of mass, impersonal, and capable of endless transformation is brought indirectly to awareness by means of direct descriptions of some aspects in our culture's lineages. In this case, the process of *indirection* includes a language by which the priority of subjectivity for experience and thought is replaced by the priority of *lineage* and its transmission. And while I am persuaded of the importance and descriptive accuracy of this move, I will place emphasis on the performative aspect of such thinking (rather than on the issue of accuracy) in order to show a way of descriptive thinking that valorizes memory and attempts to carry out its work in an indirect communication of memory's loss in memory's enactments. In this way I will show that loss and nondetermination can be given expression indirectly in a genealogical manner of placing and specifying determined, bygone occurrences. Such indirect "presentation" happens as involuntary remembering *in* memory's losses, although my direct approach to this indirection will raise problems that I will need to address.

LOCATING THE PRESENT-PAST

Memories embedded in our musculature, dreams, sicknesses, feelings, and relations; memories expressed as preferences, attractions, aversions, anxieties; memories that give unconscious depth, range, and force to our "immediacies:" involuntary memories form our everyday lives and unexpected interruptions in them, although we seldom think about involuntary memories or recognize them when they happen. But they do happen. We find a significant measure of the present-pasts' manifestation and presentation in involuntary memories which add to the singularity, determination, and affection in our bodies and in the body of our imaginations and systems of self-regulations and recognitions. Pathologizing memories, healing memories, controlling and fateful memories: they are among the patterns of our lives and define our human occurrences. We deny them at the cost of self-deception.

As important as these memories are in their determinations of the ways we come to presence and compose our subjectivity, they constitute only one of several domains of involuntary memory. I would like to look at one of these domains—an institutional one—with an emphasis on the question of ways whereby we might think appropriately as we account for this domain and speak about it. How can we give increased alertness to these memories which do not begin or continue in their courses because of volitional actions on our part? Can we speak of the present-past as it takes place in institutions in a manner that allows the present-pastness of which we speak to appear in its involuntary happening? Can we understand institutions as instances of indirect communication of involuntary memories?

I have indicated frequently in the previous chapters that the occurrences of the past-present include losses in what come to presence in memory. Such losses are not more characteristic of voluntary memory than involuntary memory. I have been addressing memorial occurrences in the transpiration of forces that are memorialized in such figurations as Mnemosyne, Lethe, Apollo, and Dionysus. I shall turn to the nonmythological figurations in institutions that are memorial, involuntary, forceful, nonsubjective, and, strangely, embody nonetheless a kind of awareness as humans live in them and by means of them. As I make this transition from mythology to institutions, consider one of Mnemosyne's figurations. She is the goddess of poetry and poets, and poets in Ancient Greece were those who could see immediately into the past, to the origins of things or to the past great ages of their people. People found these past "things" to be invisible to mortal sight and to require for their presenting by sight and song the help of this goddess. Inspired memory is the poet's power to give perceptive presence to what is not perceptively present. J. P. Vernant points to another function of the poet that accompanies his inspiration: poems may include long catalogues of the names of gods, warriors, ships, and horses. These seemingly unpoetic lists "enable a social group to piece its 'past' together. . . . They constitute, as it were, the archives of a society that has no writing."[2] This is a society that exists in lineages of gods as well as people, and the poets provide the genealogies of originary gods and people. They rank and classify them along with their ships and horses, identify their families and their origins, and in this way they tell the stories of their society's time by means of codified, detailed legends and myths. Poems in this era spoke of what is originary for the present and of the processes by which the present came to be. They speak, however, of origins and processes that have much less to do with linear time than with divinely established destinies and the mysterious linkages of divine and human lives. The poets *relate* the past and its figures, but in this seemingly unpragmatic activity they establish both a definitive past and a meaningful present in which deathless beings live. They tell a people who they are and where they came from by reference both to bygone days and to an eternal present that is not linear in its disclosure.

Vernant says that the genesis of the world, as related to the poets by Mnemosyne and her daughters and then sung to others by the poets, unfolds by means of genealogies: "The rhythm of this past depends not upon a single chronology but upon genealogies. Time is, as it were, understood in the account of the relations between generations."[3] The primal beings of the past, such as Gaia or the Titans (including Mnemosyne) remain in present effect in the "night of the underworld."[4] And those who gave identity to bygone times "are still present to those who see them. They dwell on the earth, shade-like, or under the earth or in the ocean, or on the island of the blessed. They are available to the poets' eyes as they live timelessly on the edge of time. The poet sees the 'things' of the past in their remarkable, obscure, ageless present." "Never for a moment does the journey back through time make us leave contemporary realities."[5] Rather, poetic sight into the past constitutes a region of discovery of what is contemporary, although invisible and hidden—a discovery of the depths and heights of being that determine present lives without the notice of people in their ordinary awareness and knowledge.

Poets' memory thus eliminated "the barrier that separates the present from the past." "It provides a bridge between the world of the living and that beyond to which everything that leaves the light of day must return."[6] In this movement the Lethic element is *like* the darkness through which the poet, by Mnemosyne's power, sees clearly. But the power of Lethe as well as the good sense of everyday understanding are lost in the immediacy of divine sight. Linear time and its Lethic envelopment are largely ignored. Time is not reconstituted by the poet. Re-membering is not a part of the process. Rather, past things are seen contemporaneously just as they are in their incorruptibility.

Forgetting ordinary present time, however, for the poet of present, bygone time, is a moment of liberation from the misery and nearsightedness of the present age: knowledge of who lived then and how they lived in a time vastly more privileged than the poet's own time "enables [the poet] to escape from the time of the fifth race which is so fraught with fatigue, wretchedness, and anxiety": we find the balm Mnemosyne's gift in its association with Lethe, the god of forgetfulness.[7] Discernment of the past in the oblivion of the present time composes at once discernment of an eternal present that gives freedom from a profound ignorance and the deathlessness that accompanies it. Immortality and salvation are found through this memorial, poetic knowledge.

Note that in this context oblivion is connected with a turn to the present-past. Lethe is the "power" of forgetfulness that is mirrored in human superficiality, ignorance, and consequent misery, the power that is the element through which and beyond which the poet sees what truly is. Without inspired poetic knowledge and memory—Mnemosyne—humankind is lost on earth, surrounded and suffused by a darkness that people cannot perceive, much less see through. I shall connect this ancient sense of memory and knowledge to contemporary genealogy. But first I note a turn of emphasis in the name of Mnemosyne's and Lethe's imagery in order to highlight a moment that is different from the *return* to origins that I have been considering, a moment that will also provide a helpful distinction when I consider twentieth-century thought.

A second orientation for Mnemosyne and Lethe is found in the role that they play in some forms of Greek eschatology that are valorized by belief and reincarnation.[8] In this role they are oriented toward the soul prior to its incarnation and toward the future of souls after physical death rather than toward sight in the present-past. Instead of bringing to mortals the secrets of origins, Mnemosyne now brings the means by which souls can reach the end of time and, in the context of some religious practices that were oriented around reincarnation, put an end to the cycles of generations. Mnemosyne's role in providing liberation from "the world of oblivion" remains, but now that oblivion appears before the souls' earthy life and must be overcome by a recollection discipline. Lethe is that through which the soul passes in coming back into physical life; Lethe is the element by which the soul forgets all that it has learned and suffered in earlier lives, and consequently Lethe is associated even more strongly than earlier with condemnation and misery. Mnemosyne is the power of remembering that carries the soul back through its many lives and to the many sources of its own life as her devotee engages in the act of the soul's recovery. Mnemosyne provides the knowledge by which the soul can free itself from the body's deathly forgetfulness. The waters of Lethe are crossed as the soul comes to earth: "The water of oblivion is no longer the symbol of death, but of a return to life and to existence within time."[9] By virtue of this water the soul forgets the lessons of its past earthly life and simply lives out again and blindly the travails of mortal existence. By such forgetfulness the soul is condemned to infinite *repetition* of forgetfulness, mortal experience, partial knowledge; it is "chained" to the "wheel of birth and death." It becomes merely a leaky sieve as the Platonic image that I noted in chapter 2 has it. The emphasis falls not on origins but on each soul's prenatal loss of a sense of itself as well as on the prenatal significance of Lethe.

Now the poet is not the primary perceiving mediator of Mnemosyne's blessings. The individual, rather, learns the discipline of memory and by memory's movements is transported back in time and beyond "this" time to other times and other lives. In this way people gather the knowledge and lessons by which their souls find themselves—beyond the power of temporality and now beyond the power of its earthly blindness and mistakes. And when its body dies and is prepared for rebirth, it can make informed choices. If it can avoid Lethe's water (on the left) and come by the road on the right to Mnemosyne's spring-fed lake, it can receive the lake's sacred water and become a deathless god with its complete knowledge of what is and is not. Memory, purification, salvation, past lives, and eternity are joined in this imagery, with which forgetfulness is allied in a hopeless recycling of the soul who in its impurity cannot recall life beyond its present life. "The very effort involved in remembering is in itself a 'purification,' an ascetic discipline. It constitutes a truly spiritual exercise."[10] This ascetic exercise of memory—this discipline—that the Pythagoreans and others carried out was focused on a person's past lives and will be reflected obliquely in our contemporary disciplines of philosophical genealogy. While the soul's past lives will not focus this contemporary memorial work, the living past in our culture and its institutions, the cultural force of the living past in our affections and recognitions—in our minds' involvement in institutions—will provide a centripetal center for our thought. We are not looking for eternity, but we might look for liberation or understanding or new possibilities which, though far distant from "salvation," nonetheless arise through a transforming discipline of memory.

Earlier in this chapter I referred to embedded memories and to experiences of emptiness, to something like a space (or nonspace) left as a breath passes. I connected that kind of happening to an aspect of nondetermination embedded in present-past events and gave a promissory note that I would return to this connection. Within the context of the promissory note, and not yet in its fulfillment, I note that the ancient Greek interpretations that we are now considering of the soul's collection of itself by means of remembering its past lives is an interpretation that is connected to "concentration on the soul's breath."[11] The exercise of this concentration was directly linked to recollection, to the soul's "eternal nature," and to memory of the soul's deathless difference from body. Memory of specific events of the past was not indicative of anything significant for itself, but was simply a technique used in order to "get in touch" with ones' soul in a movement toward the fulness of pure being. The benefit of the soul's difference from body was sometimes found by means of trances in which a soul would travel to the "beyond" of its other lives as well as the beyond of the "element" (Mnemosyne) through which the journey took place. In this journey it discovers all of the errors that it has committed and by which it has been contaminated. And in this case, the defilement of Lethe's forgetfulness is overcome, whether the journey be retrospective or a "vertical" and ecstatic ascension to present and complete, timeless being. In these instances, the soul finds its measure in Mnemosyne's enactment and in the purity that she is now understood to require, a requirement which means elimination of Lethe's power of forgetfulness. The soul finds itself, not by means of empty indetermination, but by fullness of being—immortal being—to which it turns. Lethe is defeated. Without loss, memory now is considered in the context of completion and perfection, and the enlightened soul, free of temporality, exists in timeless being. Lethe, on the other hand, as a force that gives temporality to the soul in the form of self-forgetfulness, self-alienation, and infinite repetition, is absent from the soul's timeless self-enactment. Now the soul never forgets itself. It suffers no forgetfulness at all. *Anamnesis* (memory) brings completion. The soul is free of non- determination in the sense that it is without forgetfulness, intrinsic need to change, intrinsic uncertainty, and anarchic disorder. It cannot die, and it now knows what is and is not, what has been, and what will be. Memory is imagined to be without loss, and Lethe figures a region "before birth from the powers of which the pure soul departs. Lethe does not name the soul's destiny when the soul comes to the end of time by means of memory's transcendence.[12] Inspired memory, rather, begins timelessly and leads to the end of time in timeless being without Lethe's forgetfulness. Mnemosyne thus figures a separation from temporality that promises salvation and divinity, that is, deathlessness and freedom from the force of human suffering. Time is experienced primarily as "a power of destruction which irremediably ruins everything that . . . makes life worth living."[13]

In this particular complex of images, beliefs, and thoughts, the highest human aspirations thus include transcendence of (escape from?) time. The Pythagorians, for example, returned to bygone events only for the purpose of reaching the soul's timeless and true dwelling places. Ages, periods, sequences, genealogies, significant moments and deeds—all that constitute a memorable past—are no more than passing steps toward a catharsis of the soul which is imprisoned by its sojourn in time. The recalling of past things is grounded by Mnemosyne's clear and unfettered power to transmit the soul to true memoria—to the truths of her eternity before unbroken presences of being. Mnemosyne's "flow" has become a timeless transmission that carries the soul to its destiny of no forgetfulness and hence of no change, affection, suffering, or death. It seems that Mnemosyne's gift is not one of freedom from transformation and loss. She no longer gives temporal perspective. Rather, she gives the soul to find itself in eternity. Mnemosyne is here a sign solely of completeness, not one that includes fragmentation or fissure or loss of life in the coming of life. Lesmosyne seems to be forgotten in this figuration. (Does Lethe smile obscurely in this accomplishment?)

We have found Mnemosyne and Lethe functioning differently in two of their figurations, but there are also similarities. Mnemosyne is a power of saving knowledge, a power by which time is transcended, a power

in which an inspired person can be in perceptive and transformative touch
with Truth and Eternal Presence. In both mythical structures the fragmentation of earthly time, its turbulence, instability, and mortal existence indicate inferiority in ontological status and a kind of existing that is aligned
with ignorance, suffering, and death, all of which are inimical to
Mnemosyne's and the soul's true nature. And yet, in spite of these unper-
suasive beliefs and the dominant conception of time, the power of
Mnemosyne continues to transmit the past and human awareness through
time in such a way that what happened no longer repeats itself in finite
lives. She also continues to be a power of liberation from the otherwise
overwhelming finite present with its destiny of blind oblivion. She is a
power that relieves mortal suffering and ignorance. And her linkage to
Lethe also continues although in the negative and externalized way of
overcoming Lethe's power. Lethe has been expelled from Mnemosyne's
own event and territory, and that means that forgetfulness is experienced
as external to memory, that memory's event is in unblemished touch with
radiant eternity. Finally, Mnemosyne continues to be an impersonal
"agency" of memory, that is devoid of mass, but her transmission is to a
perceptive psyche to which she brings enlightenment and not, in Lethe's
absence, endless transformation.

Aristotle's conception of memory, on the other hand, is radically different from that embodied by Mnemosyne's myths. Memory (*mnemes*) is a
secondary faculty, is subject to mistake, and "belongs to the past."[14] It
occurs as "a state of affection" in either sensation or judgment; it takes
place as "the lasting part of an affection" in the form of something like a
picture. (449b–450a) It depends on a lapse of time and a distance in the
mind from an impressive occurrence, a distances that is spanned by the
mental continuation of the picture. By memory we have one kind of temporal perception that is oriented by what caused the affective picture and
by that image's "likeness to that of which it is an image" (451a). Memory is
most particularly not an aspect of the present, perceptive presentation of
things. Rather it constitutes simply an awareness of pastness and past
impressions.

Recollection (for Aristotle, *anamensis*) is no less than memory a
strictly human and individual occurrence. But it differs, in Aristotle's
usage, from 'memory.' It names a process of influence and recovery by
which one deliberately moves from impression to impression until the forgotten one is discovered (451b), "for when a man is recollecting he infers
that he has seen or heard or experienced something of the sort before, and

the process is a kind of search" (453a). One's deliberations are not "at distance, as some think that visions operate . . . but one thinks of them by proportionate mental impulse (*análogon kinései*); for there are similar figures and movements in the mind" (*kinései*) (452b). In speaking of recollecting, Aristotle understands himself to be speaking of the movements toward a retained state of mind, "a mental picture in the physical sphere," a movement that is affected by other physical states such as weight that bears on the organs of perceptions or the rates of growth and decline (435b). In thinking this way a person recovers a rational, pictorial affection in the lapse of time, or perhaps better said, a human mind recovers it. There is on Aristotle's account an emphasis not only on the deliberative function of *anamnesis* but also on a nonvoluntary aspect of memories' return, for "retained affections can present themselves persistently in an unregulated and unintended way: . . . outbursts of temper or fear, when they have once produced an impulse, do not cease even when the subjects of them set up counter movements, but continue this original activity in spite them. This affection is like that which occurs in the case of names, tunes, and sayings, when any of them has been very much on our lips; even though we give up the habit and do not mean to yield to it, we find ourselves continually singing or saying the familiar sound" (453a).

Temporalization of the past, retention of affections, and deliberate recovery of memories are all fallible and conditioned events within human minds for Aristotle, and the transmission of memories retains for him a nonvoluntary power that can be for a time beyond the individual's control. The ideas of memory's independence of directional consciousness and of something approximate to the self-enactment of memory remains in Aristotle's thought despite the thoroughness of his move to temporal, human agency in his explanation and description of memory.

Lethic forgetfulness in memory's enactment is also dimly recognized in Aristotle's essay. I say "dimly" because it receives no careful attention. But the lapse of time that is definitive of memory decisively separates the past, impressive occurrence from its present enactment, and the function of memories as affective, pictorial states of mind divides memories by a representational distance from "what" they hold. Loss of the "things" that memories record as affective states is intrinsic to memorial events, and lapses by which memories are hidden constitute conditions for the exercise of recollection. Memory according to Aristotle is characterized by loss, distance in time, forgetfulness, hiddenness, and fallibility. Memories happen as an individual's states of mind and do not have any status external to the experiences of a particular mind. Mnemosyne, with her gifts and divine grace, has fallen from view in Aristotle's common sense account, but aspects of the myths, especially in the name of Mnemosyne's early connection with Lethe, are vaguely reflected in it.

All of the myths of Mnemosyne also share with Aristotle a nonhistorical sensibility. But in contrast to Aristotle, Mnemosyne's and Lethe's mythic affiliations or lack of affiliation interconnect and depart from each other without a sense of mortal time's rule over their origins and transmissions. Mnemosyne's later myths especially carry one away from temporal fragmentation and the contingent existence of orders, including the orders of her own figurations. Mnemosyne's and Lethe's mythic externality before human emotion and mentation directs people toward superhuman insight, ritualized catharsis, and unchanging truths, not to living, finite past-present linkages in human mentation, much less in human cultural experience. Perhaps Mnemosyne's balm is found in her power to divert people away from their despair and affliction. But it also gives authority and power to special people whom she guides to rarified, sublime mystery and whom she graces with the power to return to humans with speech inspired by the mystery and her transmission of it. In many ways she is a goddess who bears humans or, later, their undying souls beyond the limits of time. The songs that she inspires sing out of a timeless presence that gives the possibility of wholeness to people who are lacerated in the brokenness of mortal time.

All that is lyrical nonsense in the context of Aristotle's account, except that he too has a view in which time produces nothing and always takes life away. Such temporality infects memory and prevents it from having the noetic power to reach truth. Memory and recollection constitute a temporal agency which contributes to a human sense of time but not to knowledge of higher, more excellent truth. And although memory does not contribute to the soul's full maturation in which (the soul) is fully and timelessly in attention to itself, memory and recollection do have the virtue of making a fallible if inward capacity to transmit past experiences into present awareness, a glimmer, perhaps, of fallible, historically constituted human beings struggling to recollect the courses and trajectories by which they have come to live the ways in which they find themselves. Even though I find that memory does not happen exclusively in individuals minds, it does happen as Aristotle saw, in loss—obliteration, really—of transcendence beyond time. The temporality of memory produces—now in spite of Aristotle's description of time—possibilities for understanding in temporal terms even the enlightenment provided by memory in lineages in which transtemporal attachments are assumed.

The loss of Lethe and Mnemosyne's figuration—a lethic loss of Lethe's 'memory'—radicalized her ritualized religious functions and her association with being without time. However, Lethe continued to figure radical loss of memory and of the benefits of timeless presence. Such losses, when combined with an understanding of meaning within the constraints of finitude, constitute involuntary memory of memory's own fragmentation. This thought is, of course, beyond the circumference of Aristotle's philosophy. But there is in his interpretation nonetheless the lethic element of forgetfulness and loss within memory's process, and this element gives memory fragmentation. Memory for Aristotle, in sharp contrast to Orphic and Phythagorean views, cannot provide wholeness or unity or extraction from time. Lesmosyne again? Hardly, but still an oblique appreciation of radical forgetfulness within memory's event.

Against this mythic and Aristotelian background (inclusive of their differences) I shall turn to ways in which institutions not only transmit and embody memories but also actively form people by the power of their memories. We are at a great distance from the mythic consciousness in which Mnemosyne and Lethe moved and in which Mnemosyne and Lethe also moved people by the drawing, transforming power of their figurations. But we remain close to the events of transmission that characterize memory as they and we experience them. In archaic and classical times in Greece, we saw that poets were the bearers of meaning whose reach was completely outside of the capacity of other people, and *Mnemosyne* was the name for the power of transmission and linkage to what people either never knew or forgot in a primordial and original event of forgetfulness. Their songs were constituted by both the spirit and the content that Mnemosyne disclosed to them. And with these songs individuals were carried beyond themselves to hear—perhaps to see—what was not now immediate and perceptible in time, to hear or see what was necessarily forgotten in temporal presence. In the radical change of awareness that marks our differences from those Hellenic devotees, we lack the grace of Mnemosyne's powerful and poetic presence. But we have memorial transmissions nonetheless that have remarkable transformative power and that give all manner of possibilities and figurations of life to arise and blossom. The prosaic, transmissional, and generative powers of institutions in their memorial aspects, though they are fragmented and mortal and certainly are not mythological gods, constitute nonetheless remarkable forces as they make present past events. Without a transcendental reach, they still have a transcending dimension in their cultural events as occurrences of transmission, formation, and carriage of people far outside the reach of their private experiences. Institutions happen as bodies of memorial life, whether for good or ill. And no matter how much we might hate them or fear them or cling to them, they pound out dithyrambic rhythms by which we are bourn by strange and largely silent lineages, by things and to things we do not name but in the force of which we live. In these complex figurations of transmission, formation, and transformation institutions carry out functions analogous to that of the archaic muses, now secularized and largely without beauty, analogous to figures who moved with powers that could convey people to what is hidden and essential for their lives. And those people who attend to institutions in their transmissional aspects? Not poets, usually, but like the archaic seers who found access to things that defined destinies and past, forming events, and who would say what they saw for the benefit of people. Everything now, in comparison to the times of mythological expression, is scaled down, without radiance or divinity, perhaps not totally lacking mystery, but without uniting, unquestioned beliefs. "We" are without the need for blindness in order to see by memory. But now we see that to which those poets and seers were blind—temporal, unstable, transforming, and decomposing things—re-membered things. Such things now help to compose the element of sight and meaning, and the region of gifted sight includes past-presence given in part through institutionalized monuments such as texts, artifacts, and ancient manuscripts. And, absent gods and seers, perhaps the memory of memory also lives in guises that only Lethe could appreciate were she here and given to admiration.

Consider perhaps the least divine and poetic of established institutions: money. The object as well as bearer of suspicion, greed, and love, money is one of the most powerful means of transmission in the world, and its insubstantial products are among the most prominent universalizing powers among diverse cultures that are otherwise bound to parochial customs and beliefs. It has massively transformed many economic practices as well as entire economies and has led to the formation of many other powerful institutions. It has played a major role in defining social standing and in the process overturned other longstanding social structures. Above all money carries experiences and constitutes experiences of the imaginal, consental formation of a primary medium in and for our lives and one on which our lives depend. It can properly function as a constant reminder of radical contingency. In its power of transmission it is an opposite of Mnemosyne's early poets. It transmits and transfers with no hint of substantive, transcendent mystery. It occasions power with no requirement of purity. It mirrors a vast indifference to individual survival and can put in suspended relief the traditions by which a people have come to know who they are. It spawned a large vocabulary and transformed words in its development: *Currency, loan, investment, banking, income, capital, profit, securities, funds, account, debit, credit, fiscal, balance*, and *change*, are only a few English words that had nonmonetary meanings that were changed by the functions of money. And all of this without a "natural" origin, a natural law, or any other noncontingent foundation, with no more than human sanction, practice, and agreement for its "laws" of exchange, and nonetheless with a staggering virtuality when one considers the significance and force of its reality. Generative, awesome in its power, originary for customs, roles, social standing, and vast, interlinking networks of exchange and identity, money establishes an organism that carries us back to mutational beginnings—it has only evolved origins without an originary "word" or act or single, unified cause. Money attracts us in its ecstasy of promise and death, in its necessity and ephemeral indifference, in its receptacle-like quality of creation without subjectivity. It draws us like a fate that is spent in our lives, like a movement secreted in our lives, like an elusive memory of illusion, medium, reality, generation, disappearance, and appearance—all at once. Without our consent or preference, we belong to money rather more than it belongs to us.

In that belonging we inherit not only money's memorialized lack of substance. We also inherit histories of exchange and transmission. Consider the origin of nonconvertible paper money during the Revolutionary War. Bills that were not based on conversion into anything else—gold, silver, tobacco, or shells—probably saved the American Revolution.[15] After the colonies declared their independence, faced with the necessity of financing a war, unable effectively to levy and collect taxes in large amounts, and without credible standing as a borrower, the new government did what it had to do: it printed money with nothing precious to back it other than enthusiastic trust in the value of independence.[16] Although my use of this example of predispositions and our money's lineage does not depend on any particular interpretation of the wisdom of those policies, my account agrees with those who find the disastrous fiscal policies during the Revolution to be justifiable given the conditions of the time. Acceptance of the paper bills constituted an act of loyalty to the

Revolution, and those who did not accept them were "enemies of liberty." In other words, during this time it was considered treason to insist on convertible money or on gold or silver in financial transactions.[17] The bills that the government printed could be exchanged and used in payment for other things, but one could not go to a bank or to the government and exchange them for a standard weight of anything. At that time, the government did not even use land on a security (as several European governments had in order to increase the availability of money). The major trading nations, however, enjoyed stable currencies with reliable, convertible values. In the interest of stability and British wealth King George II in 1751 had restrained the American "Colonies or Plantations" from printing paper bills in order to retain control of trade on this continent and to prevent the inflationary and uncontrollable consequences of large quantities of "bad money." But in 1775 in the interest of liberty and heedless of certain inflation, the colonial government began to print large sums of money. Benjamin Franklin, wrote: "This currency, as we manage it, is a wonderful machine. It performs its Office when we issue it: it pays and clothes Troops, and provides Victuals, and Ammunition; and when we are obliged to issue a Quantity excessive, it pays off by Depreciation."[18] An extravagant fiscal policy became a "machine" in the service of the Revolution and belief in the value of liberty. Further, printing money during the war occurred in lieu of taxation and embodied a certain freedom from *the* indication of oppression by the state. Money without substantial backing was essential for the birth of liberty on this continent.

I note two elements in the proliferation of government bills in this country's early history: belief in liberty and inevitable hyperinflation. The continental government's paper money was soon almost worthless—not worth "a continental," as the expression goes—and the more money people were paid, the poorer they became. By the end of the war the continental currency had lost 99 percent of its face value and was effectively in default. This situation meant that many debtors paid their creditors with worthless bills and that many well-to-do patriots lost most of their monied wealth. By virtue of its bills' lack of convertibility and intrinsic value the government was able to supply its army at will, pay its bills, and, as Franklin observed, end up Scot-free by virtue of depreciation. In effect, the government had to pay for nothing. And further, paper money violated the scarcity principle as well as the security principle relative to metals that, by general consensus, were precious: as long as the supply of what is accepted as precious is limited, its value will be reasonably steady and its exchange value will be secure. But with unsecured paper bills and no central bank to establish reserves and regulations, the virtuality of a controlled medium of exchange became radical, and ruinous inflation swept the colonies.

In spite of anxiety and financial loss, most people stayed with the Revolution: belief in the value of liberty functioned like security, not for the money itself but for the policy of exchange in spite of the worthlessness signified by the bills. If the Revolution could be carried out without wealth and if liberty from oppression could be achieved by bills empty of value, so be it. The value of valueless money resided in purposes born of the lure of liberation and faith in this revolution. It was as though the bills were borrowed in debts to this faith and lure. Hope, trust, belief, ideas—the *value*—of liberty were the sources from which the currency was borrowed. And the currency repaid its creditors with the enormous interest of a newly founded republic, democratic at least in rhetoric and free of England's tyranny. In this case paper money made, instead of wealth, a revolution from tyranny, and it substituted not only for an absence of wealth but also for republican-democratic ideals. This is a strange and compound substitution, one in which an absence (in this case of wealth) finds its figuration in bills without intrinsic value, bills whose exchange value also signifies, and in that sense figures, hope in a revolution.

This associative dimension of continental paper bills, to which I am calling attention, combines failure and success, catastrophe and victory, liberty and groundlessness, and highlights a factor common to all paper bills and bank notes: possibility for growth and disaster on the verge of insubstantiality. I cannot say with certainty whether these aspects of the continental bills played a positive role in the formation of government and society in the United States. The formations of central banking systems and the strife concerning banking in this country in addition to the formation of other monetary policies make the associative lineage of liberty and paper money extremely complex. But a suggestion does take shape: the combination of successful liberation from tyranny, the power and insecurity of bills that are not (really) convertible into precious metal or land, and passion for the freedom of self-representation present elements that are familiar in the experience of United States democracy. One might well consider the legacy of the money from 1775 to 1781 for the association in United States culture of value without permanent substance, freedom from tyranny, and for a time, an astonishing degree of optimism based on expansion and depletion of resources. Perhaps memories of their money and successful revolution took many transformations in the development of North American ideals, policies, and attitudes.

Memory and money are so strange! Happening as it does in money's "eventing" and not solely or even primarily in images of money or money as image of other things—although memories occur "there" too—money's memorial aspect occurs in transmissions and networkings. This most materialistic of things from the point of view of "spiritual" perception brings to presence and transforms in its activities many past events that marked money's development and brings them to transformative presence in events of transferal that are quite excessive to any image or representation that money might also have. This kind of institutional memory has an imageless dimension in this sense: the memorial aspects of money in its usage occur in exchanging, in situations of exchange that generate new beginnings and endings in events. They take place in transmissional processes rather than only in or through images or pictures that are retained, almost like monuments, with availability for further reference. This memory in transmissional happenings is ephemeral. It does not occur in a clearly marked space for memory or in a relatively static form. This kind of memory happens, rather, in buying and selling, saving and spending, in desiring to save or spend, in empowering moments, and it happens in the interlinking of the things it enables. Memory in this case happens when we spend money, accumulate it, gain or lose social leverage by its means, expand our experiences by its networks, or recognize things on its terms. These things *might* be put into the forms of images, just as I am giving them a particular accessibility by these words and thoughts. But images and words are secondary presentations that refer and give appearance not only to signifying images but also to various other happenings. As presentative and immediate in our lives, however, these other nonimagistic happenings are not simply signs. They happen as occurrences that transmit memories—give past occurrences currency—as they occur in other transmissional processes. Events without sign or image are neither more nor less visible than Mnemosyne's presence, yet they are as forceful as people once found her to be. Money, like many other events, composes an environment in which events of the past are transformed into influential, impacting presences, into transformations, we have seen, that also enact forgetfulness of the past as it comes as memory to presence.

Consider further involuntary memory without images. I do not want to say that such memories are without form, but rather that they are not identical with the images that carry them. The eventful forms, such as forms of exchange, are moved in part, I have said, by past events that are bourn (and born again) in dynamic, current determinations and circumstances—something like a fusion of horizons that I discussed in chapter 2. The renewed happenings of past events occur as obscure forces of influence, that is, as indirect, intangible, effective, and affective powers, something like the sounding that moves forms of music. They indwell occurrences as limits, ways of doing things, as attitudes and affections that are engendered by the processes, recognitions, trajectories, and hierarchies of value. Such influences and their lineages can be studied and described by attention to the intangible forces and elements that constitute an event. Such study is not poetic divination like that of archaic Greek seers, but it is nonetheless a study which puts us in touch with forces that elude most of our everyday awareness. Images do carry influences, but inquiring into those influences requires the inquirer to find also what is not an image in the lineage's memorial enactment as well as to find transmissions of influences that exceed images.

Foucault's study of the history of insanity in the Age of Reason is one instance of this kind of inquiry and also a study of a kind of memory that is excessive to the images that carry it. Included in the several agendas in *Madness and Civilization* is the silencing of madness in the seventeenth and eighteenth centuries and a silencing that continues to be manifest in the twentieth-century medical knowledge of insanity and in the modern mental asylum.

Foucault traces and brings to awareness a division between madness and nonmadness that has its origins toward the end of the Middle Ages. This division itself obscurely carried memory of the exclusion figured by lazar houses and by "the value and images attached to the figure of the leper" in his or her removal from the "normal" world.[19] The leper was recognized as a sign of God's anger and grace, as a revelation of God's will and care in relation to humans. *In the lepers' exclusion*, people saw the hope of God's salvation. Foucault's point is that *abandonment* of the leper in the lazar houses—something distinguishable from the lazar house as a *sign* of abandonment—was itself a constitutive element in a lineage of exclusions that bore on the formation of madness in modern times.[20]

A perception had increased in the Middle Ages of the ambiguity, power, and danger of madness that appeared to separate these afflicted ones from the sense of divine grace and revelation that had previously bound them to the communities that banished them. The mad were increasingly associated with folly and with an element of cosmic anomie and deception, with what Foucault calls "unreason," in the midst of order and lawfulness something "strange" and not lawful came to figure the recognition of the madman. Or, if 'natural' is the lawful, something unnatural figured the mad. They appeared to be living epiphanies, not of something past or pending, not even of God's judgment and will, but of something in the world now that is menacing and chaotic, something divided from normalcy, nature, law, and God's will.

Foucault shows that in the modern period exclusion by means of institutionalization combined with an unconscious terror before the chaos of nonrationality, a consequent desire to contain, "correct" and "normalize" the mad by way of "rational" conduct and by an exercise of socially sanctioned power over their bodies—these combined elements gave a new form of abandonment: the voices of the mad were silenced. They were silenced in the sense that they could not present themselves to society in their own ways of being. They were not allowed their own self-manifestations, and the movements of their minds and bodies were submitted to the informed and rational subjectivity of those who knew themselves to be civilized. They were interpreted and presented by the syntax and practices of those who recognized themselves as reasonable and atoned as appropriate in their rationality to the nature of life and the will of God. The activity of this syntax and practice and the activity of containment and institutionalization memorialized the exclusion of lepers; the memorialized connection of this exclusion to the judgmental and salvitic nature of Reality as well as an anxiety before what appeared unordered and a sense of disease connected with exclusion. Containment of the mad also bore a trace of the chaos that their exile was intended to eradicate, and madness in its strange and ostracized differences became increasingly an object of fascination and preoccupation on the part of "normal" people. In their fascination people remained in touch with the "power" from which containment of the mad was supposed to free them. The silence of the chaotic mad was also carried by the institutionalized flow of official knowledge and rhetoric that placed and defined them.

This complex figuration of epiphany, confinement, exclusion, correction, and silencing was memorialized in the formation of mental institutions and psychiatric/psychological knowledge. Or, in other terms, the division between mad and rational people carried, *as division*, a body of many multiply dimensional memories. These memories, in their elusive quality, are expressed through the functions of institutions. These memories are found not only as divisions by which the mad and the normal are connected, but also as occurrences of exclusion by which the excluded, *as excluded*, continues to occur within the body that forced the exclusion, as confinements by which the confined continued to circulate in the society, as correction by which the errancy is preserved, and as silence by which something inarticulate is given a power of indirect communication. These memories have a double quality. On the one hand, they constitute retentions of what is lost by exclusion, and on the other, these very processes of division, exclusion, confinement, and silencing carry past events and practices and give them presence in other events and practices. These memories of past occurrences are also presented in such popular associations as those of madness, murder, immorality, and secret folly. They are presented in the establishment of "hospitals" for the mad, the freeing of the mad from prisons and houses for the poor for the purpose of correction in another kind of institution, the transformation of madness into the medical category of insanity which broadly disseminated sense of the dark mysteriousness of madness, and the modern formation of psychiatry within a framework of diagnosis, cure, and institutionalization.

Foucault shows that in these occurrences and associations the silence of the mad is sheltered and intensified and that the modern asylum is a monument to this silence. In its context of modernity, madness appears as "this ambiguity of chaos and apocalypse."[21] In the appearances of madness the ordered and rational grounds for life dissolve into an anarchy of emotions, sounds, and images; and madness also marks the end of rational time, the edge of ordered sequence, meaning, and truth. It is a deviant wildness that is kept in a "safe" house of futile containment.

The silence of the mad is measured and figured out only by the asylum. It is also measured and figured by expressions of madness that emerged out of the division of reason and unreason. In the lineage of unreason, Foucault mentions Goya, Nietzsche, Sade, Van Gogh, Hölderlin, and Artaud. Their art "*opens* a void, a moment of silence, a question without answer, *provokes* a breach without reconciliation where the world is forced to question itself."[22] In their works these artists and writers indicate a departure from the reign of reason and rational order in the world and allow opening to what is without reason. The opening and provocation are not explicit in the work's subject matter or coherence but come to expression as the art work reaches limits of order expression, sense, and meaning, incorporates the limits in its presentation, and becomes itself an expression of the ambiguity of chaos without order. It carries one to the edge of expressability, an edge where something without art or device or word gives darkness to the work's shining presence. In such works, Lethic oblivion qualifies everything else that is remembered and presented. Foucault finds in this qualification a refiguration of madness, not one that has learned to speak sanely but one that shows madness in the fading of reason, a fading with fragmented shape and form—something like memory of no memory at all, like vague lights blinking in the darkness and intensifying the darkness as they fade out without promise of return.

The one who traces lineages and their transformations, a person we can call an "archeologist" or "genealogist," may also be a participant in the artistic marking of madness' silence and Reason's limits in this sense: he, in this case, finds language and concepts by which to describe and present transformations and figurations in the seventeenth and eighteenth centuries in their own patterns of disclosure and formation. Inclusion of their silence recasts representation. One finds that the transmissions of influence, procedures, meanings, and figurations of recognition do not follow the principles and rules that govern traditional Western logics or experiences of reason and meaning. The emergence of "unreason," for example, in the context of seventeenth-century culture showed no rational grounding or fundamental meaning. It showed the different accidental connections in a discourse in which "Reason" was dominant, and a complex lineage of religious practice, disease, and exclusion. Those aspects can fit into a reasonable manner of explanation. But Foucault's account also shows an emptiness—an absence of meaning—that would not fit into an explanatory scheme. There are shifts that are made by a world without images, Foucault says of the experience of madness. This experience "remains silent in the composure of the knowledge which forgets it."[23] He holds in tension, without resolving their ambivalence, chaos and apocalypse in the context of Reason and unreason. Unreason at this time reveals itself aporetically as the limit of Reason—aporetically because in the discourse of its occurrence only Reason can reveal and delimit itself. As Foucault phrases the thought in *The Order of Things*, the space of seventeenth- and eighteenth-century rationality was constituted by the totality of Reason representing itself, and madness, we find in *Madness and Civilization*, occurs in a complete lack of the very representational space that would reveal it and confine it. The paradox of madness' disclosure is found in its lack of representational order and its silence in the context of its appearance as apocalyptic, like a flash of blinding light that shows a density of hidden darkness *in* Reason and Reason's manifestations. And Foucault provides a discourse in which Reason's authority is multiply broken by the ambivalence and ambiguity that compose without resistance his grammatical writing *and* by silence at a brink of experience and expressability to which his writing and expression repeatedly brings us.

For Foucault the disclosure of madness in the context of Reason gave rise to an identifiable lineage that includes Nietzsche, Hölderlin, Goya, Sade, Van Gogh, and Artaud. 'Emptiness as such' or 'chaos in itself' are not shown. Rather, his work shows emptiness with determinant experiences, no meaning *with* meanings, absence of order *with* order, silence *with* orders of articulation. In this dimension of the lineage that Foucault describes, an inclination falls away to turn either meaning or emptiness into entities that organize or underlie or infinitely transcend the world. And yet such nondetermination composes a memory in its conceptual event in the sense that "it" happens like a recall of making reasonable, meaningful, or sensible, a dimension like utter forgetfulness that happens without lucidity or explanation in the midst of illuminating knowledge, recognition, and truth. In both seventeenth-century madness and in Foucault's account of it nothing comes to nonpresence with present and determined occurrences.

The "art" of this kind of presentation, in contrast to the archaic bard's songs and to the Socratic art of *elenchoes* and recollection, is found as a study brings one to the edge of expressibility and meaning, to a boundary that links presentation to nothing presentable, to the passage of order into no order. If the style of presentation in its indirectness and nuance shows the boundaries of showing as well as of indication, connection, and causation, something like the experience of eighteenth-century madness is recalled in the midst of the work's sane rationality, and we can add Foucault's name to the list of those in the lineage stemming from madness' silence in the *formation of modern insanity*. This is a lineage in which the silence of madness in an age of Reason and the silence of insanity in an age of medical authority are given space for their own erruptions at the borders of crafted, disciplined presentations. These are works which not only allow space, as it were, for attentiveness to this silence. They are also works in which connections, communications, and orders, far from being governed by a sense of Reason, are found in the lineage of the eighteenth century's unreason, a lineage in which 'unorder' and 'no presence' are remembered by the contextual events of absence, emptiness, or unreason.

Transitions and transformations of established orders compose "regions" of unorder's epiphanies. I have said that in the manifestation of unorder, involuntary memory of no presence also happens, that the silence of madness, as Foucault describes it, occasions memory of limits to images, order, and meaning as well as memory of divisions which contribute to the formation of the power or presence of some institutions. These institutions are the present carriers of shifts and differentiations that the genealogist brings to interruptive, indirect expression. He gives another expression to an ephemeral, nonobjective dimension in the institutions' occurrences—a dimension without images. The art of expression is found, for example, in disclosures of uncapturable "silence" in the midst of what appears to be its interpretive master and articulate retainer. The gaps of exposure can be found in transformations or mutations in which one forceful figuration translates into another forceful figuration, the second of which is silently determined in part by loss of the first figuration. This kind of translation seems to "hold" the exclusion of what it was to carry, the events of differentiation that accompanied its arising limits and identity. Such translation appears to carry not only many of the determining factors *in that out* of which it changed but also the contingency of the happening that gave it to be limited and mutated.

Nietzsche, for example, shows that mercy overcomes the cruelty out of which it arises and which is formative of the Western experiences of justice. This overturning happens because of the vital temporality that is part of the composure of justice. The life force of justice leads by means of its affirmation beyond the life-endangering forms that transmit it. Cruelty expresses a fundamental and unconscious fear of the nonhuman way in which life force happens. It expresses an effort to contain and to control life and a body of hostile and resentful affections consequent to the futile and unsafe project. Individuals in this fundamental and negative attitude toward the force of life easily enjoy causing pain and justifying cruelty by appeal to principles and "higher" values. But Nietzsche shows as he traces cruelty in the form of some kinds of justice that mercy arises through a transformation of cruel justice as an individual becomes strong enough to affirm others in spite of the "wrongs" committed by them.[24] He also found in the "law of self-overcoming" a movement in Western culture that gave the values and stabilities of Western morality to change from within because of their own conflicted vitality.[25] This "law" is like a silent, intrinsic inclination toward change and differentiation in practices of self-sacrifice, an inclination toward change and differentiation *by means of* self-sacrifice, an inclination by which Western formations move in their internal differences and oppositions toward their own overcoming. They give themselves up, as it were, and transform themselves by the power of their own force of life, which has been formed by contradictions and, in Nietzsche's lineage, by the value of sacrificing oneself for "something higher." But Nietzsche's transitions seem to be full of life force, not of emptiness, and even though the idea of life-force is itself subject to self-overcoming on Nietzsche's terms, the idea nonetheless posits a continuing presence that provides instigation toward the most radical transformations. These transformations arise from the power of life that in Nietzsche's thought eludes the finality of any identity and "space," absent force, life, and will.

Foucault finds no life force that functions as a vital connective tissue that joins transitory elements. Even the disordering presence of will to power is lacking in his accounts of transformations.[26] In his study of orders of knowing in *The Order of Things*—orders by which things are gathered and recognized—Foucault emphasizes the mutable structures of established orders of knowledge.[27] Each of the orders he describes is characterized by a "network of analogies" which links different disciplines and provides an unconscious continuity among them. We can see a network of analogies or an "episteme," as a nonvoluntary and nonconscious field of continuity in which, for example, knowledge of language, knowledge of life, and knowledge of numbers operate by the same ordering rules and principles. This continuity is provided by the rules and principles and not by anything that transcends them or is in excess to them. But *this* knowledge on Foucault's part is also informed by the recognition that the exclusive ordering power of the rules and principles that are found in the orders of knowledge shows at once "a space of knowledge," choralike, that imposes no order on the orders that occur "in it." It is like "emptiness" that has no content to offer. And this knowledge of "the" space of knowledge is itself metaphorical and makes no claim to describe something literally or with calculable exactness. In its metaphorical quality, the descriptive knowledge knows that it reposes with nothing that can be directly described. "It" is like mere difference or simple indetermination as distinct to something that is active and present and governed by laws. In this Lethic space there is nothing to speak of and nothing to say, but "it" marks the limit of determination and order by a boundary of anomic absence. Or, from another perspective, one could say that determined, specific orders stand out, offering their gathering principles without further justification, stark in their singularities, forceful by means of recognitions, and yet, they occur in the muteness of a "dimension" that borders them, making them available for transformation and eradication—strange witnesses to unordered "space" in their established organizations. This metaphor of space means that the orders of knowledge by which we recognize things in their regularities and continuities are governed by describable and finite processes. Foucault's archeological/genealogical work includes a regular recall of the mutable limits of regularities. But this recall, although state-able in declarative sentences, is carried primarily in a manner of knowing that originates in the appearance (*with* determinant appearances) of what I have inadequately named "emptiness," "nondetermination," or "unrea-son." Foucault's knowing begins with the "madness" that appeared in recognitions and "corrections" in seventeenth- and eighteenth-century rationality. Foucault's way of knowing and recognizing orders of knowing compose an enacted memory of madness and its institutional lineage (including disciplined language and established customs). One can say much about this memory and its beginning, but declaration means little in comparison to knowledge that takes its shape in encounters with ends and deaths of orders, with delimiting "space" that seems to deviate completely from orders and yet to allow their distribution through time. In this famil-iarity and indirection, Foucault's work constitutes an encounter with no order amidst the orders of things.

Transformations of fundamental ordering principles—and the con-tinuity of transformations—take place as problems arise for a given order that the order cannot address adequately on its own terms. Orders change by virtue of problems that they create for themselves. The episteme of Similitude, for example, that preceded the dominance of representation for knowledge could not account for the differences among identities, as they were recognized within the episteme, or the processes of recognizing, or historical transformations. As it confronted this cluster of problems, this complex structure of recognitions mutated into an episteme that was focused by the rules of presentation. That is quite a different "network of analogies" in comparison to the network that constituted Similitude and the differences that developed under the power of Similitude by such means as discoveries in linguistics concerning the functions of signifiers, the divisions within disciplines, a growing attention to deception and imagination, discovery of new methods of measurement, and the growth of analysis and discrimination as means for connecting differences and similarities.[28] Foucault finds that basic transformations of orders and ordering principles happened as ways of knowing changed, that these changes were not the consequences of anything like subjectivity. Rather, a different kind of subjectivity formed, slowly, as ways of knowing changed.

He thus studies lineages of transformation, not volitional subjects, in order to understand the emergence of a time when knowledge revolved around the axis of subjectivity and representational activity.

Before I turn to an account of the detail of Foucault's description of transformations, I would like to note that we have turned from the rich experience of memory as founded in eternal truth—and from the poets who gave life meaning through songs and sight that originated in the Truth—to memories that are embodied in institutions and that carry with themselves traces of lack of determination (emptiness) which accompany their multiple determinations; and we have turned from the artists of truth to those who give articulation to these institutional memories. Cultural establishments transmit past events into present circumstances in the accompaniment of losses of determinations and events. These establishments in their transmissional aspect are themselves memorial events that present in highly mutated ways other times and beginnings that happened in their formation. Beginnings are measured in part by originary, institutional impotence as well as by trajectories of force and by sedimentations that are active in producing contexts and strange appendages for contemporary practice. Institutions (cultural establishments) carry fragmented memories, pieces, as it were, of other events, and they happened in a loss of the past that they also present in their contemporary formations.

Perhaps there is a balm that accompanies the prosaic descriptions of institutions' transmissional and memorial aspects, a balm that comes with recognitions, increased options, and above all, with language and thought that present things in the "element" that I have metaphorized as nondetermination or as emptiness: language and thought that embody recall of these Lethic divisions of memory, its kinship with unorder and nondetermination, its undisturbed quiet before the losses and boundaries that permeate things as they come to presence. In that language and thought memory's retention appears with unrecoverable losses whose traces are found in the slippage of past events into something else that we can call "presence," or in trajectories that we can control as little as we can grasp them in their flowing, undertowing, or elevating immediacy. We are bathed in memories that we do not choose or create as we live our day-to-day lives. And occasionally we can explicitly present them, like waking dreams, as we weave our futures and give ourselves occasion to add to or reduce, if only slightly, their force and form.

I turn now to some of the detail in Foucault's account of epistemic orders for the purpose of perceiving more of memory in transmission and of placing ourselves to undergo again and at another way station the question of memory's loss.

CHAPTER SEVEN

When the Company of Time Casts No Shadow: Memory of Differences and Nondetermination

A TRANSITION TO ORDERS OF DISORDER BY MEANS OF DIONYSUS' MASKS

*D*ionysus is not a good measure of madness, and he is most decidedly not a good measure of memories. In his power, civilization crumbles and seems to disappear, traditions shatter; violence, terror, and destruction are among the gifts that he brings.[1] His epiphany according to his myth is one of life in its ek-stasis, as I showed in chapter 4, outside of heritages, practical wisdom, and the connective tissues of communities, as well as of life's energy in its difference from individuals. Not even music holds its form for long in the sovereignty of his rhythms. Were the Dionysian alone to constitute the jointure of *human* life, human life would disappear, and, I believe, life too would disappear, unless life were something in itself and independent of the lives that give times and places to living events. To think of such pure ek-stasis—that is, to honor Dionysus above all powers as life itself—is surely (and paradoxically) a most metaphysical thought. Life in itself? Probably not.

So why is Dionysus not a good measure of madness and disorder, and in that measure a powerful memory of "divine" madness in the midst of civilized life—as we found Nietzsche saying that Dionysian energy was and is?[2] Foucault's description of unreason in an age of Reason appears to be in considerable debt to Dionysus and his tradition, and we would not have to strain to find connections among the silence of the mad, the formation of psychiatry, and lost touch with Dionysus: his loss would define in part the greater madness of Reason's dominance and of the normalizing procedures of medical cures. But Dionysus does not measure anything except by the difference of his destruction and loss of identity. In *his* wildness, measure and order are lost, and the values of measure fall apart—not merely quantitative measures but measure as qualities of rhythmic proportion, of life-giving boundaries, of *sophrosyne* (a balance of qualities whose entirety composes rightness and justice for all the present aspects: wisdom, I believe, in a full sense of the word). I showed in chapter 4 that Dionysus' power and existence depend on orders, and in chapter 5 that Apollo's combination of order and disorder perhaps constitutes a formation more attuned than Dionysus' folly to human experiences and events in a world that is both alien and the place of familiarity and communal life. When Foucault speaks of art in a lineage of unreason, he recognizes that madness appears within orders and by virtue of orders, that the radicality of madness is not found in a disclosure of mystical and cultic *ek-stasis* but in its disclosure of an opening, a rent, in the fabric of specific forms of rational discourse. Indeed, orders have limits according to Foucault's accounting, and their limits seem to be delimited in part by mere limitlessness. But our perceiving limits of order and their bordering a mere alienation of immeasurable limitlessness does not suggest that we turn to Dionysian madness as a model for life, a standard for vital energy, or a quasi-religious archetype for ecstasy. For Foucault the issue is one of attunement to mutational transformations, perceptiveness in orders before their own transfigurations, and an unanxious, nonhysterical encounter with nondetermination and madness as they happen—an encounter that might well issue in a transformation of madness into a different event in a different body of order. Foucault's "art" is one that allows the disclosures of madness when Reason in its Western heritage is sovereign. His art turns those experiences of madness away from their discursive origins while giving an account of those origins. In this context Dionysian energy finds its origin in a specific setting and is measured by discursive lineages and cultural formations. The image of Dionysus figures horrific and inspiring memories, certainly, but in the instance of Foucault's presentations his figuration emerges out of *one kind* of civilized denial of—and here wording is a problem because Dionysus emerges from denials of "what" has no name and casts no shadowed figure. Foucault's art is ordered and measured, but ordered and measured in part by an encounter with what an order can neither avoid nor encompass. His art is closer to Apollo as we found him than to Dionysus: unorder and order happen together, each measuring the other in its mortal combinations and yielding of individual things. For Foucault memories are embodied in institutions that constitute loci of power and order that are accompanied by destablizing processes of transformation and by absence of a substantive foundation. His art is found in descriptive presentations that are true to the orders of their transformations in an element of no thing, of no quality at all.

We can thus say that Dionysian power—the power to evacuate individuals of their identity and to disclose a weird unity of disunity—is quite dependent in Foucault's thought on both individuality and order. If we see Dionysus as a memorial figuration of loss of identity and memory, we must also see him as a mythic individuation of the experience of a radical loss of individuation, that is, see him as belonging to memorial singularization and order. I emphasize this perception of Dionysus as I turn to Foucault's account of some orders of knowledge for the purpose of emphasizing that a transition from an account of the silence of madness in modern times to an account of modern orders of knowledge is not as radical as it might seem. We have never left order's measure, although we have engaged through *Madness and Civilization* serious criticism of some ordered functions in our tradition. *The measure of order* is an ambiguous phrase: it can mean something that issues from order as well as something outside of order that shows order's due proportions and limits. And both sides of the ambiguity function in the perception that I am developing. Order establishes limits which give no-order to appear, and no-order measures the limits and reach of order. When *an* order alone dominates peoples' experiences of connection, transition, space, and time, the epiphany of no-order will be disturbing, whether that epiphany occurs as madness or in the metaphor of space with no stability at all in the texture of people's basic stabilities—or as a company of time that casts no shadow.

Consider this image that Walter Otto presents of Dionysus: "the god appears with such wildness and demanded such unheard of things, so much that mocked human order, that he first had to overpower the hearts of man before they could do him homage."[3] Otto speaks of the violence, horror, and tragedy which inhere in Dionysian occurrences and of the union of the heavenly and earthly in Dionysus' power (75, 78). By virtue of this union and his unnatural "demonic violence" he brings "breathtaking excitement" to those mortals who will also be the deliverers and receivers of his terrible destructiveness (80). He is "the wild spirit of the dreadful that mocks all laws and institutions," the one whose coming is marked by a crashing, thronging, uproarious din of pandemonium and in whose wake there is stunned and melancholy silence (92–93). "Everything that has been locked up has been released" in an extravaganza of primordial unrestraint, and "everything touched by him as well as his own being suffers violent loss and death" (95, 104). Dionysus presents the primordial mystery of life that "is itself mad—the matrix of the duality and the unity of disunity" (137).

In this presentation Dionysus composes a disclosure of new life itself, the primeval caldron which allows extraordinary creation and destruction on the part of those who came within the reach of its vapors. But Dionysus was not experienced, according to Otto, as a transcendent being by his earliest and most touched devotees. Dionysus was a god-man *with* people, in their midst, who appeared both tangibly and intangibly with them as a mask. His mask was "an image out of which the perplexing riddle of his two-fold nature stares—and with it madness." "Dionysus was present in person in the form of a mask at the ceremony of the mixing of the wine." "It was Dionysus who appeared in the mask" with "exciting immediacy" (86, 87, 89). "The mask," in short, "is pure confrontation. . . . It has no reverse side—'Spirits have no back,' the people say. It has nothing which might transcend the mighty movement of confrontation. It has . . . no complete existence either. It is the symbol of manifestation of that which is simultaneously there and not there: that which is excruciatingly near, that which is completely absent—both in one reality." Dionysus' masks make palpable the "eternal enigmas of duality and paradox" in "overpowering immediacy and inexpressible distance." The coming of Dionysus "brings madness" (91). He is the mad god of the mad, the revelation of life's madness, the god of the mask.

I suppose one could say that Dionysus is manifest in Foucault's work because Dionysus is *so* distant from it as a myth and yet quite available for it as a viable image for the force of unreason in a time of Reason. But there is an important difference between Foucault and Otto on a primary issue: Otto presents Dionysus as an immediate, universal power of "insane" ambiguity, like an archetypal image that presents something numenous, undeniable, and far beyond human grasp in its immediacy. Foucault, however, does not suggest that the ambiguity of presence and absence is an expression of something that is susceptible to the figuration of a god or of reality or of a two-fold nature. Rather, the figuration itself and the desire for such a figuration show a complex order arising out of and helping to form a designatable span of historical time. The figuration, its ambiguity, its power in its immediate communication, and its divine status are all subject to the era and ethos in which they arise. Further, Foucault's thought, in contrast to Otto's, does not suggest or show a desire for a primordial power that is disclosed by the mask of Dionysus in Ancient Greek culture and by the figuration of the mad in an age of Reason. We could say in this context that the ambiguity of Dionysus' mask which Otto describes reverts to itself by means of historical time: the eternal enigma and the expression that the mask gives it belong to a complex, dynamic structure of recognition and belief. This structure takes away the universal timelessness and presence attributed to Dionysus, empties his image of the implication of universal power, and restores him to the enigma that he reveals by the presumption of his timeless, earthly presence. The immediate duality of heavenly and earthly being in an eternal unity with only the finite unity of a mask is dissolved in the historical figurations of that idea of duality. He begins to appear as a temporal, composite figure that brings with it many beliefs, experiences, and human images. The sense of eternal-finite presence, we find, is attributable to the lineage of Reason or to a religious lineage of an image of divine disclosive presence and not to Dionysus' power in itself. In his mask we find reflected human dread before nothing at all, and we find the creation work of this dread in the images of archetypal presence of rational order.

That observation in no way denies the power of Dionysus' mask in its immediacy with some people. It rather locates the situation of its power and identifies the mask as a kind of institution, an established carrier, in this instance, of an image of a "matrix of the duality and the unity of disunity" (137). I am persuaded that the lineage of this "matrix" in Dionysus' revelation has had powerful effects in Western culture and has informed other figurations as varied as those of Christ and seventeenth-century madness. The reverberations of Dionysus' cymbals and frenzy and release of what is hidden and controlled are certainly found in Foucault's prose. But the immediacy of the god's form is gone. Genealogical description and thinking replace the affective, imagistic, connecting tissues of the myth, and the vexed temporality of conflicted cultural formations replaces the "eternal" ambiguity of Dionysus' religious. Madness, then, is, in this context, disclosure of primordial life only by virtue a specific situation that bestows disclosive power on it. It might well be descriptive of a given peo-

ple's encounter with what they recognize as errancy, unorder, and the limits of order. Or it might name a state of mind that some people undergo as
an undesirable illness. But in Foucault's writing the processes that
Dionysus names are not disclosive of an essence of life. As far as I can tell,
the value of 'essence' (as well as of 'divinity') is either in question or is
absent from his thought.

In prosaic terms we can say that Dionysus as an institution of a
mythic mangod has replaced Dionysus in his immediacy as mythic mangod. But that transformation does not necessarily invalidate experiences
that seem "Dionysian." Perhaps such experiences are more dispersed now,
as we have seen by means of the Dionysian aspects in seventeenth-century
madness as well as in Foucault's account of it. But Dionysus had an enor-
mously varied background in many cultures, and he had many different
aspects and characteristics. Masks are the fitting carriers for this god of
insubstantiality and enigma. Yet masks also 'state' the godman that has "no
back," no transcendent being to back him up as he traverses among mortals. He is not of one substance with his father, Zeus, and he is not fully
man. He is rather more like one of his early images—wine in water, water
in wine: fire water that is not subject to a reduction to its parts. Each
dimension in his figuration expresses and masks the other. In his mortal
immortality he brings distraction both to people and to gods. Heaven is
not fit for earthly existence, and the earthly is not fit for heavenly life. So
Dionysus releases each to the other in terrible disunity and possibly also in
a disclosure of some mortal souls' deepest travail in their embodied and
ununified character: Dionysus the paradoxical. And this matrix of
unity/disunity is *established* in image, cult, and, above all, as mask.

My point is not solely that recognition of Dionysus' institutional
being evacuates his divinity. The more important points are that the mask
does appear to express aspects of an eminent experience of horror and
ecstasy in some archaic cults and that we will be able to see an enigmatic
quality at the heart of stabilizing and established knowledges in our tradition that reflects elements of Dionysus' mask. Institutions too are like his
masks as they show what they also hide in identifiable appearances of both
order and nonorder. And institutions have the unsettling power to benefit
and to harm people by the same policies, practices, and values. They
release otherwise unimaginable possibilities as they undergo development
and transformation. Although 'pandemonium' would be a bit much to
describe this release, they can make a considerable and often transgressing
impact on a culture when they arrive—for example, the development of

the printing press and the other institutions that it spawned, or the arrival of Western trading policies and practices in Japan in the seventeenth century. Even as institutions function memorially, they also present their own weird and temporal circumstances, not in an incarnation of heaven and earth, but in disunifying configurations of stability, instability, determination, nondetermination, continuity, discontinuity. Not divine, not usually orgiastic, not necessarily mad or insane, but no less enigmatic, immediate, or inciting than Dionysus' masks. The masklike enigma of Dionysus appears so foreign to institutions! And yet a masklike enigma comes through institutional practices and belongs to them in their disclosures. And there *is* "a certain enigmatic wildness" in institutions—in the instance before us, in institutionalized and established knowledges—an enigma of wildness that is usually overlooked in the interest of holding firm to truths, law, and agencies. This wildness is manifest in transitions and transformations, not in the eradication of individuality in quasi-religious *ek-stasis* but in processes of institutionalization and transformation—in the creation of new kinds of individuals and losses of other forms. Such wildness comes as something like the shadowless nonpresence of mere space (or emptiness) as institutional identities and forms of power come to be to pass away.

I turn now to the question of what established knowledges mask and yet disclose in the masking.

ORDERS OF SAMENESSES AND DIFFERENCES—AND IN BETWEEN THEM

We have found that memories occur in institutionalized situations, functions, and ways of doing things.[4] We have also seen that memorial enactments are temporal in their transmissions, that "things" of the past, including exclusions and silencing, are presented and given appearance and currency in institutional movements, and that bygone trajectories of meanings, associations, affections, purposes, and much else can be carried forth through established, memorial occurrences. Not only do memories connect the past with the present, but also they provide connections in the present in multiple powers for connection and movement. These powers are transmitted out of past events with the consequence that by means of the projective dimension of past-present events in them, the future events can be perceived, if only fallibly and at least partially. Memories are foretelling occurrences as they project in present circumstances—which they help to form—defining, energetic figurations such as rules of association and exclusion, principles of exchange, and many other institutional structures and dynamics. And they have a foretelling quality in their presentations *with* lost determination and present moment: they foretell loss, instability, mortality, and seemingly continuous transformation. Their temporality, in this sense, is foretelling.

Memories seem to happen in something like insubstantial flows rather than only as relatively static images or passing recollections.[5] I am struggling with words and phrases that can perceive and remember memory in its temporality, as it were, and I am repeatedly driven in this perception and memory to metaphors of metaphors, vague approximations, subjunctive moods, and highly qualified substantives. I have chosen a manner of presentation that is neither a stream of consciousness nor surrealistic nor composed of words that are scattered on a page for the purpose of performing interruptions of meaning and sense. I have attempted to provide perceptive senses of borders, emptiness, and incongruity by means of indirections in the penumbra of direct statements and not by a performative emphasis on margins and spaces among words. I have said that in this process of presentation there is a Lethic aspect that is remembered in the repeated losses of "what" I wish to bring to appearance. There are enough losses and memorial presentations that occur through the uses and failures of available grammars, manners of expression, and indication to make unnecessary, in this essay, a further display of "something" like shadowless "space" that is unfixed, devoid of mass, impersonal, and capable of endless transformation—or I could say that efforts to give written presentation to "what" is capable of endless transformations seem endless. Yet memorial occurrences appear this way—suffused with indetermination and conflicting differences as constantly to unsettle in their occurrences their own identities and to undergo radical transformations in their transmissions.

I want now to consider aspects of Foucault's account of presentational orders in the modern period with the purpose of looking more carefully at memorial occurrences in light of interplays among samenesses and differences. I shall then turn to Derrida and Deleuze to pursue further the occurrences of difference and differenciation in their memorial aspects. I am moving toward an idea of differenciation as a manifestation of memory's loss.

SIMILITUDE AND A BIRTH OF DIFFERENCE IN BINARY
STRUCTURES: AN EXPOSITION

In the Renaissance, language was known as a three-fold structure: a formal domain of marks, commentary (or the content indicated by the marks), and text (the similitudes that linked marks to marks and marks to things).[6] The connective tissue among marks, commentary, and text was Likeness (or Similitude) and not Difference. Hence, "the signification of signs did not exist, because it was reabsorbed into the sovereignty of the Like." Different things in their dispersion were catalogued and organized in order to collect them in their likeness, and dispersion was known in terms of similarity and not unspeakable or essential differences. One could know and say what it thereby means of marks that were not essentially different from things. Signs thus showed likeness, presented likeness, and in that sense did not signify something different from the signs' reality. The happening of language was essentially like the happening of meaning and nonlinguistic things. Things themselves were marks and meanings—a mark (and not a mask) of Order or Divinity or Life—and were alike in being with language. Mountains and the word *mountains* were both signs of God's awesome order. People could read natural events just as they read marks, and marks themselves were intrinsically invested with meaning. There was no known gap among realities, marks, and meanings to require recollection out of loss, since all kinds of realities could be read *together* without loss.[7]

By the seventeenth century, however, knowledge of language began to be formed by binary structures that accentuated the difference and distance between signs and what they signify as well as among signs themselves. Language lost its intrinsic similitude with other things, and people increasingly recognized it as a differentiated region with its own way of being. "The profound kinship of language with the world was dissolved," with the consequence that language appeared as abstracted from nature and the world. Its best efforts are significations of what it is not. In *this* knowledge, it could indicate other existences, but it could not be them. Language in its difference was a sign of a gap between beings in their worth and lives and the marks that only indicated them. Language was known to mark the lives of what it signified.

The transformation from resemblance to difference also opened a new possibility for language's own enactment. It could express itself, people found in their knowledge of its binary aspect, in the singularity of its being as it represented other ways of being: literature as an autonomous region of expression began and came into its own. Language as literature could form according to its own movements and possibilities and not primarily in resemblance to something else. It could play out its difference from all other ways of existing. Literature's value was found in "capturing" a name, "enclosing it and concealing it, designating it in turn by other names that were the deferred presence of that first name." Things other than language are *presented*, in an oblique recall of Similitude, but now their presentation occurs in an endless dispersion and play of signs. By the rising priority of language's difference in its binary connection with things and its lack of resemblance to what it presents outside of itself, language generates names that announce their difference from the things that they present. Language presents not only its own life in dispersions of signs but also the presence of what it is not by means of these dispersions. An art of naming differences emerges, and this art takes a force of meaning that is all its own.

Both Foucault's account of this development and my own recounting of his work are within the impact of the movement of literature away from Similitude. Much else has intervened between early modern experiences of language and now, but the singularity of language as literature remains an important aspect of our recognition and thoughts. Even if language is disclosive of things other than itself, its disclosiveness is not found *in* its signifying relations, but, in this case, by its providing direct access to what it is not. A way of speaking or writing might well compose movements or irregularities that bring a person to perceive something that is *not* language. A likeness in movement or connections or lack of connections might well happen. But likeness in this instance happens with a difference that is not eliminated but rather is indicative of something other than language or leads one to the limits of language so that something else is apparent. The other things in their lives do not happen in language. Language in its disclosiveness does not suggest a logic of homogeneity or the sheer chance of destiny by a fortuitous presence but suggests rather an event that allows its difference vis à vis an other to break its own hegemony. This interpretation of language is not the same as the one in the seventeenth and eighteenth centuries that Foucault is describing, but it is in the lineage of language's differentiation from Similitude in that period. That differentiation is carried not only in the nineteenth- and twentieth-centuries' preoccupation with meaning, the contemporary question of alterity, and twentieth century hermeneutics, but also in genealogical thought, as we are now finding it, and in other deconstructive work as well. Foucault is giving an account of his own lineage in *The Order of Things*, and the question of memory as I am posing it, with the importance that I am giving to transmission, transformation, and loss, is also fully within the force of the discovery of language's difference and its inevitable power of dispersion and differentiation. As language and meaning gather things, they transfigure, dispose, dissimulate, and disperse those things. They dispose things in the sense of giving tendency and inclination, putting in place, eliminating, and transforming. Language and memory provide dispositions for things, and as they order them they provide differences with them in their presentation. Each makes its own claims in its occurrences, and they disperse as they gather. *Dispersion, dispossession*, and *disposition* name Lethic aspects of language's and memory's presentative events, something that does not cast shadows but that seems, by nondetermination, to determine events in their continuous and appearing transformations.

Literature, Foucault says descriptively, came to be known as a "space" that can be entered and experienced with intelligence by reference to its own Quixotic differentiating movements. It provides its own "basis" in a complex texture of disclosing and displacing signs. I am adding that we find in Foucault's language and thought, as he recalls the lineage of modern Western literature and linguistics, a display of a space of differencing that might make available to us by dispossession, dispersion, and disposition the phenomena that appear in his knowledge. I am further saying that memory as I am finding it is distinguished as a similar space, that there is a similarity of differentiation that probably indicates, in Foucault's terminology, an episteme of difference. And I am saying in addition, within the context of this book, that this display of differencing in this knowledge itself composes a memory of the kinds of losses that occur in memory's happening. Nondetermination happens with disquieting strangeness as memorial (and linguistic and literary) ordering transfigures what it determines. Language, literature, archaeological discourse, memory's loss: similar kinds of occurrences within a lineage of differentiation and dispersion.

ESTABLISHING DISCONTINUITIES

In his book *On the Advantages and Disadvantages of History for Life* Nietzsche utilizes the difference between two German words that are both translated into English as *"unhistorical:" unhistorisch* and *ungeschichtlich*.

Unhistorisch refers to the discipline of history and indicates an unhistorical attitude, a perspective that is not tied to history, a way of knowing that takes little account of history. *Ungeschichtlich*, on the other hand, can refer to an *event* that is not within the limits of historical time.[8] In this treatise Nietzsche addresses *Historie*—the reports, inquiries, and knowledge concerning what has happened—and describes an "unhistorical" (*unhistorischen*) art of forgetfulness. This "ecstacy" of forgetfulness is a temporal happening (*Geschehen*) and is thus *geschichtlich*, although it is also *unhistorisch*. In such revery people free themselves from the limits and power of the knowledge of what has been, find attunement with the lively and unconfined present moment of possibility, and focus on the emergence of possibilities that come within a limited horizon of changing circumstances.[9] They are not overwhelmed by their knowledge of what has happened—their historical knowledge with its sense of determination and accomplishment is suspended by forgetfulness as they experience the originality and newness of *this* moment. They find in this sensibility of forgetfulness the "youthful" energy for beginning, for creating events rather than experiencing events primarily in the wake of their passage. They have a sense for a future-engendering flow of life in and through limited events (a most *geschichtliche* sense!). At the same time that they are unhistorical in their emancipation from absorption into knowledge of what is past and reported, they are *überhistorische*, "transhistorical," in the sense that they are attuned to possibilities that are not actualized or known and to possibility which inheres in the determined, flowing energy of life. This is an *unhistorische* moment in time, one that is freed from the weight and accomplishment of historical knowledge and freed in an opening for occurrences that are yet to happen; and people are freed from their own actions that are attuned by the nondetermination of this opening: they are freed for origination of what has not been.[10]

An *unhistorische* moment for Nietzsche is one of discontinuity in the midst of knowledge and memory. The forgetfulness that characterizes it introduces discontinuity into the force of historical knowledge and sensibilities and unsettles those sensibilities and knowledge by establishing itself in a passing moment. One aspect of knowledge's temporality in this description thus composes a suspension of history (*Historie*) in an event of forgetting. In the moment of forgetting people stand out from the "drag" of knowledge that is dominated by disciplined recall, stands out from their "attachment" to the past.[11] I wish to emphasize the establishment of this *ek-stasis* in the movement of forgetting. The discontinuity that Nietzsche describes occurs in memories' flow as knowledge of the past. Forgetting and the discontinuity that it effects comprise an affirmation of the present moment's immediate freedom from the memory's known content of memories. Their determining power is found in excess to their determinations. They enact a dimension without content other than energy, a moment of forceful opening, on Nietzsche's account, that paradoxically establishes instability in the face of memorial connections—they enact the moment's interruption in the coming of bygone events. "Whoever cannot settle on the threshold of the moment forgetful of the whole past . . . will never know what happiness is, and worse yet, will never do anything to make others happy.[12] This is liberation from memorial knowledge, liberation by means of forgetting. Forgetting appears in this instance to correspond with times' passing moment and to provide coherence with the moment's difference from *its* past as well as from "the whole past." In the language of this book I can say that such forgetting composes memory of time's present difference from its happening as having been. It is memory of "always now, always beginning" in time's happening: an *unhistorische* event in time that is appropriate to time's present moment.

Nietzsche's interpretation of the moment, however, seems to come at the cost of memory's *geschichtliche* aspect. In describing liberation from historical knowledge by forgetting, he gives the present moment to appear as though its *Geschehen*, its happening, were not contextualized and situated by nonvoluntary predispositions and memories. Forgetting, in this early essay's account, has a transcendental quality of distance from any determination, as though possibilities came out of the occurrence of possibility as such or out of the moment itself. This attribution of *as such* or *itself* is different from indeterminant space or emptiness in the sense that nondetermination occurs with determination and does not suggest even the possibility of being in itself or as such. Like a Dionysian mask's presentation, it fades from appearance in an enigma without resolution. And yet, the moment of forgetting establishes *ek-stasis* in this sense: as historical knowledge is suspended in its active efficacy the moment constitutes a beginning in the context of its temporal and spacial placement; its placement is composed of specific limitations, possibilities, and forceful predispositions. Its limitations, possibilities, and predispositions are themselves composed of the "side shadows" of an incalculable number of present-past occurrences that are not specifically known or highlighted in their happening. Degrees of clarity, disturbance, and energy accompany an effective and affective presencing of sedimented experiences, structures of continu-

ity, patterns of attitude and disposition, manners of mentation and of
exclusion: all the things that provide nonvoluntary perspective and differentiated awareness even *in* the occurrences of forgetting. The moment
happens as a present arrangement that brings into effect a place and time
that joins previous and upcoming happenings. Its "unhistorical" quality
gives full sway to an extremely complex situation of multiple events and
trajectories. It allows mergers, exposure of what has gone unnoticed, and
turns of emphasis and is not unlike a waking dream in which nonvoluntary memories come to appearance. The ecstacy of liberation from knowledge by forgetting comes into existence in a highly determined fabric of
many threads. The ecstasy is stabilized momentarily in a memorial,
dynamic field. Its *Geschichte*—its happening in the present extensiveness
of past—is its momentary composure, its passing establishment.

Foucault's accounts of orders of knowledge accentuates this
geschichtliche dimension of the instability that characterizes the stability of
their occurrences. In his discussion of representing, as this episteme arose
in the late eighteenth century, he notes the difficulty of establishing historical discontinuities.[13] It is a double difficulty. One the one hand, he, as an
archeologist of epistemic formations, needs to establish a continuity of
access to the discontinuities that he describes; and on the other, he needs
to show how discontinuities among these figurations arose, which determinations figured them, and what developed out of both specific discontinuities and continuities: he needs to show how discontinuities were
established in eighteenth- and nineteenth-century knowledge. But he also
finds that the discontinuities do not show or indicate any determination
other than the broken continuities that border them. The "established"
discontinuities—like "moments" of emptiness—are not events that disclose a continuous being or a continuous teleological movement. They
happen, rather, as witnesses only to the changing events that establish
them.

Foucault finds these "witnesses," however, at a considerable distance
from their bygone events. His access to them occurs largely through his
reading of documents that present by signs a series of epistemic structures
that are found in this case by an episteme—*Foucault's* episteme—that
arose through broken continuities with representing. The episteme to
which Foucault's work belongs is continuous with the one he describes by
means of the discontinuities that he describes in *The Order of Things. His*
knowledge also establishes discontinuities, holds them in place in such a
way that they are referable and accountable, while at the same time they—

the discontinuities—are known as disclosive of no order at all that "occurs" in the midst of orders. How is Foucault able on his own terms to hold them in place in their Lethic aspect, to present them in that aspect according to their own movement without re-presenting them? This ability has to do with the manner in which discontinuities are established, with the specific *geschichtliche* qualities their happening shows, and with their *geschichtliche* qualities in Foucault's knowledge of them.

Foucault gives an account of discontinuities among orders of knowledge in a way of knowing that enacts with alertness (remembers) discontinuity in his presentation of it. He follows the sideshadowing of discontinuity in the eighteenth- and nineteenth-centuries' orders of knowledge which expect to overcome discontinuity. And he shows the play of discontinuity in the formation of the epistemic figuration that constitutes his own perceptiveness. His thought is "reapprehending itself," but not at the *root* of its own history that would provide, as nineteenth-century knowledge did, "a foundation, entirely free of doubt, . . . the solitary truth of this event . . . itself."[14] Archaeology, rather, "examines *each* event in terms of *its own* evident arrangement."[15] It comes to know events in their singularity as they provide types of continuities among things. This emphasis on singularity builds into its recognition a knowledge of Lethic discontinuity that accompanies and divides the determinations of epistemes which promise knowledge of the orders by which all things change. Foucault describes these epistemes with a sense of discontinuity with which the epistemes are unfamiliar. By the singularity of the events he describes he finds the discontinuity that valorizes his own discourse.

Foucault finds the emerging discontinuity within "the space of a few years" when "a culture ceases to think as it had been thinking up till then and begins to think other things in a new way."[16] "The last years of the eighteenth century are broken by a discontinuity similar to that which destroyed Renaissance thought at the beginning of the seventeenth; then the great circular forms in which similitude was enclosed was dislocated and opened so that the table of identities would be unfolded, and that table is now about to be destroyed in turn, while knowledge takes up residence in a new space—a discontinuity as enigmatic in its principle, in its original rupture as that which separates the Paracelsian circles from the Cartesian order."[17] What establishes those radical changes? Do they follow a law of transformation? "How is it that thought detaches itself from the squares it inherited before—general grammar, natural history, wealth— and allows what less than twenty years before had been posited and affirmed in the luminous space of understanding to topple down into error, into the realm of fantasy, into non-knowledge?"[18] During this time the very beings that are known radically change in "a profound breach in the expanse of continuities."[19] This breach is not like a single event, but is distributed across the entire field of knowledge, like an open fault line running through a once serene neighborhood.

We are thus considering configurations of order that allow one to recognize transcendent purposes or subjects which permeate transformation and give them a sense of certainty; and, around the axis of discontinuity we find leakage not by such purposes or subjects but by discontinuity. This finding occurs in a knowledge that recognizes such linkage *in* epistemic formations and transformations, and the knowledge and the epistemic formations and transformations establish mere discontinuity in a stability which discontinuity is known to destabilize. Mere discontinuity, that is, contentless nondetermination, is determined by the singularity whose convictions are breached in a collapse of certain knowledge and the emergence of another certain knowledge. A Lethic aspect of discontinuity interrupts continuities and composes an enigmatic connection of no connection—as I noted above, like a *moment* of emptiness. Foucault's knowledge in this sense bears in it memory of something like the forgetfulness figured by Lethe—with Mnemosyne appearing as well as the *geschicht-lichen*, established figuration of what Nietzsche called forgetfulness, figured now by the name *discontinuity*. Dionysus' mask seems to appear obscurely with the coincidence of continuity/discontinuity (determination/nondetermination)—except in this instance there are neither cultic celebrations nor a sense of divinity. *Ek-stasis* happens simply, without inspiration, in a darkness of nondetermination that accompanies the lights of orders.[20] And the one who tells of such things, far from touched by a god, brings forth a knowledge that knows its own fallible singularity by reference to a temporarily established breach of all establishment.

Such discontinuity, for Foucault, occurs in "a space of the world," has its perceptible origins in the orders of things, and it occasions the rise of new orders. It "allows" the formation of new ways of connecting and gathering things together, new ways by which things can be recognized. In this archaeology we are thus addressing connections when we speak of discontinuities, and we valorize discontinuities as we describe the formation of identities, continuities, and origins. Further, by his metaphor of space Foucault is not suggesting a line of time in which things happen, not a teleological process that might reveal an unbroken, guiding presence, such as the pythorgrean Mnemosyne, but he is addressing, rather, something like a spacial opening that belongs to events in the worlds of order. Although "space" occurs with sequences of figuration, it is not sequential. It is like contentless origin. Foucault's metaphor, the space of time, describes sequences that are neither necessary nor governed by an ontological principle. Sequences constitute one way whereby we count things. They establish *a* space of time whose arbitrariness is a measure of space without measure.

How might we describe an establishing power that places space and determines nondetermination? How might we describe such a power in a way that not only composes a memory of nondetermination in the midst of its ordered obscurity but also finds such memory in the institution that it describes?

AN INSTANCE OF ESTABLISHING DISCONTINUITY: SIGNS OF REPRESENTATION

An *instance* of a process whereby discontinuity is established? And one that is compounded by claims *about* established discontinuities, claims which also know themselves to establish discontinuities? Like a knowledge of *moments* of emptiness that also recognizes itself as a moment of emptiness? And a knowledge that I—perhaps we—are coming to know as an instance? An instance of discontinuity? I believe that the entirety of *The Order of Things* composes instances of such questions, descriptions, and self-awareness, but I shall address only one example, part of Foucault's account of the representation of the sign.[21]

In the early modern period knowledge of the sign required the sign to be *separated* from what it marks. The sign is no longer attached to the world by resemblance, but is rather separated from the world and its orders *by orders* of signs. And signs are also *dispersed.* This developing knowledge of the sign, Foucault shows, tacitly associates separation, order, and dispersion. In their orders and dispersions signs can be part of what they designate—an account about grammar, for example—or they can be separated from what they designate—an account of nature, for example. By their orders and in their dispersion, according to early modern knowledge of signs, they spread out what is known into divisions and groupings; they establish ordered distances among things—the distance of a person's aunt from his mother, for example, or the distance separating American and French cultures; signs bond—one who belongs to the church can violate the church by heresy; they provide distinction—that insignia is not of our house, or a serf is not among the nobility; and they give dissolutions—the city renounces the citizenship of mad individuals.

Further, signs establish conventions and hence allow for plays of signs in which one sign can substitute for another. 'Two' can stand for a number. A part can stand for the whole. Indeed, the agency and plasticity of signs as they were known, their power to encourage other syntheses and additional investigations, their power to produce possibilities and probabilities—this recognized combination of plasticity and agency gave rise to growing interest in imagination and fantasy, not for the purpose of raiding the script of eternal truths or making contact with ageless gods, but for the purpose of giving the play of signs its own domain. An understanding of the necessity of imagination for knowledge and in its combination with both errancy and antinomy is emerging. The timeless grounding of resemblance for this signal region is, of course, approaching a shipwreck all its own.

To this brew of dispersal, order, separation, connection, agency, plasticity, and autonomy the knowledge of the modern period added duplication and self-signification. *Duplication* meant *representation*, and *representation* as the essence of knowledge gave rise to the possibility that relations among signs—their signal orders—are not generated by a natural order of things in themselves. The bonds among signs, rather, could appear to take place inside of knowledge that is constituted by complex signs, by ideas that connect by means of signs one thing to another. In their power of duplication, one sign can represent another sign: the distance and difference of binary representation replaced the closeness of resemblance and the nonrepresentational being that characterized the knowledge of signs only a few years earlier; and the representative power of signs also moved toward a displacement of the supposed intimacy of connecting signs. Signs disperse and separate as they connect. The idea was emerging that the sign is ordered by a representing power, and an additional idea was emerging: this representing power can be represented by signifying activity. The signifier began to appear as something that is able to represent both the signified and the representing power that orders the signifying process. The sign thus became both a relation to an object and a self-manifestation of the power of signification. The sign gives expression to the agency of representation, and that agency is the basis for order, for connection, continuity, and difference in regions of knowledge and recognition: representation has become the power of presentation for the known world.

In this knowledge of the sign is a tacit combination of order, separation, connection, agency, imagination, plasticity, autonomy, duplication, representation, objectivity, and self-manifestation (i.e., self-signification). Consciousness would seem to enact a percolation of this brew, one potent enough to bring satisfaction to any member of a popular cult of Dionysus in his capacity as the god of beer and wine. That is, consciousness would have appeared this way if it did not also retain a direct relation to "natural" things and their orders, in *their* resemblances. An unnoticed split was forming between the power of representation and the unsignified order of things. One key to the vastness of this change that was underway in the knowledge of signs is found in the recognition of signs as composing their own world in separation from the world itself.

In this world of signs memory was known to occur in the realm of imaginative synthesis. Memory suggested resemblance *and* temporal differentiation *within* the activity of imagination, that is, within the autonomous activity of representation by signs. Resemblances among signs required memory and took place in processes of differentiation, separation, and duplication; and hence memory and temporal differentiation—errancy—seemed to indwell the processes that are essential to holding together everything that is signified and meant. Imagination functioned as the suture of differential signs, as the agency of memory and hence of synthesis. The requirement for the resemblance over time among differentiated signs opened order to an agency of synthesis that is generative, temporal, and fallible. Imagination had the power to give appearance to what does not exist as it (imagination) revealed continuity. Imagination in its power to present what is not present was known as necessary for knowledge, yet it also had the strange power in its spontaneity to give origins that *in their inception* were not apparently subject to finite order or time. Imagination in its timeless connection gave rise to tables of signs that established the signs' continuity and order from outside of time—not totally unlike the infallible foresight and hindsight of the ancient bards and seers who also knew truly what is now the case. Like the pure souls of those great prophets, modern tables of signs established the truth of signs by an origin outside of the errancy of imaginative syntheses, and they made possible a field of representation that enjoyed the shining truth of order outside of plays of substitution and concoction in significant combinations. The table's order for signs seemed to function, not as signs, but as

templets from another, foundational region of resemblance without signification. And yet, in contrast to the pure soul's sight among the ancients,
modern knowledge established the field of signs and imaginative power (a
power known for its fallibility) as the site for timeless contact with truth.
Imagination, even in the foundational transcendence of its own power of
fabrication and memory, is a far cry from the soul that, cleansed of its forgetfulness, is immediate to Mnemosyne's grace and hence without synthesis in its flawless memory and foresight.

In its originative process the imagination constituted in that knowledge a timeless perception thanks to which fabrication, temporal errancy,
and discontinuity were overcome by tables of timelessly ordered connections. So the tacit suggestions seem to be that there were origins in imagination's spontaneity that were outside of the orders of knowledge and
experience and that imaginative orders in knowledge and experience were
constituted by memories in highly fallible syntheses. The imagination was
"impure" and conflicted in the truths that it provided; its syntheses were
seen as necessary for knowledge, and the quandary provided by tables and
categories that held timeless truths in enactments of temporal, fallible
agency in human knowledge and recognition could not be forestalled for
long. It seems that foretelling the future, in this case by orders of measure
and classification, was found in conflict and contradiction with unreliable
syntheses within imaginative agency and not in a formation of directly
perceived, timeless necessities.

I note that Foucault shows in his description of the rise of the episteme of representation that his (and our) lineage manifests a powerful
desire to escape the limits of representation. Even when representation is
known as *the* power of disclosure, people also felt the need for presentation
that was uncontaminated by the temporality of syntheses and liberated
from the fallibility that memory embodies. For the sake of certainty—apo-
dictic certainty—there must be transcendence of the limits of representation in representational enactments, something continuing that shines
through the lapses and substitutions of imaginative syntheses and displacing relations among signs, a continuing unity that is contemporaneous
with all temporal events. Things *do* resemble each other and occur in patterns that are far more reliable than any knowledge that is reliant on memory. Surely there is knowledge that is not constituted by signs and acts of
imagination. Surely there are indications, perhaps intimations of resemblance outside of time, apperceptions of order outside of representation.
Such a desire is also part of the episteme of representation that Foucault

describes, and it constitutes part of the episteme's impossibility—its inadequacy—on its own terms. The "problem" that is embedded in the episteme and one that gained prominence in the nineteenth century is that the transmission of knowledge is provided by a representing agency that is dissatisfied prereflectively as well as reflectively with the limits of representational knowledge and its reliance on imaginatively synthesized, memory-dependent combinations of signs. This episteme is characterized by a desire for something with pure self-cohesion, with unbroken self-resemblance as the basis for representation, and this something must be known, not guessed or posited and hence grasped as a sign. But knowledge comes by means of the representing agency that desires nonrepresentational knowledge. This episteme thus occurs with dissatisfaction over the limits that it knows are imposed on knowledge by imagination and signs, and those limits allow an apperception, not of a natural and undivided unity, but of something closer to chaos or unorder or empty space in orders of presentation and transmission. This apperception is established by the divided, dispersed order of signs, by discontinuity, division, and temporal differentiation in connections and coherences among signs. This apperception also appears to play a significant role in the knowledge that Foucault establishes as he accentuates positively the madness of signs when they are compared to a vision of nontemporal, self-coherent order. Strangely, in his own experience of the undesirable limits of representation, he seems to escape those limits by bringing them to the center of his archeological knowledge: they open to no images, no syntheses, no memories, no things, no determination as they (the limits) border the syntheses and identities, not of imagination in subjects, but, for Foucault, of mutations in the occurrences of knowledges, subject matters, forms of recognition, and structures of presentation. He establishes a nonfoundational emptiness at the heart of his knowledge of the established knowledge of signs in the eighteenth century. The epistemes in both cases established something that undermines its own establishment, and in both instances, by Foucault's accounting, what is indicated is not will or desire of some other transcendental presence, but is nothing to be held by signification. The signifiers that establish this emptiness have a strange resemblance to the masks of Dionysus in their presentation of what is not subject to presentation.

To the extent that Foucault knows his own work to be organized in part by a metaphor of space—in *that* place of signification—he knows that his place of work is hospitable to all representation and epistemes as well as to similitude or experiences of blind, unconscious will. The *space* of his knowledge does not discriminate nor does it privilege whatever inhabits it. And he knows that his own work takes place in a lineage in one branch of which literature, as distinct to science, has been given a contested priority. In that branch, knowledge has been strongly impacted by a sense of forceful desire that does not represent anything but merely expresses itself and seeks liberation from all constraints, including those of representation. It is also a lineage in which one experiences attraction to differences and heteronomies in the midst of categories, laws, principles, and normalcies. His archeology (and genealogy) is in a lineage that knows the departure within it from order and measurement under the control of representation. It is a lineage of imagination, disclosure, origination, purposeless arches of purpose, and knowledges that constitute their own limits and define their own existence, as well as one that knows of epistemes of inviolate orders of similitude, continuous presence beyond the confusions of temporal orders, and ideals of certainty and clarity that are beyond imagination's work. So Foucault's knowledge finds itself in a lineage that is multiply divided and without an overarching unity that, as he might put it, mummers assurances in its undivided identity. His archeology presents its own lineage in such conflict and mutational transformation with the consequence that the plays of transcendental presence within it are undercut by its division and the empty space that it shows.

In this archaeological/genealogical knowledge, lineage replaces subjectivity as the site of synthesis and disclosure. I emphasize this displacement in order to be able to show that Foucault finds representation and its required foundations to be composed—thoroughly, definitively composed—of signs, that in this knowledge he carries out a striking experience of memory of nondetermination, and that he provides us with one way by which we can interpret memory outside of the episteme of representation, a way that maximizes the importance of memory's lapse in memory's formations. By this observation I shall emphasize the emergence of an experience and concept of memory to which this study is indebted. Memory, in short, is not of a movement exclusively of subjective mentation. It occurs in the activity and structures that we come to know, and in this kind of occurrence memory is found, among other things, in the institutions and habits of a culture—as indwelling an ethos—and not primarily in synthetic acts of imagination.[22] And, relevant to this particular section, in Foucault's archeology both a lineage and knowledge of it establish an "aspect" of memory's movement which appears also as quite unestablishable and which comes to the fore in the structures and movements that 'it' escapes.

THE SPACE OF A QUESTION

The limits of representation had been established in the 18th century by inflexible tables of order, of categories which promised completion and certainty in the knowledge of things.[23] But in the nineteenth century an unexpected mobility of epistemological arrangement emerged.[24] The earlier tables structured general grammar, natural history, and the analysis of wealth. Broadly, the disciplines came to recognize things by reference to structures, a *dynamic internal* to the known things, and the *functions* that connected and united things. Series and connections no longer inhabited a flat surface of classification but instead formed a variety of designs, from hierarchies in a vertical space to linear sequences or distant series. These emphases replaced tables of simultaneities that are contiguous and continuous with each other. The discontinuities that are formed by these different gathering spaces of organic structures were bridged by *analogy* and *succession*, and people tended to find identities in *relation among elements* rather than in independent substances that are connected by categories. These relations were not subject to visible perception but were perceived by knowledge of similarities of movement, form, and function that are at a distance from one another and *by establishing sequences of succession* in which one thing follows another in a connective chain: the importance of history was emerging as well as similarities that are not categorical but are rather like each other in the ways they connect and move within their own separate realms. As history gained importance, categorical adjacency was replaced by functional similarity at a distance. The distances among organic things were bridged by laws of succession, and the laws of succession were increasingly seen as the laws of historical development. History "is the fundamental mode of being of empiricities upon the basis of which they are affirmed, posited, arranged, and distributed in the space of knowledge for the use of such disciplines or sciences as may arise."[25] "History . . . becomes the birth place of the empirical."[26] Historical connections came to be known as giving birth to knowable things; things arise from histories, the order of history became the order of appearances.

Metaphysics in the nineteenth century thus took the form of memory. Memory instead of empirical observation was the region of imaginative synthesis, and thus it was the region of connection, law, regularity, and knowledge. The question emerged, What does thought's historicity mean? This question marked a movement in which thought became separated from surface, categorical order and came to belong to time—"to its flux and return"—because it belonged to the order of time.[27]

Foucault calls this order of history a new epistemological "space," and he identifies the connections of orders of things in association with discontinuities that required the rule of change, that is, required the laws of historical development. Not only is a departure from the order of history evident in his knowledge of that order. He also valorizes the imagery of space that suggests space without the definition of a table of categories, an imagery that probably emerged from the decline in power of the transcendental subject and of the priority of spiritual, intellectual, and mental order. His account at this point looks toward a development in knowledge that prioritizes orders of signs internal to systems of language and style, orders that are empirical in the sense that they reveal the arbitrariness and substitutableness of signs. He is articulating a knowledge that prioritizes something other than conscious organization and meaning, a knowledge that prioritizes the differences among positivities without a return to analogical identity, subjective syntheses, or a rule of universal laws. He looks toward a knowledge that does not subsume differences under a larger, connecting identity—not toward an identity of mind or even that of chaos or nonbeing, but toward a knowledge that refuses its own colonialization as it recognizes and places things. In this book Foucault is developing a knowledge that is not composed primarily of representation of representation. It is rather one that recognizes its own presentations as standing in or with or before something unorderable that accompanies representational orders, something that as unorderable is no-thing and that leaves him unclear about knowledge and its development. This much seems clear: the power and centrality of representing are fading; something about unrepresentable alterity is emerging; self-presentation of what is not representable appears to be important; and Foucault can recall aspects of his lineage in such a way that the power of differences, disjunctions, and nondetermination can be focused and enhanced in their intrinsic affiliations with identities, connections, and determinations. He is developing a knowledge that de-structures, in its operation, its own representational basis. He is developing a knowledge of events that requires another language and thought from that provided by the episteme of representation. The experimental quality of this study is found in the muteness of what it looks toward, in the transitory quality of the gains that are accomplished by the discursive power of the imagery of space and discontinuity, and in an emphasis on what he will later name the "plays of incompatible forces" that connect things. The force of this book, I believe, is found in its sense of something emerging that is not sensible in the language and conceptuality of representation, that lacks representational meaning, and that nonetheless seems obliquely available to a different articulation that is attuned to what the modern period experienced as madness and conceived as anarchy—attuned, that is, to the margins of perception in our recent lineage which gave a sense of empty space to modern knowledge while it excluded this sense from its explicit knowledge of order.

Foucault approaches such margins in his accounts by valorizing the *force* of labor, the *energy* of life, and the *power* of speech. Such force, energy, and power, he says, in the nineteenth century "prowl around the outer boundaries of our experience" and lead us to the "perhaps infinite task of knowing." They *formed* in the nineteenth century and perhaps also today an ability to identify the *existence* of objects, but not a transcendental condition for the possibility of the experience of objects. Such force, energy, and power are still outside of our knowledge but nonetheless condition our knowledge of things in their orders.[28] These still puzzling and anarchic sideshadows do not yet belong to knowledge, but rather our knowledge belongs obliquely to them in their continuous processes of destablizing epistemic syntheses: they seem to compose patterns of forces that give rise to different rules and groupings. What a knowledge belongs to—arises from—is not only another knowledge but also forces, energies, and powers in languages and practices which seem to collect things in orders that are not only orders of knowing. This much Foucault takes from the empirical wing of the Kantian tradition: Orders preexist our knowledge of them. But Foucault finds with greater emphasis than a Kantian could that knowable orders also differ from transcendental synthesis, yet they are describable as syntheses of forces. In his knowledge a revolution is at work that dissolves both the Kantian project of establishing transcendental limits for knowledge and the Hegelian project of finding the identity of history in an empirico/transcendental *Geist*. The hypothesis of forceful orders that establish their own notable and fragile continuities only to lose them in the impacts of new forces appears near on the horizon of this study. The move divides Foucault from the late modern project of detaching the synthesis of objects from the space of representation by means of mathematics and scientific empiricism: in his knowledge syntheses of forces do not seem always to be subject to mathematic regularities or to the connections of their material components or to the rules of physical forces. Organizations of forces appear rather to expose their own organic and disorganized dynamics, to include centripetal directions at the center of the centrifugal movements and to be in continuous fluctuation as one or another constellation of powers exerts organizational impact within or outside of the organization. Both methodological dogmatism and empirical certainty appear to be functions of forceful organizations within a governing episteme. In Foucault's thought the anthropological emphasis on concrete forms of existence joins with the spaces of fragmented times to form an empirically (i.e., a nontranscendental project of giving localized descriptions) placed and limited description of the lineages whose crises and disjunctions gave rise to the locale. These events are linked without a mathesis or a table of categories that would predict them or give them contemporaneity and without an absolute that would grant them relativity in their dispersal. Mnemosyne appears to be returned to her archaic inclusion of Lethe and something like forgetfulness emerges in the "form" of disjunctions and unpredictable mutations in a context of localized memory.

In the process of his archeological account, Foucault finds that language gained increasing singularity in the nineteenth century. Languages are formed by their particular rules of exchange, articulation, and representation. Whenever a discipline articulates what it knows, languages hold sway. The *singularities* of languages constitute a problem for any effort to make a language the perfect representation of what is found and known.[29] One effort to neutralize these singularities came with the formulation of a symbolic logic that would articulate a prelinguistic structure of thought that could mold a language to be universal in its exactness and meanings. Another effort was made in philology, one that would uncover the primary words that all discourses carry silently within them, to show something prior to the sentences and grammars that we speak—such as the unspoken elements of the unconscious or the primal Greek experiences, or hidden universal values, or a divine and originary revelation that holds an organizational sway in language. These are efforts to discover the "crude being" of language that underlies it, makes it possible, and exceeds its singularity. These are efforts "to make language speak, as it were, below itself, and as near as possible to what is being said in it, without it."[30] But, Foucault asks, do such efforts not articulate in a language the rules and values of *that* language? Do not such efforts interpret the "mute forms" of primal words as having an intention of meaning? Do we not formalize language and then interpret it by reference to something like a language as though there were hardly any space between the formalization and the interpretation? Do not such approaches articulate the idea of a primitive being in language just like the early moderns said was there? In such primitive being language is found to subsist in the very thing that is said to underlie language and to pervade all the singularities of languages. In both symbolic logic and in-depth interpretations something in language beyond language and yet like a language is found to be transparent to knowledge, something residing in prelinguistic thought or in the depth of the unconscious or in some originary wordlike event. Something prelinguistic is found in its order, whether by means of logic or interpretation, and this prelinguistic quasi-linguistic order is found knowable and articulable in language.

Foucault also discovers the emergence of literature, as we saw in the last chapter, in which words find their own power, their own space of connections, and in which words define their own art as writing. Literature is a body of radical intransitivity in which words fold back upon themselves, not in re-presentations of logics or prelinguistic grounds. Literature in this sense does not serve pleasure, taste, truth, or naturalness. It represents something, but is "a silent, cautious deposition of the word upon the whiteness of a piece of paper, where it can possess neither sound nor interlocator, where it has nothing to say but itself, nothing to do but shine in the brightness of its being."[31]

Literature, symbolic logic, philology, and exegesis (or interpretation of the "depth" of language) constitute a dispersion of language, Foucault says, "a multiple profusion" of language in modern knowledge by virtue of which language cannot be known as a transparent carrier of representations. Languages are known to hide origins, harbor silent beginnings, and fold back on themselves. Words and things in this profusion of knowledges appear marked by severe divisions. They are troubled by shadows, fabrications, deceptions, and unbridged distances, by penumbra of unspeakable nonthings. With the rise of "literature, words ceased to intersect with representations and to provide a spontaneous grid for the knowledge of things."[32] Language appeared in multiple, diverse knowledges without unity. Language as a category thus faded in power and emerged as a field that tolerated both orders and anarchy, tolerated both connection of sense and meaning and autonomies of expression that composed self-regulating localities. As philosophers turned to language as a center for thought, they thus turned to fields of dispersed unities, fields that challenged any attempt at thoughtful mastery of them. Multiple effort characterized twentieth-century thought to "confine the fragmented being of language once more into an impossible unity." But Foucault returns to Nietzsche's questions in his—Foucault's—effort to locate the synthesis of words and things: it is the question of power, of who possesses the right of words that describe and recognize things. Which people have the power to name? And with that question, Foucault notes Mallarme's answer: it is not I who speak but words in their literary solitude, in their enigmatic being as marks on a blank page. Nietzsche's question and Mallarme's answer define a contemporary distance that has not been crossed, the distance between the observation, it is I, this one, who speaks in the power to give things their singular recognitions, and the observation, there is no I in the word and its occurrence. There are only the words, unsubjective, unobjective, meaningless in their silent bestowal of meaning and signature on things. The question and answer address a language—a language addresses itself in this question and answer, looking for its own—not representation, but its own way of saying itself, providing a knowledge of itself that makes itself visible in a density of forgetfulness and innovation that appears to separate completely words and things that are not words.

At this point Foucault does not know what to write. He is confident that he defined the space of a question by following the collapse of early modern thought into the dispersion of the knowledges of languages. I believe that he is skeptical of the possibility of "mastering" languages' dispersion. He has obviously not chosen literature as his primary means of expression. He appears to want to develop an archeological empiricism in the rifts of languages' knowledges. He is preoccupied by the question of languages, and 'question' is affiliated with the spaces and divisions of languages' knowledges. He appears to prioritize the formation of questions that, while possibly giving rise to projects of mastery, make such projects improbably in their success. The fragmentation of language appears to be more of an originary event for contemporary knowledge than something to be resolved or overcome. Thinking has the opportunity to learn to speak in the fragmentation of its previous unities, to articulate the questions that shape its articulations, and to discover how to recognize things in their dispersions, things that are grounded in connecting discontinuities. There might be multiple unities and syntheses with many articulations that can show their own existences without showing even the possibility of mastery or the monarchy of any organization. In this sense, Foucault appears to adapt literature to thought in his archeological project of determining the lineage of the question of language. The archeologically determined locality of this project's limited range and likely transformation is emphasized by Foucault's hypothesis that orders of knowledge contain the principles of their existence within themselves (and not, for example, in a priori structures of representation). Orders of knowledge enact themselves—remember themselves—as they recognize and locate things. Within this archaeological way of knowing, orders of knowledge also enact their boundaries and inchoately remember them as they enact memorially the aspects of their lineage that give them place and time.

As an archeologist, Foucault recalls the movements and formative institutions that provide him with his recall and that he enacts in the recall (he sings their songs, in the imagery of chapter 4). In both his lyricism and discipline he gives a strange clearing for mere nondetermination, thereby remembering the weird Lethic aspect of the coming and shaping of memories. And he finds both the coming and the shaping of memories to lie outside of representing and representational agency by virtue of a lineage that presents what it cannot represent even in the episteme of representation. "Re-presentation" in a lineage would be an enactment of a now fragmented bygone event. But rather than a re-presentation, enactments within a lineage are presentations of 'things' that have been and are now beginning, but beginning as something different with only traces of bygone occurrences.

FRAMEWORKS FOR ANALYSES: AN EXCURSUS ON FULL HOUSES

In this and the last chapter I am describing occurrences of nonvoluntary memory in institutions and cultural events. I have used part of *The Order of Things* to highlight memorial presentations that are not representations, and I have said that such presentation can also occur in the enactments of knowledge of the lineage within which the knowledge of that lineage occurs. Through Foucault's metaphor of space I have highlighted enactments of the Lethic aspect of memory—enactments that are self-aware in their disestablishing establishment. In that context I have said that Foucault's archeological and genealogical knowledge composes memory of nondetermination accompanying epistemic transformations, that is, of losses of memories in memorial transmissions. I would like to turn now to Stephen Jay Gould's metaphor of the full house in order to elaborate the observation that organizations enact their own limits and by that enactment constitute memories in both their own determined formation and in their own pervasive nondetermination.

The accent now falls on variations in connections with expanding and contracting organizations.[33] I have wanted to show that a framework can account for something alien to frameworks—and to conceptualization and nomination as well. The framework gives occasion for perceptive alertness both to the limits of the framing and to an ephemeral escape from the framework that can take place within the framework. In the context of Foucault's work, I called this process "establishing discontinuity." In the occasion for perceptive alertness that the framework or establishment grants, the process is positive: the conundrum that the process provides, in which the established framework allows discontinuity and nondetermination to appear in continuities and determinations, I find something approximate to absurdity—something that does not fit its fitting, does not join in connecting things according to the framework, appears more like a trace of loss or emptiness than like an "itself." If we take variation due to an organization's expanding and contracting within organizations as our axis of description, how might such movement show nonpredictability and nondirectionality?

First an observation about trends and their interpretation. In this excursus I shall highlight an interpretation of evolution and organizations of life that turns away from the ideas and images of progress. Trends do not have to mean "progress."[34] They can appear—or seem to appear—by virtue of random patterns that are going nowhere, or by virtue of data that arise randomly.[35] Or people can perceive them on the basis of random correlations that are taken as causes (the Hale-Bopp comet appears and *therefore* a wart starts to grow on my ear). People can also see as trends events that are generated as "by-products, or side consequences, of expansions and contractions in the amount of variation within a system, and not by anything directly moving anywhere."[36] As the peripheries of an organization change or arrangements of some of its parts shift due to, say, new situations, some rhythms, velocities, possibilities, and patterns of variation within the organization might also change without a direct efficient causal linkage among them, as when the energy of an organization decreases, a second organization expands in the consequences vacuum, and a part in the second organization suddenly starts to grow rapidly. The changes do not seem to reflect the presence of a primordial direction for all the affected or effected things but simply an expanding or contracting shift in boundaries and horizons that has an indirect impact on a subgroup of things. The site of their lives is still within the slightly or considerably altered organization, although attention exclusively or primarily to the subset of things, within a perspective of directionality, might well discover signs of a broad scale or a general trend toward or away from a specific, desirable goal. The whole organization remains while there is some shifting of patterns that are inherent to it. As the field of research into language expanded in the eighteenth century, for example, an emphasis on the differences and autonomous regions of signs also grew. This growth does not indicate progress in knowledge toward higher or better goals, but a change of some aspects of linguistics within its considerably expanding perimeters. The change can be described adequately by reference to the organization that "holds" the change and without appearing to a transorganizational trend. Outside of the organization nothing appears with directionality and nothing appears to change.

Further, if variations within an organization can only go in one or a few directions, variation—from less complex to more complex creations, let us say—will show the limitations and possibilities inherent in a given organization, but they will not show a general trend of direction that is outside of the organization. Variation, rather, will be more like an ebb and flow of the organization's life in the lives of the groups that constitute it. The complexity of relations among signs, for example, appears to have had the option only to increase given the discoveries of their separate, systematic autonomies in relation to things as well as to each other. That increase (into literature, for instance) indicates something about the way knowledge of signification was organized at the time but does not indicate a larger teleology.

We are, of course, working with hypotheses and interpretations. One could easily say that the changing parameters of an organization manifest a directionality considerably in excess of the disturbed organization, that the larger organization is a smaller part of a still larger one that underwent a contraction, for example, that the perspective that I have presented is much too narrow to perceive what is really going on, or that hypotheses being hypotheses, one is preferable to another only on the basis of a hypothesis. One group's absurdity is another's rationality. Very intelligent people can believe and live for the sake of meanings that reveal trends that other very intelligent people find unsupportable, silly, or dangerously mistaken. This study carries out the hypothesis that metaphysical teleologies and purposes usually make difficult or impossible perception of the phenomena that form its axis, and that a group of hypotheses such as Gould's makes such phenomena more available for perception. If memory gives rise to variation and transformation by virtue of what some people in our tradition have called its "errancy" and which I have "highlighted" by words such as *Lethic, emptiness, loss, withdrawal, discontinuity*, and *nondetermination*, then we should expect something other than strict accuracy or rigid systematicity or empirical verifiability to affect the very lives of strict accuracy, rigid systematicity, and empirical verifiability. We can expect, perhaps even hope for, hypothetical variations, for *their* expansion and contraction and mutations: that could be a part of memory's synthesizing life in its gift of connection and beginnings by way of presentations of transformed bygone events. Living memorial hypotheses are organizations that enact with partiality and for the sake of their lives what has gone before. So I shall proceed with the hypothesis of nonprogress in the various developments of kinds of life in earthly evolutionary processes and see what it might disclose about its own life as it accounts for patterns and directions by way of nondirection in the formation of earthly creatures. By these procedures, perhaps I can shed some light on the hypothesis about memory that I am developing.

Systems undergo internal variations. When this happens, the variation is part of the system's entirety but need not define the system's entirety; for example, the purposes that direct a subgroup need not describe the system in its entirety. This emphasis can result in prioritizing the value of variation over the idea that an organization has an essence or a center by which one can perceive what is normal for that system. Organizations have rules and principles that define them, but these rules and principles are themselves subject to variation even as they govern a group of variations. Perhaps, as Gould says, most of us most of the time reify a numerical norm—the average or the most often found—or an ideal definition that reflects a 'perfect' expression within an organization—and treat them as though they were existing things, like an existing essence that manifests what is normal for the system.[37] But let's assume that variation is normal for many living organizations and that normalcy is an always passing abstraction from a contradicting, expanding, dynamic, and variational field.

One of Darwin's greatest gifts to Western culture, Gould argues, is found in his "substitution of variation for essence as the central category of natural reality."[38] Notice that we have not left the arena of taxonomy with this claim. We are rather finding a nonessential way of perceiving the development of earthly creatures, a way that must, I believe, on its own terms include itself in the claim.[39] Hypotheses that produce variations in tables of categories and patterns for perceiving things around us show, as hypothetical and variational, the high probability of terrific (maybe horrific) loss built into the fixing processes of abstraction, identification, and generalization. Hypothetical knowledge with the affirmed uncertainty that it carries bears out an indeterminateness that indwells taxonomical and observational knowledge, an indefiniteness that accompanies generalizations concerning existing things. It also maximizes a possibility for variation in its formulations and educated guesses. Hypothetical knowledge, from this perspective, is variability in practice.[40] In Gould's case, it knows of no central tendencies in biological organizations, and Darwin is the one who saw most clearly the mischief of teleological and directional categories when they are applied to the descents of earthly life.

The "engine" of variation among creatures is mutation. Darwin's phrase of choice for this process was *descent with modification* and not *evolution*.[41] *Evolution* sounded too progressive to him, although he adopted the word when it became widely current. *Descent with modification* names a process, for example, in which "all organisms tend to produce more offspring than can possibly survive; . . . offspring vary among themselves and are not carbon copies of an immutable type; at least some of this variation is passed down by inheritance to future generations."[42] The natural selection aspect of this process is found in the observation that surviving individuals are those "with variations that are fortuitously suited to changing local environments."[43] Descents develop as individuals adapt to local conditions and pass on their adapted characteristics to their offspring.[44] Descents cease, of course, when a whole group of individuals fail to adapt and they are overwhelmed by their living conditions. Developmental change is thus defined by local conditions and not by overarching trajectories, and by chancy mutations that successfully adapt to those conditions. It appears that most species and their variations failed sooner or later to adapt to environmental changes and died out. And Darwin—or at least one part of Darwin's complex mind—was not (and all of Gould's mind is not) convinced that the species that now survive (including our own) are the most adaptable in their lineage.[45] Both horses and humans, for example, appear to be extremely vulnerable to extinction when viewed through the lenses of "descent with modification," more like the flicker of a fading light in a long descent than a glorious triumph of evolutionary culmination.[46] Among the creatures who seem to be the most adaptable are rats, antelopes, insects, and, most of all, bacteria—not "higher" types of creatures, certainly not the most complex, but merely these most adaptable to constantly (viewed in terms of millions of years) changing and random local circumstances. In this knowledge, 'local adaptations' have usurped 'general progress' and 'variation' has replaced 'essence.'[47] And in Gould's presentation, the metaphor of a "full house" replaces the idea of a progressive development of species from lower forms of life to higher and better forms of life.

"Full house" names "a full system of variations over time."[48] Within the range of that metaphor Gould argues that when a process (he says "system") of descent of species is tracked from its minimal appearance to its most complex appearance, the *entire movement* over time from least to most complex is definitive of the process: instead of any group of creatures, many of the simplest creatures in the descent continue to exist in abundance (indicating remarkable adaptability), the complexity of some creatures increases, each species carries with it random and local adaptations, and the entire process cannot be understood properly by attention primarily to either the extremes or only the lineages that led to them. So human beings, in their extreme biological complexity, do not define a teleological movement in their lineage. Rather, they constitute an extreme within the entirety of a system in which increase in variety seems to be the primary characteristic of the system, when one begins with the simplest known organism—in this case, single-cell creatures. The full house of the process shows increased variation but no purposeful overall development—unless one follows the traditional model which begins with the most extremely developed creature and understands the process from its imposed standpoint. The system or process in *its* entirety (as a full house) does not support such a singular standpoint. It is defined by processes of variation over time, as well as by the huge variety of creatures that constitute the variations. The extreme "dribble" off at one end of the lineage and enjoy a part in a process that they do not dominate. To repeat: the entire system of variation over time composes the focus of the descriptions, and in the process uncountable, local sites of origins of species give a random quality to the development, survival, and demise of creatures. The *logos* of *bios* is made up of randomness and variation in relation to a marked point of departure and a volatile edge of highly complex formations.

Gould's arguments and evidence are far more developed and subtle than my cursory observations indicate, but I am interested primarily in his metaphors for determination which also show nondetermination in their hypothetical and systematic employment regarding established species. He constructs a view of evolutionary development in which human being is shifted by the image of a full house out of the controlling role it has had for progressive interpretations of descent with modification, shows why we should valorize variation and randomness in our understanding of evolutionary movement, shows the way in which the dynamics of evolution are constituted by adaptations to random localities, and attempts to enact the principle of random variation by locating himself and his work outside of any "central tendency" of destiny or truth. This last factor—his attempt to enact the principle of random variation—is the most difficult one. The explanatory functions of 'entire system,' random occasions for definitive formations, and the "reality" of variations in systematic formations all provide his theories with an abundant sense for nondetermination in the form of the value of absence of teleological trends that would provide a temporal connective tissue for the development of species. But the "art" proper to his work, that of enacting the principles of random variation, is troubled by an effort to present a scientifically respectable case for the reality of nature. And this idea of nature's reality has an ill fit with hypothetical thinking to the extent that Gould seems to suggest that his theory is objectively true outside its random placement.

I believe that a case can be made in opposition to my last observation. One can say with some justification that Gould is doing just what a good hypothetical thinker should do: he is making the best case he can, given the evidence, for his claims regarding the importance of the full house image and the methodological significance of the systemic entirety of the descent of species. With new evidence that supports other metaphors and hypotheses, he and we will shift to another descriptive and explanatory environment. But I believe that a considerably stronger case needs to be made for the importance of variation, randomness, and locality of his knowledge, that that knowledge needs to be put to work carefully *in* the self-presentation of his thought, and that the concepts of 'reality' and 'nature' need rethinking if he is to carry out *in* his own thinking the radical demands that he makes on evolutionary theory.[49]

I make these observations in order to emphasize that the framework that presents the nondetermination in the system of species descent also needs a framework that enacts with self-awareness its own presentation of nondetermination as it determines random locality in biological development. With a successful move in that direction, I expect that the concept of 'analysis' would undergo radical change and that the division between science and literature would be considerably narrowed if not obliterated.

Gould has taken a wonderful step toward showing that science is composed of both the determination and the emptiness of relations among signs, and he has prepared a way toward understanding science in terms of localized variations. Science as a framework for unframeable nondetermination? That too suggests a revolution in a cherished and reasonably secured lineage of "exact" knowledge that enjoys in it the life of the Platonic tradition.

A second aspect of Gould's hypothesis that I emphasize is the manner in which he shows that random localizations are held in species mutations in the form of adaptations. The woolly mammoths, for example, memorialize both a descent from minimally hairy elephants and radical environmental changes.[50] Indeed, all species track "local environments by natural selection."[51] By means of the hypothesis "natural selection can only produce adaptation to immediately surrounding (and changing) environments" Gould is in the process of showing that variation over time describes the movement of species descents and that species embody the memories (my term for the local conditions in which they developed and the mutations from which they carry). In fact, they carry only such memories and show as well no overarching teleology. They embody origins and modifications in specific environments, and in the randomness of their modifications they embody an absence of movement with transcendental grounding. According to Gould's interpretation, species embody no memory (again, my word) or indication of universal purposiveness but bear instead characteristics that revert back to their own lineages. This 'randomness' is an abstraction referring to no thing at all. It means that lineage and locality constitute a full house as far as developed characteristics and direction of change are concerned. In this sense, time, in the determined sense of a means for calculating, would seem to happen only in local knowledges and neither universally nor as a natural connective tissue for species in separate lineages. Time appears as a convention for counting, marking, and typologizing. There is, of course, no originality in the idea that time itself does not exist. But I find that idea a helpful reminder now as I consider, in the context of memory, the imagery of separate localities without common, connecting purposes or movements. Perhaps 'time' at best indicates the apparent inevitability of beginning and ending—or their simultaneity in moments within random events. Perhaps time can name mortal, local involvement with nothing else to support or direct it. Perhaps time composes the spaces of full houses of memories. In any case, the indication of random aspects that species carry shows a radicality of nondetermination in the determination of species, and this randomness seems to be memorialized in species that bear mutations in witness to often by gone local conditions.

Gould closes his book with the lines that close *Origin of Species*, words that "honor life's bursting and bustling variety in contrast with the dull repetition of earthly revolution about the sun in all its Newtonian majesty."[52] These words compliment Gould's robust affirmation and enjoyment of living things (and of being one among them) with no felt need for a sense of cosmic purpose. He exemplifies Darwin's observation that "there is grandeur in this view of life." Darwin's contrast in this statement between the monotonous "fixed law of gravity" and the wild and "most wonderful" profusion of types of creatures, however, gives me pause. His and Gould's affirmation of most humans' experience of wondrous beauty, their properly unapologetic enjoyment of their own perspectives, and their privileging human sensibility highlights the immeasurable difference between them and what gives them to wonder-filled sensations. They are both amazed by what they see, by the fecundity and the processes, by the impersonal variation of types of creatures, by the sheer force of the system of descent, by (although they do not say so) the other mystery of the systems' occurrences, the mystery of the interlinking traces of marvelous and strange kinds of creatures that, without the traces they have left, would be unimaginable—and the mystery of being able to ask why and not being able to find answers outside of local human mentation. The *happening* of creatures and their descents, after all the satisfactory explanations are appropriated, strike me as mysterious—not in some spasm of mystical inspiration, but in an everyday sense of a person's being arrested and astonished by the happening and by things beyond the reach of our knowledge and consciousness—in an everyday sense of finding traces that excite us to hypothesize about what the traces are traces of— and in an everyday sense of mystery in experiences and knowledges of things so vast in their differences that we have, really, no idea how to speak of them except by means of established memories and their uncountable mutations.

I am not sure, however, that "the fixed law of gravity" with its requirement for connections of even the simplest subatomic particles after the universe's (hypothetical) explosive origin is less (or more) wondrous than the appearances of countless types of living things on the earth. I am unable to imagine the combinations of things so small that in comparison a one-celled organism looks gigantic—and from these tensy-tiny beginnings come stars and galaxies, not to mention earth, men, women, dinosaurs, viruses, and consciousness—all by virtue (in part) of the lawful power of gravity! Given a long enough endurance of humans, I expect that many presently missing connections will be established on the basis of the language and images of empirical knowledge and reasonable hypotheses. Perhaps even the law of gravity will be understood in *its* origins. Or perhaps the idea of law will itself change into something now unimaginable. But for now, the 'universe' is so mysterious that even 'space' and 'universe' are shaky signs. And, particularly when a person has no expectation of a reason for it all, the very happening of gravity, regardless of how law-abiding it is, comes with no less potential for inspiring senses of wonder and beauty than the plenipotent prodigality of creatures and their types on earth.

And when I think of types and individuals carrying memorial traces of their origins and courses of development as well as embodying such shadowless things as randomness and localization, I suspect that the knowledge and assumptions that give us to wonder make certainty in any context other than hypothetical a reasonable object for suspicion if not for downright avoidance. Perhaps words such as *loss, emptiness*, and *nondetermination* in this context allow a small, less restricted opening to what people find wondrous, sublimely beautiful, and—in the midst of all established things—mysterious. That 'what' can, as in Gould's instance, lead people to cherish particulars without the conventional, topological practices of human domination. Unpredictability, radical contingency, random variation, movement without progress, organic diversity without unity—such "things" that also characterize events of memory can contribute to a sense of value for the unrepeatable particular as well as to a rediscovery of Lethe's meaning at the heart of established orders.[53]

'The company of things that cast no shadows' composes a thought that has influenced the shaping of this chapter. I have used *discontinuity* and *nondetermination* among other words to write of the shadowless company that we keep by way of knowledges, values, images, metaphors, and other vehicles of broken continuities and local determinations. These signs of difference have their own lineage, as I have suggested, and they allow for their own recognition in an extended and localized descent. They compose vacuous parts of a complex structure—of a limited system—that establishes a limited range of recognition and specification, a usually unconscious topography in which things appear and are known. And these signs also appear in a shadowless penumbra, which seems enigmatically to determine their own contagious differentiations—not unlike Dionysus' masks, I suggest, although they also compose resistance to his formation in their kinship with it (which makes them all the more Dionysian in their departures from his divine-human imagery). The departures and mutations of the signs of difference from and in their Dionysian heritage as well as their emphasis on differentiation and nondetermination constitute memory of 'something' without shadows that I am establishing in the language of memory's loss: loss of memory that accompanies memory's textures of continuity.

CHAPTER EIGHT

Repetitions and Differenciations

In any war story, but especially a true one, it's difficult to separate what happened from what seemed to happen. What seems to happen becomes its own happening and has to be told that way. . . .The picture gets jumbled, you tend to miss a lot. And then afterward, when you tell about it, there is always that surreal seemingness, which makes the story untrue, but which in fact represents the hard and exact truth as it *seemed.*

—Tim O'Brien, *The Things They Carried*

*W*hen I speak of the past or bygone days I would like to evoke an idea of happenings that are remote and were not necessarily linked together in the ways they now appear. Although I have images of specific past events and their interrelations in my mind, I do not have an image of "the past." And although the events that draw my attention concentrate my experiences for a time, I do not think of any group of events as organizing or giving a one "true" focus for the the past. The past is (as it were) composed of so many singularities, associations, relations, unknowns, and, I assume, unknowables—*so* many events, only some of which are not lost—that a generalization like "the past" is an aide to clarity only if it indicates its own inability and limitations and inadequacies in the ways it most conveniently functions. Even a present moment in a small locality seems to be infinitely complex in its components, subcomponents, currents of movement, associations, and influences; the past, presumably

185

made up of unaccountable bygone moments, seems to be entirely beyond any circumscription. But the word *moment* that is playing an important role in these observations can suggest a point in a line of time, and that image seems to be unavoidable . Even if I use the word in its meaning of *importance* and insist that when I say "moment" I want the word to speak of something that is singled out and given significance, I nonetheless appear to have in mind a portion of something larger or a designated point "in" a line of time. The idea of lineage that I have used inappropriately suggests the analogy of a line of time, some relations on which can be isolated for attention. I also do not find viable such nonlinear claims about time as the past is futural and upcoming in the form of destiny, or that the future is already in the past. There are, indeed, senses in which such claims seem correct. Perhaps time (as such, if there were such an occurrence) does not change and people can describe its invariances—time, for example, is composed always and at once a past, present, and future; time always happens as coming-to-be-passing-away; time does not exist as a being but happens as mortality. And I have made the general claim that memory and loss of memory happened and will happen for humans—there is *that* destiny and sameness too (and I believe that there are many other rising and falling destinies). But memory happens only in instances of remembering and memories and does not itself happen autonomously any more than the past happens on its own. Words such as *the past* and *memory* are generalizations. But *past events* (*having beens*) and *memories* do address occurrences that repeat particular characteristics whose recognition is well established in our culture. I think of the past as naming in general whatever has gone on and the ways bygone things occurred. There are probably other kinds of things that the past covers and that I should mention, but I am not attempting to be exhaustive or to provide sufficient definitions. I want to indicate, rather, that instead of an image of the past (including that of a time line), I would like to speak of multiple and particular sequences and trajectories that appear presently and belong to the past, appear by means of a particular focus, such as that of a discipline, belief, skill, institution, or group of principles. I would like also to speak of memories in terms of connections and associations as well as of lost connections and absence of association. In this context, *developments, series,* and *parts of a larger group* can be appropriate words, and the image of a dynamic, complete sequence of degenerations and generations can be helpful within limits. Some of those limits are found in the welter of interconnections that do not go in a line but branch off from any image in bewildering ways, seeming to follow no general direction, and the limits are also found in the happenings of loss. The image of a line of development or decline, while convenient, is thus not a completely appropriate image of the past or one sufficient to describe the events toward which it is directed. It describes an aspect of movements among related differences, and in the case of a lineage, the "line," although perforated and interrupted by many other events, is in the regard of something present and specific. We could say that 'lineage' describes a dynamic body of influences defined by specific formulations and foci that are repeated with multiple mutations. And I have also said that a lineage composes bodies of memories that occur as movements, connections, and losses within figurations and transfigurations. These occurrences "branch" out, provide trajectories different from those that spawned them, and compose complexes of events which may or may not be viewed with linear imagery within the confines of specific interests and foci. My minimal claim is that these complexes of events may be described as linear, that 'linear' can describe an aspect of their temporal 'being' when they are viewed from the perspective of a present formation.

'The past' does not literally name 'a field' that contains lineages and events. It names rather the characteristic of having occurred or the 'ago element.' That characteristic of having occurred appears to repeat in everything that happens as memory. It names, as we have seen, both loss of presence and presencing, transformation and formation, cessation and influences; it can indicate 'passed away' and 're-membered.' The ago element thus suggests connections by means of differenciation and thereby also suggests loss of connection in processes of repetition.[1]

SINGULARITIES

> All the pictures were the same. The whole project was a numbing onslaught of repetition. . . . After I had been at it for several minutes, he suddenly interrupted me and said, "You're going too fast. You'll never get it if you don't slow down. . . . Auggie was photographing time, I realized.
>
> —Paul Auster, *Smoke*

What makes our lives singular? Living, everyday events are singular. This man is hungry. This child is hurt. She and he love each other. He cries. She laughs. They sell their house. My mother cannot take care of herself. They are planning a trip. He wipes dust off of the chair. He is limping. I am shopping at this grocery store. This dean works on a budget. I am laughing in a movie. She stands there alone. We walk down the street together. This cup of coffee is hot. I don't know how to get to Baltimore. You want a raise in salary. She is confused. Her leg hurts. These people hate those people. He is writing. He sits by a window and looks out. She wants to be good. The wind is cool on her face. These dishes are drying. He plants a tulip bulb. This tulip is here, now.

Our singularities are endless and ordinary as we live out our events.[2] No matter how we live, our lives happen in singularities of living moments that, in the eventful moment, no one else can be. We can valorize the singularity of pain and death or heroic action or sensitive perception, but each living, frivolous moment is no less singular than the most dramatic occurrence of torture or suffering. The cheerleader's toothy grin and sense of fulfillment as he jumps in the air, touching with his hands in midair both of his feet, is no less singular than is a moment of profound self-discovery in a person's struggle with himself. Events of everyday living are no less singular than events of wonder, astonishment, or goodness. You are as singular at the sink as you are in your guilt or at the alter. The singularity of events—their being their own moment and movement—is as elusive for our awareness as it is entirely ordinary.

Of course I lose the singularity of an event that I write about, although I live in the singularity of writing about it or observing it or speaking of it or understanding it. A movement is singular in its life, in an individual's living it, not in its representation or generalization, although representing and generalizing enjoy their own singularities.

The heart's beat is singular in its living moment. The neural firing is singular. The hair's movement in the breeze is singular. The urge is singular. This heel's hitting this ground in this way is singular. The bat of an eye is singular. Event upon event, the differences that divide them, their organizations and dispersions are singular. The category that unites them, the judgment that places them, the values that arrange them, the thoughts that collect them are also singular. Each is subject to violation, eradication, and repetition. Each lives its moments and "refuses" every replacement. Each passes away. Each might be subject to perception; each is both insistent and still in its moment, its moment that is only now and then touchable and can go easily—very easily—without notice. And yet, each event, no matter how complex and connected to other events, is quite there, utterly there as nothing other.

There is something not at all virtual in the inexorability of a singular event. Even the virtual event has something not virtual about it, like a movie about its own virtuality that is also its own nonvirtual, repetitional happening. The singularity of a gene's formative power is as it is in its formative moment. It is "real," we are inclined to say, not imagined at all, quite beyond the reach of the perceptions that grasp it, imagine it, and name it. There is much that is not virtual in a child's sickness, a realization that brings many new parents out of a cloud of romanticism and imagination when they see that their child, burning with fever, can die. Not virtual, real. It is one thing to see a car wreck on film. It is quite another to be in a wreck, to feel the shock of the accident, the impact, the radical movements, out of control, twisting and rolling with you tossed and thrown in them. It is one thing to watch a man who carries a ball take the impact of another three hundred-pound man and crash to the ground. It is something else to feel the impact of a force that knocks me off of my feet, stuns me, and lands on top of me with a cry of victory. And it is one thing to know that an idea exists, to survey it, and say something about it. It is another thing to think an idea, think in it, undergo its force, or undergo its birth in the life of one's own mind. Real. Not only virtual.

I knew a thirteen-year-old boy who ran a very painful first marathon. Afterward he said, "I always thought that in the movies, if I were the guy on the ground, wounded, reaching for the gun, that I would do it. I would move two inches more, get the gun, and shoot the other guy. Out there I got to where I couldn't move any more than I was moving. I thought I was going to die. I tried, but I couldn't do any more. You know, you reach a point and you can't go any farther." The nonvirtual reality of limits.

I think that Deleuze is right, that singularities *might* repeat, but that they are not subject to pervasive and necessary internal continuity or to generalization. They simply do not exist in their generalizations or in a presence that transcends their event. Generalization, categorization—we might speak of the force of law—forget the singularity of events in a singular inclusion of them. I believe that that observation is one of the bases for Heidegger's troubled linkage of Western philosophy and everydayness in *Being and Time*: everydayness names in part a habitual, Western predisposition to orders that are based both on the value of singularity—of this being—and on a loss of singularity in general orders of necessity. Western philosophy, which he both attempts to overcome and in spite of the attempt also repeats in his understanding of existentials and horizon, includes a continual loss of the singularity that one wishes to perceive and esteem in its self-disclosure.

This loss of a sense of singularity, in the context of Heidegger's thought, arises in part because of a peculiar and powerful anxiety that lives in our lives and that is constellated by the occurrences of loss, passage, and dying that occur in the singular event, that is, losses that happen in the phenomena of occurring things, in the singularity of self-showing. As loss is elided by a generality of presence, in Heidegger's description of Western philosophy, singularity is lost to a law of presence. This is a law of continuity, not nomadic repetitions, but a law of unbroken life that loses the loss and the interruptive quality of a nonreplaceable, mortal event. There is something outside of Law, outside of demanding, transcendental orders, something in the shadows of Western recognition that is more like singular, living moments than like a percept, a synthesis, an instance, an example, a representation, a part, a piece, a similarity, or a number, something troubling to Heidegger's conservativism (in spite of his radicality) and wonderful to Deleuze's revolutionary spirit (in spite of his conservation of his heritage), something disclosed in transgressions, deterioration of certainties, the dehiscence of transcendence, and the collapse of the authority of the idea of apriority. I speak of something aimed at by empiricism, cultivated by some Western ethics of love, eulogized by modern romanticism, protected by Western democracy, and reapproached compulsively by idealism: a self-showing singularity, quite there, quite within perceptive reach, never capturable or containable, not quite divine, quite usual for human beings, and not quite within the reach of our disciplined language and reflection. For Heidegger such self-disclosing singularity—I assume that you, like I, grow increasingly dissatisfied with this word—is given allowance in unmitigated questionableness in which life as such, or being, occurs in question. For Deleuze the allowing and inciting words are *difference* and *repetition*: "Repetition is not generality." "Repetition and resemblance are different in kind—extremely so." "Repetition as a conduct and as a point of view concerns non-exchangeable and non-substitutable singularities."[3] Difference is "ungrounded chaos which has no law other than its own repetition" and is thought as *differenciation*.[4]

As I spin out these thoughts from Deleuze's textual "textbook," as he puts it, toward another and different (from his) formation, I want to turn to his reflections on thought which I shall valorize by this book's issue, memory's loss. If we can avoid forgetting such loss we might be on our way to thinking with singularities in such a way as to know them in their interruption of generalization—which means, of course, dropping the *idea* of singularity in our encounter with what I am calling, with increasing awkwardness, "singularities." Even the Deleuzian, ecstatically composed assemblage of images and ideas, to the extent that they are ecstatic and composed, will come into question as I experiment with the remarkable tools that he has left helter skelter, scattered on the artifacts of his printed pages.

LIBERATION FROM COMMON SENSE AND GOOD SPIRIT

> Auggie: I've never taken a picture in my life, and I've certainly never stolen anything [which is probably a lie], but the moment I see those cameras sitting in the bathroom, I decide I want one of them for myself. Just like that. And without even stopping to think about it, I tuck one of the boxes under my arm. . . . I lied to her, and then I stole from her. . . . Anything for art, eh, Paul? Paul: I wouldn't say that. But at least you've put the camera to good use.
>
> —Paul Auster, *Smoke*

Repetitions figure losses of continuity of the same. Repetition might be conceived as habitual synthesis or as imaginative projection of expected connections, but in such accounts of repetition *habitual* and *imaginative* would need to suggest—if repetition is described—divergence, instantaneity, truncation of identity, a requirement for another beginning. If a thing simply persisted and were subject to simple or pure perception in its unbroken continuity, habit would be unnecessary. Habit arises only because differencing intervenes in the presentations of *things*—in the occurrences of things—and broken presentations require bridging, a bridging of gaps, of no presence, of insubstantial loss of presence and occurrence—loss like that found in an inconspicuous pulsation or the blinking of eyes. In considering such bridging within our problematic, I do not want to suggest an exploration of a domain of transcendental synthesis. By the time transcendental synthesis is reached, memory's loss is already lost in what we might call "secondary memory," the kind of memory that forgets its forgetting and overrides memory's loss by an image of productive formation and grounding presence by means of temporal structures. So I shall leave aside issues such as memory which is considered to be reflective action or reproductive *action* and look rather to the occurrence of difference—differenciation—to see if we can place in jeopardy both Deleuze's and my own quasi-transcendentality in approaching the happening of memory. I speak of my quasi-transcendentality because I am inclined to find an operative definition for memory's loss which will show the law of loss in memory's occurrence. And although I do not locate that loss in transcendent or subjective synthesis, I do tend to find in it an archaic and continuous aspect of eventuation, mentation, and appearance, a continuing aspect which, contrary to its seeming to happen, gives loss to be *like* a transcendental condition—not a transcendental condition, but like one, while at the same time denying the very idea of transcendental presence. Hence, I speak of a tendency toward a quasi-transcendental occurrence in the way I establish the occurrence of loss.

Deleuze's thought is complicated with regard to quasi-transcendence. He sets his problematic in transcendental thought, in responses to Plato, Descartes, Leibnitz, Husserl, Hegel, and Bergson, among many others, and in that problematic attaches himself—or finds himself attached—to the very domain that he would overthrow: a reverse Platonism, he sometimes calls his thought. I shall leave aside most of the complications that arise from this attachment and encounter only a selection of his ideas on representation and illusion. I would like to see how one can speak of such things without using the language of suggestive synthesis. If I can move in this direction I will have taken a direction away from Deleuze's attachment to a transcendental problematic, a direction that follows the arrows (to use his image) of his own originality in conceiving repetition and difference.

He says that he is after a new image of thought, an innovation that he elaborates by the word *liberation*.[5] Liberated from what? From common sense and good spirit. Our common sense operates in our recognitions, in the ways whereby we see resemblances, orders, proprieties, parts and wholes, and, above all, formations of values that are relative to one another. The term *common sense*, does not suggest primarily an ability to be down to earth and practical in contrast to an abstract or ivory tower attitude. Common sense defines, rather, our shared sense of what is what and who is who, our shared sense of reality, truth, and goodness. At its best, common sense is exercised as individuals strive in a broad communal understanding for what is best and most right, for things appropriate to seriousness of intent, things which in their proper measurement and exchange constitute something approximate to wisdom and genuine insight; as we pursue, recognize, and appropriate reason they reflect to us our deepest and most valuable commonality. The term *common sense* names a prereflective consensus and suggests an ideal formation to be thought, represented in our social orders, and reflected in our behaviors.

In this image one nonvoluntarily desires the true, the good, the right, the genuine. We may disagree over the specific determinants, but that is a secondary matter. I emphasize here the operation of this formal image of common sense in interpretation of "real" thought. Common sense is an image that often carries with it a demand for its own universality and its unrestricted power to distribute everything that is. It is closely affiliated with *heart* and *soul* and *mind* and above all with *truth*. So an information technologist may experience the satisfaction that this preconceptual image can provide when she gets the correlates right and discovers what is "really" true in the case at hand, just as a metaphysician can experience the pleasure of truth as he thinks an idea that he finds to be necessary within a specific system. I believe that Deleuze, however, is struggling with dissatisfactions that develop as people live in an image of true thought, that he wants to overturn an economy of satisfactions that our common sense makes possible, and that he wants to make effective in his thought a release from common sense by encountering *in his thought* both the disguises that define common sense and the singularities whose differencing repetitions escape the recognitions of common sense.[6]

I cannot, I believe, overstate the difficulty of this liberating undertaking. Exactly when and where we are most stirred by the prospect of truth, when and where we feel the deepest stillness of conviction, when and where an atheist is moved to prayer or the believer finds the meaning of his life, when and where the ironist smiles with paradoxical satisfaction, when and where the satirist knows her prey, and when and where philosophers know themselves as looking for wisdom: that is when and where the issue of common sense and the *question* of liberation arise. That is terribly irritating. Not only are we annoyed when someone withdraws from our field of satisfactions and adopts a critical attitude, but we are all the more vexed when we hear that our criticisms, iconoclasm, liberality, humanism, and sincerity are far from exempt from the image of thought's common sense that attaches thought to "truth." Do not Deleuze and I enjoy the truth of our exposure of thought's image as common sensical? Does this image not reinstate itself in its unconvering? The image of thought with truth in common sense appears with truthful satisfaction. Oh my! We are trapped by the truth of untruth and by a deep glee in the propriety of smashing images.

I shall forego the immense pleasure of convincing myself that everything is virtual or the pleasure of perversity and joy in seeing nihilism curled up in the heart of postmodernism. I also wish to forego the pleasure

of confession, exposing myself to universal view as an instance of the pleasures that I condemn, making myself an example of the malady we are to
avoid, and hoping by my example to lead others to a higher standard of
truth and goodness: the temptation of radical liberalism's higher right-
eousness or of the existential believer's agonized experience of his own sin.
So I am taking a ho hum attitude toward such exemplarity and turn to see
what else I can do. To what might one be liberated?

Part of what we can do is anticipated by Deleuze's combination of
image, thought, and *truth.* He has already invoked the Nietzschean observation that truth is grounded in untruth when he correlates truth and
image. As we struggle to think the truth or as we believe that we are thinking the truth, a powerful, prereflective image is at work. A prereflective
image, he says, determines truthful thought. In the work of this image the
principle of identity operates to disguise enactments of difference without
identity. Processes are set in motion of identification, distinction on the
basis of samenesses, oppositions among identities, and "memorial-imaginative reproduction."[7] Memorial-imaginative reproduction establishes
perceptual continuity, a reenactment under present circumstances of the
image of thought-affiliated-with-truth, which for Deleuze operates as an
indefinite concept—an inchoate concept of identity that is spelled out by
continuities in recognition of identities and differences. "Difference," he
says, "becomes an object of representation always in relation to a conceived identity, a judged analogy, an imaginal opposition or a perceived
similitude."[8] Our goal, however, is to think difference, or as Deleuze puts
it, to conceive of difference in itself, and that means to learn how to
encounter and recognize repetitions and singularities without representing
them under the authority of a generalized identity.

The word *encounter* in this context is particularly important. The
word now suggests something different from recognition as we usually
think of it and experience it. In an attempt to think of encounter as distinct to recognition, and because of Deleuze's quasi-transcendental problematic, we might be tempted by Levinas' account of substitution. I mean
that Deleuze is conceiving this issue in terms of a prereflective image that
operates in our consciousness in such a way that people undergo its impo-
sition in their experiences of commonality without knowing what is happening. Viewed in this way, an encounter appears to suggest a kind of
idealism in which an a priori image functions as the condition of possibility for recognizing and representing everything. In that problematic
Levinas' proposal might seem attractive, namely, that one continuously

and tirelessly substitute the other for one's own experiential enactment in a futile but nonetheless fruitful process of undercutting the agency that presents the other. In substitution and guilt before the other's unappropriability—guilt indigenous to our own experiential enactment—we encounter the other, if obliquely, as other. But that is not what Deleuze has in mind. Although he speaks of the originary violence of thought, its lack of necessity, its inevitability of trespass, illegitimacy, and destructiveness, he does not look to eliminate thought or its perversity.[9] Rather, he intends to intensify thought, because thought begins, he says descriptively, with fundamental and exterior encounter. It does not begin with recognition but with imposed and unrecognized bearings on the senses, some thing—some singular thing—in the world which can only be sensed "forces us to think."[10] In the encounter, in its moment, we do not *know* transcendentally what or who it is. On Deleuze's terms, an encounter is before active memory and association, that is, it is before transcendental synthesis. An encounter is something more like a thoroughly physical event—like something external vis à vis conscious synthesis—than it is like an event of mental enlightenment. In a transcendental perspective that sounds like no knowledge at all. Only when common sense kicks in, in the forms of signification, connection, exchange, association, and other kinds of "transcendental exercise" do we have recognition, and in recognition, the "discordant play" of singularities in sensing is limited, transformed into order, and easily forgotten.[11]

I underscore the observation that a kind of forgetfulness is inherent in recognition. We can speak of forgetting in this context only in the conviction that we can remember singularities in their difference from recognitions. I believe that Deleuze is attempting to think in and of differencing that occurs in the singularity of encounters vis à vis our usual activity of recognizing. By this process he intends to interrupt common sense and the operation of our dominant, prereflective image of thinking. There seems to be awareness in sense that is independent of our *common*, conscious recognitions, awareness that can be recognized when common sense is interrupted and violated: he is thinking in the violation, and he is developing a recognition of another kind of awareness. This recognition emerges in violation of common sense. I believe that I do not push him too far by saying that for him this other kind of recognition has been latent in the thought of Plato, Leibnitz, Kant, and many other canonized philosophies, but they were ill attuned to it because of the common sense that guided and dominated them. This dominance is spelled out in obliteration or forgetfulness of the discord in sensed singularities in the processes of recognizing them. That is a forgetfulness that defines what he calls "transcendental exercises," a term that names the functions of synthesis definitive of Western thought and practice.

This kind of forgetfulness is then definitive of Western, philosophical problematization. The sensed but ill-appropriated singularity originates problems in our image-dominated predispositions. A singularity makes problems for thought by being other to thought, yet in contrast to what Levinas says, singularities are available to thought of a different kind, available as event-effect or surface events (in the language of *The Logic of Sense*). They are available not as commonsense problems or as products of good will but as repeating particularities that are, we might say, quite perceptible and nonproblematic. Simply and contingently and differently and perhaps bewilderingly, these proliferations are not re-cognized but are encountered in an alertness that is very different from that constituted by transcendentally exercised systems of signs that are formed in the power of common sense and the image of well-intentioned, good spirited thought. Thought appears not to be necessarily determined by common sense, and Deleuze seems to be preparing for a way of thinking that is unthinkable to common sense: nonproblematic thinking, singularly perceptive thinking, and thought in differenciating repetitions are phrases that come to mind.

In order to speak of the loss in transcendental memory—of forgetting—Deleuze refers to the developed difference between empirical memory and transcendental memory. The thought of transcendence carries with it—produces—a radical distinction between the empirical and the transcendental. The law of transcendental thought (or "transcendental exercise") is that in thought we can remember what in sense experience can never be remembered, and that transcendental remembrance is remembrance of the utterly nonempirical—being, truth, pure continuity—in other words, the essentials of common sense and good will. Transcendental "memory" "grasps" what is not contingent, not riveted by differencing repetition, but what is purely originary and essential.[12] Such memory is produced by the enactment of common sense, by what is available given proper discipline and effort. There is nothing of sensible singularity and repetition there. Rather, the remembered, appearing *reality* is essential and not subject to the radical particularity of what is sensed. And for good reason: common sense in its own sense of itself precedes and is independent of sense. It appears as though it were uncorrupted by sense and constitutes perceptiveness by orders that originate in a nonsensible, intelligible region, even if that region is located outside of the mind's direct reach. It is memory of what can only be thought, and thought only in the exhaustive generality of pure thought, generalized facts, predictability, and laws.

There are other memories, however. Although Deleuze does not call them memories, he points to the discords among faculties. He has in mind all the faculties that can attack, appropriate, and order senses, such as imagination, intelligence, judgment, and idealization. These mental faculties do many different kinds of things, synthesize things in very different ways, and produce their own kinds of order. Taken together these faculties in their many instances and singularities produce all manner of arrangements, from dreams and fantasies to sciences and orthodoxies of practice and belief. But, Deleuze says, they are themselves hinged together and brought into coherence only by common sense. They appear to him in *their* cacophony to constitute something like a memory of singularities, of differences without Order, of singular differencing, of divergence from common sense. We might say that common-sensical ordering of the different faculties—hinging them together by a law of identity, giving them images that reflect essential sameness—includes a memory of their divergence, that transcendental order remembers inchoately a loss of difference in its erasure of "discord" among the faculties.[13] Transcendental exercise carries the loss that it produces and ecstatically embodies, carries such loss in a forgetfulness that defines and figures it. In that perspective the image of thought carried by common sense produces a forgetfulness of singularity that repeats itself quietly, in repetitions of the singularities of faculties in their transcendental exercises, in a diversity of singularities that exercise themselves as "universality" and that practice themselves in conversions of singularities into generalizations.

We are confronted with the possibility of speaking of memory—or at least of a kind of memory—that does not occur as transcendental synthesis. I believe that that might be like perceiving repetitions. Instead of transcendentally based *recognitions*, with the inheritances that invest the *re* primarily with "commonsensical" subjective activity and form, in this other kind of recognition we find things that happen again and again in chains of singular moments that impact us distinctively and that occur in both their own starting and their own stopping. Something that happens "there" day in and day out, like a fence or a window, or something that happens over and over again like a heartbeat or a dog's bark, impinge on us again and again, outside of our activity and outside of a law of timeless necessity. We are in their impact. They do not constitute something static, not stases that suggest permanence. They occur as pulsations in their impacts and intensities, as differenciations that make differences, without an image of permanence or truth to sew them into a whole cloth. They occur as repetition to our senses. Perhaps we count them more than we count on them, but even in counting—even in *that* ordering grid—we *perceive* their uncountability in their repetitions. Nothing transcendent there, and nothing not transcendent. That distinction drops out. Rather, differenciations produce differences of moment and occasion, passing out of the events that began with them, joining events that began without them, as when that cat walks out of this yard or when grey appears in her dark black hair. We might then experience memory in the vacuity of lost moments and occasions without a sense of a whole thing or a wholesome truth. They would be memories without unifying syntheses, but rather syntheses that themselves constitute complex, passing singularities and their occasional, further groupings, memories held in singular moments and their chains of connection, moments held in singular signs, signs of singular systems that mean only the events that they repeat by differenciation.

I want to accentuate Deleuze's encounter with the commonsense images of subjectivity and thought that are attached to truth and good will. As he follows the images' intensities and impacts and describes the ways in which the commonsense image operates, he also uncovers the production of what is traditionally called "subjectivity." He attempts to undercut the power of the commonsense image, to interfere with its productive operation, and thus to change, in his writing, the occurrence of subjectivity. He thus struggles to find a language and conceptuality that occasion a fundamental shift in the prereflective imagery. And of course his thought is impacted in this encounter by the productive work of the image of thought with truth and good will.

He finds primarily in Nietzsche's impact, I believe, the distance from this image that he needs in order to recognize it and its impact in the internal conflict without our philosophical tradition: in the conflicts that define and determine our tradition, such as the imaginal base for nonimaginal truth, the disguise and destruction of singularity in efforts to grasp and preserve it, the unacknowledged violence of thought's good will, and the conflicts of faculties in the imposed image of subjective unity. Deleuze's processes of uncovering these conflicts, the language of his descriptions, the disjointed timing of his prose, his insistent depersonalization of seemingly subjective and communal events refigure the dynamics of agency and perception. The intensity of violence in this effort toward refiguration is repellent to our good will. Can truth come of such promiscuous illegality, such trespass and transgression of the still point of Western philosophical passion? This re-membering of the "foundations" of experiential and reflective synthesis, figured by the destruction and loss of an image of thinking, is—and must be—offensive to some of our deepest instincts and motivations. That Deleuze is able to speak hopefully of "true critique and true creation" betrays the extent of his own involvement in the image he would transform and indicates the enormity of his ambition, but that should not distract us from the accomplishment of his thought.[14] In his writing the force and effect of the image of true and good thought wane; an uncommon sense forms; and, perhaps most important of all, a memory of irreparable loss in chains of singularities and in the absence of past events—a memory that seems to be traditionally suppressed or highly qualified—joins with a Western passion and obsession with singularity to form the thought of repetition without transcendence—a memory of loss in this case in which a synthesis designed to replace loss with unlost and continuing presence stubbornly compromises its own synthesizing operation. We can call this synthesis in Deleuze's thought a "sense of loss," even an "image of loss," in which the synthesis that gives sense and image brings us to its own breaking point and simply repeats itself without a transcendental carrier. In reading him we participate in a singular effort to reform the memory of Western philosophy on the basis of what that memory steadfastly forgets in its economy of truthful and well-intentioned mediations. Or, stated more closely to his words, "essential memory" in Western philosophy loses its essential quality in a process in which contingent memory fights to replace essential memory in the operation of thought's self-description.[15]

This contingent memory functions synthetically. It collects and arranges things, names them, interferes with them, loses them in their intensities, separates and divides them in the divisions of repetition that it identifies, pronounces, and signifies. Its most remarkable accomplishment, I believe, is found in its conversion of "virtuality" into "reality." By this awkward phrasing I mean that for Deleuze the singular event is encountered, not as an isolated atom of occurrence, but as something ideal, as a synthesis of passing aspects that impacts us with the force of loss, distance, limit, refusal, division, nongenerality, opposition, destructive conflict, and violation, and in such intensities drives us to an activity of engagement which we can call "thinking." We might use words such as *contingent, fragmented, imagistic, erroneous, fractured,* and *divided* to describe the syntheses of such encounters—words that describe synthetic combinations and that also remember the losses that paradoxically constitute remembered singularities. These words, as they indicate the virtual dimension of synthesized and remembered singularities, attempt to brighten and give opacity to the concrete specificity of things—that is, to things in *their* reality—*their* impact—of being present. The guiding image for mentation now is like that of a series of moving, repeating images that move us in our encounter with them, move us to fear, laughter, sadness, and all the other living affections, move us in their being there and being vaporous and strangely going away all at the same time—more like a movie than Heidegger could have appreciated, more like living things that are also, as living, signs that in their repetitions do not ever quite settle into what has been called "substances:" no *sub*, no completed *stance*, but palpable, there, and yet not whole or full or enduring—fragmented syntheses of fragile things that repeat and in their repetitions differenciate themselves and everything around them: multiple differenciations that give us pause and the possibility for alertness with them in our repeated and moving moments.

SINGULARITY AND MEMORY

Once he made a bet with her that he could measure the weight of smoke. . . . I admit it's strange. Almost like weighing someone's soul. But Sir Walter was a clever guy. First, he took an unsmoked cigar and put it on a balance and weighed it. Then he lit up and smoked the cigar, carefully tapping the ashes into the balance pan. When he was finished, he put the butt into the pan along with the ashes and weighed what was there. Then he subtracted that number from the original weight of the unsmoked cigar. The difference was the weight of the smoke.

—Paul Auster, *Smoke*

In many cases a true war story cannot be believed. If you believe it, be skeptical. It's a question of credibility. Often the crazy stuff is true and the normal stuff isn't, because the normal stuff is necessary to make you believe the truly incredible craziness.

—Tim O'Brien *The Things They Carried*

In this encounter with Deleuze I have minimized his conception of ideality and valorized the singularities that, while they are ideally synthesized, nonetheless differentiate themselves from idealization. I have also interpreted his own idealizations as intended to produce a departure from transcendental exercise and from syntheses of common sense, and, I have emphasized, in such departure he remembers the differenciations and disguising productions that have made singularities so difficult to think. I have also provided a context for this reading by indicating that the singularities of events are ordinary even though our perceptive attention to them is not always ordinary. In considering Deleuze's observations about memory and the functions of faculties, I stressed the memory of differencing and singularity that inchoately inhabit the violence of transcendental exercises and the operations of the principle of identity. I should like now to take departure from Deleuze's reversed Platonism and the attachments that accompany it and to consider a memorial dimension of singularities for which the word *ideal* is inappropriate. I wish to indicate that singularities occur as appearances that carry with them significance and what I shall call "palpability."

By *palpable* I mean manifest and perceivable. The singularity of an event does not suggest a dense, impenetrable atomic quality. Singularities are complex, usually flowing with trajectories, bearing the marks and mutations—I continue to use Deleuze's imagery—of collisions, impacts, and productions. They occur in lineages as they manifest all manner of other impacting and specific events, something like a vital and dynamic planet that holds the traces, pocks, and abrasions of many hits by celestial things, holds them not only on its surface, but in its movement, trajectory, tilt, and wobble. Singularities do not happen in isolation from other singularities. They are like scenes of occurrences that are composed of multiple, manifest references and that can leave on other singular events an imprint of their complex composures. Deleuze's image of surface impact is helpful in showing that singular events touch, sometimes with considerable force, other surfaces. Those surfaces can be perceptual and alert. They can reel under the impact's power, undergo reconstitution in the forceful imprint. They can quietly absorb the touch and, respond with it serenely, affectionately, or in silent refusal. A touch on one's arm, for example, at a sexually charged dinner can manifest desire, intention, and attraction. A touch on one's arm in the dark house, as one enters and walks to the light switch, can give terror and an appropriate sense of danger and violation. A touch when one has said, "Don't touch me," can alter a relationship forever.

These are palpable, perceptive situations in which an event is given in its manifestness, is not necessarily concocted or produced by an individual's imagination. One can, of course, produce all manner of responses, but the response will be before the palpability of a complex singular event as it comes to pass in its own manifest sense.

Singularities happen as appearances, as happenings that carry and manifest past events in their singularity. Manifest significance and meaning might crescendo or melt away in their event. They are subject to change, to the impact of other events. They may repeat, but they repeat in the fluctuations and impositions of other events. They are social and cultural, *produced*, as Deleuze says, filled with palpable senses, manifest with or without contributions from the one impacted by them. They do indeed differenciate, leaving an individual to deal with them and their intrusion.

In their palpability, singularities thus carry memories, that is, past and yet constitutive intensities, modifications, and mutations. As repetitions they carry also loss of other impacting events, traces of other occurrences, losses of ancestors' different formations, formations that now happen in truncated, perhaps mutilated, or appended and partial formations. As manifest they are available for preservation in other events such as psychological images, all manner of signs and scripts, and conscious events that hold their ghosts in chains of associations and reflections. In their repetitions and reproductions they continuously lose their palpability to other palpable events.

Singularities, I am suggesting, carry memories that an individual does not produce in perceiving them. They are carriers of past happenings, and in that past dimension they make palpable losses the occurrence of which constitute their repetitions.

Consider the following event which I believe gives expression to an ambivalence that characterizes the difference between reality and virtuality, between ideal and real, an ambiguity that constitutes a major problem that I am addressing in the context of singularity and memory. When I was growing up in a small Oklahoma town, we children habitually went to the Saturday afternoon Western at the Pix Theater, a small storefront kind of entertainment establishment that charged us a dime for entrance and a nickel for popcorn and which ran its hour and ten minute features from two o'clock in the afternoon until ten o'clock at night, with breaks only to change the reels in the projection room. Most of us frequently saw the feature twice and occasionally stayed for a third viewing. As the detail of the movie repeated in the showings, our interests often increased. We saw more, remembered more, and anticipated more. We also cheered more frequently and commented on the action with increased animation and sophistication.

One afternoon the movie featured Lash Larue with his miraculous whip and his black outfit. We all wished that we could snap a gun out of a man's hand with a bull whip the way he did or wrap the villain around the neck and pull him off a galloping horse. Toward the end of the show, Lash was chasing an especially bad man across a pasture, and we were bouncing in our seats to the rhythm of the chase and its orchestral accompaniment, eyes glued to the scene, wide with excitement, some of us holding onto the seat in front of us as though it were a saddle horn while bouncing to the rhythm of a galloping horse. The villain came to a fence and gate, jumped off his horse, threw open the gate, and raced through it and on into the distance, leaving the gate open. Lash dashed through it, and knowing the unwritten law of the West, that you *never* leave a pasture gate open, jumped off his horse, carefully closed and latched the gate, and then jumped back on his horse to resume the climactic chase.

At this point in the second showing, one of my friends named Jackie, who was as challenged as he was sweet, leapt up, ran down the aisle with one of his overall straps flying behind him, and shouted, "You go on Lash. I'll get the gate."

A singular event. Of course there was no gate to "get," and of course there was a confusion of the imaginal and the real. The scene's dimension of virtuality and the reality of the theater gave humor and absurdity to the extent of Jackie's involvement. But Jackie, when he reached the end of the aisle, also encountered the singularity of the film, its being as it was, and the singularity of the Pix Theater, and the singularity of his imaginative projection. It seems to me that the reality of the scene's images, the reality of Jackie's imagination, and the reality of his running down the aisle were all palpable, all invested with moment and force, none of them exclusively ideal or abstract or "mere" appearance. It all constituted a manifest event that is not reducible to a division of real and ideal but was rather a happening on an ordinary Saturday afternoon that happens with forgetting, remembering, and occurrence.

Jackie participated in the virtual event before him to such an extent that it was hardly *before* him. He was in it in a way a writer is in her metaphor: not as something about something, but in an expression that is itself presented and palpable in its occurrence. The screen that means separation of a scene from an audience dissolved in his experience. He became a participant, only to find the limits of his participation in a small crisis of difference which transplanted him out of his ecstatic revery back into the place of the Pix Theater. But in his ecstasy something else happened. Horses pounded across a prairie, a pursuit of the bad by the good happened, Jackie found himself outside of theory and distant observation, without contemplation; he ran to close the open gate, only to be yanked back to an aisle leading to a white screen with figures illumined on it, and by laughter. Both sides of the crisis seem "real" to me, and the difference between them seems to constitute a space for choice and decision in which Jackie might find something of who he is as he walks back to his seat.

This event with Jackie is as illusory as the movie was—and yet palpable in its presentation, not completely unlike the Dionysian occurrences (of which I spoke in chapter 4) in which people found themselves participant in the events before them. And it is not completely unlike a myth. We are confronted by an ambivalence, one that appears to characterize events in their palpability, among such aspects that are traditionally called "reality," "illusion," "truth," "untruth," and "appearance." These aspects seem to happen together at once, each disturbing the other aspects, and yet composing together, as an event, a perceptible occurrence with the power to impact other events. Differenciation seems to describe singularities in their perceptibility as well as to characterize interactions among singularities. Things in their singularity make differences, compose variation, and give obscurity and clarity at once.

CHAPTER NINE

―――――――――― ❧ ――――――――――

Gifts of Fire:
Witnessing and Representing

I have emphasized nonvoluntary memory in institutions and cultural events in addition to (and certainly not in opposition to) conscious and unconscious personal memories. In the last chapter I carried out the hypothesis that differenciation, in belonging to singular occurrences, composes one kind of forgetting. It happens in the losses of connections and in the absence of presence that differenciation shows in association with repetitions of singularities. By valorizing repetition over resemblance I was able to indicate a loss of singular moments with the coming of singular moments. This loss is manifest in events in an intertwining of virtuality and palpability. This kind of forgetting—in enacted ellipses—seems to be sewn into singular moments, to give them to come to their past as they come to presence. Such loss appears with a moment's plentitude. Or, a singularity's plentitude traces loss of plentitude.

"A kind of forgetting—and enacted ellipsis—," I said. Why not simply speak of transformations in processes of change, drop the word *forgetting*, and rather leave forgetting to the provenance of consciousness? Because forgetting, as I find it, does not refer only to an individual's conscious event; it names occurrences of loss in events of cultural transmission as well as an individual's losing mindfulness of something. If I found memory to characterize only conscious events or events of subjectivity, I should speak of forgetting only in that context. But 'mind' we have seen, is not limited to subjectivity. People live in and through institutions, and institutions live in and through people with many dimensions of transmission, with extensive and operative lineages, patterns of recognition, and formations of significance and meaning. As cultural formations are enacted—as they operate—all manner of transforming connections (and disconnections) with past events occur. Identities and other cultural events constitute continuous reminders and formative repetitions of bygone things in the enactment of which people come to consciousness and find themselves to live as they do. Mind thus happens extensively and culturally. A people's past is remembered in the mind of a culture. That past in its infinite complexity and partiality differentiates these people and is multiply carried in ways of life, patterns of belief, and institutions. Mind happens as enacted cultural remembrance and thus also in the ellipses that come with remembrance. The ways in which loss in memorial transmission happens are ways of forgetting. If I am right in affirming the hypothesis that memory accompanies appearing—that memories compose the ways things appear (e.g., the appearance of a criminal or insane person or a valuable commodity)—then memory would seem to invest and help to figure anything that is referable, recognizable, or experienceable. In this context, *Mnemosyne* and *Lethe* refer not simply to individual recall and mistakes of recall. They speak of a people's many lineages and traditions.

Further in this context, institutions are witnesses of the past in the senses that they show now (no matter how fallibly) how things were or might have been and constitute contemporary, transmissional scenes of past events. They form and hold in action—in remembrance—past events, bear them in the present, and serve as their evidence. Past events are in the keep of institutions—that is, institutions bear witness to the past. They enact past events as they transform them into present, living occurrences. I have made the case in previous chapters that such enactments bear out loss, disruption, and transposition. They compose an amnesia—a withdrawal of memory—that can seem strange in some contexts of understanding. I have noted the traces of this kind of eclipse of memory, in dimensions that appear like side shadows, in memorial transmissions, in the impalpable and unrepresentable "distance" of past events, in the loss of their own occurrences, in the sheer break with past presence that characterizes present appearing, and by the diversity and differences in remembering the "same" event. The happenings of bygone times also seem to be quite other to their present institutional enactments and their present continuities and influences. Institutions, I said, carry and manifest such traces and differenciations and compose witnesses of the bygone.

I would like to bring more closely together the witnessing and tracing aspects by considering a part of Jacques Derrida's encounter first with writing and then with what he addresses as the gift of death. In this process I will be able to develop further the observation that re-enactment of the past has a dimension that is originary but neither representational nor creative. In this "dimension" we will find witnessing to "something" without figuration in memory, without sight or sound. But there is also in Derrida's writing the image of fire with connotations of both Prometheus and the Holocaust. It is the fire of a kind of ecstasy that is reminiscent of some Dionysian occurrences, which I will continue to hold in question in this and the final chapters.

First, a return to Jackie's experience that I described at the end of the last chapter. He found himself before a screen of light and dark images in the absence of a gate to close or a hero to help. Then there were only images cast on a screen by a light shining through film, and he was left in the ruins of the living presence that his imagination had bestowed on those images. He invested an enlivened sense of nonimaginative presence in the images of the cinematic narrative that unfolded before him, and the narrative itself told a story of good and evil, of skill with a whip that was used, not by established powers to flog and punish people without power, but to enable a lone and courageous man to fight unjust and cruel individuals. The story of Lash Larue is one of a longed-for friend to someone like me or Jackie when we were up against bullying or overpowering forces. The least we could do was to help the man in his chaste pursuit of the bad guy. But no one was there. The skill lay not with a cowboy with a whip on a white horse but with absent directors, technicians, and actors—and with Jackie's projections—in producing a story that was palpable in its virtuality. The filmed story as it appeared on the screen produced a deviation from non-filmed life, and that deviation in its setting with Jackie produced a sense of "real" presence. But whatever the film's occurrence bore witness to, it was not to the presence of a prairie, a gated fence, and panting horses carrying good and bad men. Derrida's phrase, "signifiers signifying signifiers" seems appropriate in this case.

Yet, Lash Larue the actor became famous because of his appearances in films. The director and technicians, whose names I do not know, were presented in their work. One could say that the film in its shape and composition bore witness to them and signified them, that *they* appeared in appearances which were quite different from them. In the context of this chapter, I wish to say that the film attested to their work and, as we shall see, to their lives. The film occurred as their witness in its presentation of their *technè* and their singular ways of giving themselves to appear.

"History and knowledge," Derrida says, "*istoria* and *epistémè* have always been determined . . . as detours *for the purpose of* the reappropriation of presence."[1] He says this in the context of preparing to show that in our culture the dominance of phonetic writing is passing away. Instead of translating and transcribing articulated sounds into written marks, people increasingly understand writing as standing on its own, as it were, as a site of synthesis that is not reduceable to sounds, verbal articulations, or subjective enactments. Writing—a system of marks—does not compose an experience but composes rather "the arche-synthesis" that is outside of reflected or self-disclosing presence.[2] History and knowledge—narratives of "real" events and a sense of acquaintance with them by means of the narrative—have functioned to restore a sense of real presence outside of the written or articulated signifiers that provide a loss of what is signified. Derrida turns away from the traditional processes of restoring a sense of presence to the interplay of written marks (i.e., to the site of loss of presence). He *is* not denying the presence of anything, but he is saying that in language as writing the presence of what is signified in the writing does not take place. As writing is increasingly understood as non-phonetic and not merely as a supplement to sounded expression—as nonphonetic writing usurps the speaking subject in modern and contemporary knowledge—it increasingly functions as a site of signifiers without the presence of a sounding subject or "what" is signified. Signs refer to other signs, and what is signified outside of signs is continuously deferred in writing. In this sense, writing is like the film that Jackie saw (or the film is like writing), and "restored presence" is like what Jackie gave to the film in the immediacy of his excited transference.

Derrida is neither recommending nor criticizing writing. He begins *Of Grammatology* by showing that because of people's growing understanding of writing in its singularity and freedom from sounded speech many peoples' experiences of "rationality," truth, and meaning are always changing. He describes a process that he finds underway. Not only in the formal language of mathematics and cybernetics but in experiences of literatures and history a sense of originary reflected presence in writing weakens because of the impact of signs that refer to other signs in chains of deferred presence. A language occurs as itself and not as the revelation or mimesis of nonlinguistic occurrences. Such occurrences are lost in the occurrence of language: language is witness to this loss as well as composing a site of signification. Further, language is not the same as consciousness is usually said to be. It is not an occurrence of subjectivity or of living awareness on the part of a subject. It does not re-present anything. It signals signs and constitutes a program or set of marks and does not have an immediate and conscious tissue holding the signs together any more than the film and the screen constitute a living, conscious tissue. Nothing living and present connects the marks. Nothing narrates itself or speaks itself in their occurrence. The marks and their combinations stand outside of a living presence and do not harbor in their depth intrinsic meaning or a deeper narrative that takes place outside of a system of signification.

By such descriptions of writing Derrida shows that writing does not happen as events of knowledge. Any skill that might produce such events is lost to *its* own event in the written marks. And the occurrence of a narrative is also lost in writing. I am lost in this writing that you are reading, and although you may well say on the basis of what you read that I am developing certain ideas about remembering and forgetting, and I may well agree with you, I the writer am not present in this writing. You and I must make an additional move to reappropriate my presence in the writing, and we might well forget that that is lost in the writing. My presence is spilled, as it were, and drains away in the systematically connected marks. You can tear up the pages (the artifacts) but you cannot tear up the writing. It always slips away, is never quite present, and never holds something else in presence. The signs indicate each other without any presence occurring. They are only written. As the marks appear, original presence disappears, as though burned by a conflagration.

A distortion thus goes on as I make the sign of the first person nominative and signal that that sign is doing something. An 'I' in the writing is the sign of a pronoun that connects with another sign, a verb, which in turn may connect to a noun or another grammatical sign. But the pronoun, *I* does not *do* a thing. It marks a group of systematic (grammatical) connections. And if in reading this writing I say to myself, "Look at what I am doing. Read what I am saying," I may well find myself like Jackie running, as it were, to a white screen with marks on it. I *am* not there. My sense of my presence in the text is disturbed—in fact it is radically interrupted—in the differenciation of writing and its arbitrariness and in its not presenting a presence or composing the life of something else. More radical than imaginative transformations, writing loses presence by marks on a sheet. Nothing other than signs of signs takes place. It happens neither as a presence of *istoria* nor as a presence of *episteme*. Their presence, like mine, is deferred by another sign.

But at times I write as though I were talking. When that style is successful, it allows you to have the sense that I am talking to you and that we are in a conversation. I call upon your (and my) deep and inherited sense that writing is subsidiary to conversing and that some writing at its best is like speaking in each other's presence. Then it is as though my writing were witness to my presence, that it represents me and makes me available to you. But in the context of Derrida's thought, *that* sense of witness to *my* presence forgets writing by investing presence in it, and in that sense one approaches writing like Jackie approached the screen and thereby forgets that writing loses (forgets) presence by continuously deferring it. One could also say that writing remembers presence in the deferral, but that remembrance would be like remembrance-in-loss, a trace aspect that I will take up later. For now, I want to point out that this style of writing, its personalization and conversationlike manner, composes a sensibility concerning presence, narrative, and knowledge that Derrida's description of writing interrupts and considerably troubles. My way of remembering the loss of presence in writing belies the loss and quickens a traditional sense that writing re-presents presence and supplements a speaker who is present in what he says.

An option that I have not taken is to write the loss of presence by depersonalizing my style as much as possible, eliminating as much connective tissue as I could, and allowing words to resonate with something other than their own signals and losses. I might have allowed writing to signify disaster and to trace a moment in the ruin of presence . . . *in* the ruin of presence. In its continuous deferral of presence, writing witnesses—serves as a sign of—not the finitude and deadliness of a way of being or even being "itself." Writing as Derrida describes it witnesses no singularity that could die and no presence that could be finite. It appropriates no presence but holds, rather, differing from presence by way of signs, signifying other signs. If I in my writing attempted to let writing enact without resistance such ruin, if I stepped aside and let it continuously disturb encouragements toward a person's reappropriating presence, and if I thus took references to myself out of writing, I might have before me a writing that at least troubled our culture's forceful drift toward reappropriation of lost presence. I might find writing that witnesses writing as the disaster of presence and hence of person and conversation—writing that witnesses writing by troubling and discouraging the textures of narration and traditional connections that provide "logical" continuity.

I have not, however, taken the option. Writing witnesses much besides the disaster of presence. In a given writing customs and procedures appear, multiple memories emerge, however fragmented and forgetful they might be, nonvoluntary memories of events, hopes, anxieties and memories of how things appeared to hang together. Writing the ruins of writing, for example, seems to me in Derrida's instance to bring to bear, among many other things, the Holocaust, its firey ovens, and its perceived difference from all meaningful continuities. The writing of disaster is well suited for "expression" of the inexpressible whether the inexpressible occurs as unspeakable destruction and evil or as ungraspable difference in, say, other people. Such writing might also be appropriate for the Lethic occurrences of loss and radical forgetfulness.

But I have found these occurrences to mark memorial continuities. These continuities happen *with* fragmentation, and lost presence happens *with* an ungraspable "aspect." But as I write of continuity I write not only in ruin but also in re-membrance of generation and arising meaning. According to the descriptions in this book, memory in all of its appearances and determinations does not happen according to the criteria of some primal and originary reality. Memory is ungrounded if 'grounded' means that kind of reality. The "facts" of memory are themselves memorial. And if a person imagines a great formation of undefiled Truth that gives meaning to all events as though they were facts, that image lies in ruins in this account. But in the absence of such a functioning image and in the absence of a sense of tragic loss regarding the image's ruin, one finds no presence or kind of presence to happen without the Lethic perforations of loss. The Lethic with its radical forgetfulness happens in withdrawal from memorial occurrences in memorial occurrences. "It" is no more an independent absolute than a given group of connections is an independent absolute. The Lethic happens with memory, in memory's territory according to the imagery in chapter 2. It comes with presence—it "appears" like withdrawal of presence that accompanies presentations. I am emphasizing the *with* in 'loss of presence *with presence.*' Presencing occurs with withdrawal of presencing. I am suggesting that an effort to efface presence with the sense that writing only depresences or defers presence composes an oversight, that ellipsis belongs to the broken tissue, and that presencing composes writing not only in accompaniment with losses of events in their presence but also in emerging events. Memorial presencing does not seem to be describable as a line of development with a definitive transectory. But it does seem to hold regeneration in its ruin—regeneration in discontinuous loss and forgetting. I have thus chosen to write with a sense of broken presence, not pure obliteration of presence or only deferral of presence. In that writing I suggest that writing presents with ellipses in presenting, that it presents in a rich and torn fabric of eventual recall, that it composes both loss and fragmented recovery of bygone events in their presentation through signs and images, and that writing when read can be conversational with all the space for mistake, oversight, and forgetfulness that characterizes conversational exchange.

I also have not taken the option of ruinous writing because I find the one who writes to invest writing with his or her own singularities—with the way her life is composed, with the way his psyche functions: a writing is invested with a person's way of living in and through the infinitely complex discordance of inherited and culturally inherent memories. An individual's "turn of mind" comes to expression in that individual's writing. A writer finds himself answerable for his writing no matter how independently the writing undergoes dissemination and no matter how cut off from the writing the writer experiences herself to be. I am attempting to turn away from anxiety over psychological influences in thought and writing, an anxiety that is manifest, as far as I can see, in all transcendentally oriented thought. People have thought that we can reach a site of perception or disclosure that is free from the infestation of an individual's particular psychological makeup. Surely we must be able to be perceptibly in touch with what is not contaminated by psychological determinations! I do not think that the event of forgetfulness that I am describing is only psychologically structured, but I do think that all of my perceptions, experiences, and judgments, including the immediately preceding observations, are shaped in part by *my* experiences and ways of bringing things together—by *my* psyche. I do not want to forget that I am invested in what and how I write, that there is no writing "as such," no quasi-transcendental nonthing called writing.[3] Writing only occurs as this or that writing, and while we can compare writings and distill common features, one's psyche contributes also to that effort its motivation and its shape. Owning one's part in occurrences such as writing, occurrences that one cannot hold and keep, addresses the point; and no matter how "much" presence slips one's grasp and cuts away from signs and indications, a person perceives, experiences, speaks, *and* writes in the shapes his awareness takes. These shapes are invested in her writing as her writing turns from her. Her writing is witnesses to "her" psyche. So I write 'I' in order, among other motivations, to remember that my writing, which I cannot keep, bears witness to how and who I am with everything with which I belong. I wish to remember that a sense of complete anonymity holds the illusion that I, always passing, do not happen in written passage and in what I write. The ruination of loss does happen and so does the appearance, however lost I now am to it, of parts of my own life. I believe that I am answerable to and for the writing that bears witness in written appearances to my having been, even though those appearances are ones over which I exercise little or no control. As a writer I am enacted in the writing that for a brief moment was mine to alter or to let stand. This *I* is, as I have indicated, extensive and invested with multiple past and present events. But *I* does name a living event of crosscurrents, amalgamations, plays of deep influence, singular intentions and desires, and a lineage of singular experience and encounter with and in this historical-cultural complexity. In this singularity, I am answerable to and for what I write. I appear in expression in writing. I both belong and do not belong to such expression and appearance, and their departure from *me, this* event, is part of the memory of me. And yet I did act. I did write those things, and I did enact my own self-disclosure with its range of both voluntary and involuntary elements. The writing that defers me also presents my enactment along with an unarticulable loss.

I am saying that appearances—in this case, of I—can present "what" is lost in spite of losing its previous immediacy, that appearing with that loss constitutes continuities no matter how splintered and diverse they might be, that a lost presence occurs in a regained and altering presencing, and that traces of lost presence are themselves presentations. Writing in the first person and/or conversationally thus composes a process of differenciation—that of a living event in its immediacy coming to the difference of a witness that lives in signs-to-be-read. This death of a living event is composed in a rising of signs that comprise their own event of systematic references to each other. In the events of these references all manner of memories appear as I struggle with language to write about nonvoluntary memory, impacts of deconstructive thought on traditional philosophical values, Saturday afternoons in the Pix Theater in Wewoka, Oklahoma, or the force of nouns and transitive verbs in the English language.

The signifying movements by which writing takes place also memorialize forgetfulness, and that says something distinct to saying, as Derrida does, that signs are monuments to the death of presence. That claim makes sense to me with the notation that written signs do not move in their artifactual form. They are only marks on a page. But the life of signs occurs in signifying and in the events of differencing and deferring; their event is significatory, and as artifacts only they do not occur as signs, except insofar as they occur in a system of signs. Signifying marks, on the other hand, occur in relations which they themselves enact in their systematicity. I am not saying that signs are agents or that they signify only when someone objectifies them. They happen in signifying, in processes of differenciation and appearing and in presenting by differences and deferring nonetheless the presence that is lost to them in their signifying occurrences. Gaiety and enjoyment, as well as mourning, can accompany writing and its signals as they constitute their own events. But signifying nonetheless embodies memory of loss in the sense that signifying presentations in writing embody the lost presence of what is signified. The embodiment happens in signifying occurrences and is itself lost when it is represented: enactments of signs present loss of "unsigned" living immediacy. Signs can give what they signify to *have* happened, to occur as past, or to be other signs. Signs present things as having occurred or even in a deferral in which the signified thing is yet to appear in its own event. I mean that what is signified and is itself not yet present appears through signification—is presented—as now outside of its own event. "It" is signified in an event other than its own, and this signifying event carries and presents in its formations occurrences of lost (forgotten) presence. Signs embody both memory and forgetfulness of living presence in their bestowal of appearance and different presence. They have been witness to what they are not.

Do I posit primary and disclosing presence of events that is outside of signs—or outside of which signs are? Is a nonsignifier—an event outside of the chains of signifiers—something like a continuing presence that verifies the difference instituted by signs? Do I suggest that I who write am not a sign but a present one who shows unsignified reality? The yes/no responses to these questions arise from this ambiguity: loss of presence occurs with presencing, and presencing occurs with loss of presence. I-writing occurs in self-presentation, and I-written occurs in re-membering. Both I-writing and I-written witness presencing and lapses of presencing's happening. The image of presence in itself and to itself which seems to function obiquely in Derrida's account of signs—perhaps a variation on Kant's idea of thing-to-itself—and the kinds of separation that it suggests seem to me to be optional; that is, there are live options to this image and idea. Things are as they appear to happen, and this observation does not require the addition of something behind or beyond the happening that constitutes the thing's "real" presence. *That* image—of something behind the thing's happening—seems to me to be a primary carrier of a sense of continuing pretemporal presence. That large tree's density (I can walk up to it, but I cannot walk through it) or this woman in her singularity (I can be in relation to her, but she is her own event) do not happen as things to themselves in the sense that they hide something essentially real beyond their happening here as they do. They appear to come to pass, to give up presence in presencing. I shall return to this observation. For now I want to note that we are dealing with an image when we think of pure presence or presence-to-itself beyond its appearencial happening, and that immediacy of presentation does not necessarily suggest "pure" presence or "continuing" presence. Immediacies are witnesses to both presencing and loss of presence and do not require signs for their elliptical occurrence.

As I will show, Derrida's thought of "trace" is helpful for describing this strange companionship of presencing and loss of presencing, although I believe that we find more than a trace of presence in a presencing event. We find presencing in and through appearing. I-writing in relation to a writing that I wrote, for example, might be *like* an originary presence, but only like one in the sense that what I wrote presents the I who wrote without that I's continuing self-enactment. Are there presences that are primary vis à vis their memorial presentations? Yes. Does such primary presence provide a *logos* of meaning and texture that restores the lost and forgotten to the event that remembers it? No. The primary presence lost to itself appears with forgetting with loss as it comes to presence in remembrance. But loss like that does not totally absorb or obliterate that to which it is beholden. A past present enactment is held by loss and re-membering in its appearance.[4]

An event's own enactment seems nonetheless to be deferred in the differencing that "structures" memorial presencing. Derrida has never denied, as far as I know, that events take place outside of chains of signifiers, and I do not believe that he has denied that signification happens. But he does disrupt a sense of immediate presence to cognition or experience. Presence is deferred by the signs that indicate it, and in writing presence is obliterated. A blindness—I am using here a word out of his more recent work to which I shall return—signals a divestiture of enlightening directness in events. I am saying, on the other hand, that a kind of directness happens even in the dispossession that characterizes signfication. I do not want to speak in the metaphors of sight or blindness but in those of availability for encounter, bonding with "what" is not here, and witness that can compose both the presencing of something and the loss of its own event. Each of these words may suggest the others, and each intimates a manner of directness. Even deferral and differrence occur as witness to the deferred and differenced, and "what" is deferred and differenciated may not be only another sign, but can also be "what" a sign can never be: events in their own enactment appear by means of loss, forgetting, deferral, and differenciation. Such "means" of appearing can be addressed by the word *trace* and, I shall add, by the word *encounter*. In my writing, for example, you can encounter me in the loss of my own event. I come through, as it were, the signs that defer my own event and dispossess me of my enactment in writing.

TRACE AND BLINDNESS: WITNESSING THE TOUCH

I have described differenciation as belonging to those occurrences of differences in which other differences eventuate. Differenciation does not name an action by a subject. It does not name a "what" or "who." And although I write at times as though I were saying that differenciation is a state of being, I want to indicate that even in those formulations differenciation names no thing, but rather names plays of differences in which differences arise. My difference from Derrida at this point comes with finding that differenciation seems to describe encounterable occurrences in which differences originate, that they can happen as originary ("archisites") through differential play. For Derrida, the *archi* is always erased in signification.[5] But I nonetheless draw with appreciation from his description of *différance* "as the displaced and equivocal passage of one different thing to another, from one term of an opposition to another."[6] One thing defers another different thing, and fully accorded presence is delayed and never quite achieved. Displaced presentation is an aspect of what he describes: "*Différance* maintains our relationship with that which we necessarily misconstrue, and which exceeds the alternatives of presence and absence. A certain alterity . . . is definitively exempt from every process of presentation by means of which we would call upon it to show itself in person."[7] The signified is relieved of presence as "it" is relayed by signs.

But Derrida also finds Levinas' phrasing appropriate: "a past that has never been present."[8] *Différance* suggests a nonsubstantial postponement of presence, and that means that presence never was but was delayed before a realization occurred. Always out of reach, always beyond signification, always beyond meaning, presence did not come about. *Différance* intervenes as though it gave nothing before something could present itself in its own event. This maddening, obsession-giving indefiniteness crosses all of our human references, relieves presentation of presence, and bears witness to no re-presentable event. *Différance* depresents even its own name. It cannot be a present being, although it "instigates the subversion of every kingdom."[9] By this account not only is past presence totally inaccessable, but it also never quite happened.

Différance "happens" as trace of inescapable excess of meaning and excess of determined containments. So beyond determination is trace that it disappears as it appears: "the trace (of that) which can never be presented, the trace which itself can never be presented: that is, appear and manifest itself, as such, in its phenomenon. . . . Always differing and deferring, the trace is never as it is in the presentation of itself. It erases itself in presenting itself, muffles itself in resonating, like the *a* [of *différance*] writing itself . . . in *différance*."[10] Thus, even the name, the nominal determination of *différance*, is misleading. *Différance* traces excess to any nominal state and dislocates its own placement and nondeferred moment. *Différance*, on Derrida's account, belongs to nothing and thus cannot constitute a memory, much less constitute a transfer of a past present event to another presence.

And yet *différance* as trace does not seem to occur as witness to an inexpressably radical nondetermination that subverts, ungrounds, and gives to tremble every power and domination of assumed presence. Trace happens in the processes of substitution and differencing among signs (including, as I just noted, the sign *différance*). If I were to bring together as generously as possible Derrida's language and my language in this book, I could say that *différance* happens as memory of the unmemorable—witness to and escape from an excess of meaning and sense, as witness to nothing subject to determination. This writing in the *a* of *différance*, appears to me to compose memory of loss of determination in determination, to express resonance with a beginning of nonrepresentable disappearance, to indicate limit to presentation. The oblique references in this language to *différance*'s sideshadowing by the disappearing trace—this elliptical and diverting manner of referring—composes a memorial event of forgetting. The 'of' in 'of forgetting' is ambiguous: I write of a linguistic event that remembers its own forgetting—it belongs to forgetting and forgetting belongs to it. As I see it, and in contrast to Derrida's account, the language of trace and *différance* presents "the" unpresentable in its witness of unholdable disappearance. This language re-members its own forgetting without calling to presence any forgotten event. It presents itself in its "own" loss of presence. I do not find this presentation far from the image of Lethe within Mnemosyne's realm. Each witnesses the other.

"A certain alterity . . . is definitively exempt from every process of presentation by means of which we would call upon it to show itself in person."[11] In this previously quoted statement Derrida indicates a secret aspect of presentation which is lost to presentation—indeed, forgotten in the very occurrence of presentation and lost as well to perception and expression. "Lost to sight," we might say, or "unhearable" in what is heard, or "traced in withdrawal." Whether "the" secret of complete alterity is masked by a phrase such as *mysterium tremendum* or by the narrative of Abraham's command from God to sacrifice his son, or by faith in an invisible God who sees me, or by the ungraspable life of another person, or by a sense of mystery in life, *secret* signifies what is lost by disclosure or explanation or figuration. Everything regarding the secret of alterity is dissemblance, and only if the sign holds secret the secret is alterity signified.[12] Secrecy is similar to the masked Dionysus in this sense: in secrecy one confronts nothing that happens, or if something happens, it happens in withdrawal from presentation. In the mask of Dionysus the devotee apparently confronts sheer enigina that is indicated by absence of presence behind the mask, absence that is manifest as no-presence-there, by an invisibility that accompanies the visibility of a mask—similar to a dissolution of individual consciousness when one is reaching drunken oblivion. Or, in Walter Otto's phrase, the mask revealed "something" simultaneously there and not there.[13] The secret in some cases is not presentable or thinkable—the other's own event, for example, or a bygone event's immediacy. "It" is hidden, yet maddeningly so because its obscurity is manifest as obscurity. Even in the case of secrets that are in principle disclosable—as when you know that something is being kept from you, you feel it, sense it, and yet have no clear knowledge of what "it" is—a person confronts something presented in obscurity and hiddeness. It is there; it is witnessed in obscurity. One is besieged by a thoroughly clouded revelation, held by it, and held away from it. In that case a secret happens as testimony to something given and withheld, something both presented and not presented: an elliptical disclosure.

If I use 'secret' as well as 'trace' to name the withdrawal of what is presented in its presentation, I indicate nothing visible, explicable, or conceivable. In Derrida's early writing a loss of immediate presence composed the invisible secret of signification. In *The Gift of Death* he refers to "absolute invisibility" and to "wholly other" in the context of Kierkegaard's account of God's command to Abraham (Abram) to sacrifice his son, and also in the context of a broader Western experience of *mysterium tremendum*—"an absolute dissymmetry" between one and the other.[14] In these instances (and others to which I shall refer) 'secret' in our lineage suggests obliteration of presence, but in *The Gift of Death* Derrida also refers to my finding myself, in this lineage, in the "gaze" of the secret which is never gazed by me. In such gaze, I am to respond to "what" is quite beyond any form of perception and in relation to which any sign constitutes a deception, even a betrayal of the secret that hides itself beyond recognition in "its" sight of me. I *am* before the secret in the sense that I confront myself as gazed in numinous secret. And secret is before me in the sense that whenever I recognize myself or find myself, the secret already is happening. I occur quite singularly in this gaze, exposed beyond my accounting, and hence exposed to the dissolution and dilapidation of "my" self.[15] "I" am in being placed outside of myself beyond my power of inititation or prevention, dilated immeasurably in the gaze of something not determined, gifted, as it were, by secret with the necessity of response, not to my own nature, but to an inaccessable other that (not even a who, not even really "that") dissolves those limits which decide my determination. This is like being in the gaze of no thing, no reality, that gives *me* to die not only at the end of my time but also in the transcendance of the gaze—nothing that gives me confrontation with nothing determinable and takes me out of myself. I may cry out. I may pray. I may attempt to refuse. I may hate in hopelessness. I may think about it. But I *do* respond. I *am* already in response to "what" I cannot give myself when I occur. And I deny the non-determinable secret at the cost not only of losing a sense for "it" but also of turning everything into a constricted system of determinations that holds all things to their finite, exposed, and functioning significance: no secret, all exposed, no mystery, strangulation by unsecreted identification.

The paradoxical aspect of the singularity of humans in the gift of secrecy (as presented in our lineage) is found in the discovery that the very singularity that arises in a person is also taken away by the language that figures it.[16] Derrida uses Kierkegaard's *Fear and Trembling* as an opening to the tradition that shows the language and the *formulation* of responsbility that thrust a person into a general communicability and practice that is as understandable as it is communal. In their commonality, language and responsibility lack secrecy. The exceptional and extraordinary in a singular individual's response with the gaze of secrecy are transformed into rules, concepts, and practices that provide a sense of continuous human obligation and criteria for intention and action. In that transformation the "self" is lost, forgotten, in its dissolving, subliming confrontation with gifting nondetermination. The responsible, communicating self is found in a shared generality that articulates a nature which includes and defines all individuals. Secrecy is intolerable for the obligatoriness of ethics. To share a secret, on the other hand, "is not to know or to reveal the secret, it is to share we know not what: nothing that can be determined."[17] One becomes a witness to what cannot be communicated directly, a secret preserved in its secrecy and in the utter singularity of the individual's self-fracturing encounter of it: the witness of those who find themselves in the transcending gaze that relieves them of commonality and the shelter of communicable self-disclosure. They find themselves alone in exposure to none but the other. One's responsibility arises with the occurrence of "the" secret—no one else can be one's response; no one else happens "here" with the secret. And, as Derrida emphasizes, responsibility arises, not in or through subjectivity, but in the loss of subjectivity that figures the occurrence of other-as-secret.

These observations by Derrida constitute part of a fragmented genealogy of secrecy, responsibility, and loss of subjectivity in Western experience. Secrecy, responsibility, and loss of subjectivity in the combination that he describes compose aspects of Western Christianity and its faith in a God utterly beyond knowledge and disclosive perception, an absolute Other who sees us without our seeing other-in-secrecy, and gives us to be responsibility in a secrecy and mystery of invisible and inconceivable revelation. The radical and heretical strand that he follows might be taken by "authorities" as anarchic and something to overcome, but it might also be read as showing the sublime responsibility of those individuals who seem to have died to themselves and their determinations in a numinous secret's happening. These are individuals who seem to die to themselves and to all principles of exchange that would serve themselves. They seem to give themselves to the gift of numinous secrecy and to live (or attempt to live) in that response, to respond to others in their response to sublime secret. Or one might say that as they renounce their own determinations, they are in response to the secret of life. In such renunciation and response they seem to find the secret of responsibility, to be the followers of God whom they do not see but before whom they come into self-sacrificial autonomy with the full contingency of deathly, unfounded human life. One's purposes in life have their origin in the death of human authority regarding all of one's finite determinations. One dies to one self in the invisible, mysterious call of the other whose trace is found in an awe of secrecy and in an indefensible and ununiversalizable sense of obligation.

The secret gaze that gives both death and responsibility is thus invisible—as invisible as one's having to die. I noted the absolute dissymmetry that characterizes one's finding oneself visible before the other of invisible secret. One seems to belong to a gaze that one cannot see. Further, the consequences of one's self-renunciation are not foreseeable, and the origin of the gaze before which one seems to find oneself is not subject to human insight. The occurrence of the gaze is not subject to exposure by sight or prediction. 'Secret,' as Derrida presents it, signifies secret without objectivity or subjectivity, secret which gives rise to responsibility outside of subjectivity or objectivity, secret without subjectivity or objectivity that gives rise to a person's subjectivity as well as to ways of living that hold sacred the secret of life and death. One could respond with worship and "obedience" by holding secret the secret and living with values and attitudes to which its gift gives rise. In this context one is a witness to a secret, a witness in ignorance and blindness, a witness by one who is touched and moved by nothing that one can justify in generally shareable terms. One offers one's self as a sacrifice to this mystery and finds in the response of such an offering at least a meager answer that is appropriate to the gift of secrecy.[18]

Any expectation of a return gift for one's own sacrifice constitutes perversion of witness to and in the secret: an expectation of eternal life, for example, or of an ultimate meaning for life, or of any other benefit. Secret cannot be secret and institutionalized in any way. It does not happen in any economy of exchange. It constitutes no promise or basis for reasonable expectation. There is only the *giving* of secret, not some given, not some thing that is given. Any co-respondence of giving with a determinant giver introduces an institutionalization of secret. Derrida wedges out of our lineage this radical implication of numinous secret, divides it from systems of reward or repayment or calculated benefit (leaving, I believe, Pascal's wager in ruin). If Christ were the revelation of *a* spiritual economy of sacrifice and reward, the revelation of a gift as distinct to a secret event of giving, then he would be no more than an instance of an economy of exchange and soulish commerce. I believe that this means that one can be religiously responsible only as a heretic and radical, only in departure from the Lord who, in a major strand of Christian tradition, brings the promise of life and immortality to light, destroys the powers of darkness and death, and opens the kingdom of heaven to all believers, the Lord who gives "men" certainty and an indestructible foundation for truth and goodness when they believe "on him." Only the coming of Jesus as secret, however, the gifting of secret which gives people to die to themselves without promise or surity, without an economy of gifts—only the *giving* of secret would avoid "the long history of the origin of responsibility . . . a history of cruelty and sacrifice, of the holocaust even . . . the fault as debt or obligation . . . a history of the economy of 'contractural relationship' between creditors . . . and debtors."[19] With gifting, as with dying, there is no price to be paid for the sake of an exchange of something for something else. It comes as it comes in secret, and if it is to be shared, it is shared in secret without recompence.

This wedge (Derrida calls it a "nucleus") of noninstitutional secret in our lineage would seem to put in question all institutions and movements toward institutionalization.[20] Derrida presents it as a radical ellipsis in Western life, spirit, and responsibility. He presents it as marking a death of institutionalized responsibility, morality, law, and religion in the midst of their lives. Secret infests all that is public and countable, and secret is presented as the death of human spirit *in* the arising of human spirit. It unsettles human assertion by its gift of no human determination to which and by virtue of which a human find his/herself able to respond. Secret bears witness to nothing that can be institutionalized.

Bears witness? How is this "self-destruction" of institutionalized justice, law, and assurance a witness?[21] It occurs in a self-destruction of the choosing subject as it chooses to give itself over to the gift of secret and to renounce normativity and normalcy in the midst of standards and everyday life. The witness appears to be borne by a reconstitution of the self away from its own prescriptions and into a consciousness without a conscious origin or justification. This is a witness of belief in which *belief* means, not persuasion concerning the truths of a religion or a creed, but both trust in the secret and permission in secret for secret's suasion in one's life. A person gives secret leave to govern one's life beyond legality or command or restraint. The gift of leave to secret in one's life is witness to secret's giving responsibility in the gift of itself. Secret bears witness to nothing that can be institutionalized in its gift of itself as secret in the event of which the power and trajectory of any authority are suspended. There is nothing that can be repeated or directly said in a public domain. Derrida suggests that there is a primordial aspect in this witness, that it lies behind or beyond its paradoxical instantiation in Christianity and Western morality, and that Western codifications of justice, responsibility, and religion believe this aspect. One is *able* to give credence, for example, to the Christian doctrine of atonement according to which God gave human kind the possibility of salvation by the gift of God's self-sacrifice because of (perhaps 'because of,' because one is never sure) another credence: something spectral and invisible in our lineage seems to hold us invisibly in view, giving us to die to every other hold and in that ellipsis giving us to respond in spite of ourselves before sheer mystery. We are able to respond in the divesture of all enduring things. We find ourselves answerable in the loss of all that we feel that we can keep. We are *able* to respond in the mystery of complete otherness in everything that links us and constitutes our worlds. On Derrida's account our lives seem to be impacted by secret before any practice or any individual's experience comes to the fore. Secret, possibly (this is not subject to defined clarity or informed decision) is primordial in our lives, like a cry at birth; perhaps it is before our lineage, outside of it, and not determined by it as secret. Perhaps it transcends our lineage and makes possible people's trusting response to it. Perhaps it is sheer transcendentality, always outside in its gifting. Perhaps it makes possible its corruption in the Christian sense of atonement by means of God's self-sacrifice in Jesus of Nazareth.[22] For even if the atonement is credible and public, it hides still the secret of God's redeeming gift and people's believing response as they find themselves saved in this trust—in the trust of God's gift as creditor to the debtors who may return this trusted gift in their gift of themselves.[23] *That* is a secret witness by the believer's trust, a secret that is not subject to rational or public discernment. So even in experiences that are explained and proclaimed by the doctrine of the atonement, secret remains enveloped in the occurrence and unillumined by the doctrine.

Nietzsche's question in *On the Geneology of Morals* (which Derrida quotes) also constitutes a witness to "the" secret: "how can one *believe* this history of *credence* or *credit*?" Derrida has responded to Nietzsche's observations in his (Derrida's) notations on the secret that eludes the *doctrine* of atonement. Nietzsche wonders how people could possibly believe that God personally immolated himself (sic) for the debt of humans, that God himself (sic) personally and out of love paid a human debt by a pound of his (sic) own flesh.[24] But Derrida observes that Nietzsche's words also seem to bear witness to more than they say, perhaps to a secret that is carried like a "specter" by his own discourse. Derrida asks what makes possible Nietzsche's question, even if it is rhetorical? "For what makes a rhetorical question possible can sometimes disturb the structure of it."[25] What calls through the question and from beyond it? The question, Derrida says, began "by accreditation from the other"(insofar as the question is believed). The occurrence of belief and its secret seem to haunt Nietzsche's words like a withdrawn origin for his question. He is indebted to the trust that he calls into question. And further, "Nietzsche must indeed believe he knows what believing means, unless he means it is all make-believe." Did Nietzsche hear his question as his own fabrication? Or did he himself engage in believing (trusting) that this belief occurred as he asked about the possibility of that belief? Did his words secretly affirm the secret of this belief, leaving it both operative and in secret? Did he receive a gift of giving even as he suggested ridiculousness in one's giving credence to the doctrine of the atonement? Is such believing witness to a gift of giving? And did the secret betrayal of the secret by the doctrine inhere in Nietzsche's ridicule of the doctrine? Was he true to secret as he included the doctrine? Did he share a secret that bonded his discourse with the secret of trust between a believer and the inexpressible origin of her believing? To what does Nietzsche's question bear witness? Derrida suggests, without deciding the issue, that even if Nietzsche heard fabrication in his own belief he knew what believing means. He seemed to write in response to the coming of an other, to "what" he could never say or mean. His writing seems to bear the trace of a withdrawn other for which any name composes a betrayal. Beyond dogma and antidogma comes a gift of giving that presents the author with otherness to his own life, a present to which he is always already responding.

This invisible gaze of the other, traced in a gift of giving and figured as other to whom I am, seems also like an unrecoverable touch by what is never subject to human grasp in any form. Perhaps that is like the touch of radical transition in which something is utterly lost, the touch of absence when another dies, or the touch of one's own passage out of this presence. The metaphor of touch indicates a happening in which something invisible transpires along with everything that is visible regarding the touching event, something belonging to the invisible event that is like touch—a conjunction without sight and beyond sound, a contact that is nothing other than its own event, a striking event which, like Apollo's arrow, gives impact that is not of sight or sound or smell or thought or an act of imagination, an event that carried its own power and transformation. But this language of debt? This *presenting* sense of radical otherness? This language of gift and giving? This sense of transcendance and ruination and misplaced selfhood? This presentation of the institutionalized and thus lost secret? This felt requirement of constantly overturning a language's communicability in order to allow the trace of the linguistically incommunicable? Is secret remembered, or is loss without secret remembered? Perhaps Nietzsche bears hearing at this juncture: perhaps too much re-membering takes place when "gift" is added to death and when "other" is added to loss. Perhaps anxiety seams the assertion of "secret" and its quasi-religious discourse.

The *presentation* of invisible secret as a withdrawn contact, this *account* of something, even something as elusive and indeterminant as secret, outside of the power of representation, this *sense* of secret gifting—are not the presentation, account, and above all the sensibility already events that belong to an established lineage? Are they not saturated with memories—rich memories—of a past presence figured in part by Lethe's spectoral association with Mnemosyne and by the ancient bards' sense of gaze and gift that infinitely transcend everything subject to finite expression? Are we not in the past (and transformed) presence of Pythagorean (and Eleusinian) mysteries? Are we not, in these presentations, accounts, and sensibilities that we find in Derrida's work, in touch with dreams, memories, and figurations that are enacted in the institutions of our lives? Is our lineage, in its memorial and nonvoluntary power, not the site and impulse for our responses? I believe that Nietzsche might have a last word in this exchange: a movement to invisible gifting expresses an ideal that sacrifices finitude without secret for the sake of secret that undecidably suggests the possibility of something-not-knowable, an ideal that has helped to discipline our heritage.[26] Many Westerners have longed for a giver so secret that it is (or, as often expressed, He is) not subject to its most decisive gift, death; so secret in its touch that it bestows upon us something that can be remembered only in the witness of trusting (and self- sacrificing) belief. Many have longed for something secret that compels our obsessions—or the obsessions of our most sensitive and gifted souls, something so secret that our least justifiable, most precious, least explicable, most sublime moments may appropriately come to expression in the strange metaphor (that also cannot be a metaphor) of gifting by the unknowable. In such moments even the mystery of death receives the mysterious investment of meaning beyond sight and articulation: death dies to itself in its being given. And in its dying event, it bestows the gift of giving. This seems to me to be a wonderful and ancient and beautiful *is-toria* whose secret, as it were, bears no secret at all. Its surface is where its secret begins and ends and bears witness to secret's loss.

The institution of noninstitutionalizable secret or gift or beginning might well bear witness to neither image nor shape: an absence of secret, in which absence we find happening all that is mysterious in our lives, an absence of trace other than a trace of lethic darkness in the arrival of memories. In that case, presences bear witness to other presences in presentations that re-member the bygone in lethic darkness without secret.

Lethic darkness without mystery or secret? Something like oblivion that invests even our ecstacies—our gifts of fire—with a depthless, heightless surface? Mere absence of light? A discourse of absence without gift or the fire of Prometheus or of holocaust?

CHAPTER TEN

A Symptom of Life in the Absence of Light

I turn to a "symptom of life," a witness that is accompanied by an absence of light and a pervasive sense of loss of life first by references to passages in Levinas' *Totality and Infinity*, a work that is saturated by an almost overpowering sense of loss of God in the occurrence of God's call to His people, a sense of perpetual loss of the other human being in all experiences of the other human being. A person *might* find presentation of another person to occur in the coming of the other to full presence in flesh and blood as well as in image, role, and objectivity. But Levinas finds the experienced presentation of the other to occur, not in full presence, but in loss of the other. The other's presentation occurs in an indelibly destructive transformation whereby the specific other is lost to an experiential uniformity that is imposed by the experiencing subject. The other is lost through the enactment of subjective uniformity and interiority by the one who forms the other in recognition, lost in an experiential nominalism whereby the other happens as the experiencer's dynamic structure in which the other does not live in his or her own event. For Levinas we look in the wrong place when we look to experience as the site of the other's own manifestation. The other happens, rather, in withdrawal from experience, in a radical refusal of experience, in an absence of experiential presentation, in something that appears to be closer to an absence of light than to enlightened perception.

According to Levinas a radical separation is a condition of subjective interiority and an individual's enjoyment of being at home in the world.

Neither disclosure nor writing memories overcomes this separation. Separation, in contrast to the descriptive claims that I have made, originates in an individual's autonomy and, congruent with what I have said, is a condition for an individual's self-expression. The relation of autonomy is exterior, not one of inward intimacy, but one which "reveals" itself in a coincidence "of the expressed with him who expresses, which is the privileged manifestation of the Other, the manifestation of a face over and beyond form." Separation is also the condition for one's forming the other in one's own inward experience and for the occurrence of discourse between and among humans. Pervasive of this description by Levinas is, as I say, a sense of loss that is not overcomable by intimacy or immediacy or an I-Thou occurrence. Loss of the other person's autonomy and self-presentation pervades any appropriation of the face-to-face event, leaves exteriority in place, and prevents such an event from becoming usable evidence or intuition or cognition.[1] Nothing like immediate illumination allows the other's own presence to be experienced. The face to face, in Levinas' description of it, is not an experience, and as far as experiences can reach the other occurs in an absence of light. But there is also a movement of return to meaning in Levinas' account of Infinity that, while not eliminating the sense of loss, overrides it in a forceful way. This return is in meaning and to meaning, a return that holds separation in place before Infinity, a separation in this instance that belongs to Infinity and its revelation but one that occurs nonetheless as command and giver of obligation. This return issues in ethics, in a way of living that is, in *Totality and Infinity*, commanded by the face. I shall write of the absence of light first by references to the return of light's dominance in Levinas' forceful account, a return that I find ironic as it replaces at the core of his thought the absence of light on which the return depends. In this process, I would like to interrupt a movement of *return* to meaning and light that one frequently encounters in our traditions and one that loses the Lethic sense that I have found important for an account of her life of memories.

I wish also to write about the absence of light in a presentation of a sense of life in which the absence of light is not congealed into a definitive category or way of life or within a formation of Law or Gospel. That metaphorized as absence of light happens as in ordinary life transformations as people come to live and die in many changes that carry with them more than enough possibilities of sorrow, loss, and affirmation. This desire on my part places me before the excellences of the everyday life, I mean, before the stabilities of living, before decisions, commitments, carefulness, attentiveness, beneficial organizing, responsibility, and reliability that give our lives definition and character. Without such stabilities we are lost to the everyday's often blind destructiveness—whose magnitude cannot be overstated. Everyday living is partially a matter of repetitions for the sake of lives. Our lives and those about us require dependability, trustworthiness, firmness of resolve, courage for promise, strength for steadiness in duress and desire, strength for moderation, care, balance, foresight, and self-control. The discipline of the everyday is found in regulation, in care for consequences, and in fineness of insight and knowledge. These are hard things, not given to *ek-stasis* so much as to figurations of attitude and creations of sites for living, for environments that allow people to cope with and survive the onslaught of impulse, opposition, failure, death, desire, suffering, and the pathologies of mistreatment and mistake that form us and injure us. The everyday is the space for understanding as well as misunderstanding, for coping with the oppositions that a culture carries, for support, kindness, passion and love. It is the space in which we attempt to come to terms with the inevitabilities of human life and resist or lend support to whatever destroys our lives or gives them endurance, happiness, and joy. It is the space of grief and renewed life. As we come into our individual and collective identities and integrations, however, we come into our ability to occasion pain and suffering, to facilitate situations of needless sorrow, an ability that comprises at once our ability to love, limit, enhance, affirm, and occasion new life.

In and through everyday life there is something like darkness, like an absence of light, attention to which, as we have seen, is vital for our senses of possibility, place, regulation, beliefs and recognition. There are many ways to speak of this "dimension"—some of the phrases that I have found to arise in such speaking are "indeterminacy in changes and in reference to the future," "the impenetrable aspect of pastness," "the unconscious," "sheer mystery," "the relativity of human perspective," "the unovercomeable limits of reason," "the presence of death," "the finitude of meaning," "the withdrawal of being," and "the inaccessibility of the other." One temptation I have considered is to illuminate the darkness of indeterminacy with interpretation, speculation, or conviction, to look for information or signs or experiences that will lend, if not brightness, at least perceptibility and illumination to the dark. However, such options, appear to embody both a witness to and a forgetfulness of the absence of light as people invest meaning in it, as they carry a sense of it in attitudes that transform it into feelings of illuminating and meaningful connections.

"Darkness," however, seems to be its own "connection." It persists even in the stances that would transform it, and it does not yield to memories and hopes that would give it definition and figuration—not even to the sign of secret.

Some of the everyday benefits of attention to the absence of light are reticence in conviction and belief, pause before impulse, stillness before uncertainty, affirmation of unclarity, hesitation before universalization, a sense of nonresolution to accompany each everyday resolution, and a sense of the limits of signification, interpretation, and justification. We might have the sense that our grip on things leaves something ungripped and that release of what we experience is appropriate to the urgency or palpability that comes with the experience. It seems that the bedrock of experience is perforated by something not at all like bedrock, that an unilluminable porosity pervades what seems solid or overwhelming to us in its moment. Such porosity can give us pause, to question, to blink, to exert caution. Possibility also arises in this porosity, comes with the occurrence, under-mining any pretence to infinite endurance—unsettling possibility, unset-tling chance, or unsettling mutability—an unsettlement of definitions and irrevocable figuration. One kind of strength in everyday human life seems to happen in part as a capacity to affirm "the Lethic" in an absence of its possible resolution into "light."

I am writing about a dimension of occurrence in everyday life about which we can do nothing and yet attention to which can sometimes miti-gate the destructiveness of illuminating immediacies. It is a dimension that opens our experiential certainties and inspirations to question, that puts in question our illuminations and insights, that strangely holds in question our urgencies and felt imperatives. It gives us to act by reconsideration, to be attuned to destructiveness exactly when we are most clear about what seems to be life embracing. It can give moment to the value of delay, to looking again at what appears valuable for us, to holding off closure by interpretation or felt, deep satisfaction. It is a dimension in which light is absent, one that is obscured and forgotten most when our clarity and felt certainty are strongest. It is an aspect of experience and occurrence that places in jeopardy our traditions of clarity in disciplined knowledge as much as in belief, in calculation as much as in inspiration, in personal immediacy as much as in communal certainty. By the best of our lights we feel right in certain events. Exactly there is our greatest danger for destruc-tiveness in an absence of light that gives Day to be the daughter of Night.

This is a dimension without memories which pervades all the light of determination that memories can bring.

THE WORLDLINESS OF "INNER," PRIVATE EXPERIENCE

Levinas says that "the present of the *cogito* . . . maintains itself all by itself—be it only for an instant" (54). He speaks of "this instant of sheer youth," that is, an instant that is infinite and ahistorical. "Interiority," he says, "is the very possibility of a birth and a death that do not derive their *meaning* from history." "Interiority institutes an order different from historical time in which totality is constituted, an order where everything is *pending*, where what is no longer possible historically remains always possible" (55). In such "infinity" of interiority there is a flow of life "where life has meaning." There is "fecundity" which gives continuous resurrection beyond death. "Interiority is not absorbed into the universal time"; it constitutes "a dimension in being, a dimension of non-essence, beyond the possible and impossible." The "secret" of the time of interiority "interrupts" the continuity of historical time (57). It makes separation and interiority possible.

This extreme privatization of interiority, of the *cogito*, appears to me to constitute a descriptive error, an error that has a powerful Cartesian history in our recent culture. But the claim is not limited to the lineage of Descartes or to Levinas' thought. It seems to pervade all philosophical and religious disciplines that center themselves on inner discovery or withdrawal from the world for the sake of discovering one's self. It is found in ascetic mysticism in which people follow a discipline of denial to free themselves from distraction before an inner life or inner light. It is found in the Socratic lineage of knowing one's self in an effort to discover truth and in some contemporary psychological procedures for self-discovery. The error seems to me to arise out of a traditional function of the dualism of inner and outer, the dimension of historical time and inner occurrence, and out of a location of the individual's event of life in a pure and ahistorical dimension. This inner event is taken to be something pure, without contingent content, "an instant of sheer youth," as Levinas beautifully phrases it. Nietzsche, too, uses the image of youthfulness, (as we saw in chapter 6) when he speaks of the advantage of history for life, a youthfulness that arises not from knowledge of what has happened but from a creative turning of what is known to the service of pure vitality and creative movement in the determinations of our continuing lives.[2] Life's quality of youthfulness may refer to a pure and singular event, to its irreplaceability, to its freedom and ownness, and, often (in writings other than Nietzsche's) to both its sacred aspect and its linkage to the timeless aspect of all things. The turn to *inner* life in this context, a turn crucial for Levinas' account and in contrast to Nietzsche's, can be found in the work of various thinkers as a turn to our kinship with either a ground or a groundlessness of all that occurs, to our kinship with essence or unessence; and we are thought to undergo this occurrence without contingent distraction in whatever form this standing-out-of-history takes. Humans undergo something like time-lessness that is outside of all other events. In this interpretation, the "inner" of a life is one's immediate contact with something like the time-lessness of time or being beyond the determined specificity of any particular, perhaps being within an eternal yes-no that is captured in no figuration and withdraws from any understanding that would fix "it" or "hold" it or render it intelligible. The extreme privatization of inwardness in such an occurrence can thus lead to far more than a triumph of the subjective in a definition of experience. It can also allow for the indeterminate presence of Infinity.

For now, I shall leave aside Levinas' originality in his account of totalization and nontotalization. I turn away from this part of his account because it assumes what I wish to question, namely the idea of inwardness and the assumption that the inner exists in stark difference to the outer. I wish to develop a series of suggestions that might turn us toward the possibility that the idea of inwardness is marked by too much "youthfulness" in the claims that assert its ahistoricality, regardless of the subtlety and brilliance in which such youthfulness or Infinity is conceived.[3] I wish to emphasize, however, that in Levinas' thought an absence of light is not completely forgotten and that his way of attending to it provides an ambiguity regarding illumination and nonillumination that figures a central problem in this study of memories and memories' loss.

Immediacies are enactments of culturally and psychologically constituted states of mind. Other ways to view immediate occurrences is to see them as pure ahistorical events, as a pure happening of timelessness of contact with something, as the self-enactment of a subjective faculty or capacity, or as a life in its living moment. Buber's difference from Levinas, for example, is found in his account of the immediacy of I-Thou occurrences, which are not at all inward, but are rather more like the immediacy of a between in which inwardness is infinitely transcended by two beings. In contrast to such views, it seems to me—and this book in its entirety bears witness to this belief—that immediacies occur as self-enactments of sedimented (memorial) elements. The sedimentation is deep and vast, as I have indicated. It composes a memorial fund. It includes the structures and experiences sedimented in a language, in a personal psychological history, in the complex hierarchies of a society, and the broader cultural sedimentation that is found in a specific society's way of life. Out of such memorial sedimentation come visions and dreams, unspeakably moving experiences of divinity or beauty or value, urgent inclinations toward some kinds of connection and away from others. In some religious practices, people regularly are touched immediately by "the Spirit" and undergo life-transforming ecstasies in such "gifts of fire." In our culture we are immediately horrified by practices that are experienced as salutary in other societies. A specific grouping of psychological conditions can lead to happy immediacies of experience that other psychological conditions find immediately unacceptable or bizarre. What we may term "inwardness" is a lively, multiply determined condition made up of such sedimentation that is expressed as desire or lack of it, attractions and inclinations, systems of significance, inchoate forms of recognition, senses of uncompromisable values, and a sense of life. That we live these kinds of events—that we *are* them in their (and our) moment—suggests a dimension of purity or timelessness only if a person affirms some of the values and meanings that characterize the sedimented occurrence and provide a basis for interpreting them as pure and timeless. Such values and meanings are enacted as one experiences things or people or as one thinks or feels. If the sedimentation alters and values and meanings change, the way one experiences or thinks or feels with regard to the events of experiencing, thinking, and feeling will also change. Hence a society's or group's recognition of the importance of training people in very specific ways and with very specific procedures: training teaches the individual how to experience, think, feel, and live. By education and acculturation and the transmission of memories we help to form the immediate occurrences of our lives that we are able to recognize as youthful.

These culturally and psychologically constituted states of mind, in addition to being memorial, are worldly, historical, and belong to a public. They are world relational. An 'I' occurs as a 'we.' Although, in our traditions, the movement might feel inward as we turn away from perceptions of things around us or as we give accounts of what we as subjects contribute to recognitions and experiences, the movement itself, its feeling, and a sense of privacy or subjectivity that accompanies the movement are themselves the bearers of incalculably rich traditions of practice and sensibility. A greater or lesser sense of individuality, a sense of divinity or mundanity, a sense of life or loss of life, a sense of futurity or determination—all bear lineages in which feelings and significances and meanings have been formed into a domain that is enacted both communally and individually, at once, in what is called "inwardness." In contrast to Levinas' statement, the meaning of "sheer youth" is quite historical in the sense that it is already meaningful in a tradition of practices and teachings that give priority to singular, inward lives and that give a feeling of life and timelessness in the immediacy of "interiority." Interiority is a richly psychological and communal state that brings with it meanings that we find as we come into a feeling of incalculable moment and worth. Both a complex history and a complex community are enacted in the meaning of interiority and Infinity.[4]

Inwardness thus constitutes a primary connection of an individual with a world of memories and meanings. It is often found in our lineage in a contrasting definitive relation with what is inappropriately called "exteriority;" it brings with it a sense of boundary and boundlessness, it can set itself apart from other constituted experiences such as the perceptions of "external" things and elements subject to quantification and qualitative judgment. Inwardness has come to mean singularity as well as commonality in value, sameness of experience and sense in unique individuals, sameness in some religious or quasi-religious meanings (that are taken to indwell people's inwardness). It is in contrast to many other meanings and significances. It happens in an enmeshment of traditions, languages, and experiences whereby we experience ourselves as like or unlike uncountable public options and values. To be "inward" is to be in public traditions, communal histories, and social connections.

And the solitude, the aloneness in some events? I believe that Heidegger's account in *Being and Time* of "my ownness" is accurate to this extent: only this one lives his or her event of connections. The individual is a specific occurrence of the common meanings that provide sense of place, distance, homelessness, self, and no self. One is a singular occurrence of nonsolitary relations, and Levinas, I believe, is right when he says that such an event is not replaceable by any other event except at the cost of violence. But being one's own event is neither external nor internal when those words are given ontological significance. Being one's own event carries the connections that speak of the way *we* are but does not compose something in and to itself, as though separated from the time and meanings of communities, lineages, emotions, or psychological formations borne by languages and practices. One's life is a specific event of such relational "things," immediate to itself in the complexity and thievery of its occurrences, communally coming to pass in its own moment, never finalized, never disconnected, and never "outside" of the determinate time of its happening. The I happens as a we; to appear as I means to co-appear with others in a matrix of shared memories.

MEANING IS THE FACE OF THE OTHER

People who are familiar with Levinas will have noted an awkwardness in the previous section. I have given the possibility of a different account of inwardness from the one he gives in order to establish the likelihood that what we call "inner experience" is thoroughly relational, historical, communal, and psychological. But he does not establish his interpretation of Infinity solely by reference to the *cogito* or inward immediacy. His account in *Totality and Infinity* is directed by what he calls the "primordial event of face to face," by externality; and, he says, meaning and signification originate in this primordial and external occurrence. "Meaning is the face of the Other, and all recourse to words takes place already within the primordial face to face of language" (206). Although he does think of human consciousness as characterized by a "constitutive freedom" that is always young and forever constructing experiences, that is the region that is interrupted by the face-to-face occurrence which is not a subjective synthesis and not an experience. It is other to subjective enactment and to transcendental consciousness. I have also put in question the accuracy of transcendental accounts of consciousness and left room for a different understanding of disclosure in comparison to transcendental accounts. But Levinas, quite in contrast to transcendental theories, says that the face-to-face event constitutes a prerational "discourse" that "commands" an internal discourse (207). Such an event is prior to memories as well as transcendental synthesis and constitution. It is "an original relation with exterior being"(66). In this priority it is significant but not produced by subjectivity. This signification "is infinity." "Significance is infinity, that is, the Other"(207). It marks the limit to idealism and the priority of subjectivity for understanding our world and our obligations. The face-to-face event "overflows" any grasp or symbolization of it, or, as he says, "the inexhaustible surplus of infinity overflows the actuality of consciousness"(207). By the face, consciousness is "subjected to the other." Reason and experiential subjectivity, far from mastering the other, are solicited and shaken by the other's address—by this primordial encounter—and a nonrational plurality overflows the universal orders of rational synthesis.

This is a strange situation in terms of my present attention to absence of light. Were one to make 'light' a synonym for 'consciousness,' the other in its infinity of address would be quite without illumination. But the interpreter would then do a disservice to Levinas' account of discourse, meaning, and signification as the primordial event of the face before me. Although unencompassable by consciousness, this event can be found to be saturated by the light of the meaning of Infinity and consciousness to be crossed by the darkness of its own inward and rational orders. The face-to-face event is the origin of ethical relation, not a mystical union, certainly, but a relational occurrence of discourse that happens before comprehension can take place—this is relation of discourse, which makes comprehension possible. It is a relation that can be taken as an elaboration of the faith, the trust that in the beginning God gave relation in giving creation.[5] He swept over the darkness that covered the deep, swept over the face of the waters, and uttered the words "Let there be light." And with His words, light came. Light came to the face of the deep. Light was pleasing to God, and He divided it from darkness. It was a great and primordial wonder, not in a distance of desire but in an exteriority of word, an exteriority of infinite, light-giving word which gives first, before everything else, Meaning and the possibility of response. Before signs, before mortality was a division of light from darkness in the word and sweep of God's deed that implants the firstness of face before all that is alien or familiar, the firstness of the connection of address in the infinite light of God's creation.

Murder, on the other hand, brings darkness according to Levinas. It is the radical refusal of the gift of Infinity, of Meaning and Light, a radical diminishment of a light that carries all creation with it. Murder comes in many forms, and any refusal of discourse, any violation of the face is a step in the direction of one of those forms. For Levinas, the absence of light is like the absence of God, an unspeakable sacrilege before the gift of life-in-Meaning, a separation from the primordial gift of relation, a dark oblivion to what God saw as good in the creation of the world as he gave it light. For him, sheer indetermination in no sense happens: God is the Ruler of the Universe, and that includes the dark openness of indetermination.

A SENSE OF THE ABSENCE OF LIGHT IN RELATIONS

Absense of light does not appear to be constituted at all. The phrase indicates something like primordial separation in the occurrences of things. I am thinking of occurrences as the happenings of appearances, as the shining of things in light, in their emerging into presence and passage. I join Levinas in affirming that things (and faces) do not appear primarily as a consequence of transcendental synthesis or any unifying process of perception and experience. Appearances—things in the light—are already there as we come to experience them, already in the light of appearing. I have located the site of appearing in a memorial world of social and cultural forces and factors, in lineages of happenings that are presented through the memories that are bourn by aspects of a culture. The light of appearing seems to be erased by withdrawal of light, by oblivion for which the phrase *utter darkness* seems appropriate—something like, I have said, the sense that Lethe and Hades' Lethic element of complete darkness carries in their mythological formations, an element that does not shine at all, that harbors no promise of illumination or anything that approximates the quasi-determination of 'Infinite.' A sense of absence of light does put in question totalities and totalization—systems of illumination that promise either completion or sufficiency of reference and identification. A sense of the absence of light might challenge the adequacy of knowledge and consciousness in any relation. It might expand into attentiveness to singularities, scattered pluralities, shifting configurations that give rise to unpredictable possibilities and transformed landscapes of appearances, attentiveness to loss, fragmentation, incompleteness, and a vague nonempirical dimension that accompanies our empiricities. In this context I can use affirmatively words such as *unencompassable, unspeakable, ecstatic in relation to all determinations.* But I would not use words such as *Infinite, Eternal, Divine, Sacred, God, God beyond God, Ground of Being,* or *the One Who Calls.*

I would not use such words because they say too much, cast too much light, invoke lineages in which Light conquers darkness and revelation gives meaning to absence of light and guidance regarding "it." Such words give meaning to absence of light, enlighten it, and place it within a broad scheme of theological and often religious appropriations. Such words take away the radicality of pausing and waiting with reticence before utter lack of explainability and meaning. There is nothing to be done or said before it. My words now, my initiation regarding absence of light, my giving it significance in my observations also reflect a pause that stills a desire on my part to draw meaning from it. The pause is spelled out in hesitation and reluctance within the traditions of explanation and meaning that move me to say more, to do more in an intention to make absence of light friendly or worshipful or part of a larger scheme of things or an origin of mysterious patterns of cosmic and universal direction. It gives pause to the incipient force of traditions toward totalities of practice and light. Absence of light does not lend itself to formations of identity. It leads nowhere and does nothing.

A sense of the absence of light, on the other hand, may have an active and affirmative aspect. In that sense I might feel the limits of identification and meaning. In those limits, I might cultivate an anticipation of transformation and attentiveness to indeterminant possibility. I might attempt to stay lightly with the truths that seem inescapable to me. I might accentuate differences and feel tentative in the certainties that connect them. A sense of unpredictability might accompany my strategies, plans, and demands. A predisposition toward release might pervade my sense of endurance and proper repetition. In desiring axiomatic fixations and return to past experiences, I also might attempt to mitigate the fixations and efforts to return to the immediacy of what is in the past. In a sense of the absence of light I might connect with people and things without a requirement for a sense of Infinity or transcendent call or another form of higher affirmation and presence. In a sense of the absence of light, light appears limited, subject to misleading clarity, liable to tragic error, and crossed by what it can never be. In such a sense, people and things can appear in an elemental fragility that is defined in part by the event of loss in their appearance, they can appear as subject to the values that determine them and prey to the trajectories that a community's best lights give them. People and things also appear in an absence of light that lets us in our sensibility remember the noncompletion of everything that gives them to be open in bygone determinations and in the "upcoming" toward which they move in their transitions and transformations.

RETURN TO INFINITE MEANING

Levinas identifies 'Infinity' with 'Other' as though this identification were not formed in memories. Infinity "shimmers" in the event of face (207). In that event (not in one's sensibility), one is submitted to the Other, to the

Infinite, to "an Absolute" beyond description or inscription. One is before an infinite exteriority that is beyond subjective enactment and symbolization. One is before Limitlessness when limit is defined by the structures and dynamics of subjective synthesis: an "absolute gap of separation," Levinas says. Yet, "in welcoming the Other I welcome the On High to which my freedom is subordinated. But this subordination is not an absence"(300). With that enlightening move to the On High comes an eradication of absence of light, an eradication that carries beyond being to a Source of all being and an Origin of all language. With that turn, propriety, appropriateness, and the authoritativeness of tradition enter with the force and strike of light and produce a determination of ethics and practice. We find ourselves within a revelatory trace of the On High, a trace in the Infinite's withdrawal that restores nonetheless a full range of determination that is lost to absence of light. We are again within a moment of disclosure ruled by "Meaning" and "Signification," a unitary and originary moment that is both fleeting and absolute, beyond view and yet complete "Goodness" in which "the primordial production of being" is founded. "Goodness," he says, "is transcendence itself" (p. 305).

This return to Meaning and Goodness in Levinas' thought is not like a return to the lost humanism of the Enlightenment, although I find his return dangerously close to an unappropriated desire for something lost. It is like a desire for Meaning that is lost in one kind of subjective appropriation of the Other. But Levinas does not assign Meaning to the creation of a finite will and certainly not to the creation of a limited sensibility. Rather his is a return to Meaning that includes a sacrifice of will; it is an occurrence of welcoming and of substitution of Other for myself as he develops that thought later in *Otherwise Than Being*. In a sacrifice of will one undergoes a return to Meaning, to Other, to a momentary and utterly fleeting presence-at-a-distance that is only traced in its withdrawal from appropriation and in a renewed, external call to one's inwardness. Meaning is not captured, but returns, as already there, from the losses inherent in experience and recognition. It is an ahistorical return, one not invested by error or death, a return that belongs to the Other, an unappropriable, shimmering epiphany of the On High, of Infinity which is the Meaning to which Levinas' thought, always attuned to its loss, returns.

In Levinas' account, this On High is not defined by memory, is never lost to itself, never divided or split or severed from itself in Its trace. As I see it, the On High is closed in on Itself in endless occurrence; It is presented by Levinas as infinitely, undividedly Other. Meaning does not evaporate from It. It is without dehiscence. It is like an eternal call to Meaning from Meaning, without absence in Its Meaning and Goodness. And even these statements lose the On High, so completely Other as It 'is.'

How might we speak of such significations as these that Levinas employs to speak out of his central thought? He is not speaking of eternal presence in the sense of something that is always accessible if one knows how to gain access to it. The Other is always in withdrawal from finite encounters and is encountered most appropriately in a welcoming sacrifice of spontaneous autonomy. But we can observe the power in his thought of return to something already accomplished—Meaning and Goodness that are not of history or time but are beyond any futurity of realization or past-ness of occurrence. We are certainly of time in the sense that we lose touch over and over again with the Other. Our histories constitute narratives of failures before the face of the Other. We cannot expect a future eschaton of full and appropriate presence with the Other. So we are called to return, return to Signification Itself, called from outside of time to the Other To Time, called from loss of meaning to Meaning Above All.

This interpretation of Meaning is not one of Meaning in *its* loss or in its memorial occurrence. It is an interpretation of *our* loss of Meaning. Meaning's loss is at a distance from Meaning, and our hope rests with return, not by a finite generation of meaning, but in Meaning's continuous 'already there' in the face of loss. For Levinas, however, loss of meaning occurs in the Face of Meaning, not in loss and death in Meaning's occurrence. For him, we, lost, are gifted by returns to Meaning. In this context I find his thought closed by his sense of Infinite Meaning to the Lethic aspect of appearances and affirmations. Such absence occurs for him *in* the light of Meaning. It occurs for me by virtue of his insistence on a return to Meaning in the context of Infinity and in an absence of memory's loss which gives Infinity to narrative and not to withdrawn existence.

My thoughts arise from the observation that Levinas' claims are based in a lineage of signification that returns again and again, in a defini-tive movement, to a universal significance that is placed outside of critical reach and that lends significance to all orders of experience and that is given a standing that is outside of the circumscription of memory and finite time. I am presupposing in these remarks that meanings arise in losses of meanings through memorial transformations, that significations are historical, memorial configurations, that return of meaning from loss is far from guaranteed, and that openness in the world occurs with absence of light that is figured in losses of meanings. I associate openness with renewal and transformation with absence of light, and the signification of Infinity, of eternal light, seems to me to figure an important degree of closure to transformations at the heart of what gives our lives meaning. When a signification signifies itself as its own subject we have closure to the limitation, danger, and deathliness of that signification. It incites, instead, continuous return to itself. Such continuous return figures what I am calling "closure" to the finite world of darkness and of regeneration in processes of unrecoverable losses and unpredictable figurations. The metaphor of absence of light addresses the inappropriateness of timeless and ideal signifiers that close themselves to the processes that form them and carry them in the erosions of memories—processes that are darkened to oblivion if the signifiers become the objects of insistent and compelled repetition. Such repetition constitutes a refusal of meanings' lives by the light of Meaning, a signifier closed upon itself by a powerful exertion of forgetful will and intention. Refusal of this kind of signifier and its repetition embodies a belief that meaning without Meaning will return with renewal of life through crises of forgetfulness, loss, and death, that absense of light composes a methaphor for a symptom of life that is without life or illumination or meaning.

CHAPTER ELEVEN

Gifts without Fire:
Thinking and Remembering

This art of transfiguration in philosophy.

—Nietzsche, *Joyful Wisdom*

Graver's mistake had been that he had never been able to think in dark enough terms to have any real understanding of what it was he had been dealing with. Arnett had hinted as much. Instead of thinking in terms of data or kilos or dollars, instead of thinking in terms of bits of information or accumulative intelligence, he should have been thinking in less tangible terms. He should have viewed his work at the bottom as a struggle of abstractions. His career had been devoted to shedding light on the subject of mystery, to illuminating the darkness through knowledge, albeit secret knowledge. He thought now that he had a right objective through all those years, but he had employed the wrong technique in trying to achieve it and maybe, even, he had been looking in the wrong places for the answers. Perhaps it was not the business of shedding light on people's deeds that he should have been concerned with, because after all, when light arrived the essence of darkness was changed. It was no longer darkness. It seemed to him that he was arriving too late in the sequence of events. Perhaps he should have been trying to understand instead the character of darkness itself and what it was that happened when men's desires were shaped and formed in absence of light.

—David Lindsey, *An Absence of Light*

243

I remember vividly the experience that made viable and exciting for me the prospect of becoming a philosopher. I was a junior in college and preparing for my first philosophy exam. I and two friends were sitting in a booth in the student union and talking about one of Plato's dialogues, probably *The Republic*, although I'm not sure. During the conversation I experienced the interconnection of several ideas and saw in my mind something by virtue of those connections that I had never seen before, while in the happening I was also aware of the happening. At first I was startled. I involuntarily jumped slightly, and my skin tingled. I felt a rush of excitement, and although I do not remember what I said, I remember well the feeling that I can now express by the words, I am seeing it! I am seeing it! The complex and, at least to a degree, self-aware idea intensified and reverberated in my mind. I had a sense of intense pleasure, approximating a kind of joy, accompanying my excitement. I believe that was my first experience of self-aware, "philosophical" thinking—no matter how limited it was—and since then I have not been able to think of thought as abstracted from experience. It *is* an experience, different from other kinds of experiences, but an experience nonetheless that is as bodied and concrete and alive and autonomous and defined by relations and connections as every other experience is.

As I think of and with this memory I arrive at the topic of this chapter as well as continue an activity that defines the book: Thinking in, about, and with memories most of which are not voluntary, an activity that is as "real" and as "virtual," as singular and as communal in its touch as other experiences that we attribute to mind or spirit or soul. Thinking is as "real" as love, fear, serenity, excitement, hope, depression, belief, and, of course, it is as "real" as memories are. I shall first draw thinking and remembering close together and then elaborate this closeness by a description of thinking that emphasizes its dimensions of abstraction and concreteness, its disclosure and oblivion: these dimensions will return us briefly to the images of Mnemosyne and Lethe as well as those of Apollo and Dionysus. I shall conclude with a reflection on the subjunctive mood and on the eventfulness of thinking and remembering together.

I have said that cultural practices and institutions embody memories, that these memories are not subjective in any usual sense of that word, and that past events are transformed—re-membered—in their cultural, presentational enactments. Such memories are invested in our ordinary communal lives and in our recognitions, feelings, and beliefs. I pointed out that such memorial occurrences include loss of the past events that they give to appear, that they are characterized by mutations and transformations, and that in their Dionysian aspect they dismember bygone events as they re-member them and give them to appear. I thereby pointed out that something other than subjective activity occurs in this kind of nonvoluntary memory, that as people live in their cultures they compose enactments of cultural memories, and that these memories and their enactments are already active when a person recognizes them or recognizes anything else. In that sense we belong to memories and to their nonvoluntary occurrences: hence the emphasis that I place on people's alertness extending beyond their personalities and particular life histories in these memories to which their lives belong. Our selves and our lives are extensive in the vast reach of cultural re-membering. The complexity of the Dionysian myths themselves that I discussed in chapter 3 seems to figure this memorial complexity of loss, mutation, and appearance that has formed one of the primary themes of this study.

These observations suggest that thinking too belongs to nonvoluntary re-membering. I will say later in this chapter that a thinking occurrence, though inseparable from what comes to appearance in thinking, may be distinguished in its difference from what is appearing. I wish now, however, to highlight the dimension of re-membering that occurs with what appears in thought.[1] When I first became aware of thinking as I sat with friends in the student union, I was encountering statements by Plato on the nature of the forms. What I saw and found myself seeing was what I would now call a "complex metaphysical concept," and although I do not believe that what I saw was even approximately as subtle or as complex as Plato's notion, I am reasonably certain that in that event I underwent a way of thinking that attuned me to what textbooks (not entirely correctly in my opinion) call "Platonic idealism." Ideas in their separation from bodies, true entities, entities whose being is ordered by the Good, entities that provide in their immortality patterned criteria for existing, mortal things: these ideas appeared in their interconnections in my thinking, and I saw something that I had never seen before. I saw something that resonated with my Christian heritage far beyond what I could measure. I could not have said how that resonance took place, but I felt that something illuminating had happened, that *this* complex idea about eternal forms and their good order made sense, that they somehow took on temporality and a kind of flesh that existed in imagelike, shadowy ways that in spite of their imperfect approximations of their truth provided ways to see beyond time and flesh to higher life. A lineage, albeit one that came to presence obscurely, took place in my mentation, a history whose presentation depended far less on accuracy or conceptual clarity than on interpretation, resonance, feeling, and institutional transmissions of particular strands of Western culture. What appeared carried with it a lineage that opened to me in that small but eventful thinking aperture. And it opened in large part because I already belonged to it in a cultural awareness that was saturated with the influences and reformulations of Plato's heritage. A considerable segment of my culture was recalled in that event that I personally found so startling. I discovered something about my self-in-culture preparatory to a much more extensive understanding, and I experienced something like a homeland in this small ecstasy of personal-cultural memory.

I believe that the re-membering of Plato in Western culture has been so extensive, mutated, and multiply re-membered that I would not exaggerate by saying metaphorically that Dionysus rules the Western Platonic lineage. Plato's writings have been consumed and re-membered by schools, by Stoics and Epicureans, and Church Fathers, as well as by mystics, rationalists, translators, existentialists, idealists, analysts, politicians, laws, and moralities. These appropriations and refigurations are themselves multiply re-membered. Losses and recoveries form a seemingly infinite web of threads of memories, many of which blend with others in an entanglement of influences that bears witness to no weaver, no giver of design or management or command. The transmissions of Plato's influence show no basis for belief in the existence of the forms that he seemed to think were available for intellectual perception (nor do they show that the forms do not exist). This ungraspable memorial complexity was opened up on the verge of my first real encounter with Plato's writings. The complexity happened in the religion and morality that I had learned, in the creeds and prayers that I had heard and said in church and in the sermons and books and folk wisdom that drew from the knowledge, thought, and faith in the Christian traditions, as well as in the poetry, novels, and essays that I had studied. All of that and much more figured into my moment of philosophical ecstasy in which Plato came to me as a philosophical father. He was already there when I recognized him, and one of his places of dwelling was the I who recognized him—I am tempted to say that his place of dwelling was my I, but I did not and does not belong to me. It belongs in this instance to a body of memories that do not compose a subject and that are not mine to own.

I believe that just as a person who has encountered and come to know his own death cannot really speak out of that knowledge and be heard by another who has not also found an intimate knowledge of his own death, people cannot think similar thoughts without sharing similar cultural, institutional memories. The limits of shared memories define the limits of thoughtful understanding. Bodies of knowledge and method also enable people to communicate with other people who share in such knowledge and methods. People can communicate on the basis of similar experiences; and to think, and not just to consider or examine something in common, but to find disclosure happening by virtue of mentation— that seems also to require an enactment of common cultural memories. Thinking seems to enact memories that indwell language, practice, and institutions, the memories that determine, situate, and compose the appearance-in-thought, memories that help to provide the light that an appearance-in-thought brings with it and that makes it intelligible and understandable. Without a play of shared memories a thought would not appear to be possible much less shareable or encounterable.

I have also said in this book that memorial occurrences are recreations—even if they are composed of "stolen" memories (c.f., chapter 2)—of past occurrences, not re-presentations of something there and stable as a point of reference, but recreations in the sense that lost events are returned, turned in what we call "memory" from having happened to present happenings. In memories there is nothing there that we can return to other than eventful, re-membered remains—often mutated with other remains—of events. Rather than disseminating only disorder, however, memories create orders in their recreation (re-membering) of bygone times. The memorial dimension of thinking thus does not mean only an absence of light, but it also means the arising, the coming out of things *in* their uncovering and presentation—and 'uncovering' in this context is ambiguous insofar as the word suggests that something already established comes out from its cover. Things are uncovered in thinking as they happen in enactments of thought, as they come to stand, if only for a moment, as something happening in the virtual palpability of mentation. Such occurrences are appropriately described with metaphors of light: when I *finally* come to think something, for example—to "see" it—something that I have been struggling to find, such as a connection among several thoughts, or the meaning of something that I perceived, I can say that I am enlightened; or when something dim becomes clear and prominent I can say that it is brighter or more illumined. (Some people experience brighter and darker states of mind, times when the environment of their thinking is clear and radiant, and other times when appearances occur in a twilight or with shadows.)[2] In such a metaphorical sense, thinking can be an occurrence with degrees of light or an experience of the coming of light. Memories, even in their obscurity, can also be enlightening, and that is, I believe, a common experience for thinking—its Apollonian aspect, I could say, when darkness remains with the "strike" of light and the arrival of clarity. I shall return to this thought toward the end of this chapter.

I have given accounts of two different types of memory: the memories of bygone events and the self-presentation of memory, which I have called "memory's self-presentation." I introduced this book with an account of a personal memory from my childhood, an account that raised the questions of memorial transformations, bringing past events into present events, and the self-presentation of memory and memory's loss in memorial occurrences. This latter type of remembering—memory of memory, memory's self-presentation—is one in which the tempura and re-composing aspects of memory come to appear: past-in-presence, presence composed of presentation of "the past," bearings and trajectories for the upcoming, and, strangest of all as I see it, no presence accompanying presence in occurrences of re-membering.

I want to show that thinking appears to happen not only *in* the impact of memories-in-transformation but also with many of the same qualities and dimensions that characterize memory's self-presentation. Thoughts are determined (in part) by describable lineages of bygone events—by their impacts, the crevices they begin to cut, the fluid shapes they give to conscious acts—and by an eventfulness very much like that of memory. I do not want to say that thinking is identical with remembering, but I do find that as thinking happens memory happens, that in the occurrence of thinking memory comes to self-expression—memory in memory of itself. When a person is self-aware in thinking she can also be self-aware in memory's self-presentation. This coherence of remembering and thinking is a surprise to me. I had thought that remembering and thinking compose quite different and separate events. But they seem rather to be like each other and, at times, almost indistinguishably to interpenetrate each other. Thinking happens with memory's enactment. Or I can say that in thinking memory comes to the fore, is available self-presentationally in thinking for thoughtful perception. But the reverse does not seem to be the case: remembering does not necessarily mean that thinking is going on. I find no basis for saying that thinking occurs in the lives of institutions, for example, or in nonvoluntary personal memories, but these kinds of memories do seem to happen when thought happens and memory of memory—the self-enactment of memory—thus does appear to happen when thinking happens—and the lives of institutions and nonvoluntary personal memories do seem to come into play whenever thought occurs.

The metaphor of gifts of fire which arose in chapter 9 elaborated a kind of ecstasy in which some people find themselves in mystical and quasi-religious, if not thoroughly religious experience. Derrida turned such gifts toward the gift of death as he let the sacrifices of self, desire, commitments, and the pleasures of ordinary life rise to prominence in his descriptions of gifting. It is a dangerous gifting, we saw, one through which ashes, the detreus of fire, is obliquely figured. As I turn to an account of remembering in thinking I understand myself to turn to events of self-presentation in thought, and these events can be elaborated as a kind of gifting that, while appropriate to some ecstatic words—thinking happens with an ec-static dimension—is not appropriately characterized by the metaphor of fire. Thinking is not a mystical occurrence that would properly give rise to religious or quasi-religious responses. (Although what a person thinks may well give rise to religious states of mind or beliefs in mystical occurrences.) Thinking would appear to be mystical only in discourses that exclude thinking events from ordinary life. As I see it, thinking need not be set apart from ordinary life, although many ordinary lives are not determined by thought. Many lives also are not characterized by careful analysis, and in our history many ordinary lives were not characterized by reading and writing. But analysis, reading, and writing nonetheless may be aspects of everyday living. From the perspective of those lives, however, analytical knowledge or communication by writing or perception by reading can seem mysterious, or vaguely dangerous, just as perspectives that are unmodified by thinking can find thinking and its dimensions unordinary and mysterious and if not dangerous, at least uncalled for. Other people find that they lose touch with ordinary life when they think, that thinking makes them extraordinary. Possibly, people who think are in a numerical minority and in that context are extraordinary. And quite possibly what some people think so distracts them and preoccupies them that they become spacy and inattentive to many of the details in day-to-day living. It is surely the case that when I am thinking I am engaged in activity different from carrying out a routine activity such as driving a car or subtracting numbers. But thinking can also join such activities and by joining them modify them and affect their occurrences. Thinking in its difference from other events can nonetheless compose an everyday dimension of a person's life.

To the extent that 'fire' functions as a metaphor for mystical gifting and inspiration and hints at faceless consumption, it is inappropriate for thinking. And yet there are the Dionysian aspects in thinking that I have described. This is an aspect that does not require the sacrifices and excesses and disassociations that mark religious Dionysianism. The Dionysian dimension that I have in mind is one in which thinking occurs in excessiveness to its "stance;" that is, it is an ec-static dimension. But it does not need to happen with entities that call one to sacrifice himself for the sake of something that is "higher" and possesses incalculable worth. The ec-static dimension of thinking happens as the *occurring* of things that present themselves in thought and that are composed of a field of memories. 'Present themselves' means that in thinking, appearances happen that thought does not create (like a craftsman creates a new design for a pot) or produce (like a press produces the artifacts that we call "books"). In the context of thinking, things appear, become manifest, and as far as I can tell no agent fully produces them or gives them meaning for the first time. Things appear in thinking with meanings, and appearing, as we have seen, brings with it memories and memory's loss. So a person might speak of gifting when she describes thought, but the "gifts" are not of fire or of calls to sacrifice one's self for the sake of something inexplicable, shapeless, and beyond measure. Thinking comes in its own measure; it occurs in the measure of its own event. It does not call for sacrificial emulation or for unthinking union with something or for dissociation from one's body or for blind enmeshment in one's body. The dying that continuously goes on in thinking is ordinary for thought, and one of the most serious challenges is for thinking to become accustomed to "itself" in its uncertainty as finite appearances come to pass. The dying due to passages in thinking is neither a call for sacrifice nor a sacrifice. It is one aspect of thought as things arise and pass away in its occurrence. Thought is one way by which people can find themselves perceptively open with what is quite other to them. I have emphasized that such opening is multiply determined and without unified harmony or structural consistency. But things do appear in thinking and as thinking, and I will say that palpability and abstraction happen as thought occurs. And there is, of course, much that is thought is not. But it nonetheless composes an opening in the world and with the events in the world that is quite remarkable. The quality and intensity of wonder, for example, that can happen in thoughtful mentation, or experiences of desire, mourning, refusal, serenity, or love that can happen in it bear witness not only to thought's flesh but also to singular and special events of engagement with things. Thinking constitutes passages of exposure which encounter things and in which things can happen with vividness and unreplaceable energy. Appearances in thought can touch people in powerful ways, not primarily as gifts of fire, but like "gifts" nonetheless that an individual cannot produce or image.

I would like now to take a step back from these broad observations and consider first in a limited way what philosophers do preparatory to accounts of processes of thinking with occurrences of memories and memories' loss.

WHAT WE PHILOSOPHERS DO

At our best, as I see it, we philosophers in the Western, pre-Socratic and Socratic lineages speak from the developing edges of our knowledge and thought. Our speech and writing show a certain tentativeness on these edges, and not just because of the limits of what we know. Our thinking is different from reporting and establishing results. It is different from calculation, quantification, or discovery of evidence. I will say in more detail that it is also not sufficiently defined as theorizing, observing, interpreting, or analyzing, although all of these things may be involved in processes of thinking. The difference of thinking happens in processes of appearing in which the occurrences of Mnemosyne and Lethe are not lost but rather are found in a tentativeness that seems to inhere in thinking appearances. But I am getting ahead of myself.

Exploring, testing, appreciating failure as well as success, fearing the blind alley, weighing consequences, exhilarated by flights of imaginative vision, worried about relevance and responsibility, seldom possessed by originality, hitting the same limits again and again: philosophers may give new forms to what people know as well as create new knowledge and perspectives. We are to discriminate by thought, to see things with a clarity achieved by hard discipline and learning, to analyze and dismantle, to learn how to listen to differences outside of our conceptual comprehension, and to check both our values and our truths by differences that are present to us. We are also to produce knowledge, to give form and movement to ways of seeing, to redraft thoughts, to give attention to ignored things, to effect differences in speaking, writing, hearing, perception, affection, and value. I emphasize this exploratory and tentative side of philosophical thought because when we perceive by thought in a manner that recoils with awareness in and on its own process, we perceive processes that are always coming to pass, processes that can virtually follow their coming to be bygone. In this recoil, this self-awareness as things come to appear and disappear in thinking, we can be self-aware in the processes that make all finalities and completions uncertain. Finalities and completions appear with uncertainty as they come to pass. That is the situation that gives rise to continuing critique, exploration, substitution of values, and the reformulation of patterns of perception in our ordinary, thinking lives. It is also the situation that can motivate intense attention to the way thoughtful things appear, to the occurrence of appearing, and to a certain tentativeness that belongs to our lives.

Thought gives rise to further thought and language. I cannot overemphasize, in this context, this originary power in thought—although I pause to note the caution that language also gives rise to thought and were I thematizing language at this moment I would speak of *its* originary power. Thought's life finds part of its measure in the future to which it gives rise, in its youthfulness. As we find what appears and find as well the appearing of appearing, as we find language and concepts for criticism, as we develop styles of presentation and perception, we not only belong to traditions and languages, we can become in that belonging active members of processes that form tradition, add further determinations to language, and provide changed figurations of things and meanings. We can be, as thinkers, on the edge of things' coming to appear and arriving in thought. Learning how to recoil on such an edge with self-awareness and without losing touch with the shapeless emergence of shaping things is part of the artistry of thought. This recoil on the edge can constitute, I believe, a kind of awareness that occurs as disciplined exploration, as an uncertain freedom in intersections of odd or unfitting things with our certainties, ideologies, and literalized truths. This recoil that is on the edge of the thinkable and that brings with itself its own precipitousness is also a space of responsibility to an unrealized future and to what is beyond thought's preview, a responsibility that we shall see is not necessarily alien to Dionysus' event. This edgy responsibility probably has less to do with our ethnic values, our shared "universals," or our subjective integrity than with alertness before differences, interruptions of clarity of intellect, intersections of familiar patterns and tendencies with what seems to be some other world, preservation of thoughtfulness, and appreciation for the passing of everything that appears. It is a responsibility to the arising of language and thought, to the loss of what has been, to all that plays in the metaphors of darkness, as well as of light, and to the coming passage of whatever is taking shape in thought and language.

As philosophers we can thus be engaged in the transformation of language and thought, and we can be responsible to the originary aspects in the occurrences of thought. I could say prosaically that we are responsible to both the falling apart of things as they appear and to the future shape of what is thought and said, or I could speak dramatically and say that we are responsible to the edge of our world's appearance. However we phrase it to ourselves, I suspect that by thinking we are in a space of answerability to the processes of transmission and transformation in which thinking and speaking take place.

One way to transform appearing things is to preserve them in reasonably stable movements of presentation, metaphors for which are a museum, a contract, a methodology, or a canon. We might display things in order to encourage assenting attention to them, repetition of them, or insistence on their imitation. We can also preserve things by listening to their echoes, taking account of them as they transform into memories, as we move away from them, or as we carry their remains in emotions such as admiration, identification, fear, or hatred. And we can love what has been, hold past things dear in our conceptual narratives, the values by which we connect things, images, and ways of doing things. But however we preserve things, we engulf them in a new and changing life that marks and constitutes *their* loss in *our* retention of them.

Another way to transform things is to use them "toward their loss." I employ the word *use* to indicate both a danger and an opportunity. I do not want to name, in this instance of responsibility to the transformation of things, our use of things in order to accomplish our purposes or satisfactions. That is one way to use things, and it can be an entirely legitimate kind of activity with things. I have in mind, rather, attention to things as they come to remain after their time—to memories—after they have come through their vitality, their ability to make difference. Memorial appearances, I have said, can be more or less vivid, more or less defined by the movement and control of other memorial appearances and forces. An appearance, for example, that interrupts a normal organization or flow of things can have unusual vividness and vitality. So also can a meaning or value or person who provides organizational presence and force for other things. All appearances, I suspect, have some degree of force of presence. They occur on their own in the networks of things to which they belong. Their occurrences, in their movement, are more or less vivid, more or less forceful, more or less vital, more or less—*appearential* we might say, as they come forth as self-enactments.

As events of thought, like memories, become enmeshed in other events and experiences and pass away and beyond *their* ability to make a difference, they come to belong to memories, new figurations of vitality, and appearances that take them up, as it were, into other forces that transform bygone events into other images, narratives, or constellations of values. Thinking can be responsible to its nonpreserving aspect, to this transformativeness in its life, *as* it gives new life to appearances in transformations of past and present events—in justice to their transformation we might say. In this emphasis, thought can appear as a vital factor in the manner in which the transformation of appearances gives emerging shape and presence to an upcoming time. One of our originary possibilities as philosophers becomes effective as we engage affirmatively in such transformations, as we think things anew, as we learn how to recognize, evaluate, read, and speak transformatively. Our activity as thinkers can happen in the transformations of what appears in thought and language. Thought and language compose our element. Hence our kinship with artists who also find their activity in transformation through presentation and who give new life to appearances that are passing away—and hence thought's Dionysian, re-membering dimension.

We philosophers are often uncertain regarding what we do. We wonder if we are relevant enough. Is teaching philosophy our only or our primary "real" work? Would we be policy makers and trusted advisors to those who make policy and who form and change society if we did what we really should do? We often feel guilty if our work does not effectively address terrible problems such as hunger, overpopulation, war, and social injustice. We at times think that as philosophers we should write for popular, intellectual publications such as the *New York Review of Books* or *Harper's Magazine*. We often define the domain of philosophy as a space of presumed universality and expect ourselves as philosophers to be effectively engaged, in the light of universal values, in transforming bureaucracies, laws, and the management of politics on local and international levels.

Perhaps these are instances of bad conscience and of what Nietzsche might call "resentment." We as philosophers can turn the *life* of transform-

ing thought and language against itself, and by that turning we can produce states of mind that deny their own living moment and refuse to carry
out the performative work that constitutes them. I note that the limits of
philosophy are severe, that its possibilities for life take place in restrictions
that are demanding and far from encompassing all the issues and activities
that move us. Our opportunity as citizens is found in many forms of
responsibility to our communities, but those are often not the same kinds
of responsibility as that of thought. Our opportunity as philosophers is to
think, and the life of thought happens in response to the originary transformations and transfigurations of appearances and thoughts.

I could pause to dwell on the importance of such activity, on its relevance, if you will, for the quiet and usually undramatic formation of cultures and civilizations. I could describe the power of such activity by
reconsiderations of its apparent lack of political and social power, the
extremity of its fragility, and its endurance through—its being in—
processes of transmission, transformation, and self-overcoming. But I shall
make at this point only the claim that thought occurs as a self-enacting,
self-aware event of appearances and develop this claim by consideration of
two strategies of thought. I want to show that our engagement in thought
belongs in part to Dionysus and that it might happen as an originary activity that is properly outside of the jurisdiction of applied ethics, applied
politics, other kinds of immediate relevance. In this manner, I want to situate a discussion of thinking in its memorial dimension.

STRATEGIES FOR THINKING (WITH ATTENTION TO ITS DRAWING POWERS)

Thinking can be abstract in many ways. In its occurrence it can draw away
from things, separate from them, divide things into their parts, bestow
generality upon them, derive formulations from them, transform them
into lists and associations, into images and words. Thinking can have the
violence of dragging things into views that counteract their own happening and ways of inhabiting their worlds. It also draws things toward futures
that are not their own, projects them, and gives them feelings, moods, and
mental life that they have not known. Thoughtful abstractions can occur
in definitions, mental organizations, poetic constructions, or evaluative
hierarchies.

Thinking, however, is not only abstract in those senses. In its
abstractness it is an occurrence of appearance and construction.

Thinking's draw of things not only can divert them from *their* occurrences; thinking also conducts them by its own continuing occurrences into lively associations and plays of force and meaning. Thinking is movement that constitutes recognition, intelligence, and other kinds of order. Thinking brings about feelings, senses, and orientations. It brings about increase and decrease of energy and plays of influence that are usually beyond our objective perception.

The self-enactment of thinking, in fact, seems never to be abstract. It happens as the coming and passing of appearances, the coming and passing of ways of life; it is like a process of loss and regeneration of presence. Thinking seems to bear itself out from itself, to bear itself beyond itself in its own loss and regeneration. It seems to attract itself, to draw itself, to give itself its own draft, to live out of its own history, to exceed the agency that it also enacts. Thinking seems to be temporally extensive and not confined to a present moment.

As an occurrence of abstract construction, thinking appears to be presentative. It presents both things and itself. Its abstractness is thus multiply relational. It is not at all like a fully constituted, already present substance that expresses itself in various repetitions of a preestablished, closed region of laws or rules. Rather, these laws and rules are themselves relational. Thinking appears to find its laws and rules—its prescriptions—out of its own organizations, and its own organizations seem to be plays of appearing things in processes of collision, counterflow, translation, mingling, and transgression. The orders themselves and thinking's own self-enactment seem to be subject to the forceful transpositions of things as they come to appear. Appearing (itself) appears to be subject to self-transformation under the impact of the manners in which things come to appear. Appearing (itself) comes to appear differently in different periods of thought, to withdraw from its formulated and established draw of things, to slip the hold of its own formulations. The rules and necessities for a given way of thinking are subject to transition, loss, and reconstitution. Thinking as presentative seems to live in such transformations. As thinkers we undergo both the formation and deformation of the regularities by which we identify and relate with things. As relational, thinking is drawn by its own transformations in its activity of forming a world of appearances. The nonabstract creative happening of thought occurs in its relational, abstract activity.

I understand myself, by these words, to be thinking about thought. So far I have engaged in an abstract process that attempts to develop words and conceptual relations which direct our attention to the plays of relational forces that constitute thought. I have also given emphasis to the self-enactment of these plays of forces in an effort to begin to create the possibility of recognizing thought as neither primarily the activity of an agent nor primarily an object of agency but as a self-enactment that requires a sharp modification of subject-object-dominated manners of expression and conceptualization—that is, a sharp modification of an image of thought as primarily re-presentational. But by that very process I have also given emphasis to my own agency and to thought as an object of my attention. I have thereby embodied in these thoughts conflicts and contradictions: I have intensified my own agency in thinking about thought while I have thought that language controlled by agency and its objectifications is seriously misleading with respect to thought. I have thus given appearance to thinking in a construction that seems to occur within a dualism of subjective activity and objective reception of that activity at the same time that I have presented thought as outside of that dualism. As thought appears as a focus in my thinking, the other ideas that I have evoked, their problematic, their movements, and now their conflicts in my world of thought arise from lineages that operate far beyond my range of control and construction. But they also arise from elements that are particular to me and perhaps to a limited number of other people—and even in these qualifying observations I embody the abstraction and construction that I underscored a moment ago. In my ability to think as I have in the opening paragraphs of this chapter, I embody contemporary, historical issues such as subjectivity's questionable ability to provide the self-grounding that it seems to require, the loss of the signified's being in the connection of sign to sign, the question of thought's nonsubjectivity, the historical, temporal essence of thinking, the question of being as a motivation for Western thought, a suspicion of metaphysics, and the question of force in the appearance of things. In *this* thinking I know that I find myself in movements of thought over which I exercise at most only limited control, and I know that the control that I exercise is itself, in its formation and process, moved and constituted by events, influences, and values that are far beyond my control. My *ability* to recognize, modify, and direct is itself subject to uncontrollable elements and movements.

This thinking occurrence is complex and multiply differentiated. Both the appearances in my thinking and the event of my thinking now in *these* thoughts occur with the differences that constitute the appearances that I think; that is, differences constitutive of the appearances also constitute the thought about which I am thinking and which I am doing. Thought also appears in my thinking as an individual activity and as an occurrence of formations and processes that far exceed my individual activity. It happens as both abstract and not abstract. I am doing something that I call "thinking" and in that doing, considerably more than I takes place. Thinking appears *as something* as it enacts the occurrence of its own appearing. Occurring as subject and object and as the nonsubjective, nonobjective event of subject and object, as individually and historically determined, thinking is thus multiply differentiated, multiply drawn in its moments. It is multiply drawn in the sense that it is internally and variously differentiated and in the sense that as thinking moves, these differences of appearances as well as the differences among appearances provide drafts for thinking—directions and forms of movement that make claims on thinking in its occurrence, draw it in various trajectories of possibilities, and give it multiple forces for development and transformation. We think in differences that come with intermixing attractions and inspirations, foci of accumulation and gathering, forces of dispensation, possibilities for delineation, and regions of restraint, silence, and insight. Thought in its abstraction *appears to happen* in movements that come to go in intermixing forces which impact, attract, repel, and exceed one another.

How, then, are we to think about thought, about mentation in its thoughtful awareness with an accompanying lack of awareness, complex construction, differentiating and often conflicting forces of value, self-enactment, and determinations of knowledge? I have so far placed considerable emphasis on *appearing*. I have followed a broadly phenomenological direction by beginning a descriptive process in which thought is found in thinking appearances, and my approach so far, as it made thought its own appearing event for attention, has had a decidedly nonhistorical manner of presentation. I have been aware, as I thought and wrote, of the influences of many of our canonized philosophical figures, particularly of Plato, Descartes, Leibnitz, Kant, Fichte, Schleiermacher, Schelling, Hegel, Nietzsche, and certainly of several others in the twentieth century. But these influences are determined personally by my specific readings and interpretations. Under these same influences you might think quite differently from the way I think. In this attention to appearing I have not directly established anything about the specific, historical determinations of language, thought, and capacity that operate in and beyond my own mentation. I have drawn thought to a distinct abstractness by assertion, conceptual play, and philosophical formulation. I have made claims that depend for their clarity on your knowledge of the resources and values from which I draw. I have suggested, abstractly, that the self-enactment of thought is not abstract and constitutes its being, that its self-enactment is made up of differences which are not compatible or consistent with the ordinary rules of agreement and distinct clarity, and I have maintained that the histories of thoughts' differences are enacted as we think. In this process I have wanted to draw your attention to the nonabstract occurrence of thought as it abstracts what is there to think. How might I intensify this nonabstract occurrence of thought as I think about it?

TWO STRATEGIES FOR THINKING

In addressing this question I turn to two strategies for thinking to which I have already referred in various contexts, while continuing the emphasis that I have placed on memory. I wish to find a course outside of that historicism which contends that what we think and how we think can be adequately understood by reference to the influences that form us. I also want to avoid a notion of agency that contends that thought is an enactment of a kind of transcendent reality that gives universality and necessity to contingent influences. One strategy for conducting this course of thinking and one that is attuned to memory is genealogy.

If, on the one hand, genealogy is carried out in a historicist manner, one gives an account of the formation of historical influences which form cultural species or families whose characteristics are sufficiently defined by the determinations that produced them. This would be an external genealogy insofar as it relies on a largely efficient causal understanding of events' formations and on a linear conception of objective and subjective time. It reduces a thought to the totality of influences that define that thought.

If, on the other hand, we find in a genealogical approach a way to describe the memorial formations in knowledges and practices, and if our descriptions put in question not only the priority of efficient causation for knowledge but also the priority of a linear experience of time, we will have a strategy that is quite different from a historicist strategy. In this approach the knowledges and appearances that determine our approach are systematically put in question. Such a genealogy requires an overturning, a process of transformation *in* the work *by* the language and thought of the work. The possibility emerges that differences and otherness may well come to appear that are not in our present mentation known or perceived, that our mentation may so transform that appearances and our knowledge of them will be unimaginable to us now, indeed that mentation may so turn through and beyond itself that our problematic of appearance and time could become at best a distant memory—like human being, presumably, would become to an *Übermensch* (in Nietzsche's account). The emphasis falls now on the draw of possibilities in memorial occurrences, rather than on the stability and presence of reality, and on an emergence of appearances that is not defined by efficient causation, a totality of influences, or a process of self-realization on the part of a transcending agency.

I observed in chapters 6 and 7 that genealogical thought can trace both what appears in thinking and the very force and meaning of appearing by finding the lineages of various appearances, that is, by doing genealogical studies of orders of recognition and value, by showing how lives in their organizations give expression to past occurrences by means of transforming them, by showing the forces of grammars, conceptual connections, and groups of images *in* such forms as those of truth, virtue, law, and beauty. The historicism of our recent past is turned from a relativist idealogy to an understanding of transformations and self-overcoming that is performed within specific groups and processes as well as within the genealogical thought that describes these groups and processes. The self-enactment of thinking—its performative occurrence, which I have said is a movement of self-overcoming—is no more adequately describable by the productions of its influences than present memories are. It is also characterized by the *occurrences* of differences—by occurrences of differentiation —which are enacted in economies of relation and power and are not reduceable to any set of determinations. The *occurrences* of differences are not specific beings. They are not quite what we mean by "presences." They are marked by loss and absence in ways that, as I have often noted, we struggle in our dominant languages and concepts to know, name, and describe. Such occurrences seem to include something like an economy of mortality, a timing of absences that do not function like efficient causes, that are not instated, specific possibilities, and that seem to evaporate in their designation. The occurrences of differences seem to draw presences out of their apparent stability, to allow for all manner of mutations, and to give a motility that is different from action that is enforced by an agency. Differences in their occurrences are not like influences, and their freedom and decisiveness are not like the freedom and decisiveness of choosing. Yet they are weirdly forceful in enactments of thought.

In its differentiations thought appears to occur in processes of self-overcoming, processes that occur in mutational transformations by virtue of the losses and differences that are invested in and among the seemingly stable formations.

If, in a second strategic move, we come to know differential occurrences of mind in reference to their self-enactment and in the context of memory and genealogy, we come to this descriptive claim: the differential self-enactments of knowing and thinking are composed of multiple, countervailing differences with multiple and mutating drawing powers. Attention to their self-enactments, given their complex and unharmonious compositions, makes impossible our giving priority to efficient causation or unity and simple identity for appearances or for the occurrences of thinking and knowing (assumptions that often operate in historicists' work). These are events without simple or substantial unity. Rather, dominant forces will provide rule and identity while also carrying and undergoing within their gathering power other forces, resistances, and differences of draw. This description of self-enactment draws out the differential determinations in what we might call the "being of thought and knowledge" and de-emphasizes the role that is often assigned to efficient causation or simple identity in interpretations of historical events. In this process, appearing comes to appear quite differently from its descriptions in the thought of, for example, Kant, Dilthey, or Husserl.

Two examples of genealogical thought in which neither efficient causation nor simple identity is dominant and in which appearing is experienced, in its complexity, without encompassing or transcendental unity: First Foucault, in his *History of Sexuality*, as well as in most of his other studies, gives priority to mutation, juxtaposition, and variant, locally ordered processes of exchange in the formation of Western sexual agency. Rudimentary practices of good health in the third and second centuries B.C.E., for example, mixed with perceptions regarding desire and other perceptions regarding truth. This "mixing" is extravagant in the sense that methods to maintain cleanliness and procedures for preparing to approach what is true intermingled without overarching rules of governance and character. Disciplines of diet and a broad cultural preoccupation with desire and its dangers intermixed to form bits and pieces of insight and self-relation, such as strategies for self-inspection or of timing for physical gratification. Images for these formations, which themselves provide a context for further transformations toward dominant types of subjectivity, could be ones of cloud transformations as one nebula infuses with another to give different shapes and forces of direction, or of a social context being shifted definitively by radical changes in weather or food supply.

Something like efficient causation is involved, but the changes of form and definition as well as of forces and relations are also due to something like loss and "difference" that allow random couplings, extermination and loss of experiential elements, replacement of dominant factors by new or submitted ones. In a word, the changes of form and definition are differentiations due to all manner of re-memberings; losses of relations; fading of power structures in relations, addition, subtraction, and substitution of constitutive elements, the emergence of vacuums where there were connections; and linkages that are new to an organism. The forms of subjection the development of which Foucault describes in the *History of Sexuality* came about as ordinary feelings, practices, and knowledges of the day were connected with changing approaches to health, stability, and new social problems. Foucault finds these changes in something like space without a nature or determination, space that occurs rather much like the differing of difference that Derrida invokes through the middle voice with the self-displacing name of *différance.* The genealogical knowledge and thought produced by Foucault are organized by a thought of noncausal nonagency that I have labeled "self-enactment," one that is metaphorized by 'space,' and one that requires a destabilization of its own appearance (due to its own compositional complexity and vulnerability to organizational transformations).

Foucault's own knowledge is thus not immune to the regional genealogies and spaciality that he describes in his disciplined manner of retrieving events and knowledge in past times. The order of his knowledge, by his own account, is as impacted by the transformations of nondetermination and memorial influences as any other orders are. Foucault's knowledge of the lineage itself constitutes a transformation *within* the forces of that lineage, and at its best, on its own terms, this knowledge gives expression to shifts within the lineage thanks not only to problems that the lineage engenders for itself but also to a differencing and unconnectable aspect, an absence of foundation or transcendental agency, a Lethic dimension that runs through the connections of his thought and that is enacted in the process of his thinking. The importance of history and lineage to an important degree grows out of the historicism that his genealogy transforms. It also grows out of the value of freedom in Western experience and the violations of freedom that the social institutions commit. Social institutions often promote individual freedom, within the partial, continuing influence of monarchial sovereignty. This genealogical knowledge itself arises out of the random functions of many different truths in its lineage and out of movements within established cultural stabilities toward the formation of other and previously foreign regimes of cultural stabilization. It occurs with attention to an "element" without formation or movement, an element (I am not sure what to call "it") that is not any kind of substance—a nonelement of mere difference, we might say. This is a knowledge of difference that, in its inclusion of conflicting differences, produces experiences of identity and unity. The enactment of genealogical knowledge as *a* kind of knowledge, as *an* identity of method and discipline, says to itself, in effect, I too compose a regime of truth that is held together by connections that came together in a metamorphosis of things that eventuated in a passing system of transfers. Its own stabilizing enactment forecasts for itself its destabilization, its danger by virtue of new problems that it engenders, its unsovereignty in its time and space. The determinations that place it and enforce it are known to carry lawlessness as part of their law. This extravagant quality of carrying excess to its own identity within its identity is included in the self-awareness of this genealogical thought.

In light of this description of genealogical knowledge, which composes a method (or an art) of remembering, I find an approach to thinking with regard to past events that is appropriate to memorial enactments as I have described them. This orientation also composes one way to think with regard to cultural and thus mentational orders, a way that gives appearance to what is thought always in a context of self-enacting and usually unnoticed memories. We think within lineages of practice and institutions as well as within ways of ordering what people know are definitive in a given place and period of time. The 'within' means that our thought is as extensive as the complex and conflicted occurrences of memories, that the enactments of thought are the enactments of a culture and its lineages of events and their transformations within a Lethic dimension of nondetermination.

Consider now another and quite different approach to thought and memory. I gave an account in chapter 2 of Heidegger's reading of Heraclitus' Fragment B16. By retrieving—one kind of genealogy—the middle-voice functions in the Greek verbs, he found that he could speak of the occurrence of concealing's happening in events of appearing. Nonappearing happens with appearing, and I connected nonappearing with the radical forgetfulness that is figured by Lethe. I do not want to suggest that *something* quite absent comes to light by the phrase *concealing happens in events of appearing*. Rather, I want to underscore the importance of remembering that forgetting is included in remembering and that withdrawal of appearing happens with appearing.

In this retrieval of the middle voice I found a retrieval of an experience of concealing and forgetting, the loss of which figures powerfully in Western thought and in the performance of that thought: the self-enactment of Western thought has often concealed its own concealment as it brings things to presence in thinking. In our present context I emphasize that in Heidegger's thinking the highly nuanced senses of loss and concealment, of withdrawal of presence in the coming to presence of things in thinking, effects a radical destabilization of its own leading and stabilizing ideas and values. His thinking enacts an ungrounding of its own grounds, and this "philosophical accomplishment" comes about by means of a kind of remembering that is alert to its own event, as well as by means of a retrieval of aspects of experience and knowledge that both characterize and are concealed in his own lineage. With this emphasis one can see that differenciation appears in the self-enactment of unpresence and that such a self-enactment occurs in the thought that retrieves it. Mnemosyne's Titanic figuration thus returns to us in this observation. Heidegger's retrieval of an aspect of the Western, Greek lineage is one that is aware, in its own event, of appearing *and* concealing as well as aware that concealing occurs in many traditional thoughts and that Heraclitus recognized concealment's self-enactment in events of appearing. The awkwardness for our primary structures of recognition appears as he re-members Heraclitus' way of keeping in mind the Lethic dimension of what comes to appear.

This kind of work also leads to questions about the sense and idea of transcendence that have exercised such a silent force in Western culture. Instead of the value of unity for an understanding of experiential and epistemological diversity, we find in Heidegger's thought (as well as in that of Foucault) the values of difference, loss, and concealment and the fluid lines of passing differenciations in seemingly fixed identities. Both thought and other experiences are drawn out in fields or regimes of prevailing and countervailing memorial trajectories. The occurrence of thought, rather than a determination by something that transcends determinations, is a play of self-enacting determinations—self-enactments of appearances—that shows no transcendent identity or initiating source of order and value as they re-member both what has occurred and the occurrence of appearing/concealing. Thought is drawn—lined, as it were—by boundaries of differences among appearances and by the difference of appearing and withdrawal of appearing as things present themselves in thinking. I pointed out in chapter 9 that *in* such boundaries nothing but indetermination and differenciation take place. In this reference, were we to speak of transcendence, we would speak with regard to the occurrences of memorial fields and differential boundaries that mark the organizations of identifiable and intelligible things. Such fields and boundaries and the losses that accompany them seem to give differences. They are originary without transcendent identity or nature, as we saw in chapters 6 and 8. Others come of differenciations, not of unifying agency. The "as" structure of appearances—things appearing as singular things—includes the boundaries of things, the hermetic space where singularities leave off, trickle down, or otherwise cease to be as they are. Here, in the boundaries among appearances in thought, is "where" we *might* speak of transcendence, except there is neither unity nor sacrality nor presence nor gifts of fire: nothing happens that we ordinarily associate with identifiable transcendence in the boundaries among appearing things. The self-enactment of boundaries—their happening—is like a happening of differenciation with all the strangeness that our tradition associates with the ending of identity—an association that can quickly become mysterious when it is affiliated, perhaps anxiously, with death, sacrality, sacrifice, an irretrievably lost past, or an indeterminate future.

Such genealogical thought thus gives accounts not only of what appears but also of its own appearing and of the happening of appearing (itself). In this instance we have addressed a genealogy of differenciation that calls for a study of differenciations in the occurrences of appearing.

The self-enactment of difference and boundaries in remembered events, I am suggesting, calls into question many prevailing senses of transcendence, particularly when such senses are expressed by the idea of transcendental subjectivity as a condition for the possibility of thought. In the genealogical approach that I am describing, such senses of transcendence—senses that determine the way things appear—weaken, and lose the force. Exploratory vocabularies and conceptualities form that do not suggest the meanings of transcendence that have characterized our major traditions: such meanings as otherness with a radically different identity from that of its contingent appearance, transtemporal being, sacrality, and unconditioned being. Difference, not a determinate transcendence, emerges with organizing and perceptive force in thought concerning appearances. In this emergence we find alertness to a kind of self-enactment that shows a Dionysian, ambiguous occurrence of determination and indetermination in processes of appearing. I shall return to consider this alertness when I address thinking in its remembering and forgetting dimension. Heraclitus, of course, was no friend of Dionysian practices, but his remembrance of concealing and his thought of forgetfulness—in Heidegger's reading of him—nonetheless bring him into Dionysus' realm in a manner that allows us to give place to the remarkable event of thought in its remembering with forgetting, an event that does honor to the appearance of Dionysus by virtue of which nothing is quite like it presents itself to be. Heidegger's genealogy in this instance helps us to hear Dionysus as well as Lethe in the orders of appearance by which we know the limits of disclosure and of the endurance of identity. Something different from transcendence seems to transpire in the *ek-stasis* of Dionysus' presence. I have figured that difference by an interpretation of memory's loss, that is, by an account that valorizes indetermination in accompaniment with memorial occurrences, and we now find this dimension of memory and memory's loss to characterize thought.

Genealogy thus may be taken as one strategy for thinking that finds its measure of concreteness in the lineages of mutation and forgetfulness that form appearances. It also finds its measure of concreteness in the memorial dimension of thought which enacts boundaries that, although they are without identity, nonetheless define identities. This dimension of thought enacts differences that are ungoverned by a unifying power of subjective transcendence. Such a strategy appears to give an opening for thought outside of the restrictive values that are often given to traditional ideas of intentionality, representational knowledge, and transcendental identity as bases for all orders. Stated in other words, this kind of genealogy finds its determination in the occurrences of complex lineages that are remembered in accounts that people give of them. These accounts compose occurrences of thought in which its lineages, often in bits and pieces, come to thoughtful and transformed appearance.

I turn now to a second strategy for thinking, which I shall call "reading." As I describe this strategy I will also address a question that has persisted in the background of this chapter: Does thought transcend its own appearance?

As I indicated in chapter 4, I use the term *reading* to suggest an alternative to *interpreting*, not because interpretation is eliminated in reading, but because more than interpreting takes place in reading. Reading is one among many means of transmission, and one in which thinking can take place in direct engagement with a text that serves as an occasion of transmission.

Consider Heidegger's account of *Auseinandersetzung*.[3] His use of this word has special significance in his lectures on Nietzsche in which Nietzsche appears as an opponent in a struggle over what is most essential for thought. He wishes to confront Nietzsche's thought in its difference, its strength, and its own self-determination, that is, in its questions and convictions, its own gathering *logos* and moving force. I wish to emphasize that for Heidegger this confrontation—this *Auseinandersetzung*—is the site in which the thinking of Nietzsche, the thinking of Heidegger, and their interaction take place. I want to show that is a site of re-memberance which has a dimension of self-enactment that is outside of any constituting agency.

Heidegger is looking not so much for a debate with Nietzsche as for an engagement in which thinking takes place *between* them, an engagement of thought in which their differences of thought appear. Such an engagement does not culminate in agreements, conclusions, or comparisons. It constitutes a process, a performative exchange, in which the reader must also engage if he or she is to "understand" what is happening. In this engagement, I can say descriptively, a connecting distance occurs; one stands over against the other; a decisive difference is achieved as the thoughts of the two thinkers come into contact by means of Heidegger's thinking. It is a clash of thoughtful moving forces, a *Streit*, Heidegger says, a thoughtful confrontation of minds at odds with one another in their separate enactments, a confrontation that is also an occurrence of re-membering. The strange phenomenon that I shall point out is that not only does Heidegger re-member Nietzsche's thought, but Heidegger's thought is also re-membered in the engagement.

In addition to its conflictual dimension, I note a certain irreconcilable divisiveness in Heidegger's imagery. The word *Auseinandersetzung*, according to Grimm, draws "together in one word what remains separate in living speech while at the same time inverting the natural order of the words, that is, putting the preposition *Aus* in *ein aus dem andern* ahead of the other words."[4] "A most ponderous compound," Grimm says. *Auseinandersetzung* suggests setting things apart from one another, and in Heidegger's usage it also suggests a setting apart that occurs *in* thoughtful confrontation. It does not suggest a fusion of meanings or something on the order of an exchange of ideas. Heidegger's thinking confronts Nietzsche's thinking in a radicality of difference that for Heidegger gives renewed thought and enacts a departure from what he identifies as Nietzsche's nihilism. The setting apart and particularization that characterize *Auseinandersetzung* do not work toward a resolution but toward a preservation of difference and opposition—an en-countering—in thought.

This engagement of difference also preserves a thoughtful exchange: in its self-enactment, the *Auseinandersetzung* maintains a separation that composes the engagement of thought. It thus has the force of connection, gathering, and binding together and suggests, like the word *de-cision*, both division and relation. In *Auseinandersetzung* separate thoughts and ways of thinking belong together in their opposition and difference. *Auseinandersetzung* is decisive for thought. It provides a *logos* for thought and gathers or binds together in differences what ordinarily remains separate, and in that process it gives rise to nonvoluntary connections that alter both ways of thinking.

On Heidegger's terms this means that thinking happens in *Auseinandersetzung*'s occurrence. This thinking appears in the strife of the differences and not solely by virtue of Heidegger's effort. Differences come to belong together in departure and strife. The one belongs to the other in an appropriating event of differential engagement. In this conflict of thought, the gathering determinations of different ways of thinking are joined. Thinking comes to pass like a hinge of moving, incompatable elements. A *wesentliche* event happens, an event that becomes definitive for the thinking encounter (and in that sense is essential) as it comes to pass. In the terms of this study, a reading occurs, and on these terms reading happens as recollective transformative thinking.

I have expanded Heidegger's use of *Auseinandersetzung* beyond his use of it primarily in his encounter with Nietzsche to apply to a way of reading, and for now I leave aside his showing that in *Auseinandersetzung* occurs a unique engagement with Nietzsche's own fulfillment of the leading question of Western thought—the question, what is being? Heidegger, in this *Auseinandersetzung*, turns Nietzsche's question, beyond what he found in Nietzsche's thinking, to the question of being's truth. I am directing our attention, rather, to what I consider to be characteristic of reading in the restrictive sense that I am taking the word: reading can be an encounter in which the difference of a person's thought is engaged and re-membered by a process that transforms it. This process itself composes a process of thinking that is distinct to the thought of the reader who engages the thought found through the read text. Such reading occurs as an engagement that preserves the differences of the thoughts—*draws* the differences—and finds its own future in the differenciation that happens in the reading. In this kind of occurrence a transformation takes place in which the engaged differences modify each other. It is a type of exchange that composes a mutation in which the engagement is "more" than the sum of the engaged ideas and concepts. All aspects of the encountering thoughts may undergo transformation: Heidegger's thought as well as Nietzsche's for example, is re-membered in such an event.

I note briefly the question of fidelity and appropriateness vis à vis the engaged other. Heidegger often uses the word *Zwiesprache* to name his engagement with another thinker. It emphasizes no less than *Auseinandersetzung* the irreducible particularity and otherness of the encountered thoughts. The *Zwiesprache* does not promise a dissolution of difference or a supersession of the differences into a higher order of univocity. But *Zwiesprache* does call our attention more specifically to a *dialogos* and to a less polemical exchange than an *Auseinandersetzung* does. *Zwiesprache* gives more emphasis to transformation by engaging and joining in an en-*counter* with the differences of another thinking.

The current situation of a *Zwiesprache* with Greek thought, Heidegger says, for example, takes place in widespread and largely unalert confusion in our talk of being.[5] This is a confusion that is inherent in Greek thought as well as in our scholarship and interpretation. It arises, Heidegger says, with an utter lapse (*Abgrunds*), that is, a Lethic dimension that characterizes our occurrence, one that characterizes the happening of being in our coming to pass away. We *are* in a kind of "confusion" in relation to the occurrence of being. In a *Zwiesprache* with Anaximander, Heidegger does not attempt to get into Anaximander's head or to transpose himself into Greek culture, and he pays maximal attention to the lapse that characterizes our connection to Anaximander. He finds in that lapse "something" that has to do with the fatal occurrence of life, and that means that Anaximander will be re-membered as he is engaged. He attempts, in respect to the particularity and difference of Anaximander's thought, to "heed this confusion" that is intrinsic to the lapse, and to turn to the confusion that happens in his own thinking in a way that allows him to recognize the limits of time that allow the confusion to arise. This is a process of naming the confusion from a distance provided in part by the lapse and in part by something other to the confusion, something heard by Heidegger in his reading of the language of Anaximander's fragment.

The particular other in Heidegger's engagement is Anaximander's language. As Heidegger works and reworks the fragment and relies as much on his own hearing of Greek as on the standard philological studies, as he confronts that language, finds his knowledge of it rebuffed, agonized, and set apart in *its* particularity, he pays attention to his confusion in the arising differences and separation between him and the language of the fragment, to the limitations of the disciplines that give him initial, scholarly access to the fragment, and to the language's own relentless recalcitrance before his thought. What he calls the unrelenting power (*zähe Gewalt*) of confusion, combined with a disclosive aspect over which the confusion cannot establish full sovereignty, give, in the *Zwiesprache*, a distance before the fragment's language that allows for recognition of the limits of what Heidegger and others have to say about it, as well as recognition of an impenetrable and unseeable dimension that accompanies it.

My emphasis falls on this provision of distance and difference. They constitute the *Zwiesprache*. This joining of differences, this drawing of differential lines and trajectories in the occurrence of *Zwiesprache*, gives a power of disclosure to the particular players in the encounter. It happens as differences in interactive connection with each other without resolution, without discussion that is dominated by an unquestioned, modern ideal of accuracy, and without an effort toward interpretive conquest as Heidegger engages Anaximander's language in interaction with his own thought. This engagement includes an alertness to the fateful transformations that occur in the transmission as well as attention to a dimension of forgetfulness that cannot be overcome.

In the engagement of *Zwiesprache*, Heidegger says, a situation might eventuate which gives rise to a different encounter (when compared to, say, interpretive or critical reading) in the very event of holding differences together. It might eventuate in a different experience of speaking and thinking. The confusion is not wiped out by a higher knowledge. Rather, the confusion "abides," is a definitive part of the encounter of the reading-thinking situation. As we turn to Anaximander's language in this way, we are turned by it, not as though we were silenced by it, but turned as we find ourselves confused before its bewildering impact. It gives us to experience our confusion in our encounter with it. If Heidegger sets the agenda in his reading and molds the text by *his* questions, he also modifies this dominance in two ways: he finds his obsession with the question of being and with the question of the truth of being to be *in* the transmission of Western thought, and he constructs his approach to thought within images (like those of *Holzwege* and country paths) that affirm the particularity, singularity, and momentary quality of his own work. The force of his agenda is qualified and put in question in part by its self-assessment and in part by the thinking and language that he encounters. His agenda, his assessment of his agenda from within the agenda, the transmissional setting of his thinking, and the self-presenting of the complex situation of his thought with the difference of "what" he encounters by his thinking and language all compose the *Zwiesprache*. And a *Zwiesprache* composes an event of thinking not only in Heidegger's encounter with Anaximander but also with Nietzsche and many other thinkers.

The singularity of such a "conversation" is found in its own event in which we find ourselves participant. *In* it our language and thought can undergo modification. Our directions and values regarding difference and identity can begin to change. Rather than "effecting a resolution" as the translators render "*zu einem Austrag bringen*," our confusion in the conversation with regard to being brings our mentation and the other thinking together and engenders a direction of language and thought both in the engagement and beyond the perspectives that compose it. In this event, "something" comes in the encounter that is not identical with our ideas, the other thinking, or the confusion. Something like a new beginning can come through the history of reading and thinking in Anaximander's wake. Such turning and modification are found in the shifts in Heidegger's thought, such as that after *Being and Time*, in the early 1930s, in his turn to the poets, and in the growing force of time as *Geschick* in his thought. These turnings arose, I believe, out of *Zwiesprache* which moved his ideas beyond their own meanings and directions—by mutations that Heidegger did not completely control, they (the *Zwiesprache*) changed the course of his mentation and composed sites of mutation and joining that he did not "do" but that nonetheless composed a thinking that gave things to appear differently in his engagements with them.

I break off here my reading of Heidegger on *Zwiesprache*. I stop before turning to his words on the destiny of being's disclosure. I hesitate before his thoughts on inevitability in language and thought, pausing without comment before his perception that "what is Greek is the dawn of that destiny in which being illuminates itself in beings and so propounds a certain essence of man: that essence unfolds historically as something fateful."[6] My hesitation constitutes a limiting caution as I think of a domination of the thought of inevitability in his work and thus a loss in his work of a full sense for the mutational movements of memory that continuously transform and refigure ideas of destiny as well as of the organizing thoughts that perceive destinies. In this context, I stop also before the phenomenological claim to presuppositionless thinking and its allergy to psychology and accidental mutation in the formation of the appearing of what appears, and hence, to my mind, its allergy to a dimension of the art of thinking with alertness in the transformations, institutional extensiveness, and personal histories that compose appearing. In the instance of these histories I find inadequate attention to memories, as distinct to inevitabilities, and to the determinant openings provided by memories as distinct to the idea of 'presuppositionless.' One of the arts of thinking happens by means of awareness in the mergers, mutations, and re-membrances in thinking, and a further art can come with thought that remembers its remembering as distinct to providing itself with an image of freedom from ontic determinations and from the inconstancy of basic questions and problems: an art that unties those knots of insistence that so often compose the obsessions of thought that are centered on an image of something unifying and unchanging and continuously, unceasingly repeated in all appearances.

For the art of thought is to give expression to the *particular* differenciations that both unsettle and settle the appearing of thought's presentations and to give expression to uncertainty and instability in the force of appearing as such. Thought may present the differences that take place in the happening of its references and significations and in the differences in the appearing of its particular values. Thought presents these differences in the emphases of its perceptions, in the fragments of its whole truths, and in its particular sense of destiny and inevitability. A small act of rebellion, attraction, stubbornness, commitment, habit, or laziness on the part of the one who thinks can quiet or kill or stimulate the fragile configurations in a *Zwiesprache.* The very thoughts of appearance, destiny, being, difference, and other are closer to an artistry of inherited and continuously differentiated differenciations than to stern and unchanging destiny. "The necessity of art" is itself a work of re-membering and mutation in the art of thinking—so other to the unthought is appearing in thinking, so irregular, so much drawn in its eventful moment by its own differential figurations in its remarkable, inestimable events of appearing. The art of thought arises in confrontation with accidents, temperaments, social changes, and in the ebb and flow of different memories. The art of thought comes with its presentation of itself as alert differenciation, as differential and self-aware perceptiveness.

There is nothing more alive (or less alive), more happening, more "there," more liable to death and extinction than thought. That is the difficulty: an event of thinking composes its own appearing event and is not identical with anything else in its alert, presentational differenciation. It is in its own event quite extended, quite given to accidents, bodies, mixtures, and confusions of all kinds. Thought is protean in its necessities, inconstant in its requirements, and seemingly always inclined to anchor itself in the certainty of whatever organizes it. Tribes, disciplines, religions, ideologies, obsessions, and absolutes all can belong to an appearance of thinking. So can grounds, gods, and natures. All of them—like these thoughts I now write—are real and abstract, concrete and fleeting, subject to the artistry of reasons and the powers of images, the limits of which we encounter in the impact of other artistic works. The grounds of thinking and appearing are themselves presentational images and thoughts with all their vivid force and ability to transpire. Presentations as such and gathering *logoi* belong to lineages which themselves are subject to fundamental alteration as they appear. The shared aspects that make possible *Auseinandersetzung* and *Zwiesprache* and that constitute their self-enacting inevitability belong to thought's instability, to its time of coming to pass, and to its appearing event.

I find in Heidegger's way of thinking an opening to think before unrecoverable differences, an opening to differentiate with him in encounters with thoughts whose singular happening neither he nor I can ever share. Heidegger's own difference does not happen like a simple identity with me and distinct to me, but like a complex sound that is at once comprehensible and not comprehended in its multiple determinations. Present in withdrawal, he says, in the withdrawal and obscurities, I might think again, not to re-*cover* and resolve something there, but to encounter what appears there, something that is also lost in its appearance, to encounter "it" in "its" loss amidst things that appear comprehensible and apparent. Reading can provide that experience. It can compose one kind of thinking that maximizes its losses as it finds presentations and its own moving, re-membering force in trajectories that begin again and again without completion or a definitive destiny.

These remarks suggest the possibility of a discipline of remembering to accompany thoughtful reading, of a genealogy of reading. Such a genealogy is composed, of course, of readings that find openings and multiple origins and occurrences of transformational repetitions, a way of reading that thinks in terms of its own re-membering of the lineages that give it form and motivation. Such work would be less interpretive, less given to commentary than to thinking further in the lineages that produce this value of reading. Such thought finds its vitality and future in its encounters and in the thinking that arises in the encounters. The values of wisdom and truth as well as of unity and rightness can undergo transposition as the values of differenciation, imagination, social and psychological change, possibility, and, probably, of friendship, appropriateness with loss, and *dia-logos* come into their own: Reading for a discovery of Truth decomposes into a reading that recognizes itself as re-membering *in* the encountered appearances of what comes to appear in reading.

THOUGHT AND ETHOS

The limits of thought are multiple and severe. These limits are found in the appearing of the things that appear in thinking, in their memorial eventuation. The appearing of what is thought not only provides limits to what can be thought, but it also provides multiple limits among the differences that compose the memorial legacy: the Hermes aspect of multiple borders I called it in chapter 2. Thought seems also to be limited by an absence of static transcendental grounding and by loss of presence in presencing (i.e, by abstracting, for example, as I said earlier). Thought is characterized, in its limitations, by degrees of intensity, vividness, and senses of vitality or weakness. It feels in its moments and duration, and it can turn on itself destructively, toward itself affirmatively, and out of itself by transformation: it has many agencies and receptors. Its *logoi* are like gathering processes that from time to time, in their engagements, enact imaginistic relations, rules for connecting things, patterns of associations, movements of attraction and revulsion, and feelings of dependency, aggression, and sublimity. These *logoi* themselves are constituted by other processes of memorial engagement. Thought, in its limits, is engaged with appearing things, and we live memorially in thinking as we do in our other physical enactments.

I would like now to focus on some aspects of thought's productive capacity, on its youthfulness in Nietzsche's phrase. It is composed of inclinations, and it produces inclinations. I have said that thought draws, that it gives perceptions, that it makes differences, that it gives emphasis, direction, significance, and meaning, while it is also constituted in these same elements. Thought lets things appear *as* what and how they are *in* concrete particularizing and re-membering events of abstraction. How and what we think are thus not incidental to how and what we value, and how and what we value are not incidental to how and what we think. When the appearances of things change either by thought or by other shifts in value— including the way in which appearance as such appears with evaluations—the experiential world changes.

If we act politically and change laws or governmental structures or practices regarding citizens, if we rethink certain memories and reconstitute them in certain ways, we contribute to the changing of thought. We set a new agenda, as we say, and bring to bear different forces of value in comparison to other practices and policies. These differences, for example, might give a different appearance to the insane, as we found Foucault showed in *Madness and Civilization*. Or they might change the appearances of meaning and gender, normalcy, illness, or criminality. If we act philosophically and follow, let us say, transformations in our lineage of the appearance of transcendental grounding for thinking and encounter them in such a way that in our thinking the transformation is intensified and a strong inclination toward such transformation develops, our thinking, in its engagement with this movement, may produce relations of thought and language for which the transformation of the appearance of transcendental grounding and its lineage become originary. In *this* thinking the values of presence, permanence, transcendence, order, time, and difference shift, become differently nuanced and altered in their trajectories of purpose, affirmation and refusal. We undergo such a process, and we can play active roles in it. In the multiplicity of our agencies and *logoi*, we will feel the threats, losses, and dangers that accompany the changes. (An individual can feel both the threat and the promise of particular changes, or one can feel deep anxiety over changes that he or she helps to inaugurate and carry forward: different aspects of our selves may respond differently to the same process.) Some appearances and manners of affiliation pass away *in the transitional thinking*. Ignored, submitted, or even scorned things can gain affirmative value. *In such thinking* we experience a life change. We are involved in the production, the engendering, the *phusis*, of a different way of life in comparison to those ways of life in other kinds of thought or in ways of thought to which we have come to feel at home.

Within the limits of thinking, in this life—call it, perhaps, the "life of mind?"—the lives of many things are involved—the life of the market place, for example, or the state house, or a monetary system, or perhaps of one's own family, certainly the transformed lives of many bygone events and the memories that the transformation in thought inchoately re-members. But even with such included differences, we can feel in our thinking abstracted or alienated from the very ways of life that also compose and carry impacts in moments of thought. We can feel this way because of the intensity of the thinking event which, although it is composed of many transmissions, is itself a different kind of occurrence when compared to those whose fragments and re-collections play parts in the thought. In thinking, appearances nonetheless happen which form and decompose values, and in which different manners of language arise, connections occur, perceptions change, some feelings gain and lose power. In the living activity of thinking much that is familiar can change and change enough to make what was familiar seem foreign in processes that waiver between feelings of lively engagement and estrangement.

In its productivity and self-enactment thinking composes and gives ethos and connection. Its evanescence and its susceptibility to transformation and transferral in its occurrence, combined with its ability to make decisions, differences, and guidelines; its apparent kinship with dreams, insubstantial flights of vision, error, dismemberment; its involvement with memories; its power to affect predictions, calculations, authorizations, and imperatives; its ability to fixate, pathologize, express itself, and reflect itself in its activity, its narrative and poetic capacity: such experiences of thinking belong to us and we to them. We are of thought. To give ourselves "professionally" to thinking, with the severity of its limits and its self-enacting distance from nonthinking events, may well appear to be a strange commitment when other things appear in their lives so solid, sensuously concrete, and fixed by the destinies that come from events other than events of thinking. But thinking appears nonetheless to be thoroughly political and laden with value in its difference from the unthought and to be the site of origins and departures that are as concrete as any that we can experience. It incites our lives and gives us to be the least stable, the most dangerous, the most inventive, the most destructive, and the least reliable creatures on earth. In that, I suspect, arises the responsibility of thinkers. And from that we can assume that the appearance of our responsibilities constitutes some of our liveliest and most inventive, most destructive, most memorable, and most dangerous thoughts.

OBSERVING IN A SUBJUNCTIVE MOOD

Throughout this chapter (as well as throughout the book) I have faced an ambiguity between memory (as such) and memories as well as between thoughts and thinking (as such). I have not wanted to say that there is a universal "thing," memory, and its specific enactments, rememberings. And yet crucial for this study is the claim that when memory happens, loss of memory also happens. I understand that to be a general claim about occurrences of remembering. But I would need to drop the word *memory*, and write only about rememberings and forgettings if I were to avoid more effectively a suggestion that 'memory' names an existing thing. And even if I used that strategy I could easily fall back into phrases that suggested the existence of general characteristics. In this chapter I have written not only of memory and forgetting, but of thinking, reading, and genealogy, and I am now at a point where I want to emphasize memory's and thought's belonging together and to show that thinking brings remembering with it. As a partial hedge against the tendency (and one with many memories composing it) to think of memory and thought as things with characteristics, I emphasize that I am observing shared characteristics of two sorts of events and that I see no basis for saying that 'sorts' does anything more than name groupings of similar aspects. Thoughts and memories happen as the "same" in many ways but not as identical in any way.[7] Hence the phrase *rememberings are characterized by not remembering* means the same as *memory occurs with loss of memory.*

There is an additional vexation. I affirm the observation that thinking is not the same kind of event that observing is. They are not antagonists, but I want to reserve the words *thinking* and *thought* for distinctive occurrences of self-alert perceptions which are neither an object nor necessarily the work of an individual and in which something appears that an individual does not solely structure or enact. Heidegger's enactments of *Auseindersetzung* and *Zwiesprache* as he accounts for them constitute two examples. My descriptions of Heidegger's work constitute examples of observation, although these descriptions may take place in a context of thinking. If I am right in the primary claims of this book, events of both thinking and observing include determinative enactments of memories. But in this chapter I face the question of thoughts' distinctiveness. I have said that thinking is not identical with what is thought in this sense: what appears in thinking has both the characteristics of a thinking event and the singular characteristics of a specific appearance. And yet, on the terms that I have established, I could not carry out an eidetic reduction in order to find the subjective situation or substantive event that makes all thought appearances the same. But I have also said that thinking occurs as an event of disclosure that is not necessarily an enactment of subjectivity, but is an enactment of appearing in which something (the "what") comes to pass with a degree of clarity as well as with obscurity and with a vast range of memorial associations, trajectories, and temporal enactments. And one of the characteristics of thinking appears to be "its" inseparability from thought, while two other characteristics seem to compose the disclosiveness of what is disclosed and self-awareness in the disclosive event which in their occurring with disclosed things do not seem to be a "what," or a disclosed entity.

At this juncture the power of observation finds a limit. Anything that is observed appears as an object of observation, and thinking (like most other enactments) does not occur as an object of observation. It occurs as a happening, seems to be beyond our observational reach. We lose "it" in "its" occurrence as we observe "it." That is a situation with which we—I and those who read this book—are familiar: something is lost in an appearance. That "something" can be a bygone event or a Lethic "aspect" in memory. And now I find that thought in its disclosiveness is lost in my observation of it.[8] Might thought happen as disclosiveness that occurs with nonobservational alertness? Could there be alertness in disclosive occurrences that is not objective or subjective and that can come to expression indirectly in many instances of indication?

Might this question of thinking be addressed appropriately in the mood of the subjunctive, addressed appropriately by an inflection that turns in the direct discourse that I have used from that course of directness?[9] "So many subjunctives," I said at the end of chapter 3 in reference to a loss of presence that came by way of memory. But at that point in the discussion I had not noted the institutional and extensive realm of memory, and I had not addressed the Dionysian/Apollonian aspects of memory and thought. Now I can address subjunctive expression in both its contrast and its similarity to expressions of the sublime that I addressed in chapter 4. The term *Sublime* means "elevated," "high," "rarefied," "uplifting." The word, I noted, suggests an opening into the mysterious and awesome from the point of view of everyday life. What is sublime at the very least approximates the worshipful, and it is always extraordinary. *Sublimity, ek-stasis,* and *gifts of fire* are associated metaphors in this study, and by associating them with the subjunctive mood and its expression they articulate something exceptional vis-à-vis an indicated state of affairs. But instead of exception by elevation, they now suggest liability to change, lack of full determination, and lack of factuality: were I to speak in the subjunctive mood I would not indicate facts or completed actions or definitive experiences; I would indicate absence of factuality adjoining a factual state of affairs. The sublime too expresses excessiveness to factuality and definition. But while sublimity carries the meaning of elevation from a lower state to a higher one—that kind of *ek-stasis*—'subjunctive' suggests something that belongs to something else, a conjunction or joining, something outside of denotation that is subjoined and added to a denotative situation. Elevation or superiority are not suggested. And while 'added' is problematic for my purposes (because I am saying that nonfactuality happens with, not as added onto or as separated from, factuality), the word nonetheless can give emphasis to simultaneity of occurrence. The subjunctive mood belongs to states of affairs in which incompletion and contingency, something not stately or directly stateable, are joined with statement and fact. If something were expressed in that mood it would lack the indicative mood that gives indication of only factuality, occurrence, and definiteness. This emphasis, articulating *that* kind of *ek-stasis*, is much closer than the meaning of sublimity to the mood in which I would like to speak of thinking. It is a mood that pervasively suggests the incompleteness of denotations with which it joins. If thinking were just like its appearance as I observe it, in a given instance, it would not occur as thinking, and if thinking were primarily perception of objects, it would not be the kind of presentative event that I have described it to be.

I thus find doubtful my own efforts to describe the way thinking "really" happens, and that means that I turn away from any method of reduction that would find and describe thinking, 'itself,' in its difference from what is thought.

I believe that this turn might mean that thinking as I have observed it requires for its occurrence enactment of a nonfactual dimension of appearing that is joined with appearances and that composes an awareness that is unique to its own event. That would be an awareness that is not reducible to another kind of awareness, such as observational awareness. It would seem to be an awareness that is joined with disclosure. And that would indicate in this context the question of whether awareness enacted with disclosure were a memorial event.

I am thinking of disclosure, and what I think is in the influence of many philosophers, cultural practices, systems of exchange, and lineages of narration. But disclosure in thinking? It would seem to happen like Apollo's strike, as though it occurred with a nonorder of en-lightenment, as though it brings an initiation into a citizenship of thought that tolerates many and not necessarily coordinated laws—as though it brought the power of appearing without enforcement of any way of appearing. Thinking seems to happen as though it bore memory of things in their emerging into presence and passing from presence, as though it could not forget a Lethic enactment of obscure dissociation and concealment, as though it *were* memory of presencing enacted as appearing. It is as though thinking were an awareness in a mutational appearing of things—an alertness with the losses and gifting of presences. Thinking seems to be like an alert "now" of appearances that happen in memory of memory's inevitability and of the inevitabilities of memory. Disclosure in thinking seems as though "it" were no thing, as though it were without a stance, as though it were virtual in the force of its touch, as though it withdrew in its strike, as though it evaporated in the power of its feel, as though 'its' perceptiveness left the imprint of a memory without factuality or stability. It is as though *mind, memory,* and *thought* were words that attempted to enable a person to speak of something that is the same and at the same time that it is not a thing at all.

When in the subjunctive mood the tangency of thoughtful occurrences is detached from the meanings of sublime and gifted inspiration, thinking appears as though it were as ordinary and as extraordinary as hearing distinctly a rising sound that faded into no sound, as usual and unusual as seeing the light of stars, and as common and uncommon as extending one's arm in space to reach—anything.

I remember thinking one afternoon how remarkable thinking is as I dug a hole for planting a rhododendron. The ground was rich and dark. I was sweating. I felt almost paternal toward the plant that I intended to nurture. As I felt myself digging, I remember, and in the day's clear brightness I had a sense of vast space behind my back and beyond the trees that shaded me. Beyond the fact that I wanted the rhododendron's flowers in early spring to break the spell of winter and to initiate a renewed sense of life, that planting also reminded me of my family's agrarian past; I was coming to "own" a home; I was using my hands for something earthy. But I did not "really" know why I was planting—or able to plant—something that would grow. I was aware at that moment of how far and invisibly distant the experience went that informed my present feelings, and I had a sense of distance in the universe that utterly dwarfed at that moment my life and place of life. I knew that each shovel of dirt contained millions of organisms, cells, subcells, and (almost) infinitely small things and traces of things. The worm in the dirt would seem vast, almost infinitely large, by comparison. And as *I* was thinking these things I felt a sense of strangeness and lightness with the unspeakable, vast, almost infinitely large and infinitely small things with which I was moving as I thought and dug. In the thinking I felt a sense of wonder, not just about these facts, but in the thinking and in the sense that I belonged here and nowhere at the same time. Everything seemed at the moment to count for a lot and yet not to count at all—all of that as I shoveled, and more that I cannot say directly. As I thought, I wondered, why would this mean at this moment so much and remember so much and seem so clearly here, while "here" did not appear to be much of anywhere?

NOTES

CHAPTER ONE. INTRODUCTION

1. G. Bennington and Jacques Derrida, *Jacques Derrida*, (University of Chicago Press, 1993), 25–26, 33.

2. This is a gloss on Augustine's use of the sponge metaphor in book 7 of his *Confessions* and on Derrida's recasting of it. See ibid, 100–105.

3. "And he wondered at this trick his mind continued to play on him, this constant turning of one thing into another thing, as if behind each real thing there were a shadow thing, as alive in his mind as the thing before his eyes, and in the end he was at a loss to say which of these things he was actually seeing. And therefore it happened, often it happened, that his life no longer seemed to dwell in the present." Paul Auster, *The Invention of Solitude* (Penguin Books 1982), 135.

4. Chapter 10 will return to this theme. The unrelenting roar of the sea all around me is immense, too. I can single out some of its sounds as its waves strike the land. But mostly it covers everything by sound and seems to shake the house I'm in like an avalanche of inchoate memories.

5. See for example Diane Ackreman, *A Natural History of the Senses* (Random House, 1980); Louis Thomas, *The Life of a Cell* (Viking Penguin, 1972); Stephen Rose, *The Making of Memory* (Doubleday, 1993).

CHAPTER TWO. MNEMOSYNE'S LOSS
AND STOLEN MEMORIES

1. Michael Grant, *Myths of the Greeks and Romans* (World Publishing Co., 1962), 105–107.

2. See Karl Kerényi, "Lesmosyne, Über die Quellen Erinnerung und Vergessenheit," *Humanistische Seelenforschung* (Werkausgabe I, München/Wien, Langen Müller, 1966), 311–22. Tr. *Spring* (Zurich, 1977), 120–130.

3. Ibid.

4. Ibid, 16ff, 41ff. Detienne in *Masters of Truth*, points out that by virtue of writing Hesiod's *Theogony* is quite different from the oral tradition of the twelfeth through the nineth century B.C.E. But he does follow the "model" of sung speech and so may be considered a transitional figure between oral tradition and a culture based on writing. This is a relevant point for this study insofar as memory in archaic times in Greece was associated primarily with poetic speech, while through Hesiod the carrier of memory was written words. This difference might well contribute to an increasing emphasis on memory as a mediator of passed events rather than as an immediate enactment of truth. Detienne argues that Mnemosyne's meaning in the archaic period was found as "she" occurred in voicing.

5. Kerényi "Lesmosyne," 10a.

6. Ibid.

7. This is a controversial claim that Kerényi values. I shall not engage the controversy since my purpose is simply to find an image that leads beyond its imagery in preparation for a nonmythological account of memory's loss.

8. *Was Heisst Denken* (Tübingen, Niemeyer Verlag, 1971) Fourth edition, 6ff. *What is Called Thinking* tr. Fred Wick and J. Glenn Gray, (NY: Harper Torch Books, 1968), 10ff.

9. See also his *Parmenides*, Gesamtansgabe, Vol. 54 (Klostermann, 1992), *Parmenides* tr. A. Schuwer and R. Rojcewicz; (Bloomington, Indiana University Press) see especially part I, pections 2, 3, and 5.

10. *Vorträge und Aufsätze* (Neske, 1954), 271; Heidegger, *Early Greek Thinking*, tr. David Ferrell Krell (Harper and Row, 1975), 121.

11. Ibid., 108–9; Ger., 256–57.

12. Ibid.

13. See Detienne, *Masters of Truth*.

14. Derrida, *Of Grammatology* (Johns Hopkins Press, 1976), 30ff. Derrida, *De la Grammatologie* (Les Éditions de Minuit, 1967), 46ff.

15. Ian Hacking develops this problem especially well in the final chapter of *Rewriting The Soul* (Princeton University Press, 1995). In the course of this section I will engage several of the ideas that he raises in this provocative book.

Positively, I will appropriate several of his descriptive accounts of the contemporary knowledge of multiple personality disorder and disassociative identity disorder. But I will take a direction quite different from his 'realism' which I find to constitute a disorder of its own.

16. I am using this disorder to provide a broadly drawn example. Such a disorder is now known in some "official" publications and societies, although it is in question among many theorists and clinicians. I do not wish to address the issue of the extent to which the disorder is an invention of recent years. Like all knowledges, I suspect, it has the advantages and disadvantages of imaginative and social construction that accompany and help to define a body of recognized experiences. I remind myself that my knowledge and the traditions to which I belong have those same advantages and disadvantages. The advantage of this "disorder" for my purposes is that it presents, perhaps in exaggerated form, some aspects of memory that I wish to valorize, and these aspects remain not only to jeopardize any conclusiveness that might be attached to the diagnoses of multiple identity disorder, but also any definitive rejection of such diagnoses. It also has the advantages of challenging some types of conventional, clinical wisdom and of taking early childhood abuse as *both* literal and figurative in a context that is frequently undecidable. I shall emphasize the undecidability. For five studies of sexual abuse in a Jungian context, see *The Journal of Analytical Psychology* 40 (1995): 5–76.

17. I have used 'memory' and 'memories' as the subjects for many of the verbs in this paragraph. I do not know the extent to which an individual intends or does not intend the theft of which I speak. No doubt we can individually garnish a remembered scene and turn fragments into narratives. But I suspect that much of that work is also done in the formation of memories and their appearances before we have a chance to do our own imaginative work with them.

18. See, for example, "Modern History of Child Sexual Abuse Awareness: Cycles of Discovery and Suppression," in *Child Abuse and Neglect*, E. Olafson, D. L. Corwin, R. C. Summitt, 17: 7–24; and Ian Hacking, *Rewriting the Soul*, chapt. 4.

CHAPTER THREE. ON ORIGINATING AND PRESENTING ANOTHER TIME: THE ART OF TRAGEDY

1. The following paragraph constitutes a gloss—an engagement with—the opening paragraphs of J. Derrida's "Tense," in *The Path of Archaic Thinking*, ed. K. Maly State University of New York Press, 1995.

2. See chapter 8 for a further discussion of this issue.

3. This idea will be elaborated in chapter 4.

4. I will elaborate this account of Apollo in chapter 4.

5. These remarks and those following are taken from the *OED*, *Klein's Etymological Dictionary*, *Webster's Dictionary* (second edition), and *Lydell and Scott's Greek Dictionary*.

6. This observation will also be developed further in chapters 6 and 7.

7. As I will elaborate in the next two chapters, Nietzsche does not use the term *sublime* to describe Dionysian ecstacy. I depart from his restriction of the word to Apollinian occurrences because of the meanings that I here point out.

8. Nietzsche's ideas of the Dionysian are always within highly disciplined forms. He is unsurpassed in his affirmation of self-overcoming in his own thought, which constitutes the Dionysian dimension in his thought, but when that dimension is compared to Dionsyian practices as they are reported to have happened in Greek festivals, his Dionsyianism appears to be extremely qualified and civilized. Dionysus is for him more of an ironic figure of life energy that is never captured by figuration, and his own mentation is far more Apollonian than he appreciated. My reasons for these remarks will become apparent in chapters 5 and 7.

CHAPTER FOUR. POWERS OF TRANSFORMATION WITHIN A MEMORIAL READING: NARRATIVES OF DIONYSUS

1. Although I have consulted many sources to provide the following summary, I have frequently drawn from the following studies: Robert Graves, *The Greek Myth*, vol. 1, 103ff (who gives an especially helpful account of Dionysus' deeds and names); Michael Grant, *Myths of the Greeks and Romans*, E. R. Dodd, *The Greeks and the Irrational*; Walter F. Otto, *The Homeric Gods*; Werner Jager, *Theology in the Early Greek Philosophers*; Bullfinch *Book of Mythology*. See also chapter 7 where I discuss Dionysus further and in a different context.

2. J. E. Harrison suggests that the term *tragedy* may be derived from *tragos*, which means "spelt," a grain from which Athenians derived beer, and not from *tragos*, "goat," as Virgil claimed. See Graves, *Greek Myth*, 108 n. 3.

3. The following remarks are based on Euripides' *Bacchae*.

4. These remarks differ from Nietzsche's account of the aftermath of Dionysian experiences, as we shall see later in this chapter. He contends that after such ecstatic transcendence the everyday world becomes boring and depressing for the Dionysian initiate. I am departing from his account here in order to note the possible salutary force of everyday life in the face of losses of stability and identity that the "barbarious" Dionysian revelry brings. I also wish to emphasize the

importance of our recognizing the Dionysian aspect in all of life. Without that recognition we are prey to Dionysian excess in the name of civilized life. But, as I shall show, Nietzsche's contention is descriptive of the after effects of that revelry with which Dionysus is most often associated, a revelry that often gains a quasi-religious significance and to which some people attribute insight into the 'real essence' of life.

5. Later in this chapter I will point out that in the context of Nietzsche's account of Dionysian energy, the word *sublime* is inappropriate. At this point I will allow the word to stand on its own in reference to the occurrence of loss without reference to Nietzsche's meaning for it.

6. Nietzsche, "Attempt at Self-Criticism," *The Birth of Tragedy*, section 1. Hereafter noted as "Attempt."

7. "Attempt," section 3.

8. Ibid., section 1.

9. Ibid.

10. Ibid.

11. Ibid., section 2.

12. Ibid., section 3.

13. "Still, the effect of the book proved and proves that it had a knack for seeking out fellow-rhapsodizers and for luring them on new secret paths and dancing places. What found expression here was anyway—this was admitted with as much curiosity as antipathy—a *strange* voice, the discipline of a still 'unknown God', one who conceived himself for the timebeing under the scholar's hood, under the gravity and dialectical ill humor of the German, even under the bad manners of the Wagnerian. Here was a spirit with strange, still nameless needs, a memory bursting with questions, experiences, concealed things after which the name Dionysus was added with one more question mark. What spoke here—as was admitted, not without suspicion—was something like a mystical, almost nomadic soul that stammered with difficulty, a feat of the will, as in a strong tongue, almost undecided whether it should communicate or cancel itself. It should have *sung*, this 'new soul'—and not spoken." "Attempt," section 3.

14. The following paragraph is based on "Attempt," section 4.

15. Ibid.

16. Ibid.

17. Ibid., section 6

18. Ibid., section 5.

19. Ibid., section 7.

20. Ibid.

CHAPTER 5. THE "POWER" OF NONDETERMINATION WITH DETERMINATIONS IN APPEARANCES

1. I take the term *odd* from J. S. Clay, "Tendenz and Olympian Propaganda" in *Apollo: Origins and Influences*, ed. Jon Soloman (Tucson: University of Arizona Press, 1994, 19ff).

2. Nietzsche, *The Birth of Tragedy*, 34. Kaufmann translates *Schein* in this sentence as "mere appearance" which I find misleading by the apparent suggestion that there is something more permanent than *Schein* (Shine) to which we might refer. For Nietzsche, in the context of this sentence, the other quite different existence from shining appearance is Dionysian—different from Apollo's occurrence, certainly, but not different by virtue of greater permanence or durability.

3. Nietzsche, *The Birth of Tragedy*, 35.

4. Ibid.

5. Ibid., 35, 36. Translation altered in the first sentence of the quotation. Nietzsche is quoting Schopenhauer.

6. Ibid., 37.

7. Ibid.

8. Ibid., 38.

9. Ibid., 41.

10. Ibid., 42, 43.

11. The original, unchanged lines are in Nietzsche, *The Birth of Tragedy*, 42-43.

12. These sentences are a gloss of the first part of the first paragraph on p. 43.

13. Nietzsche, *The Birth of Tragedy*.

14. This sentence is a gloss on the phrase, "that consummate immersion in the beauty of mere appearances" (*Schein*). Ibid., 44.

15. Nietzsche, *The Birth of Tragedy*, 43–44.

16. Ibid., 45.

17. Ibid.

18. The example that Nietzsche uses is Raphael's *Transfiguration*. See Nietzsche, *The Birth of Tragedy*, p. 45, for his elaboration of Raphael's painting.

19. Nietzsche, *The Birth of Tragedy*, 43.

20. Ibid., 48ff.

21. Translation altered. Kaufmann has "pleasure, of mere appearance" (*Schein*).

22. Kaufmann translates *Gleichness* as "symbols." I have changed the translation to "similitude."

23. Nietzsche, *The Birth of Tragedy*, 53.

24. Ibid., 54. In this strain language memorializes its own loss in music and thus in primordial nature.

25. Nietzsche, *The Birth of Tragedy*, 59.

26. Ibid., 60.

27. Ibid.

28. Ibid.

29. Ibid., 4.

30. Had Nietzsche presented a more conflicted and Titanic Apollo, nature in its appearance would have been shown to be still more divided because there would have been no movement of nonconflict even in the shining of figuration or in primal unity. They would have come to appear in reference to Dionysian disunity and complicated by Apollinian disunity. 'Primal unity' in his account is a concept that forgets the lack of harmony in shining—in coming to appear—and thus lends itself to the sentimentality and romanticism that Nietzsche later regretted.

CHAPTER SIX. INSTITUTIONAL SONGS AND INVOLUNTARY MEMORY: WHERE DO "WE" COME FROM?

1. Indirect communications happen in many ways. As a mood or disposition that "shades" what we say directly and gives it rhythm, expression, tone, inflexion, and gesture; as posture or movement; as context; as glance or blink or a

small wrinkle by one's eyes; as rate of breathing, relaxation of a muscle group, by, as I will say at the end of the book, even the subjunctive mood in our language. But indirection happens also *as* one attends to something—to hope or fear or something loved. The attention and the attended can affect how one relates to something else or speaks of it or of something else. Some people develop the skill of giving 'something' that is not directly expressed intensity and appearance through something else that is said or painted or sung or written. The thing sung or said is not simply a sign of this other. It belongs to the other in the communication, accords with the other's expression as the other appears in its own, quite distinct expression. The communication that I want to notice in this chapter arises from attention to nondetermination or emptiness, a kind of attention that is like overhearing something without objectivity, something both elusive and palpable, like something fading at the edge of a glance or on the brink of meaning, or like the moment I described in chapter 3, when a sound ceases. I remember seeing a border of snow and no snow where heavy snowing stopped.

2. Vernant, "The Mythical Aspects of Memory and Time," *Myth and Thought in the Greeks* (London and Boston: Routledge, 1983), 78.

3. Ibid., 79.

4. Ibid.

5. Ibid., 80.

6. Ibid. The poet is considered to be blind to "day-things" and perceptive of what lies beyond the day's light.

7. In the oracle of Lebadeia, for example, "where a descent into Hades was enacted in the cavern of Trophomius we find Lethe, forgetfulness associated with Mnemosyne, forming with her a pair of complementary religious powers. Before venturing into the mouth of hell, the questor, who has already undergone rites of purification, was taken to two springs named respectively Lethe and Mnemosyne. He drank from the first and immediately forgot everything to do with his human life and, like a dead man, he entered into the realm of Night. The water of the second spring was to enable him to remember all that he has seen and heard in the other world. When he returned he was no longer restricted to the knowledge of the present moment: contact with the beyond had revealed both past and future to him." Through this rite one transcends the opposition of death and life, "and he can move freely from one world to the other." "Memory appears as a source of immortality." Vernant, "The Mythical Aspects," 80.

8. These remarks are based primarily on Vernant, "The Mythical Aspects," 82ff.

9. Ibid., 83.

10. These observations refer to texts by Empedocles. In reference to the Pythagorian discipline of remembering, Vernant says, "The obligation laid on the members of the (Pythagorian) fraternity to recall all of the events of the day gone by, each evening, had more than the moral value of an exercise in soul-searching. The effort involved in remembering, if undertaken following the example of the sect's founder so as to encompass the story of the soul throughout ten or even twenty different lives, would make it impossible for us to learn who we are and to know our own psyche—that daemon which had become incarnate in us."

11. Vernant, "The Mythical Aspects," 83.

12. "Once it has atoned for everything, the soul, being centered in its original purity, can at last escape from the cycle of births, leaving generation and death behind it, and can gain access to the form of unchanging and permanent existence which is the prerogative of the gods." "Memory is exalted because it is the power that makes it possible for men to escape time and return to the divine state." Vernant, "The Mythical Aspects," 88.

13. Vernant, "The Mythical Aspects," 89. Consider in this context the following statement by Aristotle in *Physics* 221 a–b: "For things to exist in time they must be embraced by time just as with other cases of being "in" something; for instance, things that are in place are embraced by place. And it will follow that they are in some respect affected by time; just as we are wont to say that time crumbles things and that everything grows old under the power of time and is forgotten through the lapse of time. But we do not say that we have learnt, and that anything is made new or beautiful by mere lapses of time; for we regard time itself as destroying rather than producing, for what is counted in time is movement, and movement dislodges whatever it affects from its present state. From all this it is clear that things which exist eternally, as such, are not in time; for they are not embraced by time, nor is their direction measured by time." This thought that time destroys and does not produce anything new or beautiful is close to the mythological 'idea' that by Mnemosyne's eternal power of transmission humans come to what time cannot give: new birth into eternal truth and the beauty of a timelessly pure soul in truth's light.

14. The Greek is *hā dè mnéme toû genoménon* and is translated by W. S. Hett as "memory is of the past." "On memory and recollection," 449b, *Aristotle, Loeb Classical Library*, vol. 8, pp. 288ff. Further citations will be from this volume.

15. See John Chown, *A History of Money from AD 800* (Routledge, 1994) chapter 24; and John K. Galbraith, *Money: Whence It Came and Where It Went* (Houghton Mifflin, 1975), chapter 6.

16. The trust, however, was supported by other means of persuasion. A resolution passed on January 11, 1776, stated: "Any person who shall hereafter be

so lost to all virtue and regard for his country as to refuse the Bills or obstruct and discourage their currency shall be deemed published and treated as an enemy of the country and precluded from all trade and intercourse with its inhabitants." For discussions of opinions by those who condemn the fiscal policies of the revolutionary government see ibid.

17. Chown, *A History of Money* 219. Quoted from an act of Congress in 1775.

18. Quoted in Galbraith, *Money* 59.

19. Foucault, *Madness and Civilization* (Vintage Books), 6.

20. Foucault uses 'structures' in referring to the "remainder" of abandonment in combination with theological beliefs and religious experiences that carries a transition from lepers to the mad. This is a word that he soon gave up and one that I shall also drop with the notation that I am placing abandonment and exclusion outside of the language of structures at the same time that I recognize that structures "carry" such intangibles. The past occurrences of abandonment and exclusion in the formation of the asylum, like other nonvoluntary memories, are not identical with the bearing structures and institutions: not separate from them in their lineage but also not identical with them.

21. Foucault, *Madness and Civilization* 281.

22. Ibid., 288, my emphasis.

23. Ibid., xii.

24. Nietzsche, *On the Genealogy of Morals*, (Vintage Books, 1967) Walter Kaufman, 2nd essay, sections 8–11.

25. Ibid., 3rd essay, sections 27–28.

26. In my opinion, Nietzsche's idea of will to power should be read as strategic and temporary, as an idea whose functions are to show the temporal instability of all "stabilization" and to show human communality in something that lacks identity. In that reading, will to power lacks the possibility of providing unifying meaning and, in combination "the law of self-overcoming," moves to unsettle its own grounding aspect. Foucault's account of transition and transformation is appropriate to this reading and its turn from the thought of grounding. But one can show that Nietzsche *also* organizes his thought in the force of the idea of will to power and thereby goes considerably beyond its merely strategic employment as he makes claims for the existence of will to power.

27. The reminder of this paragraph is a gloss on Foucault's "Forward to the English Edition" (Vintage Books, 1970) 9–24.

28. Ibid., chapter 3, 2ff.

CHAPTER SEVEN. WHEN THE COMPANY OF TIME CASTS NO SHADOW: MEMORY OF DIFFERENCES AND NONDETERMINATION

1. See, for example, Walter F. Otto, *Dionysus: Myth and Cult*, tr. R. B. Palmer (Bloomington and London: Indiana University Press 1965), 74ff. Otto says "[Dionysus] entered the world differently from the way in which we are told other gods did, and he encounters man, too, in a very special way. In both instances his appearance is startling, disquieting, violent. And, like everything violent, it arouses opposition and agitation. Right at his birth gods arise as enemies. Terrible disturbances are engendered in his vicinity. The destruction of his mother is followed by suffering, bitter distress, and violent death for all who interest themselves in the little boy, beginning with his mother's sister, Ino, who plunges into the sea, out of her mind, with her own child in her arms. And in this way, even the revelation of the god who has become a man creates wild emotion, anger, and opposition among mankind. The daughters of Minyas refuse to follow his call and with good reason, for he rips the ones he has affected out of their wifely decency and mates them with the mysteries and madness of the chaos of night."

2. Walter Otto makes the same claim in terms stronger than Nietzsche's. See Dionysus, especially pp. 133ff.

3. Ibid, 78. The page numbers of this book will be written parenthetically in the text for the next two paragraphs.

4. Gary Morrison says, in a context different from this one, "even unactualized possibilities may somehow leave their mark on history . . . it is as if one possibility out of many became actual but carried another as a sort of recessive gene, invisible to the eye but capable of affecting future generations of events. In this way, a present somehow grows partly out of an unactualized as well as actualized part." He calls this situation of constitutive, unactualized possibilities in literature "sideshadowing." *Narrative and Freedom: The Shadow of Time*.

5. Charles Simic writes, "The company of time and eternity / which, begging your pardon, / Cast no image / As they admire themselves in the mirror" "Mirrors or 4 A.M., *Walking the Black Cat: Poems* (N.Y.: Harcourt, Brace and Co.) 2.

6. This section composes, in part, a gloss on *The Order of Things*, chapter 2, part 5.

7. Memory in the Renaissance is, of course, a highly textured and arrest-ing subject. I have chosen not to give an account of it beyond a few observations on the language of Similitude because of its complexity and range. Adequate con-sideration of it in the context of memory's loss requires a separate study.

8. Herman Paul (*Deutsches Wörterbuch*, eighth ed.) states that *Geschichte* has the basic meaning of "event" or "happening" and is closely associated with *Geschehen*, "what has taken place." It also has taken on the meaning of a report or account of specific events, their interconnection and unfolding, although it refers primarily to the events that are recounted. This dictionary has no entry for *Historie*, from the Latin cognate *historia*. Rather, under the entry *Geschichte*, it states that the word *historia*, was influenced by the Latin word and came to mean "inquiry." It stresses, however, that the proper German word for *historia* is *Erkundung* "inquiry" and not *Geschichte*.

9. Nietzsche, *On the Advantages*, section 10. Friedrich Nietzsche, *On the Advantage and Disadvantage of History for Life*, trans. by Peter Preuss (Indianapolis: Hackett Publishing Company, Inc., 1980).

10. Nietzsche speaks in this section of what gives the character of eternity (*der Ewigen*) to life. I am interpreting *der Ewigen* by reference to its root meaning of *ehe je*, "always before," or "always now." The opening of present time into the future is always before what is upcoming and always now. Hence, the *eternal* (*ewig*) or ever opening aspect of time.

11. "But he also wondered about himself, that he cannot learn to forget but always remains attached to the past: however far and fast he runs, the chain runs with him. It is astonishing: the moment, here in a wink, gone in a wink, nothing before and nothing after, returns nevertheless as a specter to disturb the calm of a later moment. Again and again a page loosens in the scroll of time, drops out, and flutters away—and suddenly flutters back again into man's lap. Then man says 'I remember' and envies the animal which immediately forgets and sees each moment really die, sink back into deep night, extinguished forever." Nietzsche, *On the Advantages*, section 1, pp. 8-9.

12. Nietsche, *On the Advantages*, section 1, p. 9.

13. Foucault, op. cit, II. 7.

14. Ibid., 217–18.

15. Ibid., 218; emphasis added.

16. Ibid., 217.

17. Ibid.

18. Ibid.

19. Ibid.

20. We could also reverse this comparison and say, "in the brightness of discontinuity that accompanies an obscurity of order." Orders hide many things as well as disclose other things.

21. *The Order of Things*, I: 3. 3–5. Only *one* example, only one *example* of established discontinuity? An excision from *The Order of Things* that represents the establishment of discontinuity in a bygone knowledge that recognized representation as establishing continuity? Perhaps only the excision, as it ruins the example I put forward, will save me from intolerable contradiction. But I shall defer that issue until later (perhaps then it will constitute only a memory).

22. Although an investigation into biological or botanical or genealogical "memory" is not within the purview of this book, such a study might have in common with this work recognition of the importance of memory that is beyond imagination and all other subjective forms of syntheses. Nonpersonal memory—transmission of bygone experiences and formations—shares kinship with some of the myths that I have considered in their presentation of implacable differences from the myth maker or the knower or human-centered experience. Memory beyond subjectivity or Subjectivity: a very strange phenomenon for those of us who are at home in an episteme of subjectivity.

23. The commentary portions in this section refer to *The Order of Things*, part II, pp. 7, 8.

24. Ibid., 217.

25. Ibid., 219.

26. Ibid.

27. Ibid., 220.

28. Ibid., 244.

29. Ibid., 296.

30. Ibid., 298–9.

31. Ibid., 300.

32. Ibid., 304.

33. Stephen Jay Gould, *Full House: The Spread of Excellence from Plato to Darwin*, (Harmony Books, 1996). I utilize this controversial book without judgment concerning the accuracy of its scientific claims and in appreciation for its suggestive power, especially in Gould's interpretation of Darwin.

34. "The more important the subject and the closer it cuts to the bone of our hopes and needs, the more we are likely to err in establishing a framework for analysis. We are story-telling creatures, products of history ourselves. We are fascinated by trends, in part because they tell stories by the basic device of imparting directionality to time, in part because they so often supply a moral dimension to a sequence of events: a cause to bewail as something goes to pot, or to highlight as a rare beacon of hope. . . . But our strong desire to identify trends often leads us to detect a directionality that doesn't exist or to infer causes that cannot be sustained." Gould, *Full House*, 30. I would add, cannot be sustained except by insistent beliefs concerning some "higher" stakes. Virtually any interpretation can be sustained given a supportive community, a satisfying ritual, and stakes that are experienced as life and death matters.

35. "Take the standard illustration of coin flipping: we compute the probably of sequences by multiplying the chances of individual events. Since the . . . chance of flipping heads five times in a row is . . . one in thirty-two—rare to be sure, . . . [it is] something that will happen every once in awhile for no reason but randomness. Many people, however, particularly if they are betting on tails, will read five heads in a row as *prima facie* evidence of cheating. People have been shot and killed for less..." Gould, *Full House*, 31.

36. Ibid., 33.

37. Ibid., 38ff.

38. Ibid., 41.

39. The implications of this inclusion might go beyond what Gould wants to say insofar as it means that literal truth is continuously deferred by a hypothetical structure, and within this (hypothetical) framework what is the case is always in question. Gould might prefer at times to exclude some facts from a hypothetical framework. Or, perhaps, like me, he is comfortable with "facts" in such a framework and treats them literally until their just-so quality is shaken or eliminated.

40. Gould finds the word *nature* to be reliable, although he rejects a totally objective view of nature: "a cardinal fallacy: the assumption of a fully objective nature 'out there' and visible *in the same way* to any unprejudiced observer." However, "Objective nature does exist, but we can converse with her only through the structure of our taxonomic systems." Gould, *Full House*, 39. I have added the emphasis in the first quote in order to note that while he accepts the image of an objective nature, he does not accept the idea that it is there to be read fully and accurately by all people who have the "right" approach. "Objective nature" allows for huge variations in approaches to it according to Gould's hypothesis. The impossibility of knowing nature in itself is, I believe, also a neces-

sary conviction for a view constructed on hypothetical variations. It *might* be the case that Gould has built into the language that he uses the ideas that nature is known in itself to be without essence (and hence, by that language, making variation an essence) and that the centrality that he gives to variation approximates or imitates *the* way that nature happens, that *his* hypothesis, in its allowance for variation, mirrors nature properly. I doubt that he intends that, but these kinds of ideas may well be inevitable as long as 'nature' is used as a primary gathering concept. Or, one must make clear that *nature* is a term of taxonomy and does not have ontological status. That something—nature—is there as either a whole or as an entirety that is "internally" characterized by variation is an idea rich in reification. The word sounds to me no less taxonomical, abstract, and general than *man*.

41. Gould, *Full House*, 137.

42. 138.

43. Ibid.

44. "The summation of favorable variants over many generations leads to evolutionary change. Local improvements rise upon the hecatomb of countless deaths; we get to a 'better' place by removing the ill-adapted, not by actively constructing a better version." Gould, *Full House*, 221.

45. Gould takes careful account of Darwin's "social conservatism by virtue of which he also and also contradictorily believed in progress in species development." Although that side of Darwin's thought is important for understanding the full range of his theories, it is not important for my purposes in this section.

46. Gould observes that such human arrogance as that found in viewing humans as the crown of evolutionary development constitutes one of the threats to human survival. That kind of arrogance is comparable, in terms of geological time, to foolhardiness in the region of a shark feeding frenzy or the lightness of heart that sometimes accompanies a suicidal decision.

47. "If organisms are tracking local environments, then their evolutionary history should be effectively random as well." "This process [of natural selection] yields only local adaptation, often exquisite to be sure, but not universally advancing." Gould, *Full House*, 140.

48. Gould, *Full House*, 148.

49. I have not discussed in this context Gould's important chapter 4, "Case One: A Personal Story," which is followed by a chapter entitled "Case Two: Life's Little Joke." At that point in his work the way looks clear for a strong sense of variation in random localities in his presentation. But that emphasis fades as he develops his exciting hypotheses and allows a traditional sense of objectivity to valorize his presentation.

50. Gould, *Full House*, 139–140.

51. Ibid., 40.

52. Ibid., 230. Darwin's words: "Whilst this planet has gone cycling on according to the fixed law of gravity, from so simple a beginning endless forms most beautiful and most wonderful have been, and are being, evolved." Quoted on p. 230.

53. The last two sentences constitute a gloss on parts of Gould, *Full House*, 4.

CHAPTER EIGHT. REPETITIONS AND DIFFERENCIATIONS

1. The purpose of these observations is to direct our attention to "differenciation." In this chapter and with the help of Giles Deleuze I shall work on the idea of differenciation and repetition in the context of singularity and "virtual reality." I shall use the word *differenciation* to name enactments of difference or, closer to Deleuze's language, emergence of difference out of differences. 'Differenciation' does not name an action by a subject but rather occurrences of differencing.

2. Deleuze says that singularities are not ordinary. See, for example, The *Logic of Sense* (Columbia University Press, 1990), 52. I am departing from this claim and will return below to this departure.

3. Delueze, *Difference and Repetition* (Columbia University Press, 1994), 1.

4. Ibid, 69.

5. Ibid, 16–17.

6. See especially ibid. 130–38.

7. Ibid, 138.

8. Ibid.

9. Ibid, 139.

10. Ibid.

11. Ibid, 140.

12. Ibid.

13. Ibid, 141.

14. Ibid, 139.

15. See, for example, Deleuze's discussion of essential memory: Ibid. pp. 140 ff.

CHAPTER NINE. GIFTS OF FIRE: WITNESSING AND REPRESENTING

1. Derrida, *Of Grammatology*, tr. G.C. Spivak (The Johns Hopkins Press, 1976), 10. As I noted in chapter 6 *historia* in Latin means "narrative" or "story." The Greek *istos* means "ship's mast," "beam of a loom," or anything set upright. *Istoreo* means, "give an account of what one has learned," "record," "give a narrative," or "written account." *Episteme* means "acquaintance with something," "skill," or "experience." The deponent *epistamai*, means "know how to do," "be able to do." Its participial form *epistamenos*, means "know that one is or has." It might also suggest the enactment of a skill, that is, skill doing its thing, skilling. At this point in the discussion, I am referring to narrative and to knowledge in the form of a narrative, with the overtone of skilled—perhaps professional—knowledge. *Liddell and Scott's Greek-English Lexicon* (Oxford, 1955).

2. Derrida, *Of Grammatology*, 9.

3. In this context, Derrida's descriptions of arche writing troubles me. I see his point that in writing, "something" quite inarticulable happens and happens in withdrawal from conceptual grasp as well as from sensible expression. *Differance*, as it were, takes place. But this idea also has the problem, which Derrida recognizes, that writing sounds quasi-transcendental and is like something that is to itself. In geneological terms, one can say that some kinds of disciplined knowledge find writing to be like that, but a further step toward a quasi-ontological claims that "writing" *is* like that, even if the 'is' is crossed out, in all of its instances says too much for deconstructive knowledge.

4. A *hold* is a nonphysical bond which attaches or retains, act of holding; to receive and contain, to bear or carry—appearing, holds what appears as well as loss of what appears; to receive and contain—re-membering receives past events in mutated ways; to continue, remain unbroken—past presence is held by loss and re-membering in presence. This last sentence in the text says, however, that the continuation of past presence with present appearance happens by way of loss and forgetting— one finds continuity with, in, and through radical fractures in an event's own occurrence.

5. See, for example, Derrida, "Differénce," *Margins of Philosophy*, tr. Alan Bass (Chicago: University of Chicago Press, 1982), 14–24.

6. Ibid., 17.

7. Ibid., 20.

8. Ibid., 21. Levinas' phrase applies to the absolute alterity of the other, and Derrida accepts the phrase as inscribing a delimitation of the ontology of presence.

9. Derrida, "Differénce," 22.

10. Ibid., 23.

11. Ibid., 20.

12. See Derrida, *The Gift of Death*, tr. David Wills (Chicago: University of Chicago Press, 1995). See particularly pp. 88ff.

13. See the introduction to chapter 5 of this book.

14. Derrida, *The Gift of Death*, 90ff.

15. "To have experience of one's absolute singularity and apprehend one's own death, amounts to the same thing . . . my irreplaceability is therefore conferred, delivered, 'given,' one can say, by death." Derrida, *The Gift of Death*, 41. Derrida says this in the context of discussing the thought of Jan Patočka, but the statement also articulates an observation that I take to be appropriate to Derrida's own account of secret, singularity, substitution, and death in major strands of Western experience.

16. Derrida, *The Gift of Death*, 58ff.

17. Ibid., 80.

18. See ibid., 108ff.

19. Ibid., 112–13.

20. Ibid., 114.

21. Ibid.

22. Ibid., 114–15.

23. Derrida makes this observation by means of Nietzsche's observations in *On the Genealogy of Morals* in which Nietzsche plays on the close affiliation of *der Glaubiger* (the creditor) with *der glaube* (trust or faith) and *der Schuldner* (the debtor) and *die schuld* (guilt). The creditor is the one who gives to the debtor in the trust that the debtor is trustworthy and will repay the debt. Derrida, *The Gift of Death*, 114–15.

24. Ibid., 114. Nietzsche says "pound of flesh," thereby considerably understating the expense of God's payment insofar as God's payment of his whole body inflicts a debt that requires as repayment of a person's whole body and soul.

25. Derrida, *The Gift of Death*, 115.

26. The work by Derrida that I have encountered helps to define finite occurrences and offers no transcendental Meaning. But his conception of gift and his presentation of gifting and debt in the context of his discussion seem to me to give expression to something like Nietzsche's image of the ascetic ideal—in spite of the undecidability in which Derrida contextualizes gift and debt. Undecidability has long been an accompanyment to mystery and other in their separation from origins and finite events. Mystery happens as undecidability. It has long heralded in our tradition the gift of death *for* mortals. But death does not seem in this context to strike either mystery or gift. Perhaps death is *the* mystery in major traditional strands, but how did the sense of mystery arise, the sense that elaborates, in this case, death?

CHAPTER TEN. A SYMPTOM OF LIFE
IN THE ABSENCE OF LIGHT

1. Levinas, *Totality and Infinity*, tr. A. Lingis (Duquesne University Press, 1969) p. 66. All further page references will be to this book.

2. Nietzsche, *On the Advantages and Disadvantages of History for Life*, op cit.

3. I recall in this context that Nietzsche did not understand "youthfulness" to stand outside of *Geschichte*—historical happening—but outside of the determinations of *Historie*—outside of knowledge of historical happenings.

4. The event, the life-moment of an individual, in the rich pattern of determinations also manifests lack of determination, as I have emphasized in previous chapters. Presently I am describing lack of determination by means of the metaphor of absence of light. A life-event occurs as determinations with indeterminacy in a unique moment of transformation and repetition. In such a worldly, everyday event there is no sign of something more, of "life itself" or an immediately present Source of life. Our best and worst lights occur with absence of light, light, and no light together. Nothing more.

5. The following sentences constitute a gloss on Genesis 1 in the context of Levinas' claims about relational origin.

CHAPTER ELEVEN. GIFTS WITHOUT FIRE:
THINKING AND REMEMBERING

1. I also believe that thinking is memorial in *its* enactment, as distinct to what appears in thinking, that thinking arises with an enabling capacity which has a history of development like every other human capacity, that that history is in

some sense enacted as thinking takes place, and in this sense thinking is a memorial event that presents a complex past. I am able in this chapter to support this belief only indirectly by showing that in the appearing of things pasts come to presence and by showing that appearing, in its distinct enactment, presents bygone events.

2. I believe that this is similar to the situations that Joe Dimaggio described when he said that on good days the pitched ball looks the size of a grapefruit as it zooms toward the plate, but on bad days he never sees it and only hears it hit the catcher's glove.

3. In this part of the discussion I am indebted to Rodolphe Gasché's "Toward an Ethics of 'Auseinandersetzung'," in *Enlightenments: Encounters between Critical Theory and Contemporary French Thought*, eds. Harry Kunneman and Hent deVries (The Netherlands: Kok Pharos Publishing House, 1993). I shall use the words *Auseinandersetzung* and *engagement* to name one kind of remembering in thought.

4. Ibid., quoted, 123.

5. In these remarks, I am drawing from Heidegger, "The Anaximander Fragment," *Early Greek Thinking*, tr. D. F. Krell and F.A. Capuzzi (New York: Harper and Row, 1975), 25ff; and Heidegger, *Gesamtausgabe*, Band 5, Klostermann, 334ff.

6. Heidegger, *Early Greek Thinking*, 25.

7. In this distinction between same and identical I am highlighting the definition of same as "agreeing with each other" in the ways some things happen. Instead of the meaning of self-same, which same can have, I am using the word in its suggestion that in different situations things can appear without differences in certain of their aspects.

8. This issue becomes more complex when I observe that observation is also presentational, that in its objectivity regarding itself observing loses something of its own event. In order to carry out my limited attention to thinking, I let this complexity rest in its notice.

9. "Sub-junc' tive . . . 2. Gram. Designating or pertaining to that mood of a verb which represents an attitude toward, or concern with, the denoted action or state not as fact but as something either simply entertained in thought, contingent, possible . . . or emotionally viewed as a matter of doubt, desire, will, etc." *Webster's New International Dictionary* (Second ed., 1957). In my use of the term *subjunctive* I am emphasizing the nonfactual aspect that can be subjoined to direct, indicative observations and that gives preeminence to contingency and to what occurs beyond the clarity of categories, denotation, and the reach of theory. It is a mood of tentativeness, incompletion, and uncertainty, and hence it is appropriate for expressions regarding the coming to pass of appearances.

INDEX